ALONG THESE LINES

ALONG THESE LINES

WRITING PARAGRAPHS AND ESSAYS
Fifth Canadian Edition

JOHN SHERIDAN BIAYS
Broward Community College

CAROL WERSHOVEN
Palm Beach State College

LARA SAUER
George Brown College

PEARSON

Toronto

Vice-President, Cross Media Publishing Services: Gary Bennett
Editorial Director: Claudine O'Donnell
Senior Acquisitions Editor: David Le Gallais
Marketing Manager: Jennifer Sutton
Program Manager: Laura Pratt
Manager of Content Development: Suzanne Schaan
Project Manager: Susan Johnson

Developmental Editor: Christine Langone
Production Services: Niraj Bhatt, iEnergizer Aptara®, Inc.
Permissions Project Manager: Sue Petrykewycz
Text Permissions Research: Phyllis J. Padula, Aptara®, Inc.
Cover Designer: iEnergizer Aptara®, Inc.
Cover Image: Paul Vinten/Fotolia

Credits and acknowledgments for material borrowed from other sources and reproduced, with permission, in this textbook appear on the appropriate page within the text and on page 489.

Original edition published by Pearson Education, Inc., Upper Saddle River, New Jersey, USA. Copyright © 2012 Pearson Education, Inc. This edition is authorized for sale only in Canada.

If you purchased this book outside the United States or Canada, you should be aware that it has been imported without the approval of the publisher or the author.

3 17

Library and Archives Canada Cataloguing in Publication
Biays, John Sheridan, author

Along these lines: writing paragraphs and essays. — Fifth Canadian edition.

Includes index.
ISBN 978-0-205-91606-1 (pbk.)

1. English language—Rhetoric—Problems, exercises, etc.   2. English language—Grammar—Problems, exercises, etc.   3. Report writing—Problems, exercises, etc. I. Wershoven, Carol, author   II. Sauer, Lara, author   III. Title.

PE1408.B52 2015   808'.042   C2014-907174-4

ISBN 978-0-20-591606-1

To Mom and Dad—as always, with love and thanks.

—L.S.

BRIEF CONTENTS

CONTENTS

PREFACE

Thank you for using this book. We at Pearson Canada have tried to maintain the core strength of the original US text—its clear, step-by-step application of the writing process and its variety of exercises—while adopting a distinctly Canadian focus. The fifth Canadian edition of *Along These Lines: Writing Paragraphs and Essays* has been updated and expanded in response to the encouraging reactions and practical suggestions from faculty and reviewers.

THE WRITING CHAPTERS

We have retained what you liked most: the meticulous and intensive coverage of the writing process. This step-by-step coverage traces the stages of writing, from generating ideas, to planning and focusing, to drafting and revising, to final proofreading. Every writing chapter covering a rhetorical pattern takes the students through all the stages of writing—in detail.

These chapters are filled with exercises and activities, both individual and collaborative, because we believe that basic writers are more motivated and learn more easily when they are *actively* involved with individual or collaborative tasks. In keeping with these beliefs and with the emphasis on process, this edition of *Along These Lines* offers instructors more options than ever.

New Features

In response to the suggestions of colleagues and reviewers, this edition contains the following changes and refinements:

- A new reading for the "Writing from Reading" chapter (Chapter 2): this reading, about the rise of MOOCs (massive open online courses), is current and engaging for the college student.
- The stages of writing (previously called *Thought Lines, Outlines, Rough Lines, and Final Lines*) have been renamed to better reflect the tasks—**Prewriting, Planning, Drafting and Revising,** and **Proofreading**—and continue to serve as convenient prompts for each stage.
- Exercises have been updated and revised throughout, reflecting current Canadian issues.
- Many of the writing chapters contain new Canadian readings discussing current topics relevant to today's student.

Additional Features

Along These Lines continues to include these distinctive features:

- The **Communication at Work** box demonstrates the relevance of all forms of communication in the workplace, in every writing chapter (some include collaborative exercises for in-class work).
- Learning objectives and relevant quotations are at the beginning of each writing chapter, which give students an idea of what to expect.
- The text has a lively, conversational tone, including question-and-answer formats and dialogues.
- There is less "talk" about writing; you'll find no more than two pages of print in a row without a chart, a box, a list, an example, or an exercise.
- Small, simple clusters of information are surrounded by white space rather than intimidating expanses of small print.
- Boxed examples of the outline, draft, and final version of the writing assignment are in each chapter.
- Exercises are throughout each chapter—not merely at the end—so that each concept is reinforced as soon as it is introduced.
- You will find exercises that are not merely fill-in-the-blanks style, but collaborative assignments that have students writing with peers, interviewing classmates, reacting to others' suggestions, and building on others' ideas.
- Numerous writing topics and activities are in each chapter, providing more flexibility for the instructor.
- There is a separate and detailed chapter titled "Writing from Reading" (Chapter 2), explaining and illustrating the steps of prereading, reading, annotating, summarizing, and reacting (in writing) to another's ideas.
- Vocabulary definitions for each reading selection have been added.
- The authors have grouped selections by rhetorical pattern.
- Readings have been selected to appeal to working students, returning students, and students who are parents and spouses.
- Reading selections are on such topics as getting an education, multiculturalism, and fitting in or feeling left out.
- Readings are accessible and of particular interest to this student readership—many of the selections thus come from popular sources.
- Topics for writing are sparked by the content of the reading and designed to elicit thinking, not rote replication of a model.

THE GRAMMAR CHAPTERS

Updated, more challenging, and sophisticated exercises have been added to each chapter, and the second part of the text maintains the following features:

- Emphasis is placed on the most important skills for college readiness.
- Grammar concepts are taught step by step (e.g., "Two Steps to Check for Fragments").
- Numerous exercises, including practice, editing, and collaborative exercises, have been added.
- Paragraph-editing exercises are at the end of each grammar chapter to connect the grammar principles to writing assignments.
- An ESL appendix ("Grammar for ESL Students") is included.

Instructors will find *Along These Lines* easy to use for two reasons:

- The text has so many exercises, activities, assignments, and readings that teachers can select strategies they prefer and adapt them to the needs of different class sections.

- The exercises serve as an instant lesson plan for any class period or as individualized work for students in a writing lab.

Along These Lines: Writing Paragraphs and Essays, fifth Canadian edition, will appeal to instructors, but, more importantly, it will work for students. The basic premise of this book is that an effective text should respect students' individuality and their innate desire to learn and succeed. We hope it will help your students flourish by providing them with a foundation of respect, encouragement, and ongoing collaboration as they work through the writing process.

SUPPLEMENTS

Annotated Instructor's Edition   Accessed via the instructor-led eText on MyWritingLab and available only to instructors, the AIE is the complete text annotated by the author. Special features include teaching tips, discussion tips, ideas for group-work answers to some of the in-text exercises, and more!

MyWritingLab   Where practice, application, and demonstration meet to improve writing. MyWritingLab, a complete online learning program, provides additional resources and effective practice exercises for developing writers. MyWritingLab accelerates learning through layered assessment and a personalized learning path. With over eight thousand exercises and immediate feedback to answers, the integrated learning aids of MyWritingLab reinforce learning throughout the semester.

Learning Solutions Managers   Pearson's Learning Solutions managers work with faculty and campus course designers to ensure that Pearson technology products, assessment tools, and online course materials are tailored to meet your specific needs. This highly qualified team is dedicated to helping schools take full advantage of a wide range of educational resources, by assisting in the integration of a variety of instructional materials and media formats. Your local Pearson Canada sales representative can provide you with more details on this service program.

CourseSmart for Instructors   CourseSmart goes beyond traditional expectations—providing instant, online access to the textbooks and course materials you need at a lower cost for students. And even as students save money, you can save time and hassle with a digital eText that allows you to search for the most relevant content at the very moment you need it. Whether it's evaluating textbooks or creating lecture notes to help students with difficult concepts, CourseSmart can make your work a little easier. See how when you visit www.coursesmart.com/instructors.

ACKNOWLEDGMENTS

Thanks go to the team at Pearson Canada who contributed to the realization of this book—in particular David Le Gallais and Joel Gladstone, acquisitions editors, for their continued belief in and support of the project; Christine Langone, developmental editor, for her patience; and Karen Alliston, copy editor, for her keen eye for detail.

Thanks are also due to the instructors who provided reviews for the fifth Canadian edition: Julia Colella, University of Windsor; Chandra Hodgson, Humber College; Aurelea Mahood, Capilano University; and Kim St. Yves, Medicine Hat College. Their feedback offered valuable guidance for this edition.

Lastly, I would like to thank my family: Deon and Daniel, for allowing me the space and time to write; and most of all, Mom and Dad, whose support, encouragement, and sense of humour have always sustained me.

Lara Sauer

WRITING IN STEPS

The Process Approach

INTRODUCTION

Learning by Doing

Writing is a skill, and, like any skill, it improves with practice. This book gives you the opportunity to improve your writing through a number of activities. Some activities can be done alone; some require you to work with a partner or with a group. Some you can do in the classroom; some you can do at home. The important thing to remember is that *good writing takes practice*; you can learn to write well by writing.

Steps Make Writing Easier

Writing is easier if you *don't try to do everything at once*. Producing a piece of effective writing demands that you think, plan, focus, draft, rethink, focus, revise, edit, and proof-read. You can become frustrated if you try to do all these things at the same time.

To make the task of writing easier, *Along These Lines* breaks the process into four major parts:

PREWRITING

In this stage, you *think* about your topic, and you gather ideas. You *react* to your own ideas and add more ideas to your first thoughts. Or you *react* to other people's ideas as a way of generating your own writing material.

PLANNING

In this stage, you begin to *plan* your writing. You examine your ideas and begin to *focus* them around one main idea. Planning involves combining, dividing, and even discarding the ideas you started with. It involves more thinking about the point you want to make and the order of details that can best express your point.

DRAFTING AND REVISING

In this stage, the thinking and planning begin to shape themselves into a piece of writing. You complete a *draft* of your work, a rough version of the finished product. And then you think again, as you examine the draft and check it. Checking it begins the process of *revision*, "fixing" the draft so that it takes the shape you want and expresses your ideas clearly.

PROOFREADING

In this stage, the final version of your writing gets one last, careful *review*. When you pre-pare the final copy of your work, you *proofread* to identify and correct any mistakes in spelling, mechanics, or punctuation you may have overlooked. This step is the *final check* of your work to make sure your writing is the best that it can be.

These four stages in the writing process—*prewriting, planning, drafting and revising,* and *proofreading*—may overlap. You may be changing your plan (the *planning* stage) even as you work on the *drafting and revising* of your paper. And no rule prevents you from moving back to an earlier step when necessary. Thinking of writing as a series of steps helps you to see the process as a *manageable task*. You can avoid doing everything at once and becoming overwhelmed by the challenge.

Throughout the chapters of this text, you will have many opportunities to become familiar with the four stages of effective writing. Working individually and with your classmates, you can become a better writer in *all* stages.

CHAPTER 1
Writing a Paragraph

LEARNING OBJECTIVES

After you have read this chapter and completed its exercises and assignments, you should be able to

- generate ideas for a writing topic
- narrow the range of your ideas
- distinguish appropriate topic sentences from those that are too broad or too narrow
- write an appropriate topic sentence for a paragraph
- organize and plan your paragraph
- generate supporting details for your paragraph
- draft and edit your paragraph

> *"True ease in writing comes from art, not chance, as those who move easiest have learned to dance."*
>
> ~ ALEXANDER POPE

 ALEXANDER POPE WAS AN EIGHTEENTH-CENTURY ENGLISH POET.

WHAT IS A PARAGRAPH?

Usually, students write because they have an assignment requiring them to write on some topic or choice of topics, and the writing is due by a certain day. Assume that you get such an assignment and it calls for one paragraph. You might wonder, "Why a paragraph? Why not something large, like a two- or three-page paper? After all, many classes will ask for papers, not just paragraphs."

For one thing, an essay is really just a series of paragraphs. If you can write one good paragraph, you can write more than one. The **paragraph** is the basic building block of any essay. It is a group of sentences focusing on one idea or one point. Keep this concept in mind: one idea to a paragraph. Focusing on one idea or one point gives a paragraph **unity**. If you have a new point, start a new paragraph.

You may ask, "Doesn't this mean a paragraph will be short? How long should a paragraph be, anyway?" To convince a reader of one main point, you need to make the point, support it, develop it, explain it, and describe it. There will be shorter and longer paragraphs, but for now, you can assume your paragraph will be somewhere between seven and twelve sentences long.

This chapter will guide you through each stage of the writing process:

■ **Prewriting**—how to generate and develop ideas for your paragraph
■ **Planning**—how to organize your ideas
■ **Drafting and Revising**—how to make and revise rough drafts
■ **Proofreading**—how to edit and refine your ideas

We place extra emphasis on the prewriting in this chapter to give you that extra help in getting started.

WRITING THE PARAGRAPH IN STEPS

 GATHERING IDEAS FOR A PARAGRAPH

Suppose your instructor asks you to write a paragraph about immigrating to Canada. You already know your **purpose**—to write a paragraph that makes some point about immigrating to Canada. You have an **audience**, since you're writing this paragraph for your instructor and classmates. Knowing your audience and purpose is important for writing effectively. Often, your purpose is to write a specific kind of paper for a class. But sometimes you may have to write for a different purpose or audience, such as writing instructions for a new employee at your workplace, or a letter of complaint to a manufacturer, or a short autobiographical essay for a scholarship application.

Freewriting, Brainstorming, Keeping a Journal

Once you've identified your audience and purpose, you can begin by finding some way to *think on paper*. To gather ideas, you can use the techniques of freewriting, brainstorming, or keeping a journal.

Freewriting Give yourself fifteen minutes to write whatever comes into your mind on your subject. If your mind is a blank, write, "My mind's a blank. My mind's a blank" over and over until you think of something else. The main goal here is to *write without stopping*. Don't stop to tell yourself, "This is stupid" or "I can't use any of this in a paper." Don't stop to correct your spelling or punctuation. Just write. Let your ideas flow. Write *freely*. Here's an example:

> ### Freewriting about Immigrating to Canada
>
> Immigrating to Canada. Had to leave family and friends. Stepped off the airplane and wow—it was so cold! So many things to do when we first arrived: buy winter clothes, register the children for school, find an apartment. Tried to find a job: is my accent a problem? Employers demand "Canadian experience." How can I get "Canadian experience" if no one will hire me? Should I go back to school instead? Who would take care of the children?

Brainstorming Brainstorming is like freewriting because you write whatever comes into your head, but it's a little different because you can pause to *ask yourself questions* that will lead to new ideas. When you brainstorm alone, you "interview" yourself about a subject. You can also brainstorm and ask questions within a group. Here's an example:

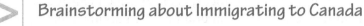

> ### Brainstorming about Immigrating to Canada
>
> **When did we immigrate?**
> January 20, 2014.
>
> **What do I remember about that day?**
> Saying goodbye to friends and family; feeling both excited and sad; exhausting flight; winter in Canada: so cold!
>
> **What is the hardest part about immigrating to Canada?**
> Loss of support network; communicating in another language; trying to find a job without "Canadian experience"; adjusting to a new culture; children becoming Westernized
>
> **What are some of the benefits of immigrating to Canada?**
> Children will have more opportunities in the future; political stability; diverse culture; improving my English skills helped me make new friends; technologically advanced; retirement benefits; universal health care; returned to school and may start a new career

If you feel as though you are running out of ideas in brainstorming, try to form a question out of what you've just written. Go where your questions and answers lead you. For example, if you write, "I returned to school and may start a new career," you could form these questions:

> What career would I consider? What's the job market like in that field? What kind of salary would I make?

You could also make a list of your brainstorming ideas, but remember to *do only one step at a time.*

Keeping a Journal A **journal** is a notebook of your personal writing, a notebook in which you write *regularly* and *often*. It's not a diary, but it is a place to record your experiences, reactions, and observations. In it, you can write about what you have done, heard, seen, read, or remembered. You can include sayings that you would like to remember, news clippings, snapshots—anything that you would like to recall or consider. A journal provides an enjoyable way to practise your writing, and it is a great source of ideas for writing.

> ### Journal Entry about Immigrating to Canada
>
> What's that saying? "When one door closes, another door opens"? It hasn't been easy adjusting to life in a new country, but almost a year after immigrating, things are starting to get easier. The first six months, however, were the most stressful of our lives: learning a new language, getting used to the winter, trying to find jobs and schools for the children. I can see another door opening: perhaps I should continue my education and pursue a different career.

Finding Specific Ideas

Whether you freewrite, brainstorm, or make entries in your journal, you end up with something on paper. Follow those first ideas; see where they can take you. You're looking for specific ideas, each of which can focus the general one you started with. At this point, you don't have to decide which specific idea you want to write about. You just want to *narrow your range* of ideas.

You might think, "Why should I narrow my ideas? Won't I have more to say if I keep my topic big?" But remember that a paragraph has one idea; you want to state it clearly and with convincing details for support. If you try to write one paragraph on the broad topic of immigration, for example, you'll probably make so many general statements that you'll either say very little or bore your reader with big, sweeping assertions. General ideas are big, broad ones. Specific ideas are smaller, narrower ones. If you scanned the freewriting example on immigrating to Canada, you might underline several specific ideas as possible topics:

> Immigrating to Canada. Had to leave family and friends. Stepped off the airplane and wow—it was so cold! <u>So many things to do when we first arrived</u>: buy winter clothes, register the children for school, find an apartment. <u>Tried to find a job</u>: is my accent a problem? Employers demand "Canadian experience." How can I get "Canadian experience" if no one will hire me? <u>Should I go back to school instead?</u> Who would take care of the children?

Consider the underlined points. They are specific challenges the writer faced in immigrating to Canada. You could write a paragraph about any one of these challenges, or you could underline specific challenges in your brainstorming questions and answers:

When did we immigrate?

January 20, 2014.

What do I remember about that day?

Saying goodbye to friends and family; feeling both excited and sad; exhausting flight; winter in Canada: so cold!

What is the hardest part about immigrating to Canada?

<u>Loss of support network; communicating in another language; trying to find a job without "Canadian experience"; adjusting to a new culture</u>; children becoming Westernized

What are some of the benefits of immigrating to Canada?

Children have more opportunities in the future; political stability; diverse culture; improving my English skills helped me make new friends; Canada is technologically advanced; retirement benefits; universal health care; returned to school and may start a new career

Each of these specific challenges could be a topic for your paragraph.

If you reviewed the journal entry on immigrating to Canada, you would also be able to underline specific challenges:

> What's that saying? "When one door closes, another door opens"? It hasn't been easy adjusting to life in a new country, but almost a year after immigrating,

things are starting to get easier. The first six months, however, were the most stressful of our lives: <u>learning a new language, getting used to the winter, trying to find jobs and schools for the children</u>. I can see another door opening: perhaps I should continue my education and pursue a different career.

Remember that if you follow the steps, they can lead you to specific ideas.

Selecting One Topic

Once you have a list of specific ideas that can lead you to a specific topic, you can pick one topic. Let's say you decided to work with the list of challenges gathered through brainstorming:

Loss of support network

Communicating in another language

Trying to find a job without "Canadian experience"

Adjusting to a new culture

Children becoming Westernized

Looking at this list, you decide you want to write about how immigrating to Canada required adjustments by your entire family.

EXERCISE 1	CREATING QUESTIONS FOR BRAINSTORMING

Below are several topics. For each one, brainstorm by writing at least six questions related to the topic that could lead you to further ideas. The first topic is done for you:

1. topic: careers

Question 1: What are the current job prospects in my field?

Question 2: What can I do with a liberal arts degree?

Question 3: Why do people move from job to job these days?

Question 4: What are the best career websites?

Question 5: Should I consider an apprenticeship?

Question 6: Should I go to college or university?

2. topic: renewable energy

Question 1: _____

Question 2: _____

Question 3: _____

Question 4: _____

Question 5: _____

Question 6: _____

   3. topic: mental health

   Question 1: _____

   Question 2: _____

   Question 3: _____

   Question 4: _____

   Question 5: _____

   Question 6: _____

   4. topic: politics

   Question 1: _____

   Question 2: _____

   Question 3: _____

   Question 4: _____

   Question 5: _____

   Question 6: _____

EXERCISE 2

FINDING SPECIFIC DETAILS IN FREEWRITING

Below are two samples of freewriting. Each is a written response to a different topic. Read each sample, and then underline any words and phrases that could become the focus of a paragraph.

Freewriting Reaction to the Topic of Travel

I like to travel. But I'd rather drive than fly. When I drive, I can decide when to stop and go. When you fly, you can get stuck on the runway for hours and never take off. Then when you're in the air, you can't get out until it's over.

   Plus, think of airline food. Disgusting soggy sandwiches or tiny bags of pretzels. And there is no leg room. I can drive and find a nice truck-stop restaurant.

Freewriting Reaction to the Topic of Pollution

Pollution. Save the planet. Smoke pollutes. Big smokestacks at the edge of the city belch smoke all the time. And even smokers pollute, especially indoors. No-smoking rules are controversial. I used to smoke and never thought about pollution. Noise pollution is a pain, too. People who live next to a highway must hear noise all the time.

EXERCISE 3

FINDING SPECIFIC DETAILS IN A LIST

Below are several lists of words or phrases. In each list, one item is a general term; the others are more specific. Underline the words or phrases that are more specific. The first list is done for you.

1. <u>The Winnipeg Free Press</u>
   newspapers
   <u>Vancouver Sun</u>
   <u>The Globe and Mail</u>
   <u>Le Devoir</u>

2. annoying TV jingles
   late-night infomercials
   psychic hotlines
   home-financing commercials
   television commercials

3. stock car racing
   sports
   cheerleaders
   stadium ticket prices
   soccer
   coaches out of control

4. coffee
   decaffeinated
   brewed
   latte
   cappuccino
   espresso

5. Norooz
   Christmas
   holidays
   Diwali
   Ramadan
   Kwanzaa

6. student services
   financial aid
   career counselling
   peer tutoring
   housing placement
   health services

EXERCISE 4

FINDING TOPICS THROUGH FREEWRITING

This exercise must be completed with a partner or a group. Below are several topics. Pick one and freewrite on it for ten minutes. Then read your freewriting to your partner or group. Ask your listener(s) to jot down any words or phrases from your writing that could lead to a specific topic for a paragraph.

Your listener(s) should read to you the jotted-down words or phrases. You'll be hearing a collection of specific ideas that came from *your* writing. As you listen, underline the words in your freewriting.

Freewriting topics (pick one):

1. post-secondary education
2. technology
3. jobs

Freewriting on [name of topic chosen]:

_____

_____

_____

_____

_____

_____

Adding Details to a Specific Topic

You can develop the specific topic you picked in a number of ways:

1. *Check your list* for other ideas that seem to fit with the specific topic you've picked.
2. *Brainstorm*—ask yourself more questions about your topic, and use the answers as detail.
3. *List* any new ideas you have that may be connected to your topic.

One way to add details is to go back and check your brainstorming for other ideas about your chosen topic—for example, the challenge of communicating in another language:

What was the hardest part about immigrating to Canada?

Communicating in another language.

What are some of the benefits of immigrating to Canada?

Improving my English skills helped me make new friends.

Now you can brainstorm some questions that will lead you to more details. The questions don't have to be connected to each other; they are just questions that could lead you to ideas and details:

Why is it important to have friends?

They provide support and encouragement.

What are some examples of how difficult it was to communicate in another language?

finding our luggage at the airport; responding to an advertisement in the newspaper for an apartment; asking for directions on the bus; setting up a bank account.

How did you improve your English skills?

At first I was very shy, and not very confident in my spoken English. I visited my local library and borrowed language CDs.

How did you start to make friends?

The librarian was very helpful and friendly, and after some time I built up enough courage to speak to her. She suggested I take English classes at the community college and gave me a course calendar.

What did you do next?

Once the children were in school, I enrolled in intensive English classes at the community college. There were fifteen other students in the class. I was so nervous the first day.

Did you make any friends in the class?

Yes; we had class every day for three hours. We ate lunch together, and spoke about our lives in our native countries; of course we spoke in English, because we all spoke different native languages. I learned much about other cultures, and practised my English at the same time.

Another way to add details is to list any ideas that may be connected to your topic. The list might give you more specific details:

winter in Canada   minus 20 degrees the day we arrived

considering a new career in office   children adjusted well
administration

If you tried all three ways of adding detail, you would end up with this list of details connected to the topic of immigrating to Canada:

said goodbye to family and friends   had to learn to navigate the public
                                      transportation system
felt both excited and sad
                                      children joined extracurricular
exhausting flight to Canada   sports and activities

loss of support network

was minus 20 degrees the day we
    arrived

had to buy winter clothes

had to shovel snow almost every day

may start a new career

what kind of salary can I expect
    as an office administrator?

what is the job market like for an
    office administrator?

children learned English quite
    quickly

had to adjust to a lack of
    sunlight in winter

children made friends quickly

children are becoming
    Westernized

needed to go back to school
    to start a new career

INFOBOX   **GATHERING IDEAS: A SUMMARY**

The prewriting stage of writing a paragraph enables you to gather ideas. This process begins with several steps:

1. Think on paper and write down any ideas you have about a topic. You can do this by freewriting, brainstorming, or keeping a journal.
2. Scan your writing for specific ideas that have come from your first efforts. List these specific ideas.
3. *Pick one specific idea.* Then, by reviewing your early writing, questioning, and thinking further, you can add details to the one specific idea.

This process may seem long, but once you've worked through it several times it will become nearly automatic. When you think about ideas before you try to shape them into a paragraph, you're off to a good start. Confidence comes from having something to say, and once you have a specific idea, you'll be ready to begin shaping and developing details that support your idea.

EXERCISE 5   **ADDING DETAILS TO A TOPIC BY BRAINSTORMING**

Below are two topics. Each is followed by two or three details. Brainstorm more questions, based on the existing details, that can add more details.

1. **topic:** advantages of going to college part-time
   details: saves money
            less stressful

Question 1:   How much money can you save? _____

Question 2:   What expenses can you cut? _____

Question 3:   What stresses can be reduced? _____

Question 4:   _____

Question 5:   _____

Question 6:   _____

2. **topic:** preparing a résumé
   details: may include references
   can use a template
   include most relevant education and experience

Question 1: <u>What templates would be most appropriate?</u>

Question 2: <u>How do you determine the most relevant information?</u>

Question 3: _____

Question 4: _____

Question 5: _____

Question 6: _____

EXERCISE
6

ADDING DETAILS BY LISTING

Below are four topics for paragraphs. For each topic, list details that seem to fit the topic.

1. **topic:** government benefits
   details:
   a. _____
   b. _____
   c. _____
   d. _____

2. **topic:** copyright infringement
   details:
   a. _____
   b. _____
   c. _____
   d. _____

3. **topic:** unusual jobs
   details:
   a. _____
   b. _____
   c. _____
   d. _____

4. **topic:** good neighbours
   details:
   a. _____
   b. _____

c. _____

d. _____

PREWRITING   FOCUSING IDEAS FOR A PARAGRAPH

The next step of writing is to *focus your ideas around some point*. Your ideas will begin to take a focus if you re-examine them, looking for related ideas. Two techniques that you can use are

- marking a list of related ideas
- mapping related ideas

Listing Related Ideas

To develop a marked list, take another look at the list we developed under the topic of immigrating to Canada. The same list is shown below, but you'll notice that some of the items have been marked with symbols that show related ideas:

W   marks ideas about **winter** in Canada

A   marks ideas about children **adjusting** to Canada

C   marks ideas about starting a new **career** in Canada

Here's the marked list of ideas related to the topic of immigrating to Canada:

said goodbye to family and friends

felt both excited and sad

exhausting flight to Canada

loss of support network

had to learn to navigate the public transportation system

A children joined extracurricular sports and activities

W was minus 20 degrees the day we arrived

W had to buy winter clothes

W had to shovel snow almost every day

C may start a new career

C what kind of salary can I expect as an office administrator?

C what is the job market like for an office administrator?

A children learned English quite quickly

W had to adjust to a lack of sunlight in winter

A children made friends quickly

A children are becoming Westernized

C needed to go back to school to start a new career

You have no doubt noticed that some items are not marked: said goodbye to family and friends, felt both excited and sad, exhausting flight to Canada, loss of support network, had to learn to navigate the public transportation system.

Perhaps you can come back to them later, or you may decide that you don't need them in your paragraph.

To make it easier to see what ideas you have and how they're related, try *grouping related ideas*, giving each list a title, such as the following:

Winter in Canada

was minus 20 degrees the day we arrived

had to buy winter clothes

had to shovel snow almost every day

had to adjust to a lack of sunlight in winter

Children Adjusting to Canada

children joined extracurricular sports and activities

children learned English quite quickly

children made friends quickly

children are becoming Westernized

Starting a New Career in Canada

may start a new career

needed to go back to school to start a new career

what kind of salary can I expect as an office administrator?

what is the job market like for an office administrator?

Mapping

Another way to focus your ideas is to mark your first list of ideas and then cluster the related ideas into separate lists. You can **map** your ideas like this:

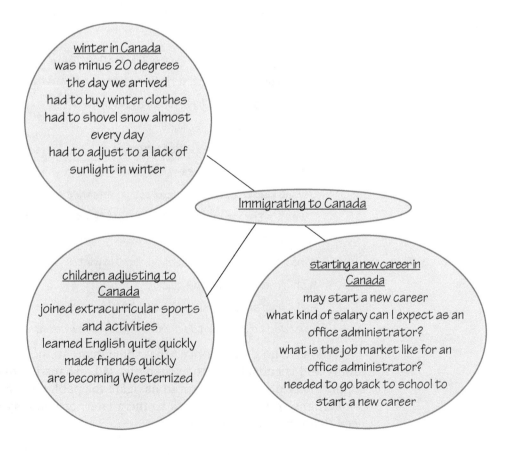

Whatever way you choose to examine and group your details, you are working toward a focus, a point. You are asking and beginning to answer the question, "Where do the details lead?" The answer will be the topic sentence of your paragraph. It will be the *main idea* of your paragraph.

Forming a Topic Sentence

To form a topic sentence, you can do the following:

1. Review your details and see if you can form some general idea that summarizes the details.
2. Write that general idea as one sentence.

Your sentence that summarizes the details is the **topic sentence**. It makes a general point, and the specific details you've gathered will support this point.

To form a topic sentence about immigrating to Canada, follow the steps. First, there are many details about the topic. It's time to ask questions about the details. You could ask yourself, "What kind of details do I have? Can I summarize them?" You might then write the summary as the topic sentence:

> Immigrating to Canada required adjustments for my entire family: adjusting to Canadian winters, the children adjusting to life in Canada, and adjusting my career.

Check the sentence against your details. It covers all three elements you will discuss: winter in Canada, the children adjusting to life in Canada, and starting a new career in Canada.

Writing Good Topic Sentences

Be careful. Topics are not the same as topic sentences. *Topics* are the subjects you will write about. A *topic sentence* states the main idea you've developed on a topic. Consider the differences between the topics and the topic sentences below:

topic:	Why courtesy is important
topic sentence:	Courtesy takes the conflict out of unpleasant encounters.
topic:	Violence on television
topic sentence:	Violence on television promotes violence in our youth.

Topic sentences don't announce; they make a point. Look at the sentences below, and notice the differences between the sentences that announce and the topic sentences:

announcement:	I will discuss the process of writing an essay.
topic sentence:	Writing an essay is easy if you invest some time and follow a simple writing process.
announcement:	An analysis of why recycling paper is important will be the subject of this paper.
topic sentence:	Recycling paper is important because it saves trees, money, and even certain animals.

Topic sentences can be too big to develop in one paragraph. A topic sentence that is *too broad* may take many paragraphs, even pages of writing, to develop. Look at the very broad sentences below, and then notice how they can be narrowed:

too broad:	Athletes get paid too much money. (This sentence is too broad because the term "athletes" could mean anything from professional boxers to college football players to neighbourhood softball teams; "too much money" could mean anything from the fees basketball players receive for endorsing products to the bonuses professional football players get if they make it to the Super Bowl. The sentence could also refer to all athletes in the world at any time in history.)
a narrower, better topic sentence:	Last year, several professional baseball players negotiated high but fair salaries.
too broad:	I changed a great deal in my last year of high school. (The phrase "changed a great deal" could refer to physical changes, intellectual changes, or emotional changes—or to changes in attitude, changes in goals, or changes in just about any other aspect you can think of.)
a narrower, better topic sentence:	In my last year of high school, I overcame my shyness.

Topic sentences can also be too small to develop in one paragraph. A topic sentence that is *too narrow* can't be supported by detail. It may be a fact that can't be developed. A topic sentence that is too narrow leaves you with nothing more to say:

too narrow:	I hate reality television shows.
an expanded topic sentence:	I hate reality television shows because they highlight the worst of human nature.
too narrow:	It takes twenty minutes to get out of the airport parking lot.
an expanded topic sentence:	Congestion in the airport parking lot is causing problems for travellers.

The prewriting stage begins with free, unstructured thinking and writing. As you work through the prewriting process, your thinking and writing will become more focused.

INFOBOX	FOCUSING IDEAS: A SUMMARY

The prewriting stage of writing a paragraph enables you to develop an idea into a topic sentence and related details. You can focus your thinking by working in steps:

1. Mark a list of related details, or try mapping to group your ideas.
2. Write a topic sentence that summarizes your details.
3. Check that your topic sentence is a sentence, not a topic. Make sure that it's not too broad or too narrow, and that it's not an announcement.
   Check that it makes a point and focuses the topic you have developed.

EXERCISE 7

GROUPING RELATED ITEMS IN LISTS OF DETAILS

Below are lists of details. In each list, circle the items that seem to fit into one group; then, underline the items that seem to belong to a second group. Some items may not belong in either group. The first list is done for you.

1. topic: shopping
   (leaves little money for savings)
   (time-consuming)
   time with friends
   supports the economy
   keep up with trends
   (crowded malls)
   lots of advertisements
   get some exercise
   (encourages materialism)
   buy things you like

   YouTube
   Facebook
   blogs
   wikis
   plasma TVs
   iPods

3. topic: falling in love
   romantic moments
   shared thoughts
   jealousy
   Valentine's Day
   mutual respect
   emotional security
   petty arguments
   shared dreams
   fear of commitment
   possessiveness

2. topic: technology
   smartphone applications
   Netflix
   laptops
   tablets

EXERCISE 8

WRITING TOPIC SENTENCES FOR LISTS OF DETAILS

Below are lists of details that have no topic sentence. Write an appropriate topic sentence for each list.

1. topic sentence: _____
   People don't have to be in great shape to take walks.
   Walking burns calories.
   It's good for the heart.
   It's good for the bones and muscles.
   It doesn't cost anything to walk.
   Walking is convenient.
   It requires no exercise equipment or gym membership.
   It can be done almost anywhere.

2. topic sentence:_____
   A popular online bookstore sold more ebooks than physical books for
       the first time this past year.
   Online pharmacies sell everything from prescription drugs to toothpaste.
   Online shopping can be done at any time from the comfort of your own
       home.
   Some online shops offer free shipping.
   In past years, some online shopping sites have experienced a breach of
       their security systems.
   Online customers have had personal information such as addresses,
       phone numbers, and credit card numbers stolen.

3. topic sentence: _____
    Ebooks are cheaper than traditional books.
    Because thousands of books can be stored on an ereader, ebooks are
        more convenient than traditional books.
    Ebooks are more environmentally friendly than traditional books.
    Many people prefer the feel of a traditional book: the texture of the
        paper, the quality of the binding.
    A collection of books in one's home gives a sense of the owner's taste.
    Antique books can be very valuable.
    Traditional books can be shared among friends.

4. topic sentence: _____
    Job candidates are sometimes late for their interviews.
    Candidates can dress inappropriately, in jeans and T-shirts.
    Some candidates chew gum during the interview.
    It's common for candidates to forget to bring additional résumés to an
        interview.
    Hiring managers' most common complaint is that candidates often don't
        research the company in preparation for the interview.
    Candidates are often uncomfortable making a follow-up phone call or
        writing a follow-up email after their interview.
    Candidates sometimes feel too intimidated to ask for clarification if they
        don't understand a question.

EXERCISE 9

TURNING TOPICS INTO TOPIC SENTENCES

Below is a list. Some of the items in the list are topic sentences, but some are topics. Put an *X* beside the items that are topics. In the lines below the list, rewrite the topics as topic sentences.

1. _____ Three reasons to learn a second language.
2. _____ Breaking a habit takes willpower.
3. _____ Canada's greatest heroes.
4. _____ Buying a house is a good investment.
5. _____ Moving up the corporate ladder.
6. _____ My brother discovered his talents in his first job.
7. _____ High-school friendships can be lasting ones.
8. _____ Why driving is stressful.
9. _____ I got a B in history because I studied and reviewed.
10. _____ It is one's civic duty to vote.

Rewrite the topics. Make each one into a topic sentence:

_____
_____
_____
_____
_____
_____

EXERCISE 10 — REVISING TOPIC SENTENCES THAT ARE TOO BROAD

Below is a list of topic sentences. Some of them are too broad to support in one paragraph. Put an *X* beside the ones that are too broad. Then, on the lines below the list, rewrite those sentences, focusing on a limited idea—a topic sentence that could be supported in one paragraph.

1. _____ Working is extremely unpleasant.
2. _____ The most challenging aspect of getting a job was the interview.
3. _____ Taxes are not fair to many people.
4. _____ Camille's honesty makes her a trustworthy friend.
5. _____ Two speeding tickets set my finances back for months.
6. _____ Leon believes in the Canadian way of life and wants it for his children.
7. _____ People should leave their neighbours alone when it comes to little things.
8. _____ Teresa hopes her children will be educated and thoughtful voters.
9. _____ Violence is ruining Canada.
10. _____ My parents fought to keep us out of a gang.

Rewrite the broad sentences. Make each one more limited.

_____

_____

_____

_____

_____

_____

EXERCISE 11 — MAKING ANNOUNCEMENTS INTO TOPIC SENTENCES

Below is a list of sentences. Some are topic sentences. Some are announcements. Put an *X* beside the announcements. Then, on the lines below the list, rewrite the announcements to make them into topic sentences.

1. _____ Lying to a spouse is a destructive habit.
2. _____ The need for winter tires will be the subject of this paper.
3. _____ The need for a new student centre will be explained.
4. _____ Moving to a new city can be a chance for a fresh start.
5. _____ Students at our college need better wireless access.
6. _____ More benches and trees throughout the city would make it more attractive to pedestrians.
7. _____ Why more student bursaries are needed is the subject to be discussed.
8. _____ This essay concerns the growing number of bike thefts on campus.
9. _____ The current law against texting while driving is not working.
10. _____ This paper will be about running a marathon.

Rewrite the announcements. Make each one a topic sentence.

_____

_____

_____

_____

_____

_____

| EXERCISE **12** | REVISING TOPIC SENTENCES THAT ARE TOO NARROW |

Below is a list of topic sentences. Some of them are topics that are too narrow; they can't be developed with details. Put an X beside the ones that are too narrow. Then, on the lines below, rewrite those sentences as broader topic sentences that could be developed in one paragraph.

1. _____ It snowed when I drove to Canmore.
2. _____ On rainy days, I have to pay careful attention to the way I drive.
3. _____ My apartment has only one room.
4. _____ Denzel missed the flight because his car broke down on the highway.
5. _____ Buy-Low is a discount store.
6. _____ Clever use of space made my tiny office look larger.
7. _____ Nilsa drives a Chevrolet.
8. _____ My parents' minivan was a great car for long trips.
9. _____ Chris takes six vitamins every morning.
10. _____ Dr. Chan studied at Dalhousie.

Rewrite the narrow sentences. Make each one broader.

_____
_____
_____
_____
_____
_____
_____

| PLANNING | **DEVISING A PLAN FOR A PARAGRAPH** |

Checking Your Details

Once you have a topic sentence, you can begin working on an **outline** for your paragraph. The outline is a plan that helps you stay focused in your writing. The outline begins to form when you write your topic sentence and make your list of details beneath the topic sentence. You can now look at your list and ask yourself an important question: "Do I have *enough details* to support my topic sentence?" Remember, your goal is to write a paragraph of seven to twelve sentences.

Consider this topic sentence and list of details:

topic sentence:	People can be very rude when they shop in supermarkets.
details:	push in line
	express lane
	too many items

Does the list contain enough details for a paragraph of seven to twelve sentences? Probably not.

Adding Details When There Aren't Enough

To add detail, try brainstorming. Ask yourself some questions like these:

Where else in supermarkets are people rude?
Are they rude in other lanes besides the express lane?
Are they rude in the aisles? How?
Is there crowding anywhere? Where?

By brainstorming, you might come up with this list of details:

topic sentence:	People can be very rude when they shop in supermarkets.
details:	push in line
	express lane
	too many items
	hit my cart with theirs in aisles
	block aisles while they decide
	push ahead in deli area
	won't take a number
	argue with cashier over prices
	yell at the stock clerk

Keep brainstorming until you feel you have enough details for a seven- to twelve-sentence paragraph. Remember that it's better to have too many details than too few, for you can always delete the extra details later.

If you try brainstorming and still don't have many details, you can refer to your original ideas—your freewriting or journal—for other details.

Eliminating Details That Don't Relate to the Topic Sentence

Sometimes, what you thought were good details don't relate to the topic sentence because they don't fit or support your point. Eliminate details that don't relate to the topic sentence. For example, the following list contains details that really don't relate to the topic sentence. Those details are crossed out.

topic sentence:	Waiters have to be very patient in dealing with their customers.
details:	customers take a long time ordering
	~~waiters' salary is low~~
	waiters have to explain specials twice
	customers send orders back
	customers blame waiters for any delays
	customers want food instantly
	waiters can't react to sarcasm of customers
	waiters can't get angry if customers do
	~~waiters work long shifts~~
	customers change their mind after ordering

From List to Outline

Take another look at the topic sentence and list of details on immigrating to Canada:

topic sentence:	Immigrating to Canada required adjustments for my entire family: adjusting to Canadian winters, the children adjusting to life in Canada, and adjusting my career.

details: said goodbye to family and friends
                          felt both excited and sad
                          exhausting flight to Canada
                          loss of support network
                          had to learn to navigate the public transportation
                             system
                          children joined extracurricular sports and activities
                          was minus 20 degrees the day we arrived
                          had to buy winter clothes
                          had to shovel snow almost every day
                          may start a new career
                          what kind of salary can I expect as an office
                             administrator?
                          what is the job market like for an office administrator?
                          children learned English quite quickly
                          had to adjust to a lack of sunlight in winter
                          children made friends quickly
                          children are becoming Westernized
                          needed to go back to school to start a new career

After you scan that list, you're ready to develop the outline of the paragraph.

An outline is a plan for writing, and it can be a type of draft in list form. It sketches what you want to write and the order in which you want to present it. An organized, logical list will make your writing *unified* since each item on the list will relate to your topic sentence.

When you plan, keep your topic sentence in mind:

> Immigrating to Canada required adjustments for my entire family: <u>adjusting to Canadian winters</u>, the <u>children adjusting to life in Canada</u>, and <u>adjusting my career</u>.

Notice the underlined key phrases, which lead to three key parts of your outline:

> adjusting to Canadian winters
> children adjusting to life in Canada
> adjusting my career

You can put the details on your list together so that they connect to one of these parts:

adjusting to Canadian winters
   —was minus 20 degrees the day we arrived; had to buy winter clothes; had to shovel snow almost every day; had to adjust to a lack of sunlight in winter

children adjusting to life in Canada
   —children joined extracurricular sports and activities; children learned English quite quickly; children made friends quickly; children are becoming Westernized

adjusting my career
   —needed to go back to school to start a new career; what kind of salary can I expect as an office administrator? what is the job market like for an office administrator?

With this kind of grouping, you have a clearer idea of how to organize a paragraph.

Now that you've grouped your ideas with key words and details, you can write an outline.

As you can see, the outline combines some of the details from the list. Even with these combinations, the details are very rough. As you reread the list of details, you'll notice places that need more combination, places where ideas need more explaining, and places that are repetitive. Keep in mind that an outline is merely a very rough organization of your paragraph.

INFOBOX   **AN OUTLINE FOR A PARAGRAPH**

topic sentence: Immigrating to Canada required adjustments for my entire family: adjusting to Canadian winters, the children adjusting to life in Canada, and adjusting my career.

details: **adjusting to Canadian winters**
It was minus 20 degrees the day we arrived.
We had to buy winter clothes.
We had to shovel snow almost every day.
We had to adjust to a lack of sunlight in winter.

children adjusting to life in Canada
The children joined extracurricular sports and activities.
The children learned English quite quickly.
The children made friends quickly.
The children are becoming Westernized.

adjusting my career
I needed to go back to school to start a new career.
What kind of salary can I expect as an office administrator?
What's the job market like for an office administrator?

As you work through the steps in designing an outline, you can check for the following:

Coherence: Putting Your Details in Proper Order

Check the sample outline again and you will notice that the details are grouped in the same order as the topic sentence: first, details about adjusting to Canadian winters; next, details about how the children adjusted to life in Canada; and then, details about adjustments you'd like to make to your career. Putting the details in an order that matches the topic sentence is a logical order for this paragraph.

Putting the details in logical order makes the ideas in your paragraph easy to follow. The most logical order for a paragraph depends on the subject of the paragraph. If you're writing about an event, you might use **time order** (such as telling what happened first, second, and so forth); if you're arguing some point, you might use **emphatic order** (such as saving your most convincing idea for last); if you're describing a room, you might use **space order** (such as from left to right or from top to bottom).

The format of the outline helps to organize your ideas. The topic sentence is written above the list of details. This position helps you remember that the topic sentence is the main idea, and the details that support it are written under it. The topic sentence is the most important sentence of the paragraph. You can easily check the items on your list, one by one, against your main idea. You can also develop the **unity** (relevance) and **coherence** (logical order) of your details.

When you actually write a paragraph, the topic sentence doesn't necessarily have to be the first sentence in the paragraph. Read the paragraphs below, and notice where each topic sentence is placed.

Topic Sentence at the Beginning of the Paragraph

Health care should be the federal government's priority over the next few years. With an increasingly aging population and fewer younger taxpayers to replace them, Canada is going to encounter a strain on its health-care resources in the near future. Hospital waiting times are on the rise, and more elderly people are going to require home health care or placements in nursing homes. Incidences of certain cancers are on the rise. Many Canadians do not have a family physician, and thus visit already overburdened emergency wards when they get sick. Modern lifestyle choices in diet and exercise, with the addition of daily stress, have increased the incidence of disease. If the government does not enact a plan to address these challenges, our health-care system will soon be overwhelmed.

Topic Sentence in the Middle of the Paragraph

Trees lined both sides of the street. Sidewalks were wide, allowing for pedestrians to take leisurely walks. Quaint, independent stores with large windows invited passersby to window shop. Benches were provided for the weary to rest. The street was the perfect example of "defensible space," a space designed to be welcoming and to deter crime. The cobblestone street made an appealing sound as cars rumbled by. People enjoyed drinks on patios as their dogs lay nearby.

Topic Sentence at the End of the Paragraph

In the following paragraph, taken from an article entitled "Arts Education Does Pay Off" by Livio Di Matteo (1999), the topic sentence is placed at the end of the paragraph.

Canada's universities—particularly the humanities and social sciences—face a major challenge. This has led to government funding initiatives in science and technology that fail to recognize the importance of a liberal arts education. Yet supporting a humanities and social science education is justified on sound economic grounds, not just on the civic and academic grounds used.

Since many of your paragraph assignments will require a clear topic sentence, make sure to follow your instructor's directions about placement of the topic sentence.

CHECKLIST | **FOR AN OUTLINE**

✓ **Unity:** Do all the details relate to the topic sentence? If they do, the paragraph will be unified.

✓ **Support:** Do you have enough supporting ideas? Can you add to these ideas with even more specific details?

✓ **Coherence:** Are the details listed in the right order? If the order of points is logical, the paragraph will be coherent.

EXERCISE

13

ADDING DETAILS TO SUPPORT A TOPIC SENTENCE

The topic sentences below have some—but not enough—detail. Write sentences to add details to the list below each topic sentence.

1. **topic sentence:** Procrastination is the thief of time.

   a. <u>Putting off applying to college may mean missing the deadline and having to wait until the following semester.</u>

   b. _____

   c. _____

   d. _____

   e. _____

   f. _____

   g. _____

2. **topic sentence:** In a technological age, libraries are even more important.

   a. <u>Families who cannot afford home internet access can conduct research and read emails at their local library.</u>

   b. _____

   c. _____

   d. _____

   e. _____

   f. _____

   g. _____

3. **topic sentence:** A parent can show his or her love without spending a great deal of money.

   a. <u>Attending a child's school events shows interest.</u>

   b. _____

   c. _____

   d. _____

   e. _____

f. _____

g. _____

4. **topic sentence:** The first day of college can be confusing and tense.

a. A student may not know how to find the classroom for his or her first class.

b. _____

c. _____

d. _____

e. _____

f. _____

g. _____

EXERCISE

14

ELIMINATING DETAILS THAT DON'T FIT

Below are topic sentences and lists of supporting details. Cross out the details that do not fit the topic sentence.

1. **topic sentence:** Computers can limit or harm a small child's growth.
    details: Some children spend too much time indoors on their computers when they could be outdoors.
    They may lose out on the health benefits of exercise.
    They may rely on the computer as a substitute for interacting with real friends.
    In some cases, a child who spends too much time in cyberspace can become very uncomfortable around others.
    As a child, I always had several friends at my house.
    Computers can expose children to questionable pictures or photographs.
    All children should be encouraged to read.

2. **topic sentence:** Everywhere I look, I see how music influences fashion.
    details: Music celebrities wear a certain style.
    Soon, the style becomes a fad.
    One diva will be famous for her hairstyle.
    Then her fans want their hair styled the same way.
    Another celebrity is photographed in trendy clothing.
    He creates a line of clothing named after him, crossing into the fashion industry.
    Many stars in the music world have to look good.
    If a popular musician wears a certain kind of jewellery, like a necklace or bracelet, many fans want the same jewellery.
    Music is a universal language.

3. **topic sentence:** People give many reasons for texting while driving.
    details: Some people say they don't know it's illegal.
    Others say the text will "only take a second."
    Police officers can pull drivers over and give them fines.
    Some people claim that they must text, as it's "an emergency."

A few say they think texting is safer than calling.
Many deny they were even texting.
Some say it's a work-related text.
Some students text in class.

<table>
<tr><td>**EXERCISE**
15</td><td>**COHERENCE: PUTTING DETAILS IN THE RIGHT ORDER**</td></tr>
</table>

These outlines have details that are in the wrong order. In the space provided, number the sentences in the right order: 1 would be the number for the first sentence, and so on.

1. **topic sentence:** Our garage sale was a disaster from start to finish.

   _____ By noon, we had nothing left to sell, and people were still coming.

   _____ People began to arrive at 8:30, before we had put out all the merchandise.

   _____ These early arrivals grabbed all the best bargains, even before we had a chance to put on price tags.

   _____ We started setting up at 8:15, thinking we had plenty of time.

   _____ At mid-morning, our yard was full of people, most of them complaining because we had so little left to sell.

   _____ The latest arrivals left, complaining because they had made a trip for nothing.

   _____ We were up at 7:30 a.m., putting Garage Sale signs around the neighbourhood.

   _____ We spent the afternoon cleaning up.

   _____ That evening, we swore that our next sale would start earlier and include more merchandise.

2. **topic sentence:** A parent's job is never done.

   _____ At work, I have to keep an eye on the clock to make sure I leave in time to pick up my son from school.

   _____ After dinner, it's time for his bath.

   _____ Then there's the daily scramble to make the school bus.

   _____ We have dinner together.

   _____ The first order of the day is to wake up my son.

   _____ The race is on to pick him up on time.

   _____ Breakfast usually consists of cereal for him and a large cup of coffee for me.

   _____ We read a story before he gets into bed.

   _____ Only after he's in bed do I realize that I still have to put away all his toys.

3. **topic sentence:** Losing my car keys was a stressful experience.

   _____ I rushed out the door, reaching for my car keys on the counter, where I always left them.

   _____ I grabbed some keys, but they were my brother's house keys.

   _____ I was late for work, as usual, so I hurried out of the apartment.

   _____ When I had done a thorough search of the counter, I panicked.

   _____ Trying to be calm, I looked more closely at the counter, searching for my car keys under a pile of mail, behind a stack of magazines, next to the spice rack.

_____   My next step was a frantic search of my entire apartment and the car.

_____   Unable to find my keys anywhere, I called my boss to tell him I would be late.

_____   Then I called a friend, who gave me a ride to work.

DRAFTING AND REVISING

DRAFTING AND REVISING A PARAGRAPH

Drafting a Paragraph

The outline is a draft in list form. You're now ready to write the list in paragraph form, to "rough out" a draft of your assignment. This stage of writing is the time to draft, revise, edit, and redraft. You may write several drafts in this stage, but don't think of this as an unnecessary chore or a punishment. It's a way of taking the pressure off yourself. By revising in steps, you're reminding yourself that the first try doesn't have to be perfect.

Review the outline on immigrating to Canada on page 23. You can create a first draft of this outline in the form of a paragraph. (Remember that the first line of each paragraph is indented.) In the draft of the paragraph below, the first sentence of the paragraph is the topic sentence.

> ### A First Draft of a Paragraph
>
> Immigrating to Canada required adjustments for my entire family: adjusting to Canadian winters, the children adjusting to life in Canada, and adjusting my career. It was minus 20 degrees the day we arrived. We had to buy winter clothes. We had to shovel snow almost every day. We had to adjust to a lack of sunlight in winter. The children had to adjust to life in Canada. The children joined extracurricular sports and activities. The children learned English quite quickly. The children made friends quickly. The children are becoming Westernized. I had to make adjustments to my career. I needed to go back to school to start a new career. What kind of salary can I expect as an office administrator? What is the job market like for an office administrator?

Revising

Once you have a first draft, you can begin to think about revising and editing it. **Revising** means rewriting the draft by making changes in the order of the sentences (coherence) and in the content (unity). **Editing** includes making changes in the choice of words and in the length, pattern, and kinds of sentences (style), in the selection of details (support), and in sentence structure and punctuation (grammar). It may also include adding **transitions**, which are words, phrases, or sentences that link ideas.

One way to begin revising and editing is to read your work aloud to yourself. Listen to your words, and consider the questions in the following checklist.

✓ Am I staying on my point?
✓ Should I take out any ideas that don't relate?
✓ Do I have enough to say about my point?
✓ Should I add any details?
✓ Should I change the order of my sentences?
✓ Is my choice of words appropriate?
✓ Is my choice of words repetitive?
✓ Are my sentences too long? Too short?
✓ Should I combine any sentences?
✓ Am I running sentences together?
✓ Am I writing complete sentences?
✓ Can I link my ideas more smoothly?

If you apply the checklist to the first draft of the paragraph on immigrating to Canada, you'll probably find these rough spots:

- The sentences are very short and choppy.
- Some sentences could be combined.
- Some words are repeated often.
- Some ideas would be more effective if they were supported by more detail.
- The paragraph could use a few transitions.

Consider the following revised draft of the paragraph and notice the changes, underlined, that have been made in the draft. You'll also notice some errors that will need to be corrected at the proofreading stage.

A Revised Draft of a Paragraph

Immigrating to Canada required adjustments for my entire family: adjusting to Canadian winters, the children adjusting to life in Canada, and adjusting my career. It was minus 20 degrees that day we arrived in january. We had to buy winter clothes for the entire family: hats, gloves, scarfs, parkas, and boots. We

sentences combined

had to shovel snow <u>almost every day, and had</u> to adjust to a lack of sun light in

detail added

winter. <u>In the morning, it was difficult to get out of bed when it was still dark</u>

transition added
details added; repetitive words eliminated

<u>outside. In adition,</u> the children had to adjust to life in Canada. <u>At school, they</u> <u>joined extracurricular sports and activities such as chess club and the soccer</u>

detail added; sentences combined

<u>team. The children learned English quite quickly, speaking it all day at school, and</u> <u>this helped them make friends quickly.</u> <u>Indeed, I beleive</u> the children are becoming

transition added; detail added
transition added

Westernized. <u>Immigrating to Canada meant</u> I had to make adjustments to my

detail added

career, too. I needed to go back to school to start a new career and <u>discovered</u> <u>office administration at the community college.</u> What kind of salary can I expect as an office administrator? What is the job market like for an office administrator?

When you're revising your own paragraph, you can use the checklist to help you. Read the checklist several times; then reread your draft, looking for answers to the questions on the list. If your instructor agrees, you can work with your classmates. Start by reading your draft to a partner or a group. Your listener(s) can react to your draft by applying the questions on the checklist and by making notes about your draft as you read. When you're finished reading aloud, your partner(s) can discuss the notes about your work.

EXERCISE

16

REVISING A DRAFT BY COMBINING SENTENCES

The paragraph below has many short, choppy sentences. The short, choppy sentences are underlined. Wherever you see two or more underlined sentences clustered next to each other, combine the clustered sentences into one clear, smooth sentence. Write your revised version of the paragraph in the spaces above the lines.

Paragraph to Be Revised

My brother is a baseball fanatic. He wakes up in the morning thinking about the game. <u>He reaches for the newspaper. He checks out all the baseball scores.</u> He talks about baseball during breakfast. He can't stop talking and thinking about baseball during work. <u>He talks about his favourite teams during his break. He has baseball conversations during lunch. With customers, he argues about the sport.</u> My brother's clothes reflect his obsession. <u>He has seven baseball caps. There are three baseball jackets in his closet. He owns at least twelve shirts marked with team insignias.</u> For him, it's always baseball season.

EXERCISE

17

ADDING DETAILS TO A DRAFT

Complete this exercise with a partner or a group. The paragraph below lacks the kind of details that would make it more interesting. Working with a partner or a group, add the details in the blank spaces provided. When you're finished with the additions, read the revised paragraph to the class.

Paragraph to Be Revised

Popular movies come in a variety of forms. Some offer exciting action sequences. The action may involve war, in a movie like _____, or a dramatic chase, in films such as _____ and _____. Other popular movies feature tragic love stories. _____ is this kind of film. Every year, one kind of film especially popular with children is the blockbuster animated feature, like _____ or _____. Equally popular are the outrageous comedies that appeal to teens or college students. Movies such as _____ and _____ are perfect examples of these comedies. Clearly, there are films to suit all tastes and ages.

PROOFREADING PROOFREADING AND POLISHING A PARAGRAPH

The final version of your paragraph is the result of careful thinking, planning, and revising. After you've written as many drafts as you need, you then read to polish and proofread. You can avoid too many last-minute corrections if you check your last draft carefully. Check that draft for the following:

- spelling errors
- punctuation errors
- grammar errors
- word choice
- a final statement

Take a look at an earlier draft of the paragraph on immigrating to Canada. Corrections are written directly above the crossed-out material. At the end of the paragraph, you'll notice that a concluding sentence has been added to unify the paragraph.

> ## Correcting the Last Draft of a Paragraph
>
> Immigrating to Canada required adjustments for my entire family: adjusting to Canadian winters, the children adjusting to life in Canada, and adjusting my career. It was minus 20 degrees that day we arrived in ~~january~~ January. We had to buy winter clothes for the entire family: hats, gloves, ~~scarfs~~ scarves, parkas, and boots. We had to shovel snow almost every day, and had to adjust to a lack of ~~sunlight~~ sunlight in winter. In the morning, it was difficult to get out of bed when it was still dark outside. In ~~adition~~ addition, the children had to adjust to life in Canada. At school, they joined extracurricular sports and activities such as chess club and the soccer team. The children learned English quite quickly, speaking it all day at school, and this helped them make friends quickly. Indeed, I ~~beleive~~ believe the children are becoming Westernized. Immigrating to Canada meant I had to make adjustments to my career, too. I needed to go back to school to start a new career and discovered office administration at the community college. What kind of salary can I expect as an office administrator? What is the job market like for an office administrator? Although immigrating to Canada may have been intimidating and required many adjustments by my family, our future looks bright, and I am looking forward to it.

Giving Your Paragraph a Title

When you prepare the final version of your paragraph, you may be asked to give it a title. The title should be short and should fit the subject of the paragraph. For example, an appropriate title for the paragraph on immigrating to Canada could be "Immigrating to Canada" or "Adjusting to Life in Canada." Check with your instructor to see if your paragraph needs a title. In this book, the paragraphs do not have titles.

The Final Version of a Paragraph

Below is the final version of the paragraph on immigrating to Canada. As you read it, you will notice a few more changes. Even though the paragraph went through several drafts and many revisions, the final copy still reflects some additional polishing: some details have been added, some have been made more specific, and some words have been changed. These changes were made as the final version was prepared. (They are underlined for your reference.)

> ### A Final Version of a Paragraph (*changes from the previous draft are underlined*)

Immigrating to Canada required adjustments for my entire family: adjusting to Canadian winters, the children adjusting to life in Canada, and adjusting my career. It was minus 20 degrees that day we arrived in January. We had to buy winter clothes for the entire family: hats, gloves, scarves, parkas, and boots, <u>and on the same day we arrived</u>. We had to shovel snow almost every day, and had to adjust to a lack of sunlight in winter. In the morning, it was difficult to get out of bed when it was still dark outside, <u>and still more difficult to get the children out of bed and off to school</u>. In addition, the children had to adjust to life in Canada. At school, they joined extracurricular sports and activities such as chess club and the soccer team. The children learned English quite quickly, speaking it all day at school, and this helped them make friends <u>easily</u>. Indeed, I believe the children are becoming Westernized. Immigrating to Canada meant I had to make adjustments to my career, too. I needed to go back to school to start a new career and discovered office administration at the community college. What kind of salary can I expect as an office administrator? What is the job market like for an office administrator? Although immigrating to Canada may have been intimidating and required many adjustments by my family, our future looks bright, and I am looking forward to it.

Reviewing the Writing Process

This chapter has taken you through four important stages in writing. As you become more comfortable with them, you'll be able to work through them more quickly. For now, try to remember the four stages.

INFOBOX	THE STAGES OF THE WRITING PROCESS

Prewriting: gathering and developing ideas, thinking on paper through freewriting, brainstorming, mapping, or keeping a journal.

Planning: planning the paragraph by combining and dividing details, focusing the details with a topic sentence, listing the supporting details in proper order, and devising an outline.

Drafting and Revising: writing a rough draft of the paragraph, then revising and editing it several times.

Proofreading: preparing the final version of the paragraph, with one last proofreading check for errors in preparation, punctuation, and mechanics.

EXERCISE 18

PROOFREADING TO PREPARE THE FINAL VERSION

Here are two illustration paragraphs with the kinds of errors that are easy to overlook when you prepare the final version of an assignment. Correct the errors by writing above the lines. There are ten errors in the first paragraph and nine errors in the second paragraph.

1. Mature students can have additionall responsibilities that make college life particularly stressfull. It may have been many years since they've been back at school, so they may feel apprehensive about returning to a classroom setting. They're classmates are often younger, so mature students' may have trouble making friends; they often have jobs or familys, so matures student may not be able to stay after class to socialize. A mature student, in addition to a full coarse load, may work up to thirty hours a week to support her family. She is likely exhausted by the time she arrives home to her family. After spending time with her children, she will work on her school assignments. Often mature student's sacrifice sleep, getting well under the recomended 8 hours per night. May be more bursaries are needed to support these mature students.

2. Insufficient parking is a serious prolem for student's at Carlyle College. Very often, students are forced to drive around the filled rows for ten or twenty minutes, looking for a solitary space. if they find one, it is at the end of a long row. And by the time they find it and have walked the long way to there classroom, they are late for class. They run the risk of missing a quiz or being penalize in some other way. For those who cannot find a space, there are even more risky alternatives. Some students parks in a faculty spot or in a fire Lane. These students risk getting a ticket and a fine, but they must weigh this risk against missing class. Carlyle College administrators need to reconize students' parking dilemmas and provide more parking spaces for students who just want to get to class on time.

Lines of Detail: A Walk-Through Assignment

This assignment involves working within a group to write a paragraph.

Step 1: Read the three sentences below. Pick the one sentence you prefer as a possible topic sentence for a paragraph. Fill in the blank, if necessary, for the sentence you chose.

   a. Holding down a part-time job while at school can be challenging for a college or university student.

   b. Our society places too much emphasis on material possessions.

   c. _____ was the most stressful period in my life. [fill in the time in your life]

Step 2: Join a group composed of other students who picked the same topic sentence you picked. In your class, you'll have "job" people, "possessions" people, and "stress" people. Brainstorm in a group. Discuss questions that could be used to get ideas for your paragraph.

   For the job topic, sample questions could include, "What are the most challenging aspects of working and studying?" or "How does this challenge affect other areas or aspects of a student's life?" For the possessions topic, sample questions could include, "What kinds of possessions do people want?" or "Do certain age groups want different possessions?" For the stress topic, sample questions could include, "Why was it so stressful?" or "How did you overcome the stress?"

   As you discuss, write the questions, not the answers, below. Keep the questions flowing. Don't stop to say, "That's silly" or "I can't answer that." Try to devise at least ten questions.

Ten Brainstorming Questions

1. _____

2. _____

3. _____

4. _____

5. _____

6. _____

7. _____

8. _____

9. _____

10. _____

Step 3: Split up. Alone, begin to think on paper. Answer as many questions as you can, or add more questions and answers, or freewrite.

Step 4: Draft an outline of the paragraph. You'll probably have to change the topic sentence to fit the details you've gathered. For example, your new topic sentence might be something like,

Holding down a part-time job while at school can be challenging because of _____, _____, and _____.

or

Our society places too much emphasis on material possessions, such as _____, _____, and _____.

or

_____ was the most stressful period in my life because _____.

Remember to look at your details to see where they lead you. The details will help you refine your topic sentence.

Step 5: Prepare the first draft of the paragraph.

Step 6: Read the draft aloud to your writing group, the same people who met to brainstorm. Ask each member of your group to make at least one positive comment and one suggestion for revision.

Step 7: Revise and edit your draft, considering the group's ideas and your own ideas for improvement.

Step 8: Prepare a final version of the paragraph.

Writing Your Own Paragraph

When you write on any of these topics, follow the four basic stages of the writing process in preparing your paragraph.

1. Begin this assignment with a partner. The assignment requires an interview. Your final goal is to write a paragraph that will introduce a class member, your partner, to the rest of the class. In the final paragraph, you may design your own topic sentence or use one of the topic sentences below, filling in the blanks with the material you've discovered:

There are several things you should know about _____. [fill in your partner's name]

or

Three unusual events have happened to _____. [fill in your partner's name]

Before you write the paragraph, follow these steps:

Step 1: Prepare to interview a classmate. Make a list of six questions you might want to ask. They can be questions like, "Where are you from?" or "Have you ever done anything unusual?" Write *at least six questions* before you start the interview. List the questions on the following interview form, leaving room to fill in short answers later.

Interview Form

Question 1:_____

Answer: _____

Question 2: _____

Answer: _____

Question 3: _____

Answer: _____

Question 4: _____

Answer: _____

Question 5: _____

Answer: _____

Question 6: _____

Answer: _____

Additional questions and answers: _____

_____

_____

Step 2: Meet and interview your partner. Ask the questions on your list. Jot down brief answers. Ask any other questions you think of as you're talking; write down the answers on the additional lines at the end of the interview form.

Step 3: Change places. Let your partner interview you.

Step 4: Split up. Use the list of questions and answers about your partner as the prewriting part of your assignment. Work on the outline and draft steps.

Step 5: Ask your partner to read the draft version of your paragraph, to write any comments or suggestions for improvement below the paragraph, and to mark any spelling or grammar errors in the paragraph itself.

Step 6: When you've completed a final version of the paragraph, read the paragraph to the class.

2. Below are some topic sentences. Select one and use it to write a paragraph.

Experience is the best teacher.

My daily commute provides several irritations.

Reality TV shows are not realistic at all.

College is a good place to _____ and _____.

3. Write a paragraph on one of the topics below. Create your own topic sentence; explain and support it with specific details.

a favourite activity	the best gift
applying for a job	one stress-buster
a sad occasion	the best time of day
a challenging class	bullying
my biggest regret	texting
an exciting sport	a proud moment

MyWriting**Lab**

CHAPTER 2
Writing from Reading

LEARNING OBJECTIVES

After you have read this chapter and completed its exercises and assignments, you should be able to

- read a piece of writing and identify its thesis and main ideas
- make notes of the main ideas in a piece of writing
- write a summary and a paraphrase of a piece of writing
- avoid plagiarizing a piece of writing
- respond to a piece of writing
- write an essay test effectively and efficiently

"Say all you have to say in the fewest possible words, or your reader will be sure to skip them; and in the plainest possible words or he will certainly misunderstand them."

~ JOHN RUSKIN

▼ JOHN RUSKIN, BORN IN THE NINETEENTH CENTURY, WAS KNOWN FOR HIS ART AND SOCIAL CRITICISM.

Reflecting

What do you think John Ruskin meant by this? Do you agree or disagree?

Want to learn more about Ruskin? Go to www.victorianweb.org/authors/ruskin/index.html to find out about his life and works.

WHAT IS WRITING FROM READING?

One way to find topics for writing is to draw from your ideas, memories, and observations. Another way is to write from reading you've done. You can *react* to it; you can *agree* or *disagree* with something you've read. In fact, many college assignments ask you to write about an assigned reading: an essay, a chapter in a textbook, an article in a journal. This kind of writing requires an active, involved attitude toward your reading. Such reading is done in steps:

1. preread
2. read
3. reread with a pen or pencil

After you've completed these three steps, you can write from your reading. You can write about what you've read or you can react to what you've read.

AN APPROACH TO WRITING FROM READING

Attitude

Before you begin the first step of this reading process, you have to have a certain **attitude**. That attitude involves thinking of what you read as half of a conversation. The writer has opinions and ideas; he or she makes points just as you do when you write or speak. The writer supports his or her points with specific details. If the writer were speaking to you in a conversation, you would respond to his or her opinions or ideas. You would agree, disagree, or question. You would jump into the conversation, linking or contrasting your ideas with those of the other speaker.

The right attitude toward reading demands that you read the same way you converse: you *become involved*. In doing this, you "talk back" as you read, and later you react in your own writing. Reacting as you read will keep you focused on what you're reading. If you're focused, you'll remember more of what you read. With an active, involved attitude, you can begin the step of prereading.

Prereading

Before you actually read an assigned essay, a chapter in a textbook, or an article in a journal, magazine, or newspaper, take a few minutes to **preread** it: look it over, and be ready to answer the questions in the prereading checklist below.

CHECKLIST | FOR PREREADING

- ✓ How long is this reading?
- ✓ Will I be able to read it in one sitting, or will I have to schedule several time periods to finish it?
- ✓ Are there any subheadings in the reading? Do they give any hints about the reading?
- ✓ Are there any charts? Graphs? Boxes of information?
- ✓ Are there any photographs or illustrations with captions? Do the photos or captions give me any hints about the reading?
- ✓ Is there any introductory material about the reading or its author? Does the introductory material give me any hints about the reading?
- ✓ What is the title of the reading? Does the title hint at the point of the reading?
- ✓ Are any parts of the reading underlined, italicized, or emphasized in some other way? Do the emphasized parts hint at the point of the reading?

Why Preread?

Prereading takes very little time, but it will help you immensely. Some students believe that it's a waste of time to scan an assignment; they think they should jump right in and get the reading over with. However, spending just a few minutes on preliminaries can save hours later. And, most important, prereading helps you become a *focused reader*.

If you scan the length of an assignment, you can pace yourself. And if you know how long a reading is, you can alert yourself to its plan. A short reading, for example, has to come to its point fairly early. A longer essay may take more time to develop its point and may use more details and examples.

Subheadings, charts, graphs, illustrations, and boxed or other highlighted materials are important enough that the author wants to emphasize them. Looking over that material *before* you read will give you an overview of the important points the reading contains.

Introductory material or questions will also help you know what to look for as you read. Some background on the author or on the subject may hint at ideas that will come up in the reading. Sometimes, even the title of the reading will give you the main idea.

You should preread so that you can start reading the entire assignment with as much *knowledge* about the writer and the subject as you can get. Then, when you read the entire assignment, you'll be reading *actively*, for more knowledge.

Forming Questions Before You Read

If you want to read with a focus, it helps to ask questions before you read. Form questions by using the information you gain from prereading.

Start by noting the title and turning it into a question. If the title of your assigned reading is "Reasons for the War Measures Act," you can ask the question, "What were the reasons for the War Measures Act?"

You can turn subheadings into questions. If you are reading an article on beach erosion, and one subheading is "Artificial Reefs," you can ask, "How are artificial reefs connected to beach erosion?"

You can also form questions from graphs and illustrations. If a chapter in your history book includes a photograph of a Gothic cathedral, you could ask, "How are Gothic cathedrals connected to this period in history?" or "Why are Gothic cathedrals important?" or "What is Gothic architecture?"

You can write down these questions, but it's not necessary. Just forming questions and keeping them in the back of your mind helps you read actively and stay focused.

An Example of the Prereading Step

Take a look at the article that follows. Don't read it; *preread* it.

Free for All

Jesse Brown

Jesse Brown, a contributor to Toronto Life, *examines the impact of mobile computing and social media. Here, he describes his experience with Massive Open Online Courses (MOOCs).*

I'm studying sociology at Princeton in my spare time. I'm also taking game theory at Stanford, computer programming at the University of Toronto and **equine** nutrition at the University of Edinburgh. I attend class in my underwear, watch cartoons during lectures and cheat on tests with help from some of my hundreds of thousands of classmates. The classes I'm enrolled in are called MOOCs—Massive Open Online Courses, available for free to knowledge-hungry students of life like myself through the educational website Coursera.

MOOCs are a global phenomenon with Canadian roots. The term was coined in 2008 by Dave Cormier, a web communications manager at the University of P.E.I., to

equine: regarding horses

describe an Internet-based course designed by professor George Siemens of Athabasca University in Alberta and Stephen Downes of the National Research Council. Twenty-five University of Manitoba students signed up for a course on connectivist theory and were joined by 2,300 virtual students from the general public, who participated free of charge via the web.

The MOOC concept stalled until 2011, when Stanford offered three open online courses and received a staggering 350,000 registrants from 190 countries. A couple of the Stanford profs involved with the experiment were encouraged enough to drop everything and launch Coursera, a self-described "social entrepreneurship company." And there have been other launches, notably Udacity and EdX, a joint venture of MIT and Harvard. In a matter of months, MOOCs attracted millions of students from around the world and millions of dollars in venture capital. Coursera alone has enrolled 2.6 million students and secured $16 million in investment. But according to **evangelists**, MOOCs are not about money—they're about revolutionizing post-secondary education.

evangelists: people who believe very strongly in the subject at hand

Last July, U of T signed up as a Coursera partner. Students can't earn course credits for taking the classes, nor do they pay any fees. And no money changes hands between Coursera and U of T—at least not yet. If profits emerge in the future—through nominal tuition fees or by selling their database—Coursera says the money will be shared with partner universities.

My computer programming class, one of seven MOOCs offered by U of T, attracted more than 100,000 registrants. Yes, I'm participating for the purpose of writing this article, but I'm also hoping to learn something about programming. Without reading the honour code—which I assume says something about promising not to cheat—I click a button swearing to uphold it, and class begins.

I half expect a bunch of videotaped lectures. I'm half right. While the course is taught via a series of short videos starring my teachers—senior computer science lecturers Jennifer Campbell and Paul Gries—the videos weren't created by pointing a Handycam at a lectern. They were designed specifically for the web, and the **production values** are pretty good. When the teachers code, I watch them code. Difficult concepts are rendered simple through live-drawn illustrations. When the class gets ahead of me, I pause the video, or play it again from the start. When I grasp the point of the lesson, I hit 1.5X to speed things up. I rarely grasp it.

production values: quality of a media production; can include aspects of lighting, pacing, video quality, and the like.

My homework consists of multiple-choice and short-answer exercises, coding assignments and a three-hour final exam. All work is auto-graded, but other MOOCs also use peer assessment to evaluate assignments. I visit the course's discussion forums to hang out with my fellow students.

So how did I do? Not great. I dropped out. Programming fundamentals started off fun, kind of like a **TED talk**, but then it turned into actual work, so I gave up. I also dropped out of sociology, game theory and equine nutrition. I'm not alone.

TED talk: TED (Technology, Entertainment, and Design) is a conference where speakers give lectures on current and innovative ideas

Of all those students who enrolled in the coding class, only 9,000 completed it to earn a "statement of accomplishment." I learn this upon visiting Jennifer Campbell in her office at U of T's Bahen Centre for Information Technology on St. George. I'm a little star-struck by the nice-looking teacher I've been spending so much time with at home, and I resist the urge to blurt out, "Hey, I know you from the Internet!"

Campbell is disheartened by her MOOCs completion rate. When she taught the same course in a real classroom last fall, 85 percent of students saw it through. Of course, those students needed to pass. I didn't, though I still got something out of it.

I ask Campbell what the experience was like for her. "Fun," she says. "But I missed the face time with students." Participating in online discussions with thousands is no replacement for the one-on-one chats she has with students during her office hours.

And yet the advantages of MOOCs are undeniable. They drive the cost of a world-class education down to nothing. They make knowledge accessible to all. They let you pace your learning—and emerging companies are developing technology that will enable MOOCs to learn how you learn in order to adapt to different styles. Open captioning allows anyone to translate a MOOC, so you can take courses taught in different languages. All of this explains why they're popular, but there is a legitimacy problem. To become a viable alternative, MOOCs will have to grant course credits, which would improve the dismal completion rates and allow committed students to distinguish themselves from dabblers.

The obstacles to this are many. MOOCs need a reliable identity verification system to prevent cheating. They need richer assessment of oral and written work that goes beyond machine-graded multiple choice and peer assessment. Most of all, they need to offer meaningful interaction and discussion with scholars.

A couple of daring schools (Georgia State and San Jose State) are planning to provide these services in the months ahead, charging and sharing tuition fees with MOOC sites and providing bona fide, transferable credits to students.

It's a horrifying idea to education traditionalists, the reduction of our institutions of higher learning to mere support systems for "classroom in a box" websites. But perhaps it's time to shed romantic notions of **ivory tower symposiums**. Toronto's undergrad students are crammed into vast auditoriums by the hundreds—Psych 101 at U of T maxes out at 1,500 students per lecture. The days when U of T luminaries like Northrop Frye and Marshall McLuhan taught intimate classes of 19-year-olds are well behind us.

It won't be long before our universities shift their big introductory courses online. Tuition needn't change, and few students will complain—most will prefer it. But that's just the opinion of one equine nutrition dropout.

ivory tower: sheltered academic isolation, often providing abstract, impractical advice

symposium: meeting or conference

The Results of Prereading

By *prereading* the article, you might notice the following:

The title is "Free for All."

The author is a columnist for *Toronto Life.*

There are some vocabulary words you may need to know.

The introductory material says that the essay is about online courses.

You might begin reading the article with these questions in mind:

What could the title, "Free for All," mean?

How big is a "Massive Open Online Course"?

Reading

The first time you read, try to get a sense of the whole piece you're reading. Reading with questions in mind can help you do this. If you find that you're confused by a certain part of the reading selection, go back and reread that part. If you don't know the meaning of a word, look in the margin to see if the word is defined for you. If it's not defined for you, try to figure out the meaning from the way the word is used in the sentence.

If you find that you have to read more slowly than you usually do, don't worry. People vary their reading speed according to what they read and why they're reading it. If you're reading for entertainment, for example, you can read quickly; if you're reading a chapter in a textbook, you must read more slowly. The more complicated the reading selection, the more slowly you'll read it.

An Example of the Reading Step

Now *read* "Free for All." When you've completed your first reading, your answers to the prereading questions you formed will probably be like these:

Answers to Prereading Questions

"Free for All" could mean that the courses are free, or could refer to the expression "free for all," meaning that the courses have so many students that there is little organization.

A "Massive Open Online Course" could include hundreds of thousands of students.

Rereading with Pen or Pencil

The second reading is the crucial one. At this point, you begin to *think on paper* as you read. In this step, you make notes or write about what you read. Some students are reluctant to do this, for they're not sure *what* to note or write. Think of making these notes as a way of learning, thinking, reviewing, and reacting. Reading with a pen or pencil in your hand keeps you alert. With that pen or pencil, you can do the following:

Mark the main point of the reading.

Mark other points.

Circle words you don't know and define them in the margin.

Question parts of the reading you're not sure of.

Evaluate the writer's ideas.

React to the writer's opinions or examples.

Add ideas, opinions, or examples of your own.

It's easiest to do this right on the page, although if you're reading a library book or a book that doesn't belong to you, you can use sticky notes or make notes on a separate sheet. There is no single system for marking or writing as you read. Some readers like to underline the main idea with two lines and to underline other important ideas with one line. Some students like to put an asterisk (a star) next to important ideas, while others like to circle key words.

Some people use the margins to write comments like "I agree!" or "Not true!" or "That's happened to me." Sometimes, readers put questions in the margin; sometimes, they summarize a point in the margin, next to its location in the essay. Some people make notes in the white space above the reading and list important points, while others use the space at the end of the reading. Every reader who writes as he or she reads has a personal system; what these systems share is an attitude. If you *write as you read*, you concentrate on the reading selection, get to know the writer's ideas, and develop ideas of your own.

As you reread and write notes, don't worry too much about noticing the "right" ideas. Think of rereading as the time to jump into a conversation with the writer.

An Example of Rereading with Pen or Pencil

For "Free for All," your marked article might look like the following:

Free for All

by Jesse Brown

American university located in New Jersey

I'm studying sociology at (Princeton) in my spare time. I'm also taking game theory at Stanford, computer programming at the University of Toronto and equine nutrition at the University of Edinburgh. *Cool!* I attend class in my underwear, watch cartoons during lectures and cheat on tests with help from some of my hundreds of thousands of classmates. The classes I'm enrolled in are called MOOCs—Massive Open Online Courses, available for free to knowledge-hungry students of life like myself through the educational website Coursera.

MOOCs are a global phenomenon with Canadian roots. The term was coined in 2008 by Dave Cormier, a web communications manager at the University of P.E.I., to describe an Internet-based course designed by Professor George Siemens of Athabasca University in Alberta and Stephen Downes of the National Research Council. Twenty-five University of Manitoba students signed up for a course on connectivist theory and were joined by 2,300 virtual students from the general public, who participated free of charge via the web.

The MOOC concept stalled until 2011, when Stanford offered three open online courses and received a staggering 350,000 registrants from 190 countries. A couple of the Stanford profs involved with the experiment were encouraged enough to drop everything and launch Coursera, a self-described "social entrepreneurship company." And there have been other launches, notably Udacity and EdX, a joint venture of MIT and Harvard. In a matter of months, MOOCs attracted millions of students from around the world and millions of dollars in venture capital. Coursera alone has enrolled 2.6 million students and secured $16 million in investment. But according to evangelists, MOOCs are not about money—they're about revolutionizing post-secondary education.

University of
Toronto

Last July, (U of T) signed up as a Coursera partner. Students can't earn course credits for taking the classes, nor do they pay any fees. And no money changes hands between Coursera and U of T—at least not yet. If profits emerge in the future—through nominal tuition fees or by selling their database—Coursera says the money will be shared with partner universities.

My computer programming class, one of seven MOOCs offered by U of T, attracted more than 100,000 registrants. Yes, I'm participating for the purpose of writing this article, but I'm also hoping to learn something about programming. Without reading the honour code—which I assume says something about promising not to cheat—I click a button swearing to uphold it, and class begins.

I half expect a bunch of videotaped lectures. I'm half-right. While the course is taught via a series of short videos starring my teachers—senior computer science lecturers Jennifer Campbell and Paul Gries—the videos weren't created by pointing a Handycam at a lectern. They were designed specifically for the web, and the production values are pretty good. When the teachers code, I watch them code. Difficult concepts are rendered simple through live-drawn illustrations. When the class gets ahead of me, I pause the video, or play it again from the start. When I grasp the point of the lesson, I hit 1.5X to speed things up. I rarely grasp it.

My homework consists of multiple choice and short-answer exercises, coding assignments and a three-hour final exam. All work is auto-graded, but other MOOCs also use peer assessment to evaluate assignments. I visit the course's discussion forums to hang out with my fellow students.

So how did I do? Not great. I dropped out. Programming fundamentals started off fun, kind of like a TED talk, but then it turned into actual work, so I gave up. I also dropped out of sociology, game theory and equine nutrition. I'm not alone.

only 9%

Of all those students who enrolled in the coding class, only 9,000 completed it to earn a "statement of accomplishment." I learn this upon visiting Jennifer Campbell in her office at U of T's Bahen Centre for Information Technology on St. George. I'm a little star-struck by the nice-looking teacher I've been spending so much time with at home, and I resist the urge to blurt out, "Hey, I know you from the Internet!"

Campbell is disheartened by her MOOCs completion rate. When she taught the
drastic difference in completion rates
same course in a real classroom last fall, 85 percent of students saw it through. Of course, those students needed to pass. I didn't, though I still got something out of it.

I ask Campbell what the experience was like for her. "Fun," she says. "But I missed
There are also drawbacks for instructors.
the face time with students." Participating in online discussions with thousands is no replacement for the one-on-one chats she has with students during her office hours.
advantages of MOOCs
And yet the advantages of MOOCs are undeniable. They drive the cost of a world-class education down to nothing. They make knowledge accessible to all. They

let you pace your learning—and emerging companies are developing technology that will enable MOOCs to learn how you learn in order to adapt to different styles. Open captioning allows anyone to translate a MOOC, so you can take courses taught in different languages. All of this explains why they're popular, but there is a legitimacy problem. <u>To become a viable alternative, MOOCs will have to grant course credits,</u> which would improve the dismal completion rates and allow committed students to distinguish themselves from dabblers.

obstacles
<u>The obstacles to this are many.</u> MOOCs need a reliable identity verification system to prevent cheating. They need richer assessment of oral and written work that goes beyond machine-graded multiple choice and peer assessment. Most of all, they need to offer meaningful interaction and discussion with scholars.

A couple of daring schools (Georgia State and San Jose State) are planning to provide these services in the months ahead, charging and sharing tuition fees with MOOC sites and providing bona fide, transferable credits to students.

<u>It's a horrifying idea to education traditionalists, the reduction of our institutions of higher learning to mere support systems for "classroom in a box" websites.</u> But perhaps it's time to shed romantic notions of ivory tower symposiums. Toronto's undergrad students are crammed into vast auditoriums by the hundreds—Psych 101 at U of T maxes out at 1,500 students per lecture. The days when U of T luminaries like Northrop Frye and Marshall McLuhan taught intimate classes of 19-year-olds are well behind us.

It won't be long before our universities shift their big introductory courses online. Tuition needn't change, and few students will complain—most will prefer it. But that's just the opinion of one equine nutrition dropout.

What the Notes Mean

In the sample above, the underlining indicates sentences or phrases that seem important. The words written between the lines or in the margin are often summaries of what is underlined. The phrases and words *only 9%*, *drastic difference in completion rates*, and *obstacles*, for instance, are like subtitles or labels added by the reader.

Some of the added words are reactions. When Brown describes how he took multiple courses in his underwear or watched cartoons during lectures, the reader notes, "Cool!" Several words in the margin are definitions. For example, the term "U of T" in the selection is defined as *University of Toronto* in the margin.

The marked-up article is a flexible tool. You can go back and mark it further. You may change your mind about your notes and comments and find better or more important points in the article.

You write as you read to involve yourself in the reading process. Marking what you read can help you in other ways, too. If you're to be tested on the reading selection or asked to discuss it, you can scan your markings and notations at a later time for a quick review.

EXERCISE	**READING AND MAKING NOTES**
1	

Below is a paragraph from "Free for All." First, read it. Then reread it and make notes on the following:

1. Underline the advantages of Massive Open Online Courses (MOOCs).
2. Circle a word you don't know and define it in the margin.
3. In the margin, add another possible advantage of a MOOC.
4. At the end of the paragraph, summarize the point of the paragraph.

Paragraph from "Free for All"

And yet the advantages of MOOCs are undeniable. They drive the cost of a world-class education down to nothing. They make knowledge accessible to all. They let you pace your learning—and emerging companies are developing technology that will enable MOOCs to learn how you learn in order to adapt to different styles. Open captioning allows anyone to translate a MOOC, so you can take courses taught in different languages. All of this explains why they're popular, but there is a legitimacy problem. To become a viable alternative, MOOCs will have to grant course credits, which would improve the dismal completion rates and allow committed students to distinguish themselves from dabblers.

Main point of the paragraph: _____

_____

_____

WRITING A SUMMARY OF A READING

There are a number of ways you can write about what you've read. You may be asked for a summary or paraphrase of an article or chapter, or for a reaction to it, or to write about it on an essay test. For each of these, this chapter will give you guidelines so that you can follow the stages of the writing process.

A **summary** of a reading tells the important ideas in brief form in your own words. It includes (1) the writer's main idea, (2) the ideas used to explain the main idea, and (3) some examples used to support the ideas.

When you preread, read, and make notes on the reading selection, you have already begun the prewriting stage for a summary. You can think further, on paper, by *listing the points* (words, phrases, sentences) you've already marked on the reading selection.

PREWRITING	GATHERING IDEAS: SUMMARY

Marking a List of Ideas

To find the main idea for your summary and the ideas and examples connected to the main idea, you can mark related items on your list. For example, the expanded list below was made from "Free for All." Five symbols are used:

h **history** of MOOCs
e the author's **experience** of taking a MOOC
— the **drawbacks** of MOOCs
+ the **benefits** of MOOCs
s what it will take for MOOCs to be **successful**

A List of Ideas for a Summary of "Free for All"

e attend class in underwear

e watch cartoons during lectures

h MOOCs are free through Coursera

h MOOCs available around the world but began in Canada

h interest in MOOCs took off in 2011, when hundreds of thousands registered for three courses and Coursera was developed

h millions of dollars invested

MOOCs expected to change post-secondary education

e students cannot earn credits, but do not pay tuition for courses

e students must adhere to an honour code

e course delivered through short videos of good quality; videos can be replayed

e assignments and exercises automatically graded, though some courses assign grades through peer evaluation

— very small percentage of students complete MOOCs compared with traditional courses

— instructor missed face-to-face interaction with students

+ MOOCs make education more affordable

+ MOOCs make courses more accessible

+ students can learn at their own pace

+ MOOCs can be designed to adapt to different learning styles

+ technology can translate courses from different languages

s MOOCs will have currency only when credits are granted

s MOOCs require systems to prevent cheating

s MOOCs will require grading schemes that are more thorough

s students will need more interaction with their instructors and each other

— courses may reduce post-secondary schools to supports for online courses, but some first-year university courses are already very large

The marked list could be reorganized, like this:

history of MOOCs

MOOCs are free through Coursera

MOOCs are available around the world but began in Canada

interest in MOOCs took off in 2011, when hundreds of thousands registered for three courses and Coursera was developed

millions of dollars invested

the author's experience of taking a MOOC

students cannot earn credits, but do not pay tuition for courses

students must adhere to an honour code

course delivered through short videos of good quality; videos can be replayed

assignments and exercises automatically graded, though some courses assign grades through peer evaluation

drawbacks of MOOCs

very small percentage of students complete MOOCs compared with traditional courses

instructor missed face-to-face interaction with students

courses may reduce post-secondary schools to supports for online courses, but some first-year university courses are already very large

benefits of MOOCs

MOOCs make education more affordable

MOOCs make courses more accessible

students can learn at their own pace

MOOCs can be designed to adapt to different learning styles

technology can translate courses from different languages

what it will take for MOOCs to be successful

MOOCs will have currency only when credits are granted

MOOCs require systems to prevent cheating

MOOCs will require grading schemes that are more thorough

students will need more interaction with their instructors and each other

Selecting a Main Idea

The next step in the process is to select the idea you think is the writer's main point. If you look again at the list of ideas, you'll note that one idea is unmarked:

MOOCs expected to change post-secondary education

You might guess that it's unmarked because it's more general than the other ideas. This may allow you to conclude that this is the *main idea* of the reading selection:

Massive Open Online Courses (MOOCs) are expected to change post-secondary education.

Once you have a main idea, check to see if it fits with the other ideas in your organized list. Do the ideas in the list connect to the main idea? Yes. The author examines how very different *his MOOC experience* is from a traditional course, and then describes both the *drawbacks* and *benefits* of MOOCs. Finally, he concludes that there are several elements required for MOOCS to be *successful*, and that ultimately, MOOCs will change the face of post-secondary education.

Once you have a main point that fits an organized list, you can move to the *planning stage* of a summary.

EXERCISE	MARKING A LIST OF IDEAS AND FINDING THE MAIN IDEA
2	**FOR A SUMMARY**

Below is a list of ideas from an article called "How to Ride Ups, Downs of Learning New Skills." Read the list, and then mark it with one of these symbols:

X = examples of different learning styles

S = steps in learning

A = advice from successful people

After you've marked all the ideas, survey them, and think of one main idea. Try to focus on an idea that connects to the title, "How to Ride Ups, Downs of Learning New Skills."

List of Ideas

_____ Kids tend to learn by trial and error and are ready to learn from their mistakes.

_____ Excitement and confidence replace fear and confusion, since the learner can say, "I know this."

_____ If you want to increase your success rate, double your failure rate.

_____ Confidence and comfort levels are highest when the course begins.

_____ Another student prefers to study alone to avoid distractions.

_____ Focus all your energy on improving, learning, and achieving your goals.

_____ Utter confusion, frustration, and discomfort make the learner feel lost.

_____ Some adults view change with suspicion and uncertainty and are uncomfortable moving into new situations.

_____ One student enjoys studying with a group to exchange ideas and bolster her confidence.

Main idea: _____

_____

_____

_____

PLANNING   DEVISING A PLAN: SUMMARY

Below is a sample of the kind of outline you could do for a summary of "Free for All." As you read it, you'll notice that the main idea of the prewriting stage has become the topic sentence of the outline, and that the other ideas have become the details.

> ## Outline for a Summary of "Free for All"
>
> **topic sentence:**   Massive Open Online Courses (MOOCs) are expected to change
>   post-secondary education.
>
> **details:**
>
> history of MOOCs
>
>   Massive Open Online Courses (MOOCs) are free through the website Coursera.
>   Millions of dollars have been invested.
>
> author's experience of taking a MOOC
>
>   Although students cannot earn credits, they do not pay tuition for courses.
>   Students must adhere to an honour code, which includes no cheating.
>   Courses are delivered through short videos of good quality; videos can be
>   replayed for review.
>   Assignments and exercises are automatically graded, although other
>   courses assign grades through peer evaluation and feedback.
>
> drawbacks of MOOCs
>
>   A very small percentage of students complete MOOCs compared with
>   traditional courses.
>   Instructors can miss face-to-face interaction with students.
>   Courses may reduce post-secondary schools to supports for online courses,
>   but some first-year university courses are already very large.
>
> benefits of MOOCs
>
>   MOOCs make education more affordable.
>   MOOCs make courses more accessible; anyone with internet access can
>   take them.
>   Students can learn at their own pace.
>   MOOCs can be designed to adapt to different learning styles.
>   Technology can translate courses from different languages.
>
> what it will take for MOOCs to be successful
>
>   MOOCs will have currency only when credits are granted.
>   MOOCs require the implementation of systems to prevent cheating.
>   MOOCs will require grading schemes that are more thorough.
>   Students will need more interaction with their instructors and each other.

In the preceding outline, some ideas from the original list have been omitted (they were too detailed for a summary), and the order of some points has been rearranged. That kind of selecting and rearranging is what you do in the planning stage of writing a summary.

DRAFTING AND REVISING: SUMMARY

Attributing Ideas in a Summary

The first draft of your summary paragraph is the place where you combine all the material into one paragraph. This draft is much like the draft of any other paragraph, with one exception: When you summarize another person's ideas, be sure to say whose ideas you are expressing. That is, *attribute* the ideas to the writer. Let the reader of your paragraph know

1. the author of the selection you are summarizing, and

2. the title of the selection you are summarizing.

You may wish to do this by giving your summary paragraph a *title*, such as

A Summary of "Free for All" by Jesse Brown

(Note that you put the title of Brown's essay in quotation marks.)

Or you may want to put the title and author into the paragraph itself. Below is a draft summary of "Free for All" with the title and author incorporated into the paragraph.

A Draft for a Summary of "Free for All"

"Free for All" by Jesse Brown claims that Massive Open Online Courses (MOOCs) will change the face of post-secondary education. MOOCs became popular in 2011, when hundreds of thousands of students registered for three courses and the website Coursera was developed in response. Millions of dollars have been invested in the site, and students can now take courses for free. Brown himself enrolled in several MOOCS: sociology at Princeton and game theory at Stanford. He also took computer programming at the University of Toronto and equine nutrition at the University of Edinburgh. He describes his own experience taking the computer programming course. While students cannot earn credits toward a degree, they do not have to pay tuition, either. Students are expected to adhere to an honour code, which Brown assumed includes a stipulation of no cheating. Brown found that the course was delivered through a number of short videos of good quality. He found it helpful that he could replay these videos to review concepts. Assignments and exercises were automatically graded through multiple-choice questions, though other courses assign grades through peer evaluation. Brown, through discussions with his instructor, discovered some drawbacks to MOOCs: a very small percentage of students complete MOOCs compared with traditional courses. Brown dropped out of his programming, sociology, game theory, and equine nutrition courses. His instructor missed the face-to-face interaction with students. MOOCs' detractors are often concerned that such courses may reduce post-secondary schools to supports for online courses, but Brown argues that some first-year university courses are already very large. He continues to describe the benefits of MOOCs: they make education more affordable. MOOCs also make courses more accessible, so more people can take them. Students can learn at their own pace, and they can review whenever they need to. Technology is being developed so that MOOCs can be adapted to different learning styles, and technology can already translate courses from different languages. Brown suggests that there are several elements required for MOOCs to be successful. To encourage students to complete a MOOC, credits must be granted. Such courses will require a more robust grading system, more than mere multiple-choice tests or peer review. Systems must be implemented to prevent cheating. Above all, students will need more interaction with their instructors and each other. Given the significant advantages MOOCs offer, it may not be long before many students are able to take their introductory courses through MOOCs.

When you look this draft over and read it aloud, you may notice a few problems:

1. It's wordy, and repetitive in places.
2. Some of the sentences are choppy.

Revising the draft would mean rewriting to eliminate some of the wordiness, to combine sentences or smooth out ideas. Also, when you state that Brown interviewed his instructor and drew conclusions, you are clearly giving the author credit for his ideas. Giving credit is a way of attributing ideas to the author.

Note: When you refer to an author in something that you write, use the author's first and last name the first time you make a reference. For example, you would write "Jesse Brown" the first time you refer to this author. Later in the paragraph, if you want to refer to the same author, use only his or her last name. Thus, a second reference would be to "Brown."

PROOFREADING

PROOFREADING AND POLISHING: SUMMARY

Look carefully at the final version of the summary. Notice how the sentences have been changed, and words added or taken out. "Brown" is used to show that the details and conclusions given came from the essay.

> ### A Final Version of a Summary of "Free for All"
>
> "Free for All" by Jesse Brown claims that Massive Open Online Courses (MOOCs) will change the face of post-secondary education. MOOCs became popular in 2011, when hundreds of thousands of students registered for three courses and the website Coursera was developed in response. Millions of dollars have been invested in the site, and students can now take courses for free. Brown enrolled in several MOOCs offered in different countries but describes his experience taking a computer programming course. Currently, MOOCs do not count as credit toward a degree. Students are expected to adhere to an honour code, which Brown assumed includes a stipulation of no cheating. Brown found that the course was delivered through a number of short videos of good quality, and found it helpful that he could replay these videos to review concepts. Assignments and exercises were automatically graded through multiple-choice questions, though other courses assign grades through peer evaluation. Brown, through discussions with his instructor, discovered two drawbacks to MOOCs: a very small percentage of students complete MOOCs compared with traditional courses, and his instructor missed the face-to-face interaction with students. MOOCs' detractors are often concerned that such courses may reduce post-secondary schools to supports for online

courses, but Brown argues that some first-year university courses are already very large. He continues to describe the benefits of MOOCs: they make education more affordable and courses more accessible; students can learn at their own pace; technologies are being developed so that MOOCs can address different learning styles; and MOOCs can already be delivered in different languages. Brown suggests that several elements are required for MOOCs to be successful. To encourage students to complete a MOOC, credits must be granted. Such courses will require more robust grading systems, more than mere multiple-choice tests or peer review. Systems must be implemented to prevent cheating. Above all, students will need more interaction with their instructors and each other. Given the significant advantages MOOCs offer, it may not be long before students around the world are able to take their introductory courses through MOOCs.

Writing summaries is good writing practice, and it also helps you to develop your reading skills. Even if your instructor does not require you to turn in a polished summary of an assigned reading, you may find it helpful to summarize what you have read. In many classes, mid-terms or other exams cover many assigned readings. If you make short summaries of each reading as it is assigned, you will have a helpful collection of focused, organized material to review.

WRITING A PARAPHRASE OF A READING

A **paraphrase** is like a summary: you use your own words to express the ideas found in a reading in the same order. However, a paraphrase is usually as long as or longer than the original because its purpose is to restate the entire content in different words rather than stating the main ideas, as in a summary. Because of its potential length, you generally won't be asked to write a paraphrase of anything longer than a paragraph or so.

Let's see how it works. Ever heard "A bird in the hand is worth two in the bush"? or "The early bird catches the worm"? These statements are *proverbs*, frequently used sayings that express common truths. However, proverbs can be difficult to understand if you haven't heard them all your life. How would you explain "The early bird catches the worm" to a recent newcomer to Canada?

You might say, "Well, 'The early bird catches the worm' means that people who wake up early benefit more than people who don't." You have just *paraphrased* the proverb.

EXERCISE **3**	**PARAPHRASING**

Paraphrase the following proverbs, working individually or in a group.

1. You are what you eat.
2. When the cat's away, the mice will play.
3. A rolling stone gathers no moss.
4. Too many cooks spoil the broth.
5. Once bitten, twice shy.
6. A penny saved is a penny earned.

7. Many hands make light work.
8. A chain is only as strong as its weakest link.
9. A friend in need is a friend indeed.
10. Least said, soonest mended.

Paraphrasing a Paragraph

Paraphrasing is very similar to summarizing, only you don't have to distill as much information; remember that a paraphrase is usually as long as or even longer than the original. So, in keeping with the summary-writing steps, follow these paraphrasing steps:

Step 1: Read the passage three times. The first time, read to understand the passage; the second, read to define any terms you don't understand. Lastly, read the passage looking at paragraph structure and the order in which the ideas are presented.

Step 2: Start to translate the ideas into your own words, maintaining the same order in which they were presented in the original passage. When reading the paraphrase, the reader should hear *your* voice, not the original author's.

Step 3: Revise your paraphrase for unity and coherence. Does it contain all the important ideas? Do the sentences flow together?

Step 4: Edit your paraphrase for spelling and grammar.

communication at work

Employers demand good communication skills, both spoken and written. Read the following paragraph, taken from an article entitled, "Employers Complain about Communication Skills" by Jim McKay (2005), and consider its paraphrases:

> Communication skills often top the list of qualities employers seek not just for entry-level jobs but for executive and blue-collar positions as well. But the qualities persistently are at the bottom of what potential recruits bring to an interview. When the National Association of Colleges and Employers recently asked employers what skill was most lacking in college job candidates, good communication skills was first.

An unacceptable paraphrase:

> Communication skills are the most important qualities employers look for, not only for entry-level jobs but other positions as well. However, recruits don't often bring these qualities to interviews. The National Association of Colleges and Employers said good communication skills were most lacking in college job candidates.

This paraphrase is unacceptable because much of it has been copied from the original (see *italics*); changing a few words here and there and changing the sentence structure (see underlining) don't mean you have paraphrased. You must also indicate *where* you found the information.

An acceptable paraphrase:

> Employers often say that communication skills are the most important qualities they look for, for virtually any position. However, they also say that these qualities are among those they see the least in job interviews. Employers told the National Association of Colleges and Employers that they found communication skills were the most deficient quality in recent college graduates (McKay, 2005).

EXERCISE 4	PARAPHRASING A PARAGRAPH

The following passage is from a *Toronto Star* article entitled, "Mass Collaboration: Harnessing the Power of Global Ideas" by Sharda Prashad (2007). Write a paraphrase of the passage.

> Mass collaboration, a large number of people and companies coming together on the Web to innovate and create value, is evidenced in the operating system Linux, the online encyclopaedia Wikipedia, and the virtual communities of YouTube and MySpace. While owners of traditional bricks-and-mortar businesses might be quick to dismiss mass collaboration as a new-fangled notion that won't reap profit, in *Wikinomics* the authors emphasize that profits and mass collaboration go hand-in-hand.

_____

_____

_____

_____

_____

_____

_____

_____

A Note on Plagiarism

> *"Borrowed thoughts, like borrowed money, only show the poverty of the borrower."*
>
> ~ LADY MARGUERITE BLESSINGTON, COUNTESS OF BLESSINGTON

Plagiarism is the act of copying someone else's words or ideas and passing them off as your own, even if done inadvertently. It is a serious academic offence, one that usually incurs some sort of academic penalty; check the academic policy of your college or university to find out what its stand is on plagiarism, and consult with your instructor if you have any questions or concerns about your own work.

Keep in mind that you do *not*, necessarily, have to copy from the original word for word for your summary to be considered plagiarized. Similar sentence structure and phrasing are also signs of plagiarism, and these may be the most difficult for students to identify. This section of *Along These Lines* will deal specifically with plagiarism issues common to summary writing. Additional plagiarism issues specific to researching and documenting outside sources such as books, newspapers, magazines, and electronic sources are addressed in Chapter 12, "The Research Process."

The following excerpt is from an article by Maura Welch (2006), originally published in *The Boston Globe*, and ironically about online plagiarism:

> Beth gets more than 500 hits per day at her blog, Cursed to First, which
> serves as a very personal homage to the Red Sox and the Patriots, so she

knew that spicy entries like "Chicks dig the long ball" were being read. She didn't realize until recently that they were also being ripped off.

Last month, an alert reader informed Beth that her blog was being plagiarized. Dozens of Beth's blog entries had been stolen, word-for-word, over six months. Names of people in her life were changed to the names of people whom the plagiarist apparently knew, creating the impression that she had lived Beth's experiences and had thought her thoughts.

On the same day that this was published, the following was published on an ebusiness website:

Beth's blog got more than 500 hits per day, mostly from Red Sox and New England Patriots fans, not an unusual occurrence since she lives in Boston.

But one of Beth's regular readers told her that her blog was being plagiarized on a regular basis, word-for-word over the past six months. The thief simply changed the names of Beth's friends in her post to those in the thief's post (which was, of course, actually Beth's).

This was considered plagiarism, and the article on the ebusiness website was removed.

INFOBOX   **PLAGIARISM IN A PROFESSIONAL CONTEXT**

Plagiarism also occurs in more traditional professional contexts; one notable example is that of Jayson Blair, a former staff writer with *The New York Times*. In 2003, Blair confessed to lying and/or plagiarizing in multiple articles he wrote for the newspaper. Blair resigned and went on to write a book about his journalistic experiences, but *The New York Times*'s reputation was tarnished. See an interview with Jayson Blair at www.msnbc.msn.com/id/4457860.

EXERCISE 5   **IDENTIFYING PLAGIARISM**

1. With a partner or in a small group, discuss the excerpt from *The Boston Globe* (above) and the excerpt from the ebusiness website. Why is the second considered plagiarism?

    _____

    _____

    _____

    _____

    _____

2. W. R. Inge once said, "Originality is undetected plagiarism." Writers throughout the ages have argued that one writer builds on another's thoughts and that the results ought not to be considered plagiarism.

What do you think? Is there a difference between expanding an idea and plagiarism? What should the consequences be for professional instances of plagiarism? What do you think of the Jayson Blair incident?
Be prepared to discuss your views in class.

_____

_____

_____

_____

_____

EXERCISE 6 — IDENTIFYING PLAGIARISM IN A PARAPHRASE

In the following, read the original passages and their paraphrases. Identify whether each paraphrase is acceptable or unacceptable, and rewrite those that are unacceptable.

1. *original:* MOOCs are a global phenomenon with Canadian roots. The term was coined in 2008 by Dave Cormier, a web communications manager at the University of P.E.I., to describe an Internet-based course designed by Professor George Siemens of Athabasca University in Alberta and Stephen Downes of the National Research Council.

   paraphrase: Belying their global reach, MOOCs found their start in Canada at the University of P.E.I., where an internet-based course had been developed.

   rewrite:

   _____

   _____

2. *original:* They were designed specifically for the web, and the production values are pretty good.

   paraphrase: These videos were designed specifically for web viewing, and their production values were good.

   rewrite:

   _____

   _____

3. *original:* Campbell is disheartened by her MOOC's completion rate. When she taught the same course in a real classroom last fall, 85 percent of students saw it through.

paraphrase: Campbell is disappointed by the completion rate in her MOOC. Eighty-five percent of her students passed the same course in a real classroom last fall.

rewrite:

_____

_____

For more information on plagiarism and strategies to avoid it, visit the "Avoiding Plagiarism" section in Pearson's MyWritingLab.

WRITING A REACTION TO A READING

A summary or a paraphrase is one kind of writing you can do after reading, but there are other kinds. You can write a **reaction** to a reading by writing on a topic related to the reading or by agreeing or disagreeing with some idea within the reading.

Writing on a Related Idea

Your instructor might ask you to react by writing about some idea you got from your reading. If you read "Free for All," for example, your instructor might have asked you to react to it by writing about some other trend in post-secondary education. You can begin to gather ideas by freewriting.

PREWRITING GATHERING IDEAS: REACTION

Freewriting

You can freewrite in a reading journal, if you wish. To freewrite, you can

- write key points made by the author
- write about whatever you remember from the reading selection
- write down any of the author's ideas that you think you might want to write about someday
- list questions raised by what you've read
- connect the reading selection to other things you've read, heard, or experienced
- write any of the author's exact words that you might like to remember, putting them in quotation marks

A freewriting that reacts to "Free for All" might look like this:

> Freewriting for a Reaction to a Reading
>
> **"Free for All"—Jesse Brown**
>
> Brown says that MOOCs will change post-secondary education, and that many introductory courses at university are really large anyway, so what's the difference? Being able to replay a lecture would be really helpful. Online completion rates are really low. Do students need more face-to-face interaction? It seems that instructors miss that interaction, too.

Freewriting helps you review what you've read, and it can give you topics for a paragraph that is different from a summary.

Brainstorming

After you freewrite, you can brainstorm. You can ask yourself questions to lead you toward a topic for your own paragraph. For instance, brainstorming on the idea of student–instructor interaction could look like this:

> #### Brainstorming after Freewriting
>
> Brown's programming instructor said that she was disappointed in how few of her online students completed the course. Completion rates for online courses are dismal compared with completion rates for similar traditional courses. **Why is this the case? Is it merely because MOOCs don't yet give credits?**
>
> In part, yes. Many students can't stay motivated.
>
> **Could there be other reasons?**
>
> Perhaps multiple-choice tests don't give enough feedback for students to understand how they can improve. Students may not feel enough engagement with other students or the instructor.
>
> **Do instructors also feel a lack of engagement?**
>
> Brown's instructor did say that she missed the "one-on-one" chats she had with students during office hours.

Could you write a paragraph on the importance of student and instructor engagement in MOOCs? If so, your brainstorming, based on your reading, might lead you to a topic.

Developing Points of Agreement or Disagreement

Another way to use a reading selection to lead you to a topic is to review the selection and jot down any statements that provoke a strong reaction in you. You are looking for sentences with which you can agree or disagree. If you already marked "Free for All" as you read, you might list these statements as points of agreement or disagreement:

> #### Points of Agreement or Disagreement from a Reading
>
> "Most of all, [MOOCs] need to offer meaningful interaction and discussion with scholars."—agree
>
> "It won't be long before our universities shift their big introductory courses online . . . few students will complain—most will prefer it."—disagree

Then you might pick one of the statements and agree or disagree with it, in writing. If you agreed with the first statement that "MOOCs need to offer meaningful interaction and discussion with scholars," you might develop the prewriting part of writing by listing your own ideas. You might focus on how such interaction helps your own learning process. With a focus and a list of reasons, you could move to the outline part of writing from reading.

PLANNING   ## DEVISING A PLAN: AGREE OR DISAGREE

An outline might look like the one below. As you read it, notice that the topic sentence and ideas are your opinions, not the ideas of the author of "Free for All." You used his ideas to come up with your own thoughts.

An Outline for an Agree or a Disagree Paragraph

topic sentence: Face-to-face interaction is important for students to be successful.

details:

with other students   It's much easier to make friends and maintain relationships when you meet on a regular basis. Students will be able to develop a supportive network to help each other with assignments and study for tests and exams. These relationships can extend to other courses.

with the instructor   When students feel that their instructor knows them and cares about their learning, they're more likely to be invested in the course. They may feel more comfortable asking for help. In a traditional classroom setting, the instructor can be more responsive, answering students' questions as they arise.

DRAFTING AND REVISING   ## DRAFTING AND REVISING: AGREE OR DISAGREE

If your outline gives you enough good points to develop, you are on your way to a paragraph. If you began with the ideas above, for example, you could develop them into a paragraph like this:

A Draft for an Agree or a Disagree Paragraph

Face-to-face interaction is important for students to be successful. It's much easier to make friends and maintain relationships when you meet on a regular basis. Students will be able to develop a supportive network to help each other with assignments and study for tests and exams. These relationships can extend to other courses. When students feel that their instructor knows them and cares about their learning, they're more likely to be invested in the course. They may feel more comfortable asking for help. In a traditional classroom setting, the instructor can be more responsive, answering students' questions as they arise.

PROOFREADING   ## POLISHING AND PROOFREADING: AGREE OR DISAGREE

When you read the previous paragraph, you probably noticed some places where it could be revised:

- It could use more specific details.

- It should attribute the original idea about the importance of student interaction to Jesse Brown, probably in the beginning.
- It requires a conclusion.

Below is the final version of the same paragraph. As you read it, notice how a new beginning, added details, and a conclusion make it a smoother, clearer, and more developed paragraph.

Final Version for an Agree or a Disagree Paragraph

In "Free for All," Jesse Brown indicates that for MOOCs to change post-secondary education, they must provide "meaningful interaction and discussion with scholars." It's true: face-to-face interaction is important for students to be successful. It's much easier to make friends and maintain relationships when you meet on a regular basis; lifelong friendships have begun when two nervous strangers sit next to each other on the first day of class. Students will be able to develop a supportive network to help each other with assignments and study for tests and exams. They may share notes or form a study group. These relationships can extend to other courses. When students feel that their instructor knows them and cares about their learning, they're more likely to be invested in the course. They may feel more comfortable asking for help. In a traditional classroom setting, the instructor can be more responsive, answering students' questions as they arise. An instructor who can read and respond to the dynamic in her class will add to her students' investment in the course. Students need such face-to-face interaction to be successful, true; however, this interaction will also benefit their instructor, and the institution itself, in the form of a more engaged student body.

Reading can give you many ideas for your own writing. Developing those ideas into a polished paragraph requires the same writing process as any good writing, a process that takes you through the steps of thinking, planning, drafting, revising, editing, and proofreading.

WRITING FOR AN ESSAY TEST

Most essay questions require a form of writing from reading. That is, your instructor asks you to write about an assigned reading. Usually, an **essay test** requires you to write from memory, not from an open book or notes. Such writing can be stressful, but breaking the task into steps can eliminate much of that stress.

Before the Test: The Steps of Reading

If you work through the steps of reading several days before the test, you'll be halfway to your goal. Prereading helps keep you focused, and your first reading will give you a sense of the whole selection. The third step, rereading with a pen or pencil, can be particularly helpful when you're preparing for a test. Most essay questions will ask you to summarize a reading selection or to react to it. In either case, you must be familiar with the reading's main idea, supporting ideas, examples, and details. If you note these by marking the selection, you'll be teaching yourself about the main point, supporting ideas, and structure of the reading selection.

Shortly before the test, review the marked reading assignment. Your notes will help you focus on the main point and the supporting ideas.

During the Test: The Stages of Writing

Answering an essay question for a test may seem very different from writing at home. After all, on a test, you must rely on your memory and write within a time limit, and these restrictions can make you feel anxious. However, by following the stages of the writing process, you can meet that challenge calmly and confidently.

- **Prewriting:** Before you begin to write, think about the question: Is the instructor asking for a summary of a reading selection? Or is he or she asking you to react to a specific idea in the reading by describing or developing the idea with examples or by agreeing or disagreeing? For example, in an essay question about "Free for All," you might be asked (1) to explain what Jesse Brown thinks are the advantages of Massive Open Online Courses (a summary); (2) to explain what he means when he says that MOOCs are "about revolutionizing post-secondary education" (a reaction, where you develop and explain one part of the reading); or (3) to agree or disagree that "most students will prefer" MOOCs for introductory courses (a reaction, so you have to be aware of what Brown said on this point).

  Once you've thought about the question, list or freewrite your first ideas about the question. At this time, don't worry about how "right" or "wrong" your writing is; just write your first thoughts.
- **Planning:** Your writing will be clear if you follow a plan. Remember that your audience for this writing is your instructor and that he or she will be evaluating how well you stick to the subject, make a point, and support it. Your plan for making a point about the subject and supporting that point can be written in a brief outline.

  First, reread the question. Next, survey your list of freewriting. Does it contain a main point that answers the question? Does it contain supporting ideas and details?

  Next, write a main point and then list supporting ideas and details under the main point. Your main point will be the topic sentence of your answer. If you need more support, try brainstorming.
- **Drafting and revising:** Write your point and supporting ideas in paragraph form. Remember to use effective transitions and to combine short sentences.
- **Proofreading:** You probably won't have time to copy your answer, but you can review it, proofread it, and correct any errors in spelling, punctuation, and word choice. This final check can produce a more polished answer.

Organize Your Time

Some students skip steps; they immediately begin writing their answer to an essay question without thinking or planning. Sometimes, they find themselves stuck in the middle of a paragraph, panicked because they have no more ideas. At other times, they find themselves writing in a circle, repeating the same point over and over. Occasionally, they even forget to include a main idea.

You can avoid these hazards by spending time on each of the stages. Planning is as important as writing. For example, if you have half an hour to write an essay, you can divide your time like this:

- 5 minutes: thinking, freewriting, listing
- 10 minutes: planning, outlining
- 10 minutes: drafting
- 5 minutes: reviewing and proofreading

Focusing on one stage at a time can make you more confident and your task more manageable.

Lines of Detail: A Walk-Through Assignment

Here are two ideas from "Free for All":

1. Massive Open Online Courses (MOOCs) will "revolutionize post-secondary education."
2. For introductory courses, most students will prefer a MOOC to a traditional course.

Pick one of these ideas, with which you agree or disagree. Write a paragraph explaining why you agree or disagree. To write your paragraph, follow these steps:

Step 1: Begin by listing at least two reasons why you agree or disagree. Use your own experience with post-secondary courses to come up with your reasons. For example, for statement 1, you could ask yourself these questions: Does this mean all post-secondary education? University only? College? For statement 2, you might ask questions like these: Will students prefer MOOCs for introductory courses only? Do MOOCs lend themselves to other courses? Answering such questions can help you come up with your reasons for agreement or disagreement.

Step 2: Read your list to a partner or to a group. With the help of your listener(s), you can add reasons or details to explain the reasons.

Step 3: Once you have enough ideas, transform the statement you agreed or disagreed with into a topic sentence.

Step 4: Write an outline by listing your reasons and details below the topic sentence. Check that your list is in a clear and logical order.

Step 5: Write a draft of your paragraph. Check that you have attributed Jesse Brown's statement, that you have enough details, and that you have combined any choppy sentences. Revise your draft until the paragraph is smooth and clear.

Step 6: Before you prepare the final copy, check your last draft for errors in spelling, punctuation, and word choice.

Writing Your Own Paragraph on "Free for All"

When you write on one of these topics, be sure to work through the stages of the writing process in preparing your paragraph.

1. Jesse Brown writes about the impact MOOCs may have on post-secondary education. MOOCs, like many other educational advancements, rely

heavily on technology. Think of the impact technology has had on education. How does technology affect your learning process? Does it help or hinder? Write a paragraph describing the impact technology has had on education, good or bad.

2. Brown notes that his online programming course had an "honour code," and that successful MOOCs would have to ensure that students not cheat. Why do you think students cheat on assignments and tests? Do students not have enough time to prepare? Are they afraid to ask for help if they don't understand the material? Are they lazy? Write a paragraph in which you describe why you think students cheat.

Writing from Reading: The Writing Process

To practise the skills you've learned in this chapter, follow the steps of prereading, reading, and rereading with a pen or pencil as you read the following selection.

Cursive Is Dying, Kids Can't Sign Their Own Names—And That's a Huge Problem

Amber Daugherty

Amber Daugherty studied journalism at Humber College in Toronto. She has worked as a reporter for The Globe and Mail *and as a producer for Bell Media.*

Before you read this selection, consider these questions:

> *Did you learn cursive writing in school?*
>
> *Is cursive writing an art?*
>
> *With today's technology, is cursive writing still a necessary skill?*
>
> *Can you envision situations where cursive writing would be necessary?*

We live in a digital era. It can be argued everything is the exact same as it was 10, 15 years ago, that we've just added more screen time to our daily lives. But there are some important—and subtle—changes that aren't all positive.

cursive writing: handwriting in script

There's now less of a focus on teaching children how to **cursive write** in schools, and while you might think, "So what? I learned how to cursive write and I don't do it on a regular basis," there are some stunning drawbacks to this.

First and foremost: signatures.

Signatures are our identifier. They are the passwords that unlock our banks, that sign our bills, that prove that we are who we say we are. And they require a basic, working knowledge of cursive writing. Those **intricate** loops and delicate swirls are pieces of a key we all need to open vaults we have chosen to store important things in.

intricate: complex, involving many parts

An article in the *Toronto Star* highlights this growing issue: Children who aren't learning how to cursive write are unable to form their personal signature.

"I do a lot of stuff on the computer," Lukas, 14, told the *Star*. "But I guess it's weird [not to learn any cursive], because it turns out I have to sign my name on some things."

Lukas couldn't sign his name when applying for a passport, something his father was shocked about.

Ontario curriculum no longer lists cursive writing as mandatory, but as an option for students to communicate, thrown into a list alongside printing and PowerPoint presentations.

Brought up in a world pushing hard for digital-first, all the time, students don't understand the importance of creating something that is uniquely theirs that doesn't come in the form of code. They aren't being taught to value that. It's surprising, particularly because there is such an emphasis in the world placed on brand creation. "Everyone is their own brand," we hear.

So we all create our own websites, Facebook pages, Twitter accounts, LinkedIn profiles, and some of those vaults our valuables are stored in can be accessed digitally, too—banks, for example. But we may be setting ourselves up for digital despair: Accounts are hacked into every day, because, as much as we'd like to believe it, the Internet isn't as secure as we'd like to think.

As recently as mid-2013, four computer hackers in Britain were handed lengthy jail sentences after organizing cyberattacks on the CIA, Sony Pictures, British National Health Services and others. They posted the personal information, including credit-card details, of millions of people, online. And there's a raging debate still happening in the United States over why exactly the **National Security Agency** has been collecting records of phone calls and e-mails of U.S. citizens.

National Security Agency: federal government agency responsible for the national security of the United States

nefarious: wicked

A signature is something that is uniquely ours. It is something we have created, that no one else can replicate (**nefarious** motives aside) in true likeness. An Internet password is none of those things. By neglecting to teach our children the value of cursive writing, with which they can create their own physical mark, are we setting them up to have their digital identities stolen, with no real, hard-copy ones to back them up?

personae: plural form of *persona*, meaning a person or character

We risk moving into an age where we all take on online **personae**—anonymous, floating heads, entrusting password-remembering sites to hold the keys to the things we value most, as we try different combinations of capital letters, numbers, and exclamation points to keep the hackers at bay. Let's not lose that piece of ourselves that once was our permission, our safety, our original brand.

UNDERSTANDING "CURSIVE IS DYING, KIDS CAN'T SIGN THEIR OWN NAMES—AND THAT'S A HUGE PROBLEM"

1. According to the article, what is the most serious drawback of not learning cursive writing? Why?

   _____

   _____

   _____

   _____

2. According to the article, what might be the rationale behind eliminating the teaching of cursive writing?

   _____

   _____

_____

_____

3. According to the author, what are we at risk of losing in the digital era?

_____

_____

_____

_____

WRITING FROM READING "CURSIVE IS DYING, KIDS CAN'T SIGN THEIR OWN NAMES—AND THAT'S A HUGE PROBLEM"

When you write on any of the following topics, make sure to work through the stages of the writing process in preparing your paragraph.

1. Using the ideas and examples you gathered in the previous exercise, write a summary paragraph of Daugherty's article.
2. "Creativity is more, not less, necessary in the technological age." Write a paragraph in which you agree or disagree with this statement.
3. What other subjects are no longer taught in school but that you feel are necessary? Why?
4. Are there some professions that still require legible handwriting? Write a paragraph in which you make a case for cursive writing by giving examples of these professions.

CHAPTER 3
Illustration

LEARNING OBJECTIVES

After you have read this chapter and completed its exercises and assignments, you should be able to

- distinguish between broad statements and specific examples
- add specific examples to broad statements and topic sentences
- generate ideas for an illustration paragraph
- write an appropriate topic sentence for an illustration paragraph
- draft and edit an effective illustration paragraph

"Example is not the main thing in influencing others. It is the only thing."
~ ALBERT SCHWEITZER

▼ ALBERT SCHWEITZER WAS A THEOLOGIAN, PHILOSOPHER, AND DOCTOR WHO WON THE 1952 NOBEL PEACE PRIZE FOR HIS WORK IN AFRICA.

WHAT IS ILLUSTRATION?

Illustration uses specific examples to support a general point. In your writing, you frequently use illustration when you want to explain to your friends why the iPad is (or isn't) the best tablet around, or why your college is (or isn't) the best, for example.

communication at work

Have you ever looked at job postings? Most job postings will say something like, "The ideal candidate must have . . . ," followed by a list of skills or experience expected of the candidate. For example, you might see a posting like this:

The ideal candidate must have

- a B.N. degree from a recognized institution
- 2–3 years' experience in the health-care industry
- excellent communication skills, both spoken and written
- excellent teamwork skills

This list, with its specific *examples* of the skills required, is an example of illustration at work. How would you describe your dream job?

Hints for Writing an Illustration Paragraph

Knowing What Is Specific and What Is General A general statement is a broad point. The following statements are general:

> Traffic can be bad on Hamilton Boulevard.
> Car insurance costs more today than it did last year.
> "It is difficult to meet people at my college."

You can support a general statement with specific examples:

general statement:	Traffic can be bad on Hamilton Boulevard.
specific examples:	During the morning rush hour, the exit to King Street is jammed.
	If there's an accident, cars can be backed up for a kilometre.

general statement:	Car insurance costs more today than it did last year.
specific examples:	Last year, I paid $150 a month; this year, I pay $200 a month.
	My mother, who has never had a traffic ticket, has seen her insurance premium rise 50 percent.

general statement:	It is difficult to meet people at my college.
specific examples:	After class, most students rush to their jobs or families.
	There are very few places to sit and talk between classes.

When you write an illustration paragraph, be careful to support a general statement with specific examples, not with more general statements:

not this:

general statement:	College is harder than I thought it would be.
more general statements:	~~It's tough to be a college student. Studying takes up a lot of my time.~~

but this:

general statement:	College is harder than I thought it would be.
specific examples:	I can't afford to miss any classes.
	I have to study at least two hours a day.

If you remember to illustrate a broad statement with specific examples, you'll have the key to this kind of paragraph.

EXERCISE **1**	**RECOGNIZING BROAD STATEMENTS**

Each list below contains one broad statement and three specific examples. Underline the broad statement.

1. Montreal's Arcade Fire is considered one of the best bands in independent music.
   Canadian bands are receiving more international recognition.
   David Bowie contributed to Arcade Fire's title song "Reflektor" after admiring its sound.

The Burlington, Ontario, band Walk Off the Earth received more than a hundred million views in four months with their YouTube video "Somebody I Used to Know."

2. Green technology is growing.
   Homeowners are installing solar panels.
   Geothermal technologies can save homeowners money on heating costs.
   Wind turbines are being used to generate electricity.

3. Canadians have been responsible for some great inventions.
   Pablum, a fortified infant cereal, was developed at the Hospital for Sick Children in Toronto.
   Frederick Banting and Charles Best discovered how to extract insulin to treat diabetes.
   In 1891, Dr. James Naismith created the game of basketball.

4. The office printer ran out of ink just before an important deadline.
   A sudden power failure caused the loss of an expensive program.
   An important backup disk turned out to be blank.
   Even computer technology isn't always reliable.

5. Many working parents struggle to spend time with their children.
   Students do their classwork and have full- or part-time jobs, too.
   Everybody seems to be short of free time these days.
   People work overtime because they need the extra money, even if they lose their free time.

EXERCISE **2**	**DISTINGUISHING THE GENERAL STATEMENT FROM THE SPECIFIC EXAMPLE**

Each of the following general statements is backed up by three items of support. Two of these support items are specific examples; one is too general to be effective. Underline the one that is too general.

1. **general statement:** High technology is not necessarily the best technology.
   support: Computers' CPUs are getting faster all the time.
   Smartphones can make us available to work at any time, increasing stress levels.
   Some studies show that the frequencies emitted by smartphones may be dangerous.

2. **general statement:** A positive attitude is a great asset.
   support: Looking on the bright side is a good thing.
   Smiling can actually improve a person's mood.
   Most people like to be around an optimist, so a positive attitude can lead to more friends.

3. **general statement:** Colleges and universities try to create a welcoming environment for new students.
   support: Students are given tours of the campus.
   I certainly did feel welcome on my first day.
   Free T-shirts foster a feeling of belonging.

    4. **general statement:** The local coffeehouse is becoming the preferred
                                  meeting place for today's youth.
        support: More and more coffeehouses are remodelling to include free
                     WiFi access.
                     Coffeehouses offer a more welcoming, relaxed atmosphere
                     than the local mall.
                     Everyone meets there.

    5. **general statement:** Most bookstores sell more than books.
        support: Many sell CDs and items for home decor.
                     They sell lots of things.
                     Most sell a variety of magazines.

| EXERCISE **3** | **ADDING SPECIFIC EXAMPLES TO A GENERAL STATEMENT** |

With a partner or group, add four specific examples to each general statement below.

    1. **general statement:** Many demands are made on a college student's finances.

        examples: _____

        _____

        _____

        _____

    2. **general statement:** Poor customer service is more common than good customer service.

        examples: _____

        _____

        _____

        _____

    3. **general statement:** With just a few changes, people can lead healthier, less stressful lives.

        examples: _____

        _____

        _____

        _____

    4. **general statement:** Online course supplements such as Pearson MyLab and Blackboard are a benefit to students.

        examples: _____

        _____

        _____

        _____

5. **general statement:** There are several places on campus where students can meet and socialize.

    examples: _____

    _____

    _____

    _____

WRITING THE ILLUSTRATION PARAGRAPH IN STEPS

PREWRITING   ## GATHERING IDEAS: ILLUSTRATION

Suppose your instructor asks you to write a paragraph about some aspect of cars. You can begin by listing ideas about your subject to help gather your thoughts and to find a focus for your paragraph. Your first list might look like the following:

Listing Ideas about Cars

cars in my neighbourhood	cars in the college parking lot
my brother's car	parking at college
car prices	car insurance
drag racing	

This list includes many specific ideas about cars. You could write a paragraph about one item or about two related items on the list. Reviewing the list, you decide to write your paragraph on cars in the college parking lot.

Adding Details to an Idea

Now that you have a narrowed topic for your paragraph, you decide to write a list of ideas about cars in the college parking lot:

Cars in the College Parking Lot: Some Ideas

vans	older people's cars, Volvos
cars with strollers	and Cadillacs
and car seats	racing cars, modified, brightly
beat-up old cars, some with	tinted
no bumpers	elaborate sound systems
a few new sports cars, gifts	bumper stickers
from rich parents	some stickers have a message
some SUVs	some brag

Creating a Topic Sentence

If you examine this list, looking for *related ideas*, you can create a topic sentence. The ideas on the list include (1) details about the kinds of cars, (2) details about what's inside the cars, and (3) details about the bumper stickers. Not all the details fit into these three categories, but many do.

Grouping the related ideas into the three categories can help you focus your ideas into a topic sentence.

Kinds of Cars

beat-up old cars, some with no bumpers	some SUVs
vans	older people's cars, Volvos and Cadillacs
a few new sports cars, gifts from rich parents	racing cars, modified, brightly tinted

Inside the Cars

elaborate sound systems	strollers and car seats

Bumper Stickers

some stickers have a message	some brag

You can summarize these related ideas in a topic sentence:

Cars in the college parking lot reflect the diversity of people at the school.

Check the sentence against your details. Does it cover the topic? *Yes.* The topic sentence begins with "Cars in the college parking lot." Does it make some point about the cars? *Yes.* It says that the cars "reflect the diversity of people at the school."

Since your details are about old and new cars, what is inside the cars and on the bumper stickers, you have many details about differences in cars and some hints about the people who drive them. The word "diversity" in your topic sentence will cover all these details.

EXERCISE 4

FINDING SPECIFIC IDEAS IN FREEWRITING

Below are two samples of freewriting. Each is a response to a broad topic. Read each sample, and then underline any words that could become a more specific topic for a paragraph.

Freewriting Reaction to the Topic of Food

What comes to my mind when I think about food? I'm hungry right now. Can't bring food into class though. Three o'clock in the afternoon is the worst: between classes and so long after lunch, I need either chocolate or coffee. Can't afford to buy food every day though. Must remember to make a lunch for tomorrow. Food on campus is so expensive! $7 for a burger and fries. Hot dogs from the cart outside are much cheaper though. I wish this city had more interesting street food. Samosas, burritos, noodles would all be tastier than hot dogs.

Freewriting Reaction to the Topic of Health

I'm healthy. Health class? I have to take a health class next term. I think it's about nutrition, vitamins, exercise. Health is a hard subject to write about. I just take it for granted that I'll be healthy. I've never really been sick. Just childhood things like chicken pox. One bad case of strep throat. That was awful. Then there was that time last year when I had to go to the emergency room. A three-hour wait! The doctor's office is not that much better though.

EXERCISE 5

FINDING SPECIFIC IDEAS IN LISTS

Below are two lists. Each is a response to a broad topic. Read each list, and then underline any words that could become a more specific topic for a paragraph.

Topic: Technology in Daily Life

lots of technology	YouTube
scanners at the supermarket	Skype
cyberspace	new breakthroughs
voice mail	mobile banking
blogs	surveillance cameras

Topic: Music

different kinds of music	music around the world
legendary rappers	my favourite songs
the best radio station	the year's most popular
people and music	downloads
country music	advertising jingles

EXERCISE 6

GROUPING RELATED IDEAS IN LISTS OF DETAILS

Below are lists of details. In each list, circle the items that seem to fit into one group; then underline the items that seem to fit into a second group. (For an example, see Chapter 1, Exercise 7.) Some items may not fit into either group.

1. **topic: losses**

lost credit card	lost self-esteem
lost moral standards	lost wallet
lost keys	lost in the woods
lost in the final period	lost notebook
lost sense of purpose	lost innocence

2. **topic: studying for a test**

cramming at 4:00 A.M.	essay test
calmly reviewing the text	notes from class
frantically reading the book	budgeting time to study
trying to memorize it all	getting a good night's sleep
staying up all night	connecting key ideas and terms

3. **topic: birthday gifts**

a CD by your favourite band	a Lexus SUV
gifts from parents	a romantic gift
airline tickets to Jamaica	new shirts

a special, framed photo   a giant birthday cake
aftershave or cologne   a complete entertainment unit

4.   **topic: travelling to college by bus**
can study on the bus   saves gas money
bus can be late   you can be late and miss it
waiting for bus in the rain   walk from bus to school
no parking hassles   variety of bus riders
traffic congestion   bus drivers

EXERCISE 7

WRITING TOPIC SENTENCES FOR LISTS OF DETAILS

Below are lists of details that have no topic sentences. Write an appropriate topic sentence for each one.

1.   topic sentence: _____

_____

The house has a beautiful hardwood floor.
It also has high ceilings.
There is a small but cozy fireplace in the living room.
The entrance hall is spacious.
The kitchen needs a new sink and refrigerator.
There is a leak in the roof over the big bedroom.
Several of the window frames are rotted.
The bathroom tile needs to be replaced.

2.   topic sentence: _____

_____

Alicia's boyfriend, Keith, teases her about her weight.
He is also critical of her intelligence, her personality, and her style.
He even criticizes her friends.
Keith is often late or fails to show up for a date with Alicia.
He gets angry if she questions him about his absence.
He tells her she is too controlling.
He never apologizes for his bad behaviour.

3.   topic sentence: _____

_____

Alex was once stopped by a police officer.
The officer said Alex had a broken taillight.
He wanted to give Alex a ticket.
Alex started his usual line of jokes and stories.
Soon, the officer let Alex off with a warning.
Another time, Alex fell during a soccer game.
He broke a bone in his foot and was rushed to the emergency room.
Instead of complaining about the pain, Alex tried to look on the funny side.
He talked about his "superfoot" and soon had the doctor and nurses laughing.

4. topic sentence: _____

_____

Sharing a room with two sisters, I always have a lack of privacy.
As I was growing up, I always had to wear hand-me-down clothes
and shoes.
We always have big family dinners where we sit down and share our news.
Whenever I need advice or a shoulder to cry on, there is always
someone to talk to.
My sisters and I have always been very competitive, fighting for
everything from our parents' attention to the last piece of cake.
I have never felt lonely in my family.
It costs a lot of money to feed a family of five.
Everyone from my grandparents to my nephews helps out when there
is work to be done.
We have only one car, so it's always very crowded whenever we have
to go somewhere.

5. topic sentence: _____

_____

When I took my first airplane trip, a stranger helped me find my
connecting flight.
Some good person mailed my wallet (and all its contents) back to me
when I lost it.
An elderly customer at the restaurant where I work gave me a ride
home when my car wouldn't start.
One day when I was holding my crying baby, a man let me cut ahead
in the supermarket line.
The crossing guard on my block always says, "Hi, how are you
doing?" when I walk by, even though I don't know him.
A boy in the city went two blocks out of his way to show me the way
to the court buildings.

EXERCISE 8

CHOOSING THE BETTER TOPIC SENTENCE

Below are lists of details. Each list has two possible topic sentences. Underline
the better topic sentence for each list.

1. possible topic sentences:

a. Canadians eat many different foods.

b. Canadians are lucky to have access to food from many countries.

People of many heritages enjoy Chinese food.
Tofu and fried rice are available everywhere.
Pho, a Vietnamese soup with noodles, makes for a cheap yet flavourful
lunch.
Pasta is a favourite dish for many people.
Caribbean jerk chicken and pastries are sold at the local college cafeteria.
My neighbour introduced me to Chelo Kabab, a famous Iranian dish.
My personal choices are Indian curries and papadums.

2. **possible topic sentences:**

    a. In a crisis, it's good to have friends.

    b. A crisis can reveal a person's true friends.

        I had plenty of friends in high school.
        Dave was my basketball buddy; we played every Thursday afternoon.
        Jiwon and I used to make jokes in our math class.
        I had known Eddie since he moved into my neighbourhood when we were both eight years old.
        Harry and I worked together at the movie theatre.
        I ran into Carlos at parties, and we became friends.
        Then I was seriously hurt in a bad car accident.
        Dave came to see me in the hospital, once.
        Jiwon sent me a funny card.
        Eddie called and said he hadn't had a chance to come to the hospital.
        I never saw Carlos again.
        Only Harry came to see me through all my months of rehabilitation.

3. **possible topic sentences:**

    a. Humour can hide a person's dark side.

    b. The ability to make people laugh is a true talent.

        Sean was always the joker in our group.
        He was lively, cheerful, and quick with a witty comment.
        He could make me break into laughter during the most serious movie.
        When I got scolded for laughing, Sean would sit, looking very serious.
        His expression made me laugh even more.
        Sean was always the centre of fun and good times.
        Then one day I saw him sitting alone in our college cafeteria.
        He didn't know anyone was looking at him.
        His expression was sad and lonely.

PLANNING ## DEVISING A PLAN: ILLUSTRATION

When you plan your outline, keep your topic sentence in mind:

    Cars in the college parking lot reflect the diversity of people at the school.

Remember the three categories of related details:

    kinds of cars

    inside the cars

    bumper stickers

These three categories can give you an idea for how to organize the outline.

    Below is an outline for a paragraph on cars in the college parking lot. As you read the outline, you'll notice that details about the insides of the cars and about bumper stickers have been added. Adding details can be part of the outlining stage.

> An Outline for an Illustration Paragraph

topic sentence: Cars in the college parking lot reflect the diversity of people at the school.

details:

kinds of cars:

There are beat-up old cars.

Some have no bumpers.

There are vans.

There are a few new sports cars.

Maybe these are gifts from rich parents.

There are some SUVs.

Older people's cars, like Volvos and Cadillacs, are there.

There are a few racing cars, modified and heavily tinted.

inside the cars:

Some cars have elaborate sound systems.

Some have a baby stroller or car seat.

Some have empty paper cups and food wrappers.

bumper stickers:

Some have stickers for a club.

There are stickers with a message.

There are stickers that brag.

As you can see, the outline used the details from the list and included other details. You can add more details, combine some details to eliminate repetition, or even eliminate some details as you draft your paragraph.

EXERCISE 9 — ADDING DETAILS TO AN OUTLINE

Below are three partial outlines. Each has a topic sentence and some details. Working with a partner or group, add more details that support the topic sentence.

1. **topic sentence:** Most teenagers have the same worries.

   a. They're concerned about their appearance.

   b. They obsess about finding the right person to love.

   c. They worry about fitting in.

   d. _____

   e. _____

   f. _____

   g. _____

2. **topic sentence:** Pets are good for their owners' well-being.

   a. You can get healthy exercise by walking a dog.

   b. Widows and widowers with pets tend to live longer.

   c. An aquarium populated with fish adds tranquility to any room.

   d. _____

   e. _____

   f. _____

   g. _____

3. **topic sentence:** Even if you don't have air conditioning, there are ways to keep cool in the summer heat.

   a. Find a big shady tree and sit under it.

   b. Wear loose cotton clothing.

   c. Buy a fan.

   d. _____

   e. _____

   f. _____

   g. _____

EXERCISE 10

ELIMINATING DETAILS THAT ARE REPETITIVE

In the following outlines, some details use different words to repeat an example given earlier in the list. Cross out the repetitive details.

1. **topic sentence:** Everybody has some advice for fighting a cold.

   My mother thinks vitamin C tablets will help.
   My grandmother believes in chicken soup with a good dash of pepper.
   My uncle says the only way to shake a cold is to go to bed and sleep it off.
   "Drink plenty of liquids," says my neighbour.
   My roommate urges bed rest.
   My sister, who is interested in alternative medicine, urges me to try an herbal tea.
   My boss says there is an old saying: "Feed a cold and starve a fever," which means that I should make sure I eat enough.
   At school, my instructor told me to take lots of fluids.

2. **topic sentence:** After many mistakes, I've learned to think before I act.

   I bought the first car I saw.
   It was overpriced and full of hidden mechanical problems.
   I chose my college major because everyone else was majoring in business and I was in a hurry to register.
   I'm not interested in my business courses.

A friend of mine insulted me, and I was so angry that I hit him.
I barely avoided being arrested.
I didn't shop around before I got my car.
My mother asked me for a favour, and I blurted out the first excuse I could think of.
I hurt my mother's feelings.
I'm stuck in business classes that bore me.
My temper got me into trouble with a friend and the law.

3. **topic sentence:** The cheapest product isn't always the best to buy.

I bought cheap toothpaste, but it felt gritty on my teeth.
Cheap dishwashing liquid is weaker than the more expensive, concentrated kind.
My $1.99 umbrella lasted through only one rainy day.
Using gritty toothpaste is like brushing my teeth with sand.
Big bags of cookies can taste dry and stale.
I bought a pack of sale-priced ballpoint pens and they leaked all over my backpack.
I loved my $2.99 shirt, but it fell apart after one washing.
What good is a bargain umbrella that turns inside out when the wind starts to pick up?

DRAFTING AND REVISING

DRAFTING AND REVISING: ILLUSTRATION

Review the outline on cars in the college parking lot on page 77. You can create a first draft of this outline in the form of a paragraph. At this point, you can combine some of the short, choppy sentences of the outline, add details, and add transitions to link your ideas. You can revise your draft using the checklist on the next page.

Transitions

As you revise your illustration paragraph, you may find places where one idea ends and another begins abruptly. This problem occurs when you forget to add **transitions**, which are words, phrases, or sentences that connect one idea to another. Using transitions effectively will make your writing clear and smooth.

When you write an illustration paragraph, you will need some transitions that link one example to another and other transitions to link one section of your paragraph to another section. Here are some transitions you may want to use in writing an illustration paragraph.

INFOBOX **TRANSITIONS FOR AN ILLUSTRATION PARAGRAPH**

for example	for instance
one example	one instance
a second example	the first instance
another example	another instance
other examples	in addition
in the case of	to illustrate
like	other kinds
such as	once

CHECKLIST | **FOR REVISING AN ILLUSTRATION PARAGRAPH**

✓ Should some of the sentences be combined?

✓ Do I need more or better transitions?

✓ Should I add more details to support my points?

✓ Should some of the details be more specific?

Look carefully at the following draft of the paragraph on cars in the college parking lot, and note how it combines sentences, adds details, and uses transitions to transform the outline into a clear and developed paragraph.

A Draft of an Illustration Paragraph

topic sentence	Cars in the college parking lot reflect the diversity of people at the school. There
detail added	are beat-up old cars, some with no bumpers, near several vans. There are one or two
detail added	new sports cars, like BMWs; they might belong to the few lucky students with rich
transition added	and generous parents. Other kinds include SUVs and older people's cars such as Volvos
transition added	and Cadillacs. In addition, the parking lot holds a few racing cars, modified and highly
detail added	tinted. Some cars have elaborate sound systems for music lovers. Others must belong
detail added	to parents because they have a baby stroller or car seat inside. Many are filled with
detail added	empty paper cups or food wrappers since busy students have to eat on the run. Many
details added	cars also have bumper stickers; some are for clubs, like the Charlottetown Athletic
	Club, while others have a message such as "Give Blood: Save Lives" or "Save the Whales."
details added	Some stickers brag that the driver is the "Proud Parent of an Honour Roll Student,"
	and some may warn other drivers, "If you can read this, you're driving too closely!"

EXERCISE

11

REVISING A DRAFT BY COMBINING SENTENCES

The paragraph below has many short, choppy sentences, which are underlined. Wherever you see two or more underlined sentences clustered next to each other, combine them into one clear, smooth sentence. Write your revised version of the paragraph in the spaces above the lines.

Mr. Gonsalves, my high-school English teacher, had a whole bag of tricks

for keeping the class awake and alert. Sometimes, a student would fall asleep.

The student would be in the back of the classroom. Mr. Gonsalves would stand

beside the sleeping student's desk and stare silently. The rest of the class would begin

to laugh. The laughing woke up the student. At other times, when Mr. Gonsalves was teaching a grammar lesson, the class would become bored. Mr. Gonsalves would startle everyone by suddenly singing loudly. He was such a terrible singer that we all jumped to attention. Once Mr. Gonsalves really went to extremes. <u>He made the whole class sing. The song was one he had written. It was a song about punctuation.</u> In every class, Mr. Gonsalves's students had to be prepared for surprises.

EXERCISE 12 — REVISING A DRAFT BY ADDING TRANSITIONS

The paragraph below needs some transitions. Add appropriate transitions (words or phrases) to the blanks.

My girlfriend Elise has some annoying habits. _____, she never lets me finish a sentence. Whenever I start to say something, Elise jumps in with her own idea or with what she thinks I am about to say. _____, she likes to plan too far ahead. On Monday, she wants to know exactly what we'll be doing on Saturday night. I'm more spontaneous and like to wait until Friday or Saturday to decide. _____, she worries too much. _____, she worries when I'm late for school. She also worries when I have a cold. She's afraid it may turn into pneumonia. Elise is clearly a talker, a planner, and a worrier, but these are all minor flaws. She isn't perfect, but she's perfect for me.

EXERCISE 13 — ADDING DETAILS TO A DRAFT

The paragraph below lacks the kinds of details that would make it more interesting. Working with a partner or group, add details to the blank spaces provided. When you are finished, read the revised paragraph to the class.

The clothes people wear to work depend on their positions. The average college student who works in a restaurant is likely to wear _____ or _____ on the job. Men who work behind the counter of an expensive men's clothing store may be required to dress in _____, while women who sell makeup in department stores often have to wear _____ and perfect makeup. If a person works as a teller in a bank, he or she cannot come to work in _____. Instead, appropriate dress is _____ and _____. Executives in financial corporations are often expected to dress in _____, _____, and _____. On the other hand, people in creative fields such as music or film production can wear almost anything from _____ to _____ when they work.

PROOFREADING

PROOFREADING AND POLISHING: ILLUSTRATION

As you prepare the final version of your illustration paragraph, make any changes in word choice or transitions that can refine your writing. Below is the final version of the paragraph on cars in the college parking lot. As you read it, you'll notice a few more changes:

- Some details have been added.
- Several long transitions have been added. The paragraph needed to signal the shift in subject from the kinds of cars to what was inside the cars; then it needed to signal the shift from the interior of the cars to bumper stickers.
- A concluding sentence has been added to reinforce the point of the topic sentence: A diverse college population is reflected in its cars.

> ### A Final Version of a Paragraph (*changes from the last draft are underlined*)

>   Cars in the college parking lot reflect the diversity of the people at the school. There are beat-up old cars, some with no bumpers, near several vans. There are one or two new sports cars, like BMWs; they might belong to the few lucky students with rich and generous parents. Other kinds include SUVs and older people's cars such as Volvos and Cadillacs. In addition, the parking lot holds a few racing cars, modified and highly tinted. <u>What is inside the cars is as revealing as the cars themselves.</u> Some cars have elaborate sound systems for music lovers <u>or for those who just like everyone to know they're coming</u>. Others must belong to parents because they have a baby stroller or car seat inside. Many are filled with empty paper cups or food wrappers since busy students have to eat on the run. <u>Bumper stickers also tell a story.</u> Many cars have bumper stickers; some are for clubs, like the Charlottetown Athletic Club, while others have a message such as, "Give Blood: Save Lives" or "Save the Whales." Some stickers brag that the driver is the "Proud Parent of an Honour Roll Student," and some may warn other drivers, "If you can read this, you're driving too closely!" <u>A walk through the parking lot hints that this college is a place for all ages, backgrounds, and interests.</u>

    Before you prepare the final version of your illustration paragraph, check your latest draft for errors in spelling or punctuation and for any errors made in typing and copying.

EXERCISE

14

PROOFREADING TO PREPARE THE FINAL VERSION

Below are two illustration paragraphs with the kinds of errors that are easy to overlook when you prepare the final version of an assignment. Correct the errors by writing above the lines. There are eleven errors in the first paragraph and nine errors in the second paragraph.

    1.   Today, when people say they want a drink of water, they could be

axsing for a number of drinks. Of coarse, there is water right from the faucet, but many people drink bottle water. There are dozens of brans of bottled water and there are also to basic kind of water in bottles. One kind is fizzy, and one kind is flat. In edition, there are many new types of water, such as water with vitamins, water with caffeine, and Flavoured water. These days, a whole row in the supermarket can be filled with ten or twenty variety of water, and restaurants may offer a choice of water, from free tap water to expensive kins of bottled water. As a result a person who asks for a glass of water has to be very specific.

2.   Every member of my family has a peculiar driving habit. My Father, for example, always drives with the windows open even if it is freezing. Riding with him, I have saw ice crystles forming on the car seats. My mother also has a strange driving habit, but her's is more dangerous. She never looks into her rear-view mirror. Instead, she just changes lane's whenever she feels like it. I always say my prayers when I get into a car with her. Unlike my mother, my brother is a very cautious driver. He was in an accident, and it scared him so much that he drives very slowly and doesn't change lanes unless he has to. I am too impatient to ride with him. Finally, my habit is quiet dramatic I blast the radio so that it can be heard a block away. My parents wont even ride with me because they are afraid they will burst their eardrums. In our family, every driver, because of some personal driving weirdness, tends to drive alone.

Lines of Detail: A Walk-Through Assignment

Your assignment is to write an illustration paragraph about music.

Step 1: Freewrite or brainstorm on this broad topic for ten minutes.

Step 2: Review your freewriting or brainstorming. Underline any parts that are a specific idea related to the broad topic, music.

Step 3: List all the specific ideas. Choose one as the narrowed topic for your paragraph.

Step 4: Add related ideas to your chosen, narrowed topic. Do this by reviewing your list for related ideas and by brainstorming for more related ideas.

Step 5: List all your related ideas and review their connection to your narrowed topic. Then write a topic sentence for your paragraph.

Step 6: Write a first draft of your paragraph.

Step 7: Revise your first draft. Be sure it has enough details and clear transitions. Combine any choppy sentences.

Step 8: After a final check for any errors in punctuation, spelling, and word choice, prepare the final version of the paragraph.

Writing Your Own Illustration Paragraph

When you write on any of these topics, follow the four basic stages of the writing process in preparing your illustration paragraph.

1. Begin this assignment with a partner or group. Together, write down as many old sayings as you can. (Old sayings include such statements as "It's not whether you win or lose; it's how you play the game" and "Money can't buy happiness.") If anyone in your group speaks a second language, ask him or her to translate and explain any old sayings from that language.

   Once you have a long list of sayings, split up. Pick one saying, then write a paragraph on that saying. Your paragraph should give several examples that prove the truth of the saying.

2. Below are some topic sentences. Select one and use it to write a paragraph in which you give examples of the topic sentence.

   I think of my friend _____ when I hear people talk of "running the rat race."

   Online course supplements such as WebCT and Blackboard are a benefit to students.

   Technology makes communication more efficient.

   Ergonomics (designing office furniture and office space so that workplace injuries and fatigue are minimized) is being considered more and more in today's offices.

   A trade is an excellent career choice.

   Women's health issues are at the forefront of the medical community's concerns.

   _____ is an example of a world-class city.

3. Select one of the topics listed below. Write a paragraph on some narrowed part of the topic. If you choose the topic of jobs, for example, you might narrow the topic to your experiences working at a supermarket.

jobs	fears	dreams	mistakes
stress	money	television	technology
computers	children	celebrities	surprises
fashion	challenges	memories	holidays

WRITING FROM READING: THE WRITING PROCESS

Who's Stealing Our Jobs? Not Who You Think

Margaret Wente

Margaret Wente writes on current affairs for The Globe and Mail. *Her thought-provoking pieces have also appeared in such magazines as* Report on Business *and* Canadian Business. *Here, she writes on the impact of technology on employment.*

I actually feel a little sorry for the Royal Bank of Canada. The villain of the week has been portrayed as a **callous** rule-bender throwing hard-working Canadians out of work to maximize its obscene profits. The online outrage boiled over. The CEO **grovelled**. The government pledged to look into it and clamp down on companies abusing the temporary foreign worker program.

In fact, the bank is behaving exactly like every other business. They're all in search of better, cheaper and more productive ways of doing things. Unfortunately, these

callous: hard-hearted

to grovel: to debase oneself, usually in apology

better, cheaper ways may not necessarily include maintaining you in your current job for the rest of your working life. We, too, could wind up training our replacements.

But don't blame greedy capitalists for your distress. Blame technology. We're going through a technological revolution so disruptive that we're only beginning to feel its impact. Advances in technology are the reason why RBC can outsource work to Indian software engineers who are paid 10 cents on the dollar. In the next stage of the revolution—coming very soon—the bank won't need people to do this work at all.

The revolution started lower down the value chain, wiping out millions of middle-class jobs that real people used to do. Bank tellers, data-entry clerks, airline ticketing processors, travel agents, office assistants and meter readers bit the dust. Entire occupations were virtually obliterated. Not all of these people were laid off; they simply weren't replaced. Today, retail workers are being let go by the thousands because more and more of us are shopping on the Internet. They won't be replaced, either.

Andrew McAfee, a research scientist at MIT who specializes in technology's impact on business, says the pace of innovation has sped up so much that our skills and institutions simply can't keep up. A lot of people have been left behind. Computers contribute enormous wealth and productivity to the economy, but not much employment, he agreed in an interview with the CBS program *60 Minutes*. In his blog, he points out that Apple, Amazon, Facebook and Google have a combined **market capitalization** of more than $900-billion, yet employ fewer than 200,000 people. That's less than the number of new jobs the U.S. must create every two months just to hold the unemployment rate steady.

market capitalization: the value of the shares of a publicly traded company

Technology-related job losses have depressed median wages and kept job-creation rates miserably low. But it's not just lower-level jobs that have disappeared. What's astonishing is how rapidly the job displacement is moving up the value chain. For example, new accounting systems that can perform higher-level tasks are putting general accountants out of work. "What would get you into a CA firm 10 years ago won't get you an interview today," one accounting professor told me. **Radiologists**—among the highest-paid professionals in medicine—are facing brutal competition from outsourcing, because anyone can read a diagnostic scan. Even those people could be replaced by computers.

radiologist: professional who analyzes and interprets medical images such as X-rays

Software legal programs (known as e-discovery) are wiping out law clerks who used to sift through tonnes of documents in search of information used in litigation. These programs are far cheaper, faster and more accurate than mere mortals. A version of Watson, the computer program that can beat every living being at *Jeopardy!*, is being developed for medical diagnostics. The giant job-search industry, which was built on recruiting mid-level professionals, is being hammered by online sites such as LinkedIn that allow companies to find workers faster and cheaper on their own.

Underlying all these changes is the exponential advance of artificial intelligence. Computer power is getting faster and cheaper all the time. It's now powerful enough to operate a self-driving car. I don't want to be an alarmist, but artificial intelligence software can now be used to grade university-level essays (not just multiple-choice tests). Computer writing engines can produce a decent sports or business story in less time than it takes a **J-school** graduate to fetch a cup of coffee. They can even be instructed to

J-school: journalism school

irreverent: disrespectful
snarky: sarcastic

serfdom: life of servitude

add tone—from straight up and dignified to **irreverent** and **snarky**. No doubt they'll eventually master opinion-writing. I too could be replaced by an algorithm.

Technological revolutions are very good for the human race, in the long run. The steam revolution liberated people from **serfdom** and poverty. But, short term, people suffer. As Prof. McAfee writes in *Race Against the Machine* (co-authored with Erik Brynjolfsson), "There is no economic law that says that everyone, or even most people, automatically benefit from technological progress." For the record, he's an optimist. He thinks the information revolution will create far more wealth and opportunity than it destroys—eventually.

Meantime, we're in for a lot more shocks. The world is changing faster than we want, but nobody has the power to slow things down. None of us will be left untouched. And that giant sucking sound may be your livelihood.

But if you're looking for villains, fancy algorithms make for lousy targets. Bank presidents and neglectful governments are much more satisfactory.

UNDERSTANDING "WHO'S STEALING OUR JOBS? NOT WHO YOU THINK"

1. To what does Wente attribute the loss of such jobs as bank tellers and travel agents?
2. Give five examples of middle-class jobs that have been replaced by technology.
3. Give five examples of higher-level jobs that have been affected by technology.
4. What conclusions does Wente draw about the future of employment?

WRITING FROM READING "WHO'S STEALING OUR JOBS? NOT WHO YOU THINK"

1. Consider how technology has affected you as a student. How has it changed the way you communicate with your fellow students? With your professors? Does it affect the way you access information, research, or study? Write an illustration paragraph in which you examine the kinds of technology you use to communicate, research, or study.
2. Wente mentions the impact technology has had on job-search strategies. Write an illustration paragraph giving examples of the internet resources available for job seekers or employers.
3. Online shopping is quickly becoming a strong competitor for traditional retail. Write an illustration paragraph examining various online shopping sites, and what traditional stores they might affect.
4. Many Canadians now own smartphones, and many cannot envision their lives without them. Consider the apps you use most often, and write an illustration paragraph in which you give examples of your favourite apps.

MyWritingLab

Go to MyWritingLab to access a diagnostic test that creates your own personalized learning path supported by rich multimedia resources and a variety of animated tutorials, all aimed at helping you improve your writing. MyWritingLab also includes a complete eText version of the book that is fully searchable and accessible through your web browser or most mobile devices.

CHAPTER 4
Description

LEARNING OBJECTIVES

After you have read this chapter and completed its exercises and assignments, you should be able to

- generate ideas for a descriptive paragraph
- distinguish between general and more effective, specific words and phrases for your descriptive paragraph
- use effective sense words and phrases in your descriptive paragraph
- create a dominant impression for your descriptive paragraph
- organize your ideas in a logical order
- draft and edit an effective descriptive paragraph

"Don't tell me the light is shining; show me the glint of light on broken glass."

~ ANTON CHEKHOV

▼ ANTON CHEKHOV WAS A TURN-OF-THE-TWENTIETH-CENTURY RUSSIAN PLAYWRIGHT AND SHORT-STORY WRITER.

WHAT IS DESCRIPTION?

Description shows a reader what a person, place, thing, or situation is like. When you write descriptively, you try to *show* something, not *tell* about it; Anton Chekhov is referring to this in his quotation above. An effective description puts the reader in that place, helps the reader understand that person, and gives the reader a feeling for that situation.

Hints for Writing a Descriptive Paragraph

Using Specific Words or Phrases   The reader will see what you're describing if you use specific words and phrases. When a word or phrase is *specific*, it is exact and precise. The opposite of specific language is *general* language, which is vague or fuzzy. Think of the difference between specific and general in this way:

Imagine that you're browsing through a used-car lot. A salesman approaches.

"Can I help you?" the salesman asks.
"I'm looking for a good, reliable car," you say.
"Well, what kind of car did you have in mind?"

"Not too old."

"A sports car?" asks the salesman.

"Maybe," you say.

The conversation could go on and on. You are being general in saying that you want a "good, reliable" car. The salesman, however, is looking for specific details: How old a car do you want? What model of car?

In writing, if you use words like "good" or "nice" or "bad" or "interesting," you will have neither a specific description nor an effective piece of writing. Whenever you can, try to use the more precise word instead of the general term. To find a more precise term, ask yourself such questions as, "What type?" or "How?" The examples below show how a general term can be replaced by a more specific one.

general word:	light (Ask "What kind?")
more specific words:	incandescent, fluorescent, early morning, dappled
general word:	novel (Ask "What genre [type]?")
more specific words:	science fiction, literary, romance, graphic, mystery
general word:	ran (Ask "How?")
more specific words:	raced, sprinted, loped
general word:	nice (Ask "How?")
more specific words:	friendly, outgoing, courteous

EXERCISE 1

IDENTIFYING GENERAL AND SPECIFIC WORDS

Below are lists of words. Put an X beside the most general term in each list. The first one is done for you.

List 1

- ____ waiter
- _X_ restaurant employee
- ____ cook
- ____ cashier
- ____ dishwasher

List 2

- ____ government
- ____ federal
- ____ municipal
- ____ provincial

List 3

- ____ community college
- ____ university
- ____ preschool
- ____ educational institution
- ____ secondary school

List 4

- ____ spring
- ____ mineralized
- ____ flavoured
- ____ water
- ____ sparkling

List 5

- ____ convenience
- ____ department
- ____ store
- ____ pet
- ____ specialty

List 6

- ____ mathematics
- ____ algebra
- ____ calculus
- ____ geometry
- ____ statistics

EXERCISE 2

RANKING GENERAL AND SPECIFIC ITEMS

Below are lists of items. In each list, rank the items from the most general (1) to the most specific (4).

List 1

_____ health-care provider
_____ surgeon
_____ physician
_____ brain surgeon

List 2

_____ *Singin' in the Rain*
_____ musical romantic comedy
_____ romantic comedy
_____ funny movie

List 3

_____ college services
_____ academic help
_____ help for students
_____ tutoring

List 4

_____ first-person shooter game
_____ video game
_____ shooter game
_____ *Halo 5*

EXERCISE 3

INTERVIEWING FOR SPECIFIC ANSWERS

To practise being specific, interview a partner. Ask your partner to answer the questions below. Write his or her answers in the spaces provided. When you've finished, change places. The goal in both interviews is to find specific answers, so you should both be as explicit as you can in your responses.

Interview Questions

1. Who has been the most influential person in your life?

   _____

2. If you could vacation anywhere in the world, where would it be?

   _____

3. What is your favourite sport?

   _____

4. What piece of technology could you not live without?

   _____

5. Name three objects that are in your wallet or purse right now.

   _____

6. What food reminds you of your childhood?

   _____

7. What would you say is the one defining moment in your life?

   _____

8. What is the most enjoyable part of your day?

   _____

9. What do you like most about your school, college, or university?

_____

10. What would you do if you won $10 million?

_____

FINDING SPECIFIC WORDS OR PHRASES

List four specific words or phrases beneath each general one. You may use brand names where they are appropriate. The first word on List 1 is done for you.

List 1

general word: bad
specific word or phrase: annoying

_____

_____

_____

_____

List 2

general word: said
specific word or phrase:

_____

_____

_____

_____

List 3

general word: nice
specific word or phrase:

_____

_____

_____

_____

List 4

general word: angry
specific word or phrase:

_____

_____

_____

_____

List 5

general word: good looking
specific word or phrase:

_____

_____

_____

_____

communication at work

Tourism plays an important role in Canada's economy. The following paragraph, from the Parks Canada website, describes the natural beauty of British Columbia's and Alberta's national parks:

> The grizzly bear stops and looks toward the sound. Sniffing the air, he searches the dim, early-morning horizon. That sweet smell of spring pervades the cool Rocky Mountain air. In the distance, Mount Victoria and Mount Lefroy mark the Continental Divide. Soon, newly sprouted wildflowers will greet the hikers who pass this way.

Note the use of specific descriptive words such as "dim," "early morning," "pervades," and "newly sprouted." Think of a place that has special meaning for you. How would you describe it?

EXERCISE 5

IDENTIFYING SENTENCES THAT ARE TOO GENERAL

Below are lists of sentences. Put an *X* beside one sentence in each group that is general and vague.

1. a. _____ Jose is an easygoing person.

   b. _____ Jose always has a new joke.

   c. _____ Jose makes faces at me in class.

2. a. _____ She criticized anyone who tried to help her at her work.

   b. _____ She expected the worst out of her job.

   c. _____ She had a bad attitude.

3. a. _____ It was a sweltering day.

   b. _____ It was 40 degrees Celsius in the shade.

   c. _____ The news warned people of the risk of heatstroke.

4. a. _____ I often have to deal with irate customers.

   b. _____ For six hours, I have to lift boxes weighing more than twenty kilograms each.

   c. _____ My job isn't easy.

5. a. _____   I want to live life to the fullest.

    b. _____   I want to travel to India and study my heritage.

    c. _____   I want to get married and raise a family.

Using Sense Words in Your Descriptions   One way to make your description specific and vivid is to use **sense words**. As you plan a description, ask yourself,

What does it *look* like?
What does it *sound* like?
What does it *smell* like?
What does it *taste* like?
What does it *feel* like?

Sense details make a description vivid. Remember, you're trying to *show*, not *tell*, so try to include details about the five senses in your descriptions. You can often brainstorm sense details more easily if you focus your thinking.

INFOBOX	DEVISING SENSE DETAIL

For the sense of ...	Think about ...
sight	colours, light and dark, shadows, or brightness.
hearing	noise, silence, or the kinds of sounds you hear.
smell	fragrance, odours, scents, aromas, or perfume.
taste	bitter, sour, or sweet—or compare the taste of one thing with another.
touch	the feel of things: texture, hardness, softness, roughness, smoothness.

EXERCISE

6

**BRAINSTORMING SENSE DETAIL
FOR A DESCRIPTIVE PARAGRAPH**

With a partner or a group, brainstorm the following ideas for a paragraph. That is, for each topic, list at least six questions and answers that could help you create sense details. Be prepared to read your completed exercise to another group or to the class.

1. **topic:** The college library is the ideal place to study.

    Brainstorm questions and answers: _____

    _____

    _____

    _____

    _____

    _____

    _____

2. **topic:** Riding the subway during rush hour makes me nauseated.

Brainstorm questions and answers: _____

_____

_____

_____

_____

_____

3. **topic:** The fireworks celebration dazzled the children.

Brainstorm questions and answers: _____

_____

_____

_____

_____

_____

_____

EXERCISE **7**	**WRITING SENSE WORDS**

Write sense descriptions for the following items.

a. Write four words or phrases to describe the texture of beach sand.

_____

_____

b. Write four words or phrases to describe how the sofa in the student lounge looks.

_____

_____

c. Write four words or phrases to describe the sounds of a traffic jam.

_____

_____

d. Write four words or phrases to describe the taste of chocolate ice cream.

_____

_____

WRITING THE DESCRIPTIVE PARAGRAPH IN STEPS

 GATHERING IDEAS: DESCRIPTION

Writing a descriptive paragraph begins with thinking on paper and looking for specific details and sense descriptions. You can think by brainstorming, freewriting, or writing in a journal. For example, because you have a sense of unease every time you go downstairs to your basement, you might decide to write about your basement. Brainstorming might lead you to something like the following list of ideas:

A Brainstorming List for a Descriptive Paragraph

Bought our house five years ago—house is fifty years old

I hate doing laundry

It's dark in the basement; there are fluorescent light bulbs

Everything is coated in dust

Doing laundry for my whole family takes me all weekend

Thick cobwebs are in every corner

Drywall is discoloured; there is a water stain

There is a clothesline in one corner

My brother doesn't mind going down to the basement

Plastic sinks and an old washer in the laundry room

Old wooden steps to the basement creak

The furnace hums

Washer makes a loud noise

Basement has a musty smell

A pair of jeans on the clothesline hangs as stiff as a board

The Dominant Impression

When you think you have enough details, you can begin to think about focusing them. Look over these details and consider where they're taking you. If you were to look at the list above, you might identify details that contribute to a particular idea:

It's dark in the basement; there are fluorescent light bulbs

Everything is coated in dust

Thick cobwebs are in every corner

Old wooden steps to the basement creak

The furnace hums

Basement has a musty smell

Reading over this list, you realize that the basement has an abandoned, otherworldly quality. Therefore, one main idea about your basement is that it can feel very different when you go to do your laundry. This idea is the **dominant impression**, or the main point of the description. It will form the topic sentence of the description paragraph. For example, it could be the following:

Going to do laundry in my basement is like entering another world.

Once you have a dominant impression, you're ready to add more ideas to explain and support it. You should try to make the added details specific by using sense description where appropriate.

| EXERCISE **8** | **ADDING DETAILS TO A DOMINANT IMPRESSION** |

Below are sentences that could be used as a dominant impression in a descriptive paragraph. Add more details. Some details, to explain and support the dominant impression, are already given.

1. **dominant impression:** My friend John had obviously pulled an all-nighter.

   details:

   a. <u>He spoke incoherently.</u>

   b. <u>He had bags under his eyes.</u>

   c. _____

   d. _____

   e. _____

2. **dominant impression:** My closet was crammed with ten years of accumulated junk.

   details:

   a. <u>Boxes piled on the top shelf threatened to fall.</u>

   b. <u>A moth-eaten sweater peeked out of a box.</u>

   c. _____

   d. _____

   e. _____

3. **dominant impression:** You could feel the tension in the school library the week before exams.

   details:

   a. <u>No one dared utter a sound.</u>

   b. <u>Some students had sat for hours without moving, heads bowed toward their books.</u>

   c. _____

   d. _____

   e. _____

4. **dominant impression:** Nothing compares to the atmosphere at an important soccer game.

   details:

   a. <u>Tens of thousands of fans packed the stands.</u>

   b. <u>The fans roared their approval and stomped their feet at every goal.</u>

   c. _____

   d. _____

   e. _____

EXERCISE

9

CREATING A DOMINANT IMPRESSION FROM A LIST OF DETAILS

Below are lists of details. For each list, write one sentence that could be used as the dominant impression created by the details.

1. dominant impression: _____

_____

_____

_____

details: People on beach towels sat elbow to elbow.
A beach volleyball game took up the remaining space.
The lifeguard could barely be seen above the players and sunbathers.
At the shoreline, parents watched small children build sandcastles and wade in shallow water.
Meanwhile, the deep water was filled with swimmers and people on floats.
CD players and radios blasted above the laughter of children, the shouts of the swimmers, and the victory cries of the volleyball teams.

2. dominant impression: _____

_____

_____

_____

details: The thunder roared while the lightning crashed and crackled, coming closer and closer.
Rain gushed into the streets.
The wind became stronger.
Leaves and tree branches flew in the air.
Doors blew shut and windows flew open.
Cars pulled over to the side of the road.
Pedestrians ran for cover.

3. dominant impression: _____

_____

_____

_____

details: The jury returned to their seats, looking down at the floor.
They would not look at the defendant or the lawyers.
No one spoke.

The only sound in the courtroom was the swish of the judge's robes as she returned to her chair.
The defendant turned pale; he clenched his hands.
The jury chairperson clutched the verdict in his fist, but his hands were shaking.
The reporters leaned forward in their seats, waiting for the verdict to be read.

4. dominant impression: _____

_____

_____

_____

details: The man in the dentist's waiting room had sweat trickling down his face.
His jaw was clenched.
He sat on the edge of his chair.
He kept looking at the clock.
His eyes were full of misery.
His hands trembled as he tried to flip through a magazine.
When the nurse called his name, he jumped.

PLANNING

DEVISING A PLAN: DESCRIPTION

You can use your dominant impression as the topic sentence of your outline. Beneath the topic sentence, list the details you've collected. Once you have this rough list, check the details and ask,

Do all the details relate to the topic sentence?
Are the details in logical order?

Below are the topic sentence and a list of details for the paragraph describing the writer's basement. The details that are crossed out *don't fit* the topic sentence.

topic sentence: Going to do laundry in my basement is like entering another world.

details: ~~Bought our house five years ago~~

~~House is fifty years old~~

~~I hate doing laundry~~

It's dark in the basement; there are fluorescent light bulbs

Everything is coated in dust

~~Doing laundry for my whole family takes me all weekend~~

Thick cobwebs are in every corner

Drywall is discoloured; there is a water stain

There is a clothesline in one corner

~~My brother doesn't mind going down to the basement~~

Plastic sinks and an old washer and dryer in the laundry room

Old wooden steps to the basement creak

The furnace hums

Washer makes a loud noise

Basement has a musty smell

A pair of jeans on the clothesline hangs as stiff as a board

Notice what is crossed out. The details about when the writer bought the house, the age of the house, how the writer feels about doing laundry, how doing laundry takes the whole weekend, and how the writer's brother feels about going down to the basement do not really have much to do with the topic sentence. The topic sentence is about how the writer feels about her basement.

Remember that, as you write and revise, you may decide to eliminate other ideas, or to re-insert ideas you had rejected, or to add new ideas. Changing your mind is a natural part of revising.

Once you've decided on your list of details, check their *order*. Remember that when you write a description, you're trying to make the reader *see* and *feel*. It will be easier for the reader to imagine what you see if you put your description in a simple, logical order. You might want to organize descriptions by *time order* (first to last) or by *space order* (top to bottom, or right to left). You might also group by *similar types* or categories (for example, all about the flowers in a park, then all about the trees). Because you're trying to *show*, not *tell*, about a person, place, or thing, you're trying to create a sense, or feeling, through your description. Your description may therefore be in order of sensory perception— that is, what you see, hear, smell, touch, or taste.

If you're describing a house, for instance, you may want to start with the outside of the house and then describe the inside. You don't want the details to shift back and forth from outside to inside and back to outside. Also, you want to make sure that you're creating a *feel* for the house: What makes this house special? If you're describing a person, you might want to group together all the details about his or her face before you describe the person's body; you'll also want to describe this person's personality and special traits. You might describe a meal from first course to dessert, and whether the meal is a special family tradition.

Look again at the details of the outline describing the basement. Because using sensory detail would be the best approach in creating a feel for the basement, you can categorize your details according to each of the senses. Now look at the following outline and notice how this order works.

> ## An Outline for a Descriptive Paragraph

topic sentence: Going to do laundry in my basement is like entering another world.

details:

visual

It's dark, so I look for the light switch.

Everything is coated in a fine layer of dust.

Thick cobwebs are in every corner.

Security gates on the windows, meant to prevent break-ins, make the

(continued)

basement feel like a dungeon.

The discoloured drywall hasn't been painted in years, and is stained a rust colour where water has leaked from the floor above.

I see a clothesline draped across one corner of the basement.

I pull a long cotton string to turn on the light bulb in the laundry room.

A dull, sickly light fills the laundry room.

There are plastic sinks and a twenty-year-old washer and dryer in the corner.

audio

The furnace hums.

The old wooden steps creak every time I take a step.

I turn on the light in the laundry room and hear a click.

Doing a load of laundry causes the washer to make a loud noise.

scent

The air in the basement carries a musty smell like wet dog.

touch

A pair of jeans on the clothesline hangs as stiff as a board.

You've probably noticed that you may not be able to separate the sensory details into convenient sections, as with a more physical description. For instance, as you describe entering the basement, you may describe the dark (visual detail) and the musty smell (scent). This approach can be more effective than describing all the visual details and then all the audio details, and so on. You've also likely noticed that the outline has more details than the original list. These details help make the descriptions more specific. You can add them to the outline and to the drafts of your paragraph.

Once you have a list of details that are focused on the topic sentence and arranged in some logical order, you can begin the stage of writing the descriptive paragraph.

EXERCISE 10

FINDING DETAILS THAT DON'T RELATE

Survey the following lists. Each list includes a topic sentence and several details. In each list, cross out the details that don't relate to the topic sentence.

1. **topic sentence:** The pond was a tranquil retreat.

   details: Few people knew of this small place.
   It was hidden from the road by a thick wall of trees.
   The road was two bumpy lanes.
   The trees encircled a shady shore of pebbles and greenery.
   Yellow wildflowers bloomed on the edges of the pond.
   The water was lightly ruffled by the breeze.
   I could hear the soft wind in the trees.
   I could hear the buzz of small summer insects.
   I was alone with my own thoughts and dreams.
   Someday, I would come back and bring a picnic.

2. **topic sentence:** My uncle Oscar was a wonderful playmate.

   details: He always had a joke for his nieces and nephews.
   When he ran out of jokes, he had a plan for a new adventure.
   Uncle Oscar died last year.
   Sometimes, he would take us exploring in the neighbourhood.
   Whenever he came over, he would arrive on time.
   He would push us on the swings for hours.
   Uncle Oscar was the one who pleaded with our parents to let us
   stay up later and play another game.
   He was my mother's brother.

3. **topic sentence:** Levar was a very spoiled child.

   details: He would interrupt his mother when she was talking to people.
   He'd pull at her sleeve or the hem of her dress.
   He'd whine, "Mom, Mom, I want to go now" or "Mom, can
   I have a dollar?"
   He had about a hundred toys.
   Whenever he broke a toy, he got a new one right away.
   Levar wore designer clothes, even to play in.
   Levar had no set bedtime; he was allowed to stay up as long as
   he wanted.
   He had a little sister, Denise.
   Levar had big black eyes with long, soft lashes.

EXERCISE **11**	**PUTTING DETAILS IN ORDER**

Below are lists that start with a topic sentence. The details under each topic
sentence are not in the right order. Put each detail in logical order by labelling
it, with 1 being the first detail, 2 the second, and so forth.

1. **topic sentence:** The plane trip went very smoothly. (Arrange the details in
   time order.)

   details: _____ Our plane departed on time.
   _____ We had no turbulent weather in the air.
   _____ We arrived at the airport in plenty of time to get good
   seats.
   _____ When we went to claim our luggage, all of it was there.
   _____ Our plane arrived on time.

2. **topic sentence:** The restaurant was dirty and unappealing. (Arrange the
   details according to space order, from outside to inside.)

   details: _____ Soot smeared the "Burgers and Shakes" sign.
   _____ Finger smudges covered the glass front door.
   _____ The chrome edges of the counter were caked with food.
   _____ Inside the entrance, we smelled the rancid odour of grease.
   _____ We approached a counter covered with crumbs.

3. **topic sentence:** The man showed off his money. (Arrange the details according to spatial position, from head to foot.)

details: _____ His designer shoes were a soft, glossy leather.
_____ His hair was immaculately styled.
_____ Two diamond earrings shone in his left ear.
_____ His wrist boasted a platinum Rolex.
_____ His shirt was silk.

EXERCISE 12 — CREATING DETAIL USING A LOGICAL ORDER

The following lists include a topic sentence and indicate a required order for the details. Write five sentences of detail in the required order.

1. **topic sentence:** The medicine cabinet in my bathroom is full of everything except medicine.
(Describe the contents of the cabinet from top shelf to bottom shelf.)

a. _____

b. _____

c. _____

d. _____

e. _____

2. **topic sentence:** The day was full of surprises.
(Describe the day from beginning to end.)

a. _____

b. _____

c. _____

d. _____

e. _____

3. **topic sentence:** The scene after the blizzard showed people at their best.
(First describe the scene; then describe the people's behaviour.)

a. _____

b. _____

c. _____

d. _____

e. _____

4. **topic sentence:** The bodyguard was an intimidating person.
(Describe him from head to foot.)

a. _____

b. _____

c. _____

d. _____

e. _____

DRAFTING AND REVISING

DRAFTING AND REVISING: DESCRIPTION

After you have an outline, the next step is creating a first rough draft of the paragraph. At this point, you can begin combining some of the ideas in your outline, making two or more short sentences into one longer one. Or you can write your first draft in short sentences and combine the sentences later. Your goal is simply to put your ideas into paragraph form. Then you can see how they look and check them to see what needs to be improved.

The first draft of a paragraph will not be perfect. (If it were perfect, it wouldn't be a first draft.) Once you have the first draft, check it using the following list.

✓ **CHECKLIST**   **FOR REVISING A DESCRIPTIVE PARAGRAPH**

✓ Are there enough details?

✓ Are the details specific?

✓ Do the details use sense words?

✓ Are the details in order?

✓ Is there a dominant impression?

✓ Do the details connect to the dominant impression?

✓ Have I made my point?

A common problem in writing descriptively is creating a fuzzy, vague impression. Take a look at the following:

> The hockey fans were rowdy and excited. They shouted when their team
> scored. Some people jumped up. The fans showed their support by cheering
> and stomping. They were enjoying every minute of the game.

The description could be revised so that it's more specific and vivid:

> The hockey fans were rowdy and excited. When their team scored, they yelled,
> "Way to go!" or "Stomp 'em! Crush 'em!" until they were hoarse. Three

fans, wearing the team jerseys of blue and white and with the team logo painted on their faces, jumped up, spilling their drinks on the teenagers seated below them. During timeouts, the fans chanted rhythmically, and throughout the game they stomped their feet in a steady beat against the wooden bleachers. The entire arena participated in "the wave" several times in an effort to pump up the teams. The speakers in the arena blasted rock music and encouraged the fans to chant, "Go Team Go!" using flashing, multicoloured signs. The atmosphere was electric. As people chanted and whooped, they turned to grin at each other and thrust their clenched fists into the air.

This vivid description meets the requirements of the checklist. Its details are sufficiently specific. These details use sense words in order to describe what the fans looked and sounded like, to give a *feel* for the place, and to support a dominant impression of rowdy, excited fans. The vivid, specific details make the point; they create an atmosphere and put the reader in the stadium.

EXERCISE **13**	**REVISING A PARAGRAPH BY FINDING IRRELEVANT SENTENCES**

Below are two descriptive paragraphs. In each, there are sentences that are irrelevant, meaning that they don't have anything to do with the opening topic sentence. Cross out the irrelevant sentences in the following paragraphs.

1. Leo looked and sounded as if he were trying to control his anger. I know what that's like because I too have been furious and had to suppress my feelings. Leo's face was nearly purple with rage and his eyes were blazing. He spoke very slowly and quietly, but his tone implied that he was holding himself back from an outburst. His jaw was tight, showing his stress. I could hear his shallow breathing as he tried to calm down. Breathing can be the key to changing your frame of mind; it's an important part of meditation.

2. The garage was crammed with junk and dirt. Empty cardboard boxes, collapsing into each other, lined one wall. Other boxes were filled with newspapers and smaller boxes. A workbench against one wall held rusty screwdrivers and an assortment of loose nails and hooks. Above the bench, a pegboard was filled with dangling hammers, clippers, and cords, some of them covered with rags and gardening gloves. My father keeps all his gardening tools in a shed in the yard. A large bag of dog food had spilled its contents across one end of the garage. To avoid this kind of mess, dog food can be stored in large plastic containers. The place was so full of debris that there was hardly room for the one car parked on the oil-stained floor.

EXERCISE **14**	**REVISING A PARAGRAPH FOR MORE SPECIFIC DETAILS**

In the following paragraphs, the details that are underlined are not specific. Change the underlined sentences to a more specific description. Write the changes in the lines below each paragraph.

1.   The Caribbean Festival ended with a delicious island dinner. To begin, banana bread and spicy conch fritters were served. The main course included snapper marinated in lime juice and broiled golden on the outside and tender on the inside. Crispy coconut shrimp, pigeon peas and rice, and mango relish completed this course. <u>The meal ended with a great dessert.</u>

   revisions: _____

   _____

2.   The classroom was a dreary place. The dull green and grey paint immediately created a sense of an old and faded schoolroom. The blackboards, covered in layers of ancient chalk dust ground into grey patterns by filthy erasers, spoke of neglect and apathy. Even the bulletin boards, which had no tacks, no notices, and no pictures, offered nothing to please the eye. <u>The student desks were awful.</u> The teacher's desk was really a chipped wooden table accompanied by a chipped metal folding chair.

   revisions: _____

   _____

Transitions

As you revise your descriptive paragraph, you may notice places that seem choppy or abrupt. That is, one sentence may end and another may start, but the two sentences don't seem to be connected. Reading your paragraph aloud, you might sense that it's not very smooth.

   You can smooth out the writing and make the content clearer by using *transitions*. Transitions are words or phrases that link one idea to another. They tell the reader what he or she has just read and what is coming next. Every kind of writing has its own transitions. Here are some transitions you may want to use in writing a description:

INFOBOX	**TRANSITIONS FOR A DESCRIPTIVE PARAGRAPH**

To show ideas brought together: and, also, in addition, as well as

To show a contrast: although, but, however, in contrast, on the contrary, on the other hand, unlike, yet

To show a similarity: all, both, each, like, similarly

To show a time sequence: as, after, always, before, first (second, third, and so forth), meanwhile, next, often, once, soon, then, when, while

> **To show a position in space:** above, ahead of, alongside, among, around, away, below, beside, between, beneath, beyond, by, close, down, far, here, in front of, inside, near, nearby, next to, on, on top of, outside, over, there, toward, under, up, underneath

There are many other transitions you can use, depending on how you need to link your ideas. Take a look at the following draft of the description paragraph about the writer's basement. Compare it with the outline on pages 98 and 99. You'll notice that more sense details have been added. Transitions have been added, too. Pay particular attention to the transitions in this draft.

A Draft of a Descriptive Paragraph (*transitions are underlined*)

Going to do laundry in my basement is like entering another world. <u>When</u> I go down the staircase, basket in hand, the old wooden steps creak every time I take a step. <u>Once</u> I reach the bottom of the stairs, it's dark, so I look for the light switch. Everything is coated in a fine layer of grey dust, and thick cobwebs are in every corner. Security gates on the windows, meant to prevent break-ins, make the basement feel like a dungeon. The discoloured drywall hasn't been painted in years, and is stained a rust colour where water has leaked from the floor above. <u>As</u> I walk toward the laundry room, I see the clothesline draped across one corner of the basement. A pair of jeans hangs from it, as stiff as a board. Pulling the long cotton string to turn on the naked light bulb suspended from the ceiling, I hear a click and a dull, sickly light fills the room. There are plastic sinks, and a twenty-year-old washer and dryer squat in the corner. Doing a load of laundry causes the washer to make a loud noise and to move, as if possessed, across the floor. I don't like doing laundry.

EXERCISE 15

RECOGNIZING TRANSITIONS

Underline the transitions in the following paragraph.

Waiting for my bus, I felt like a stranger on the scene. Under the roof of the small bus shelter, I was all alone. In front of me was a strip of dead grass littered with soft drink cans and cigarette butts. A six-lane highway was beyond the grass patch. Cars and trucks sped by me, focused on passing each other, making the green light, and getting somewhere fast. The drivers didn't have time to notice me. A few cars in the outside lane swerved toward me as they temporarily lost control. Far ahead of me, on the other side of the highway, tall buildings with blank glass fronts stared. Maybe they were staring at me, the only human being who wasn't enclosed in metal or glass.

COMBINING SENTENCES AND USING TRANSITIONS

The following description has some choppy sentences that could be combined to create a smoother paragraph. Combine each pair of underlined sentences by revising them in the space above each pair and using appropriate transitions.

The street fair was filled with tempting objects to buy and food to eat. First, there was a booth selling bright straw hats. <u>People strolled by. The vendor popped a hat on each person's head.</u> He said the hat looked stunning and tried to make a deal. <u>A stall offering shiny silver bracelets was in the same area. So was a stall selling discount CDs.</u> Food was a tremendous attraction. <u>Dozens of people crowded around an ice-cream truck. A group of people pushed to buy hot pretzels at a pushcart.</u> Food smells filled the air wherever people went. <u>Bakery smells were nearby. So was the odour of pizza.</u> They were irresistible. <u>The spicy aroma of Indian curry came. It was not so close.</u> When people reached the end of the fair, they turned around to walk through it one more time. <u>They had seen, tasted, and bought many things. They wanted to do it all again.</u>

PROOFREADING ## PROOFREADING AND POLISHING: DESCRIPTION

In preparing the final version of a descriptive paragraph, you add the finishing touches by changing words, revising or adding transitions, and sharpening details. In the final version of the description paragraph, you will notice these changes:

- The phrase "go down the staircase" has been changed to "creep down the staircase," which is more descriptive.
- Many more sense details have been added, referring to the feel and smell of the air, the sound the washer makes, and the feeling the basement gives the writer.
- In the draft paragraph, the ending of the paragraph is a little sudden. The paragraph isn't really about doing laundry; it's a description of the basement. The concluding sentence should pull all the details together and complete the feeling of the place.

> ### A Final Version of a Descriptive Paragraph (*changes from the draft version are underlined*)

Going to do laundry in my basement is like entering another world. When I <u>creep down</u> the staircase, basket in hand, the old wooden steps creak every time I take a step. Once I reach the bottom of the stairs, <u>I feel the walls closing around me and slap the wall frantically, searching</u> for the light switch. <u>Fluorescent bulbs cast a sickly light on the uneven concrete floors.</u> Everything is coated in a fine layer of grey dust, and thick cobwebs are in every corner. Security gates on the windows, meant to prevent break-ins, make the basement feel like a dungeon. The discoloured drywall hasn't been painted in years, and is stained a rust colour where water has leaked from the floor above. <u>The air is damp and cold, and carries a musty smell like wet dog.</u> As I walk toward the laundry room, I see the clothesline draped across one corner of the basement; <u>it sags sadly.</u> A pair of jeans hangs from it, as stiff as a board. <u>The hum of the furnace becomes a roar. Entering the laundry room is like entering a</u>

<u>grotto or damp cave.</u> Pulling the long cotton string to turn on the naked light bulb suspended from the ceiling, I hear a click and a dull, sickly light fills the room. <u>Dingy plastic sinks, once white and now grey, greet me</u>, and a twenty-year-old washer and dryer squat in the corner. Doing a load of laundry causes the washer to <u>screech deafeningly</u> and to move, as if possessed, across the floor. <u>I throw the laundry into the washer and escape, taking the stairs two at a time, wondering how such an alien world can exist in my own house.</u>

Before you prepare the final copy of your descriptive paragraph, check your latest draft for errors in spelling and punctuation, and for any errors made in typing or recopying.

| EXERCISE 17 | PROOFREADING TO PREPARE THE FINAL VERSION |

Below are two descriptive paragraphs with the kinds of errors that are easy to overlook when you write the final version of an assignment. Correct the errors, writing above the lines. There are twelve errors in the first paragraph and eight errors in the second paragraph.

1.   I have an old dilapidated sweatshirt that I'll allways cherish for the memmories it holds. It is a ratty-looking, grey shirt that belongs in the rag pile but I wore that shirt on many happy occassions. The greasy stain on one sleeve is a memory of how I got covered in oil when i was working on my first motor-cycle the tear at the neck reminds me of a crazy game of football. At the game where I tore the shirt, I also met my current girlfreind. The pale white blotches acrost the front of the shirt are from bleech. But to me they are a memory of the time my girlfriend and I was fooling around at the laundry room and put to much bleach in the washer. Every mark or stain on my shirt means something to me and I'll never through that old shirt away.

2.   When I finally got around to cleaning my refrigerator, I was horrified at the items I had been storing. First, I surveyed the boxes and jar's on the door shelves. Among them was a jar of gourmet salsa that some one had given me for Christmas four years ago. I also found a handful of brown rice in a bag and an empty box of vanila puding mix. I did not stop to wonder why I had kep a empty box of pudding mix, or enough brown rice to feed a small mouse. Instead, I moved on to the back of the refrigerator, where I found jars full of a mysterous green and orange fuzz. Behind the jars were shrivelled lemons and rock-hard pieces of cheese. Underneath it all was a slice of slimy pizza wrapped in ancient aluminum foil. I had no idea my refrigerator had become such health hazard.

Lines of Detail: A Walk-Through Assignment

Your assignment is to write a paragraph describing a popular place for socializing. Follow these steps:

Step 1: To begin, freewrite about a place where people socialize. For example, you could write about a place where people go to eat, or dance, or shop, or just hang out.

Step 2: Read your freewriting. Underline all the words, phrases, and sentences of description.

Step 3: List everything you underlined, grouping the ideas in some order. Maybe the details can be listed from inside to outside, or can be put into categories, such as walls, floor, and furniture, or scenery and people.

Step 4: After you've surveyed the list, write a sentence about the dominant impression given by the details.

Step 5: Using the dominant impression as your topic sentence, write an outline. Add specific details where you need them. Concentrate on details that appeal to the senses.

Step 6: Write a first draft of your paragraph. Be sure to check the order of your details. Combine short sentences and add transitions.

Step 7: Revise your first draft version, paying particular attention to order, specific details, and transitions.

Step 8: After a final check for punctuation, spelling, and word choice, prepare the final version of the paragraph.

Writing Your Own Descriptive Paragraph When you write on any of the following topics, work through the stages of the writing process in preparing your descriptive paragraph. Make sure that your paragraph is based on a dominant impression, and put the dominant impression into your topic sentence.

1. Write a paragraph that describes one of the following items:

   your school library during exam week
   your house on an important holiday
   what you ate for breakfast
   children riding the school bus
   a hospital waiting room
   people riding the subway or bus
   the best meal you've ever had
   the interior of your car
   a dentist's waiting room
   an exciting sports event
   your favourite teacher
   an irritating customer
   your first impression of a school
   a person who was a positive influence in your life

2. Describe a place that creates one of these impressions:

peace	tension	depression
excitement	cheerfulness	hurry
friendliness	danger	fun

3. Describe a person who conveys one of these impressions:

confidence	warmth	pride
hostility	fear	style
shyness	rebellion	intelligence
conformity	strength	beauty

4. Online dating services such as Lavalife.com and Match.com are experiencing a steady increase in subscribers. You (or a friend) would like to post a profile. Write a paragraph in which you describe yourself or your friend.
5. Select a photograph of a person or place. You can use a photograph from a magazine or newspaper, or one of your own photographs. Write a paragraph describing that photograph. Attach the photograph to the completed paragraph.
6. Interview a partner to gather details for a descriptive paragraph with the title, "My Perfect Room."

First, prepare a list of at least six questions to ask your partner. Write down the answers your partner gives and use these answers to form more questions. For example, if your partner says her dream room would be a game room, ask her what games she'd like to have in it. If your partner says his perfect room would be a workshop, ask him what kind of workshop.

When you've finished the interview, switch roles. Let your partner interview you. Feel free to add more questions or to follow up on previous ones.

Finally, give your partner his or her interview responses, then take your own responses and use them as the basis for gathering as many details as you can on your perfect room. Finally, build the prewriting of your paragraph. Then go on to the outline, draft, and final versions. Be prepared to read your completed paragraph to your partner.

WRITING FROM READING: DESCRIPTION

A Present for Popo
Elizabeth Wong

The child of Chinese immigrants, Elizabeth Wong was born in Los Angeles. She has a master's degree in fine arts and has worked as a writer for newspapers and television. She has also written several plays. In "A Present for Popo," Wong describes a beloved grandmother.

Before you read this essay, consider these questions:

Are you afraid of growing old?

Do you think most old people in North America are treated well?

Are they respected? Ignored?

Are you close to anyone over sixty-five?

Did you grow up in close contact with a grandparent?

Is there one person who holds your family together?

nimbly: quickly, gracefully

When my Popo opened a Christmas gift, she would shake it, smell it, listen to it. She would size it up. She would open it **nimbly**, with all enthusiasm and delight, and even though the mittens were ugly or the blouse too small or the card obviously homemade, she would coo over it as if it were the baby Jesus.

Despite that, buying a gift for my grandmother was always problematic. Being in her late 80s, Popo didn't seem to need any more sweaters or handbags. No books certainly, as she only knew six words of English. Cosmetics might be a good idea, for she was just a wee bit **vain**.

vain: excessively proud of one's appearance

But ultimately, nothing worked. "No place to put anything anyway," she used to tell me in Chinese. For in the last few years of her life, Popo had a bed in a room in a house in San Gabriel owned by one of her sons. All her belongings, her money, her very life was now **co-opted** and controlled by her sons and their wives. Popo's daughters had little power in this matter. This was a traditional Chinese family.

co-opted: taken over

For you see, Popo had begun to forget things. Ask her about something that happened 20 years ago, and she could recount the details in the heartbeat of a New York minute. But it was those **niggling** little everyday matters that became so troubling. She would forget to take her heart medicine. She would forget where she put her handbag. She would forget she talked to you just moments before. She would count the few dollars in her billfold, over and over again. She would ask me for the millionth time, "So when are you going to get married?" For her own good, the family decided she should give up her beloved one-room Chinatown flat. Popo herself recognized she might be a danger to herself, "I think your grandmother is going crazy," she would say.

niggling: unimportant

That little flat was a bothersome place, but Popo loved it. Her window had a view of several import-export shops below, not to mention the **grotesque** plastic hanging lanterns and that nasty loudspeaker serenading tourists with 18 hours of top-40 popular hits.

grotesque: incongruous; comically or repulsively distorted

My brother Will and I used to stand under her balcony on Mei Ling Way, shouting up, "Grandmother on the Third Floor! Grandmother on the Third Floor!" Simultaneously, the wrinkled faces of a half-dozen grannies would peek cautiously out their windows. Popo would come to the balcony and proudly claim us: "These are my grandchildren coming to take me to **dim sum**." Her neighbours would cluck and sigh, "You have such good grandchildren. Not like mine."

dim sum: an assortment of dumplings with savoury fillings

In that cramped room of Popo's, I could see past Christmas presents. A full-wall **collage** of family photos that my mother and I made together and presented one year with lots of fanfare. Popo had attached additional snapshots by way of paper clips and Scotch tape. And there, on the window sill, a little **terrarium** to which Popo had tied a small red ribbon. "For good luck," as she gleefully pointed out the sprouting buds. "See, it's having babies."

collage: collection of photos, pieces of paper, and so on, affixed to a backing

terrarium: a small container where plants and small creatures are kept alive under conditions imitating their natural environment

Also, there were the utility shelves on the wall, groaning from a wide assortment of junk, stuff, and whatnot. Popo was fond of salvaging discarded things. After my brother had installed the shelving, she did a little jig, then took a whisk broom and lightly swept away any naughty spirits that might be lurking on the walls. "Shoo, shoo, shoo, away with you, Mischievous Ones!" That apartment was her independence, and her pioneer spirit was everywhere in it.

Popo was my mother's mother, but she was also a second mother to me. Her death was a great blow. The last time I saw her was Christmas 1990, when she looked hale and hearty. I thought she would live forever. Last October, at 91, she had her final heart attack. The next time I saw her, it was at her funeral.

An open casket, and there she was, with a shiny new penny poised between her lips, a silenced warrior woman. Her sons and daughters placed colourful pieces of cloth in her casket. They burned incense and paper money. A small marching band led a New Orleans–like procession through the streets of Chinatown. Popo's picture, larger than life, [rode] in a flatbed truck to survey the world of her adopted country.

This little 4-foot, 9-inch woman had been the glue of our family. She wasn't perfect, she wasn't always even nice, but she learned from her mistakes, and, ultimately, she forgave herself for being human. It is a lesson of forgiveness that seems to have **eluded** her own sons and daughters.

And now she is gone. And with her—the **tenuous, cohesive** ties of blood and duty that bound us to family. My mother predicted that once the distribution of what was left of Popo's estate took place, no further words would be exchanged between Popo's children. She was right.

But this year, six of the 27 grandchildren and two of the 18 great-grandchildren came together for a holiday feast of honey-baked ham and mashed potatoes. Not a gigantic family reunion. But I think, for now, it's the one yuletide present my grandmother might have truly enjoyed.

Merry Christmas, Popo!

eluded: escaped

tenuous: slight, insubstantial

cohesive: holding together

UNDERSTANDING "A PRESENT FOR POPO"

1. Why was Popo's life co-opted and controlled by her sons and their wives?
2. Although it was noisy and cramped, why did Popo love her little flat (apartment)?
3. The author refers to presents that Popo had received over the years. List two gifts that she treasured.
4. What was the most important present, the one mentioned in the title "A Present for Popo"?

WRITING FROM READING "A PRESENT FOR POPO"

1. Elizabeth Wong uses many details about Popo's apartment to describe her grandmother. Write a paragraph in which you use many details about a person's environment (for example, her office, his apartment) to describe that person.
2. Wong's essay includes a description of a funeral in a Chinese-American family. Write a description of some custom or ritual in your family. You could write, for instance, about a wedding, a funeral, the celebration of a holiday, or a religious occasion.
3. "A Present for Popo" is a tribute to a beloved person. Write a description of someone who holds a special place in your life.
4. The grandmother in Wong's essay is an immigrant, a Chinese woman who moved to America. Describe an immigrant you know. Focus on how the person is a combination of two countries or cultures.

5. Describe an older person you know well. In your description, you can use details of appearance and behaviour. Focus on how these details reveal personality.

6. Describe yourself at age ninety. Use your imagination to give details of appearance, behaviour, and family relationships.

CHAPTER 5
Narration

LEARNING OBJECTIVES

After you have read this chapter and completed its exercises and assignments, you should be able to

- write a narrative with a point
- make your narrative interesting and engaging
- use dialogue effectively in your narrative
- add effective detail to your narrative
- draft and edit your narrative

"If you would understand your own age, read the works of fiction produced in it. People in disguise speak freely."

~ SIR ARTHUR HELPS

▼
SIR ARTHUR HELPS WAS A NINETEENTH-CENTURY ENGLISHMAN KNOWN FOR HIS PARTICIPATION IN A GROUP CALLED THE APOSTLES, WHOSE PURPOSE WAS TO DISCUSS LITERATURE AND SOCIETY.

WHAT IS NARRATION?

Narration means telling a story. Everybody tells stories; some people are better storytellers than others. When you write a *narrative paragraph*, you can tell a story about something that happened to you or to someone else, or about something that you saw or read.

Because it relies on specific details, a narrative is like a description. But it's also different from a description, because it covers events in a time sequence. While a description can be about a person, a place, or an object, a narrative is always about happenings: events, actions, incidents.

Interesting narratives do more than tell what happened. They help the reader become involved in the story by providing vivid detail. You can get that detail from your memory or observation or reading. Using good details, you don't just *tell* the story, you *show* it.

Giving the Narrative a Point

We all know people who tell long stories that seem to lead nowhere. These people talk on and on; they recite an endless list of activities and soon become boring. Their narratives have no point.

The difficult part of writing a narrative is making sure that it has a *point*. That point will be included in the topic sentence. The point of a narrative is the *meaning* of the incident or incidents you're writing about. To get to the point of your narrative, ask yourself questions like these:

What did I learn?
What's the meaning of this story?
What's my attitude toward what happened?
Did it change me?
What emotion did it make me feel?
Was the experience a good example of something (like unfairness, or kindness, or generosity)?

The answers to such questions can lead you to the topic sentence.

An effective topic sentence for a narrative is

not this: I'm going to tell you about the time I flunked my driving test. (This is an announcement; it does not make a point.)
but this: When I failed my driving test, I learned not to be overconfident.
not this: Yesterday my car stalled in rush-hour traffic. (This identifies the incident but does not make a point. It's also too narrow to be a good topic sentence.)
but this: When my car stalled in rush-hour traffic, I was annoyed and embarrassed.

The topic sentence, stating the point of your narrative paragraph, can be placed in the beginning or middle or end of the paragraph. You may want to start your story with the point, so that the reader knows exactly where your story is headed, or you may want to conclude your story by leaving the point until last. Sometimes the point can even fit smoothly into the middle of your paragraph.

Consider the following narrative paragraphs. The topic sentences are in various places.

Topic Sentence at the Beginning

When I was five, I learned how serious it is to tell a lie. One afternoon, my seven-year-old friend Tina asked me if I wanted to walk down the block to play ball in an empty lot. When I asked my mother, she said I couldn't go because it was too close to dinnertime. I don't know why I lied, but when Tina asked me if my mother had said yes, I nodded my head. I wanted to go play, and I did. Yet as I played in the dusty lot, a dull buzz of guilt or fear distracted me. As soon as I got home, my mother confronted me. She asked me whether I'd gone to the sandlot and whether I'd lied to Tina about getting permission. This time, I told the truth. Something about my mother's tone of voice made me feel very dirty and ashamed. I had let her down.

Topic Sentence in the Middle

When I was little, I was afraid of diving into water. I thought I would go down and never come back up. Then one day, my father took me to a pool where we swam and fooled around, but he never forced me to try a dive. After about an hour of playing, I walked around and around the edge of the pool, trying to get the courage to dive in. Finally, I did it. When I made that first dive, I felt blissful because I was

<u>doing something I'd been afraid to do.</u> As I came to the surface, I wiped the water from my eyes and looked around. The sun seemed more dazzling, and the water sparkled. Best of all, I saw my father looking at me with a smile. "You did it," he said. "Good for you! I'm proud of you."

Topic Sentence at the End

It seemed as if I'd been in love with Reeza for years. Unfortunately, Reeza was always in love with someone else. Finally, she broke up with her boyfriend, Nelson. I saw my chance. I asked Reeza out. After dinner, we talked and talked. Reeza told me all about her hopes and dreams. She told me about her family and her job, and I felt very close to her. We talked late into the night. When she left, Reeza kissed me. "Thanks for listening," she said. "You're like a brother to me." <u>Reeza meant to be kind, but she shattered my hopes and dreams.</u>

EXERCISE 1

FINDING THE TOPIC SENTENCE IN A NARRATIVE PARAGRAPH

Underline the topic sentence in each of the following narrative paragraphs.

Paragraph 1

I was eager to get a place of my own. I figured that having my own apartment meant I was free at last because there would be no rules, no curfew, no living by someone else's schedule. My first day in the apartment started well. I arranged the furniture, put up all my pictures, and phoned each of my friends to say hi. Then I called out for pizza. When it came, I tried to start a conversation with the delivery man, but he was in a hurry. I ate my pizza alone while I watched the late movie. It was too late to call any of my friends to come over, and I definitely wasn't going to call my mother and let her know I wanted some company. In truth, my first day in my apartment showed me the lonely side of living on my own.

Paragraph 2

Last Saturday, I took a bus downtown to have lunch with a friend. After lunch, my friend and I split the bill, and I reached for my wallet to pay my share. I was horrified to discover I had lost my wallet. My friend drove me home, and the first thing I saw was the blinking message light on my answering machine. The message said someone had found my wallet and wanted to return it. I couldn't believe anyone in the city would be so kind and honest, but losing something changed my mind. When I met the man in a nearby coffee shop, he gave me the wallet with all my money and credit cards still in it. He said he had found it on a seat on the bus and had been calling my apartment for hours. He was such a good person he wouldn't even take a small reward. He even paid the cheque at the coffee shop because he said I'd had a bad day and deserved a break!

Paragraph 3

   Yesterday, one person showed me what it means to be a good parent. I was walking in the mall, and just ahead of me a toddler was holding his father's hand and struggling to keep up. Pretty soon, the child got tired and started to cry. Within minutes, his crying had become a full-fledged tantrum. The little boy squatted on the ground, refusing to go any farther, his face purple. Some parents would have shouted at the child, threatened him, or scooped him up and carried him away. This father, however, just sat down on the ground by his son and talked to him, very calmly and quietly. I couldn't hear his words, but I got the feeling he was sympathizing with the tired little boy. Pretty soon, the child's screams became little sniffles, and father and son walked quietly away.

EXERCISE 2

WRITING THE MISSING TOPIC SENTENCES IN NARRATIVE PARAGRAPHS

Below are three paragraphs. If the paragraph already has a topic sentence, write it in the lines provided. If it doesn't have a topic sentence, create one. (Two of the paragraphs have no topic sentence.)

Paragraph 1

   When I got up, I realized I must have turned off my alarm clock and gone back to sleep because I was already an hour behind schedule. I raced into the shower, only to find I had used up the last of the shampoo the day before. I barely had time to make a cup of coffee to take with me in the car. I grabbed the cup of coffee, rushed to the car, and turned the ignition. The car wouldn't start. Two hours later, the emergency service finally came to jump-start the car. I arrived at work three hours late, and the supervisor was not happy with me.

_____

_____

Paragraph 2

   Since I gave my first speech in my public speaking class, I'm not as shy as I used to be. On the day I was supposed to give my speech, I seriously considered cutting class, taking an F on the speech, or even dropping the course. All I could think of was what could go wrong. I could freeze up and go blank, or I could say something really stupid. In spite of my terror, I managed to walk up to the front of the class. When I started talking, I could hear my voice shaking. I wondered if everyone in the room could see the cold sweat on my forehead. By the middle of the speech, I was concentrating so intensely on *what* to say that I forgot about my nerves. When I finished, I couldn't believe people were clapping! I never believed I could stand up and speak to the entire class. Once I did that, it seemed so easy to talk in a class discussion. Best of all, the idea of making another speech doesn't seem as frightening anymore.

_____

_____

Paragraph 3

Last weekend, I was driving home alone, at about 10:00 p.m., when a carload of young men pulled up beside me. They began shouting and making strange motions with their hands. At first, I ignored them, hoping they'd go away. But then I got scared because they wouldn't pass me. They kept driving right alongside my car. I rolled up my windows and locked the doors. I couldn't hear their shouts, but I was still afraid. I was more afraid when I stopped at a red light and they again pulled up next to me. Suddenly, one of the men screamed at me, at the top of his lungs, "Hey! You have a broken tail light!"

_____

_____

_____

HINTS FOR WRITING A NARRATIVE PARAGRAPH

Everyone tells stories, but some people tell stories better than others. When you write a story, be sure to

- be clear
- be interesting
- stay in order
- pick a topic that isn't too big

1. **Be clear.** Put in all the information the reader will need to follow your story. You may need to explain the time frame, the place, or the relationships of the people in your story to make it clear. Sometimes, you need to explain how much time has elapsed between one action and another. This paragraph is not clear:

> I've never felt so stupid as I did on my first day of work. I was stocking the shelves when Mr. Cimino came up to me and said, "You're doing it wrong." Then he showed me how to do it. An hour later, he told me to call the produce supplier and check on the order for grapefruit. Well, I didn't know how to tell Mr. Cimino that I didn't know what phone to use or how to get an outside line. I also didn't know how to get the phone number of the produce supplier, or what the order for the grapefruit was supposed to be and when it was supposed to arrive. I felt really stupid asking these questions.

What's wrong with the paragraph? It lacks all kinds of information. Who is Mr. Cimino? Is he the boss? Is he a produce supervisor? And, more importantly, what kind of place is the writer's workplace? The reader knows the place has something to do with food, but is it a supermarket, or a fruit market, or a warehouse?

2. **Be interesting.** A boring narrative can make the greatest adventure sound dull. Here is a dull narrative:

> I had a wonderful time on prom night. First, we went out to dinner. The meal was excellent. Then we went to the dance and saw all our friends. Everyone was dressed up great. We stayed until late. Then we went out to breakfast. After breakfast we watched the sun come up.

Good specific detail is the difference between an interesting story and a dull one.

3. **Stay in order.** Put the details in a clear order, so that the reader can follow your story. Usually, time order is the order you follow in narration. This narrative has a confusing order:

> My impatience cost me twenty dollars last week. There was a pair of shoes I really wanted. I had wanted them for weeks. So, when payday came around, I went to the mall and checked the price on the shoes. I had been checking the price for weeks before. The shoes were expensive, but I really wanted them. On payday, my friend, who works at the shoe store, told me the shoes were about to go on sale. But I was impatient. I bought them at full price, and three days later, the shoes were marked down twenty dollars.

There's something wrong with the order of events here. Tell the story in the order it happened: first, I saw the shoes and wanted them; second, the shoes were expensive; third, I checked the price for several weeks; fourth, I got paid; fifth, I checked the price again; sixth, my friend told me the shoes were about to go on sale; seventh, I paid full price right away; eighth, the shoes went on sale. A clear time sequence helps the reader follow your narrative.

4. **Pick a topic that isn't too big.** If you try to write about too many events in one paragraph, you run the risk of being superficial. You can't describe anything well if you cover too much. This paragraph covers too much:

> Starting Grade 10 at a new high school was a difficult experience. Because my family had just moved to town, I didn't know anybody at school. On the first day of school, I sat by myself at lunch. Finally, two students at another table started a conversation with me. I thought they were just feeling sorry for me. At the end of the first week, it seemed like the whole school was talking about exciting plans for the weekend. I spent Friday and Saturday night at home, doing all kinds of things to keep my mind off my loneliness. On Monday, people casually asked, "Have a good weekend?" I lied and said, "Of course."

This paragraph would be better if it discussed one shorter time period in greater depth and detail. It could cover the first day at school, or the first lunch at school, or the first Saturday night at home alone, when the writer was doing "all kinds of things" to keep from feeling lonely.

communication at work

In a job interview, you may expect to be asked a question that begins with the phrase "Tell me about a time when you..." These kinds of questions are called *behavioural* questions, and give the interviewer some insight into how you would behave in certain situations. Your response will be told in the form of a *narrative*, with a main point, in chronological order, and with as much detail as you can possibly include. Two common behavioural questions are "Tell me about a time when you went 'above and beyond' at work" and "Tell me about a time when you had to deal with a difficult co-worker or client." Your instructor may ask you to write a paragraph in which you respond to one of these questions.

Using a Speaker's Exact Words in Narrative

Some of the examples of narrative you've already seen have included the exact words someone said. You may want to include part of a conversation in your narrative. To do so, you need to know how to punctuate speech.

A person's exact words need quotation marks around them. If you change the words, you do not use quotation marks.

exact words:	"You're being silly," he told me.
not exact words:	He told me that I was being silly.
exact words:	My sister said, "I'd love to go to the party."
not exact words:	My sister said that she'd love to go to the party.

There are a few other points to remember about punctuating a person's exact words. Once you've started quoting a person's exact words, periods and commas generally go inside the quotation marks. Here are two examples:

Richard said, "Nothing can be done."
"Be careful," my mother warned us.

When you introduce a person's exact words with phrases like "She said," or "The instructor told us," put a comma before the quotation marks. Here are two examples:

She said, "You'd better watch out."
The instructor told us, "This will be a challenging class."

If you're using a person's exact words and have other questions about punctuation, check the section on punctuation in this book.

WRITING THE NARRATIVE PARAGRAPH IN STEPS

PREWRITING   GATHERING IDEAS: NARRATION

Finding something to write about can be the hardest part of composing a narrative paragraph because you may find it difficult to think of anything interesting or significant that you've experienced. Answering the following questions will help you gather topics for your paragraph.

| EXERCISE **3** | **QUESTIONNAIRE FOR GATHERING NARRATIVE TOPICS** |

Answer the following questions as best you can. Then read your answers to a group. The members of the group should then ask you follow-up questions. Write your answers on the lines provided; the answers will add detail to your list.

Finally, ask each member of your group to circle one topic or detail on your questionnaire that could be developed into a narrative paragraph. Discuss the suggestions. Repeat this process for each member of the group.

Narrative Questionnaire

1. Have you ever had a close call? When? _____ Write four details you remember about it:

   a. _____

   b. _____

   c. _____

   d. _____

   Additional details to add after working with the group:

   _____

   _____

2. Have you ever tried out for a team? Write four details about what happened before, during, and after:

   a. _____

   b. _____

   c. _____

   d. _____

   Additional details to add after working with the group:

   _____

   _____

3. Have you ever had a day when everything went wrong? Write four details about that day:

   a. _____

   b. _____

   c. _____

   d. _____

   Additional details to add after working with the group:

   _____

   _____

4. Have you ever applied for a job? Write four details about what happened when you applied for a job:

   a. _____

   b. _____

c. _____

d. _____

Additional details to add after working with the group:

_____

_____

Freewriting for a Narrative Topic

One good way to discover something to write about is to freewrite. For example, if your instructor asks you to write a narrative paragraph about something that changed you, you might begin by freewriting.

> ### Freewriting for a Narrative Paragraph
>
> ### Topic: Something That Changed Me
>
> Something that changed me. I don't know. What changed me? Lots of things happened to me, but I can't find one that changed me. Graduating from high school? Everybody will write about that, how boring, and anyway, what was the big deal? I haven't gotten married. No big change there. Divorce. My parents' divorce really changed the whole family. A big shock to me. I couldn't believe it was happening. I was really scared. Who would I live with? They were real calm when they told me. I've never been so scared. I was too young to understand. Kept thinking they'd just get back together. They didn't. Then I got a stepmother. The year of the divorce a hard time for me. Kids suffer in divorce.

Narrowing and Selecting a Suitable Narrative Topic

After you freewrite, you can assess your writing, looking for words, phrases, or sentences that you could expand into a paragraph. The sample writing has several ideas for a narrative:

> high school graduation
>
> learning about my parents' divorce
>
> adjusting to a stepmother
>
> the year of my parents' divorce

Looking for a topic that is not too big, you could use

> high school graduation
>
> learning about my parents' divorce

Since the freewriting has already labelled graduation as a boring topic, the divorce seems to be a more attractive subject. In the freewriting, you already have some details related to the divorce; add to these by **brainstorming**. Follow-up questions and answers might include the following:

How old were you when your parents got divorced?

I was seven years old when my mom and dad divorced.

Are you an only child?

My sister was ten.

Where did your parents tell you? Did they tell you at the same time?

They told us at breakfast, in the kitchen. Both my folks were there. I was eating toast. I remember I couldn't eat it when they both started talking. I remember a piece of toast with one bite out of it.

What reasons did they give?

They said they loved us, but they couldn't get along. They said they would always love us kids.

If you didn't understand, what did you *think* was happening?

At first I just thought they were having another fight.

Did you cry? Did they cry?

I didn't cry. My sister cried. Then I knew it was serious. I kept thinking I would have to choose which parent to live with. Then I knew I'd really hurt the one I didn't choose. I felt so much guilt about hurting one of them.

How did you feel overall?

I felt ripped apart.

Questions can help you form the *point of your narrative.* After brainstorming, you can go back and survey all the details. Do they lead you to a point? Try asking yourself the questions listed at the beginning of this chapter: What did I learn? What's the meaning of this story? What's my attitude toward what happened? Did it change me? What emotion did it make me feel? Was the experience a good example of something (e.g., unfairness, kindness, generosity)?

For the topic of the divorce, the details refer to a number of emotions: confusion, pain, shock, disbelief, fear, guilt. The *point* of the paragraph can't list all these emotions, but it could say,

When my parents announced they were divorcing, I felt confused by all my emotions.

Now that you have a point and a good-sized list of details, you can move to the outline stage of writing a narrative paragraph.

EXERCISE 4

DISTINGUISHING GOOD TOPIC SENTENCES FROM BAD ONES IN NARRATION

Some of the sentences listed below would make good topic sentences for a narrative paragraph. Others would not; they're too big to develop in a single paragraph, or they're so narrow they can't be developed, or they make no point about an incident or incidents. Put an X beside the sentences that wouldn't make good topic sentences.

1. _____ I bought a flat-screen television yesterday.
2. _____ I learned a lot during my co-op work placement.

3. _____ The motorist who stopped to help me on the highway taught me a valuable lesson about trust.

4. _____ My two-year battle for child custody was a nightmare.

5. _____ This is the story of the birth of my son.

6. _____ I saw true compassion when I visited the home for babies with AIDS.

7. _____ Our team's victory over the Rangers demonstrated the power of endurance.

8. _____ I've seen drugs ruin the lives of four of my friends in four years.

9. _____ The robbery took place at the convenience store near my house.

10. _____ I never knew what it was like to be afraid until our house was burglarized.

EXERCISE 5 — DEVELOPING A TOPIC SENTENCE FROM A LIST OF DETAILS

Below are two lists of details. Each has an incomplete topic sentence. Read the details carefully, then complete each topic sentence.

1. **topic sentence:** When he _____, my brother made me feel _____.

   details: My brother always borrows my clothes.
   Sometimes I wish he wouldn't.
   Last week, he took my new leather jacket.
   I went to my closet, and the jacket wasn't there.
   I wanted to wear it that night.
   Later, he came home wearing it.
   I could have punched him.
   He gave it back.
   He swore he didn't know it had a big slash in the back.
   He acted innocent.
   I told him he'd have to pay to fix the jacket.
   He still hasn't paid me.

2. **topic sentence:** An incident at a traffic light showed me _____ _____.

   details: I was stopped at a traffic light one afternoon.
   Cars were stopped on all sides of me.
   Suddenly, a driver from the car beside me leaped out of his car.
   He ran to the car in front of me.
   He started screaming at the driver of the car.
   The driver inside that car wouldn't open his window.
   The man who was screaming began to pound on the window.
   Then he started kicking the car, hard.
   I watched in terror.
   I couldn't drive out of this situation.
   I was stuck and afraid of being the next victim.
   The crazy, shouting driver stopped.
   He got back in his car.
   When the light changed, he raced into the intersection.
   I felt safer, but I was still shaken.

PLANNING   DEVISING A PLAN: NARRATION

The topic of how an experience changed you has led you to a point and a list of details. You can now write a rough outline, with the *point* as the *topic sentence*. Once you have the rough outline, check it for these qualities:

Relevance: Do all the details connect to the topic sentence?
Order: Are the details in a clear order?
Development: Does the outline need more details? Are the details specific enough?

Your revised outline might look like the following:

> An Outline for a Narrative Paragraph
>
> **topic sentence:**   When my parents announced that they were divorcing, I felt confused by all my emotions.
>
> **details:**
>   background of the narrative
>   I was seven when my mom and dad divorced.
>   My sister was ten.
>   Both my folks were there.
>   They told us at breakfast, in the kitchen.
>   I was eating toast.
>   I remember I couldn't eat anything when they started talking.
>   I remember a piece of toast with one bite out of it.
>   story of the divorce announcement
>   My parents were very calm when they told us.
>   They said they loved us but couldn't get along.
>   They said they would always love us kids.
>   my reactions at each stage
>   It was a big shock to me.
>   I couldn't believe it was happening.
>   At first I just thought they were having another fight.
>   I was too young to understand.
>   I didn't cry.
>   My sister cried.
>   Then I knew it was serious.
>   I kept thinking I would have to choose which parent to live with.
>   I knew I'd really hurt the one I didn't choose.
>   I felt so much guilt about hurting one of them.
>   I was ripped apart.

Once you have a revised outline, you're ready to move on to the drafting and revising stage of the narrative paragraph.

EXERCISE 6

FINDING DETAILS THAT ARE OUT OF ORDER IN A NARRATIVE OUTLINE

The following outlines have details that are out of order. Put them in the correct order by numbering the first event with a 1, and so on.

1. **topic sentence:** Renewing my driver's licence was a frustrating experience.

   details: _____ I got in the shortest line.

   _____ The office was packed with people.

   _____ When I got through the crowd, I went straight to the information desk.

   _____ The clerk at the information desk just gave me a form and said, "Get in line."

   _____ After an hour, I got to the head of the line.

   _____ I gave my form to the man behind the counter.

   _____ I waited in line for an hour.

   _____ The man behind the counter said, "You're in the wrong line."

2. **topic sentence:** Yesterday, I saw something that showed me the good side of people.

   details: _____ My traffic lane was at a standstill, so I had time to look around.

   _____ I was driving down the highway.

   _____ As I waited for the traffic to move, I saw a ragged man by the side of the road, holding a sign.

   _____ The sign said, "Will Work for Food."

   _____ I saw a car pull off the road, right next to the man.

   _____ The ragged man shrank back, as if he were afraid the car would hit him.

   _____ The driver motioned to the homeless man through the open window.

   _____ The driver of the car rolled down his window on the passenger side.

   _____ The homeless man crept over.

   _____ The driver handed him a big bag of food from Burger King.

EXERCISE 7

RECOGNIZING IRRELEVANT DETAILS IN A NARRATIVE OUTLINE

Below are two outlines. One of them has details that aren't relevant to the topic sentence. Cross out the details that don't fit.

1. **topic sentence:** I saw another side of my sister when her husband was in a car accident.

   details: My sister Julia is usually very helpless.

   She lets her husband Leo make all the decisions.

   She doesn't like to go anywhere without him.

Then one day she got a call from the hospital.
Leo had been in a car accident.
He was in critical condition.
Julia suddenly became very strong.
She calmly told us she was going to the hospital
to wait.
She went right up to the desk at the emergency room and
asked to see Leo.
When the nurses tried to make her wait, she demanded to
see him.
She stayed by Leo's side for twenty-four hours.
The only time she left was to talk to his doctors.
She was very firm and businesslike with the doctors.
She questioned them about the right treatment for Leo.
She got the name of a famous surgeon.
She called the surgeon and got him to come to the
hospital.
Today, Leo says she saved his life.

2. **topic sentence:** The most embarrassing thing I've ever experienced
happened to me in the supermarket checkout line.

   details: I always shop with a list of what I need to buy.
The cashier was running the items through the scanner.
Our store uses scanners now instead of cash registers.
When he was finished, he said, "That'll be $23.50."
I reached into my wallet for the money.
All I found was a ten-dollar bill.
I searched frantically through all the folds of my wallet.
There was nothing but the ten-dollar bill.
I was *sure* I'd put a twenty in my wallet when I left
for the store.
Then I remembered—I'd spent the twenty at the gas
station.
I whispered to the cashier, "Oops! I didn't bring
enough money."
He just looked at me.
The groceries were already bagged.
I had to take them out of the bags and get rid of items that
added up to $13.50.
Meanwhile, the people in line behind me wanted to kill me.
At that moment, I wished they had.

DRAFTING AND REVISING: NARRATION

DRAFTING AND REVISING

Once you have a revised outline for your narration paragraph, you can begin
working on a rough draft of the paragraph. As you write your first draft, you can
combine some of the short sentences of the outline. Then, after you've completed
your draft, you can check it for places you'd like to improve. The following list
may help you check your draft.

CHECKLIST	FOR REVISING THE DRAFT OF A NARRATIVE PARAGRAPH

- ✓ Is my narrative vivid?
- ✓ Are the details clear and specific?
- ✓ Does the topic sentence fit all the details?
- ✓ Are the details written in a clear order?
- ✓ Do the transitions make the narrative easy to follow?
- ✓ Have I made my point?

Revising for Sharper Details

A good idea for a narrative can be made better if you revise for sharper detail. In the following first-draft paragraph, the underlined words and phrases could be revised to create better details. See how the second draft contains more vivid details.

First Draft: Details Are Dull

A woman at the movies showed me just how rude and selfish people can be. It all started when I was in line with a lot of other people. We'd been waiting a long time to buy our tickets. We were outside, and it wasn't pleasant. We were impatient because time was running out and the movie was about to start. Some people were making remarks and others were pushing. Then a woman cut to the front of the line. The cashier at the ticket window told the woman there was a line and she would have to go to the end of it. The woman said she didn't want to wait because her son didn't want to miss the beginning of the movie.

Second Draft: Better Details

A woman at the movies showed me just how rude and selfish people can be. It all started when I was in line with forty or fifty other people. We'd been waiting to buy our tickets for twenty minutes. We were outside, where the temperature was about 30 degrees, and it looked like rain. We were all getting impatient because time was running out and the movie was about to start. I heard two people mutter about how ridiculous the wait was, and someone else kept saying, "Let's go!" The man directly behind me kept pushing me, and each new person at the end of the line pushed the whole line forward, against the ticket window. Then a woman with a loud voice and a large purse thrust her purse and her body in front of the ticket window. The cashier politely told the woman there was a line and she had to go to the end of it. But the woman answered indignantly. "Oh no," she said. "I'm with my son Mickey. And Mickey really wants to see *Guardians of the Galaxy*. And he hates to miss the first part of any movie. So I can't wait. I've got to have those tickets now."

Checking the Topic Sentence

Sometimes, you think you have a good idea and a good topic sentence and details, but when you write the draft of the paragraph, you realize that the topic sentence doesn't quite fit all the details. When that happens, you can either revise the details or rewrite the topic sentence.

In the following paragraph, the topic sentence (underlined) doesn't quite fit all the details, so it needs to be rewritten.

> I didn't know what to do when a crime occurred in front of my house. At 9:00 p.m., I was sitting in my living room, watching television, when I heard what sounded like a crash outside. At first, I thought it was a garbage can that had fallen over. Then I heard another crash and a shout. I ran to the window and looked out into the dark. I couldn't see anything because the street light in front of my house was broken. But I heard at least two voices, and they sounded angry and threatening. Then I heard another voice, and it sounded like someone moaning. I was afraid. I ran to the telephone. I was going to call 911, but then I froze in fear. What if the police came and people got arrested? Would the suspects find out I was the one who had called the police? Would they come after me? Would I be a witness at a trial? I didn't want to get involved. So I just stood behind the curtain, peeking out and listening. Pretty soon, the shouting stopped, but I still heard sounds like hitting. I couldn't stand it anymore. I called the police. When they came, they found a young teenager, badly beaten, in the street. They said my call may have saved his life.

The paragraph above has good details, but the story has more of a point than "I didn't know what to do." The person telling the story did, finally, do something. A better topic sentence would cover the whole story. Here is the topic sentence rewritten:

> I finally found the courage to do the right thing when a crime occurred in front of my house.

EXERCISE **8**	**COMBINING SENTENCES IN A DRAFT OF A NARRATIVE**

The following paragraph contains some short, choppy sentences, which are underlined. Wherever you see two or more underlined sentences next to each other, combine them into one clear, smooth sentence. Write your revised version of the paragraph in the spaces above the lines.

Getting lost in the city gave me my first taste of panic. When I was fourteen, I convinced my mother I was old enough to travel to my aunt's apartment in the city. My mother gave me clear directions. She wrote the address on a slip of paper. She also drew a map of the streets I had to cross once I got off the bus. I'd been to my aunt's place many times with my family. I was sure I would have no problems. When I got off the bus, I began walking confidently toward my aunt's street. However, after I'd walked a few blocks, nothing looked familiar. I convinced myself that I had to keep walking until I found a store or restaurant I knew. I walked farther. <u>Everything seemed strange.</u> The streets began to look unfriendly, even dangerous. <u>I felt the people were staring at me. They were staring with hostility.</u> Desperate, I approached a stranger. I asked him for directions. <u>He looked at me for a moment. He laughed.</u> He told me that I'd gotten off at the wrong bus stop. My aunt's street was fifteen blocks away. <u>I felt relieved. I felt foolish. I felt both emotions about my mistakes and my panic.</u>

EXERCISE 9 — ADDING BETTER DETAILS TO THE DRAFT OF A NARRATIVE

The following paragraph has some details that could be more vivid. Rewrite the paragraph in the lines below, replacing the underlined details with more vivid words, phrases, or sentences.

Roberto demonstrated what a great athlete he is when he lost the wrestling match. The match had been very close, but someone had to lose, and that someone turned out to be Roberto. After the match, the winner, Tom, was <u>getting all the attention.</u> He was acting very <u>full of himself.</u> Roberto was just <u>keeping to himself.</u> Roberto <u>looked hurt.</u> His eyes <u>were sad.</u> Nevertheless, he went to Tom and shook hands. Tom looked <u>mean</u> and <u>didn't say much.</u> Roberto, on the other hand, <u>said the right thing.</u> Then Roberto walked away, his head held high.

rewrite:

_____

_____

_____

_____

_____

_____

_____

_____

EXERCISE 10 — WRITING A BETTER TOPIC SENTENCE FOR A NARRATIVE

The following paragraphs could use better topic sentences. (In each paragraph, the current topic sentence is underlined.) Read each paragraph carefully, then write a new topic sentence for it in the lines provided.

1. <u>My visit to my old school was interesting.</u> I hadn't been back to Miller Road Public School since Grade 5, so I expected it to be changed. I just

didn't expect it to be so drastically changed. When I entered the schoolyard, I saw that the playground that had once been full of trees and bright green grass was now a muddy empty lot. All the trees were gone. The school, once a new golden-brick building, was sooty and decrepit. Several of the windows were broken. I walked into the entrance hall and saw graffiti all over the walls. The school was silent. Wandering the halls, I peeped into the classrooms. I saw rickety desks and blackboards so faded you could hardly see the words chalked on them. Then I found Room 110, my old Grade 1 classroom. I went in and sat down at one of the desks, and the room that had once seemed so big and so exciting suddenly seemed small and sad.

new topic sentence: _____

_____

2. <u>I had dinner with my family last week.</u> My two younger brothers, Simon and David, started it by fighting over who was going to sit in the seat next to my father. When we all sat down to eat, my sister provoked my mother by complaining, "Chicken again? All we eat is chicken." Of course, my mother jumped right in and said that if my sister wanted to take the responsibility for planning menus and cooking meals, she could go right ahead. Meanwhile, my father was telling David not to kick Simon under the table, and Simon was spitting mashed potatoes at David. I got irritated and said I wished that for once, just once, we could eat dinner like a normal family. So then my father and I had an argument about what I meant by a normal family. By that time, Simon had spilled his milk on the floor and my mother had caught my sister feeding chicken to the dog. We all left the dinner table in a bad mood.

new topic sentence: _____

_____

Using Transitions Effectively in Narration

When you tell a story, you have to be sure that your reader can follow you as you move through its steps. One way to make your story easier to follow is to use *transitions*, words that connect one event to another. Most of the transitions in narration have to do with time. Here's a list of transitions that writers often use in writing narration.

INFOBOX	TRANSITIONS FOR A NARRATIVE PARAGRAPH

after, again, always, at first, at last, at once, at the same time, before, during, finally, first (second, etc.), frequently, immediately, in the meantime, later, later on, meanwhile, next, now, once, soon, soon after, still, suddenly, then, until, when, while

The Draft

Below is a revised draft of the paragraph on divorce. It has been revised several ways, using the checklist. Some ideas from the outline have been combined. The details have been put in order and transitions (underlined) have been added. Exact words of dialogue have been used to add vivid details.

A Draft of a Narrative Paragraph (*transitions are underlined*)

When my parents announced that they were divorcing, I felt confused by all my emotions. At the time of their announcement, I was seven and my sister was ten. Both my folks were there to tell us. They told us at breakfast, in the kitchen. I was eating toast, but I remember I couldn't eat anything when they started talking. I remember a piece of toast with one bite taken out of it. My mom and dad were very calm when they told us. "We both love you very much," my father said, "but your mother and I aren't getting along." They said they would always love us. The announcement was such a shock to me that I couldn't believe it was happening. At first, I just thought they were having another fight. Because I was too young to understand, I didn't cry. Suddenly, my sister started to cry, and then I knew it was serious. I kept thinking I would have to choose which parent to live with. I knew I'd really hurt the one I didn't choose, so I felt so much guilt about hurting one of them. I felt torn apart.

EXERCISE 11 — RECOGNIZING TRANSITIONS IN A NARRATIVE PARAGRAPH

Underline the transitions in the following paragraph.

The salesman who called last night was a master of manipulation. He first asked for me by name. After confirming I was Mr. Johnson, he told me he was checking on my newspaper delivery. Then he asked if I'd been getting my paper regularly and on time. When I said yes, he quickly added that I could get a better deal by extending my subscription, right away, at a discounted rate for long-term customers. By that time I was getting tired of what I now knew was a sales call. Just before I tried to end the conversation, the salesman offered me a chance to win a trip to the Bahamas. Suddenly he had my interest again. While I listened to him explain the contest, I seriously thought about extending my newspaper subscription. Finally, I even thanked him for the information about the vacation contest. Maybe the next time a salesperson calls, I'll first ask him about any contests and my real chances of winning.

EXERCISE **12**	ADDING THE RIGHT TRANSITIONS TO A NARRATIVE PARAGRAPH

In the following paragraph, circle the correct transition in each of the pairs.

I ran into trouble when I was taking my art history test yesterday; (later/at once), I solved my problem. I was doing fine (after/at first), completing the matching questions about the painters and their paintings. (Then/Still), I ran into five short-answer questions about the Impressionists, and my mind went blank. I knew I had studied the material, but I couldn't remember a thing. Who or what were the Impressionists? I froze, and the harder I tried to remember, the less confident I felt. I decided to go on to the other questions on the test (before/ while) I lost my confidence. I took a deep breath and completed the rest of the test, ignoring the five questions about the Impressionists and focusing on what I knew about the remaining questions. (Soon after/Finally) I had done that, I felt much calmer, for I had found the rest of the test fairly easy. I began to feel confident (frequently/again). (Before/Suddenly), all that I had studied about the Impressionists came back to me.

PROOFREADING   **PROOFREADING AND POLISHING: NARRATION**

As you prepare the final copy of the narrative paragraph, make any minor changes in word choice or transitions that will refine your writing. Below is the final copy of the narrative paragraph on divorce. Notice these changes in the final version:

- The draft version used both formal and informal words such as "folks," "parents," "dad," and "father"; the final version uses only "parents" and "father."
- A couple of details have been added.
- A transition has been added.

> A Final Version of a Narrative Paragraph (*changes from the draft are underlined*)

When my parents announced that they were divorcing, I felt confused by all my emotions. At the time of their announcement, I was seven and my sister was ten. Both <u>my parents</u> were there to tell us. They told us at breakfast, in the kitchen. I was eating toast, but I remember I couldn't eat anything when they started talking. <u>In fact,</u> I remember <u>staring at</u> a piece of toast with one bite taken out of it. My <u>parents</u> were very calm when they told us. "We both love you very much," my father said. "But your mother and I aren't getting along." They said they would always love us. The announcement was such a shock to me that I couldn't believe it was happening. At first, I just thought they were having another fight. Because I was too young to understand, I didn't cry. Suddenly, my sister started to cry, and then I knew it was serious. I kept thinking I would have to choose which parent to live with. I knew I'd really hurt the one I didn't choose, so I felt <u>terrible</u> guilt about hurting one of them. I felt torn apart.

Before you prepare the final copy of your narrative paragraph, check your latest draft for errors in spelling and punctuation, and for any errors made in typing or recopying.

EXERCISE 13

PROOFREADING TO PREPARE THE FINAL VERSION

Here are two narrative paragraphs with the kinds of errors that are easy to overlook when you prepare the final version of an assignment. Correct the errors, writing above the lines. There are eleven errors in the first paragraph and eight errors in the second paragraph.

1. When my girl friend tossed my ring out the window, I knew she was not ready to forgive me one more time. It all started on Saturday, at MacDonald's, when I ran into my girlfriend Lakisha. I could see she was'nt in a good mood. As soon as we sat down, she asked me about Yvonne. A girl I've been seeing behind Lakisha's back. Well, of course I lied and said "Yvonne means nothing to me." However, Lakisha said she seen me and Yvonne at the mall the night before, and we looked like was rommanticlly involved. I asked, "How could you tell?" Well, naturally that was the wrong thing to say since I was admitting Yvonne and I had been together. After I asked that stupid question, Lakisha took my ring off her finger and tossed that ring right threw the window at McDonald's.

2. My son Scott's first day at preschool was an emotional one for me. i was up early on that day, planning his cloths and worrying about his fears and tears when I dropped him off at his first school. However, when I woke Scott up, I tried to be cheerful. I smiled and acted as if he were about to begin an exciting adventure. "Today is the day you get to make friends and have some fun," I said. Scott didn't seem to unhappy or reluctant as he ate breakfast. He was pleased when I let him wear him favorite baseball cap and shorts. In the car on the way to school, Scott sat quietly, but I could hardly hold back my tears. I was picturing my little boy along, afraid, crieing in a corner of the classroom. Yet when I handed him over to the friendly teacher, Scott did not protest. He took the teacher's hand and walked, wide-eyed, to a new world.

Lines of Detail: A Walk-Through Assignment

Write a paragraph about an incident in your life that embarrassed (or amused, or frightened, or saddened, or angered) you. In writing the paragraph, follow these steps:

Step 1: Begin by freewriting. Then read your freewriting, looking for both the details and the focus of your paragraph.

Step 2: Brainstorm for more details. Then write all the freewriting and the brainstorming as a list.

Step 3: Survey your list. Write a topic sentence that makes a point about the details.

Step 4: Write an outline. As you write the outline, check that your details fit the topic sentence and are in a clear order. As you revise your outline, add details where they're needed.

Step 5: In the drafting and revising stage, write and revise a draft of your paragraph. Revise until your details are specific and in a clear order, and your transitions are smooth. Combine any sentences that are short and choppy. Add a speaker's exact words if they will make the details more specific.

Step 6: In preparing the final copy, check for punctuation, spelling, and word choice.

Writing Your Own Narrative Paragraph

When you write on any of the following topics, be sure to work through the stages of the writing process in preparing your narrative paragraph.

1. Write about an event you saw that you'll never forget. Begin by freewriting. Then read your freewriting, looking for both the details and the focus of your paragraph.

   If your instructor agrees, ask a writing partner or a group to (a) listen to you read your freewriting, (b) help you focus it, and (c) help you add details by asking questions.

2. Write a narrative paragraph about how you met your boyfriend or girlfriend, your husband or wife, or your best friend. Start by listing as many details as you can, and, if your instructor agrees, ask a writing partner or a group to (a) survey your list of details and (b) ask questions that will lead you to more details.

3. Write about a time when you got what you wanted. Start by listing as many details as you can, and, if your instructor agrees, ask a writing partner or a group to (a) survey your list of details and (b) ask questions that will lead you to more details.

4. Interview an older family member or friend. Ask him or her to tell you an interesting story about the past. Ask questions as the person speaks. Take notes. If you have a tape recorder, you can record the interview, but take notes as well. When you've finished the interview, review the information with the person you've interviewed. Would he or she like to add anything? If you wish, ask follow-up questions.

   Next, on your own, find a point to the story. Work through the stages of the writing process to turn the interview into a narrative paragraph.

WRITING FROM READING: NARRATION

One Caring Teacher Set Things Right
Richard Wagamese

Richard Wagamese is a member of the Ojibway Nation in northwestern Ontario. A successful journalist, he began writing novels in 1993. His latest novel, Medicine Walk, *was published in 2014.*

Before you read this selection, consider these questions:

What are your most vivid childhood memories?
Who has been your most memorable teacher, and why?
Have you ever experienced an act of kindness that has changed your life?

I write in the dimness of morning. Outside, the world is a shape shifter. Light eases things back into definition, their boundaries called from shadow, hardening, forming, beginning to hold again and the land shrugs itself into wakefulness. Purple moving upward into pearl grey.

It's good to be up and working at this time. I can feel the power of life and light around me and as the letters form upon the screen, race each other to the sudden halt of punctuation, I understand where this need to write comes from.

It comes from this **palpable** mystery. This first light breaking over everything, altering things, arranging them, setting them down into patterns again and tucking shadow back into folds behind the trees. It comes from the need of **communion**, of joining with that Great Mystery, that force, that energy.

I always wanted to write. There isn't a time I can recall when I didn't carry the desire to frame things, order things upon a page, sort them out, make sense of them. But in the beginning, learning to write was a test, a challenge, an ordeal.

I was the only Indian kid in a mill town school in northern Ontario in the early 1960s. It was a different world then, harder maybe, colder and the idea of Indians was set like concrete, particularly in the **parochial**, working class confines of a saw mill town 200 miles from nowhere.

The school was set between the railroad tracks and the pipeline in a hollow between hills above the mill. We sat with the thick **sulphur** smell coming through the windows and the **spume** of the stacks on the horizon above the trees. In the classroom, I was ignored, set down near the back and never called upon for anything.

They said I was slow, a difficult learner, far too quiet for a kid and **lethargic**.

They said I hadn't much hope for a future and after they held me back a year, they just let me be. But I wanted to learn. I was hungry for it and I went to school every day eager and excited about the things we were given to learn.

But I couldn't see. No one had spent enough time with me to learn that.

The reason I was slow to pick things up was that I could never see the board. Even at the front of the room where they put me so they could keep a better eye on me, I could never **discern** the writing on the blackboard. Everything I learned I learned by memory, by listening hard to what the teacher said and memorizing it.

palpable: tangible, obvious

communion: a feeling of connectedness

parochial: narrowly restricted perspective

sulphur: a chemical smelling of rotten eggs
spume: column of smoke

lethargic: listless, tired

discern: to perceive; to recognize

When I was adopted in 1965, I was sent to my first big school in a southern Ontario town called Bradford, just north of Toronto.

There were hundreds of kids in that school and it seemed like I walked in waves of them on my way to school that first day. Walking through those big glass doors was terrifying for me.

I was in Grade 3 and my teacher wanted to introduce me and she asked me to write my name on the blackboard for the other kids to read. I went to the board, leaned close to it, squinted and began to write. I heard snickers at the first letter and open laughter when I'd finished.

I'd written my name upside down and backwards. To the rest of my classmates it was odd, strange and hilarious but it was how I'd learned and I felt the weight of their laughter like stones. Walking back to my seat that day I felt ashamed, stupid and terribly alone.

But I had a teacher who cared. She walked me down to the nurse's station herself and waited while I got my eyes tested.

astigmatism:
a condition that results in blurred vision

Astigmatism, the nurse told her. Terrible astigmatism. Then she listened closely to me when I explained why my writing was wrongly shaped.

I taught myself to write by squinting back over my shoulder. When we were taught to write in script, I wasn't given any teacher attention, wasn't offered any help in forming the letters.

mimicked: copied

So I watched the kid behind me and I **mimicked** what I saw on my own page. Unfortunately, what I saw was upside down and backwards and that was how I taught myself to write. I could spell everything correctly but it was all **skewed.**

skewed: crooked, off-centre

Well, I got glasses very shortly after that and my world changed. Once I could see what was written on the board, my ability to learn accelerated and I graduated Grade 3 with straight As. Especially in **penmanship.**

penmanship:
handwriting

See, for that teacher I wasn't an Indian. I was a kid in need. So she took the time to show me how to write properly. Every day, before and after school, she and I sat at a desk and we worked through the primary writing books. I shaped letters time after time after time until I gradually unlearned the awkward process I'd taught myself.

Like life, unlearning something was a lot harder than learning it. I struggled with breaking down my method and at times it seemed I would never get it right. But I persisted with the help and encouragement of that teacher and I learned how to write in the right direction. But I still shape my Gs and Ds wrong today. I still write them back to front after all this time.

I write on a keyboard these days. But there isn't a time when I set a pen to paper that I don't remember learning how to write and what it took to get me there.

See, there's a story behind every difference. There's a reason we become the people we become and it's having the courage and consideration to hear those stories that allows us to help each other. Sometimes, life turns us upside down and backwards. It's caring that gets us back on our feet again and pointed in the right direction.

UNDERSTANDING "ONE CARING TEACHER SET THINGS RIGHT"

1. The first few paragraphs of "One Caring Teacher Set Things Right" describe the pre-dawn contrast between light and dark. Why do you think Wagamese prefers to write at this time?

2. According to Wagamese, why does he feel the need to write?

3. What two meanings do "upside down and backwards" have for the narrative?

WRITING FROM READING "ONE CARING TEACHER SET THINGS RIGHT"

When you write on any of the following topics, be sure to work through the stages of the writing process.

1. Write a narrative paragraph about a time when you helped someone who was in trouble.

2. Write a story that describes your most vivid school-related memory.

3. Many people have had a teacher who has helped shape their lives, either positively or negatively. Write a narrative paragraph that describes what that teacher did to make an impact on your life.

MyWritingLab

CHAPTER 6
Process

LEARNING OBJECTIVES

After you have read this chapter and completed its exercises and assignments, you should be able to

- distinguish between directional and informational processes
- describe a step-by-step process
- use appropriate transitions for your process paragraph
- draft and edit your process paragraph

"Logic takes care of itself; all we have to do is to look and see how it does it."

~ LUDWIG WITTGENSTEIN

▼ LUDWIG WITTGENSTEIN WAS A TWENTIETH-CENTURY AUSTRIAN PHILOSOPHER.

WHAT IS PROCESS?

A **process** paragraph explains how to do something or describes how something happens or is done. When you tell the reader how to do something (a *directional process*), you speak directly to the reader and give him or her clear, specific instructions about performing some activity. Your purpose is to explain an activity so that a reader can do it. For example, you may have to leave instructions telling a new employee how to use new software or the photocopier.

When you describe how something happens (an *informational process*), your purpose is to explain an activity, but not to tell a reader how to do it. For example, you may have to explain how a boxer trains for a fight or how the special effects for a film were created. Instead of speaking directly to the reader, an informational process speaks about *I*, *he*, *she*, *we*, *they*, or about a person by his or her name. A directional process uses *you* or, in the way it gives directions, the word *you* is understood.

A Process Involves Steps in Time Order

Whether a process is directional or informational, it describes something that is done in steps, and these steps are in a specific order: a **time order**. The process can involve steps that are followed in minutes, hours, days, weeks, months, or even years.

For example, the steps in changing a tire may take minutes, whereas the steps taken to lose ten pounds may take months.

The important thing to remember is that a process involves steps that *must follow a certain order*, not just a range of activities that can be placed in any order.

This sentence signals a process.

> Changing a tire is easy if you follow a few steps. (*Changing a tire involves following steps in order; for example, you have to raise the car before you remove the flat tire.*)

The following sentence *does not signal a process*:

> There are several ways to get a person to like you. (*Each way is separate; there is no time sequence here.*)

When you're telling someone in a conversation how to do something or how something is done, that person can ask questions if he or she doesn't understand—which gives you the opportunity to add important points you may have forgotten or to throw in details you may have left out. Writing about a process, however, is more difficult. Your reader isn't there to stop you, to ask you to explain further, to question you. In writing about a process, you must be organized and clear.

Hints for Writing a Process Paragraph

1. **In choosing a topic, find an activity you know well.** If you write about something familiar to you, you'll have a clearer paragraph.

2. **Choose a topic that includes steps that must be done in a specific time sequence.**

   not this: I find lots of things to do on a rainy day.
   but this: I have a plan for cleaning out my closet.

3. **Choose a topic that is fairly small.** A complicated process cannot be covered well in one paragraph. If your topic is too big, the paragraph can become vague, incomplete, or boring.

   too big: There are many stages in the parliamentary process of a bill before it becomes a law.
   smaller and manageable: Willpower and support were the most important elements in my struggle to quit smoking.

4. **Write a topic sentence that makes a point.** Your topic sentence should do more than announce. Like the topic sentence for any paragraph, it should have a point. As you plan the steps of your process and gather details, ask yourself some questions: What point do I want to make about this process? Is the process hard? Is it easy? Does the process require certain tools? Does the process require certain skills, like organization, patience, endurance?

   an announcement: This paragraph is about how to change the oil in your car.
   a topic sentence: You don't have to be a mechanic to change the oil in your car, but you do have to take a few simple precautions.

5. **Include all the steps.** If you're explaining a process, you're writing for someone who doesn't know the process as well as you do. So keep in mind that what seems clear or simple to you may not be clear or simple

to the reader. Make sure to tell what is needed before the process starts, too. For instance, what ingredients are needed to cook the dish? Or what tools are needed to assemble the toy?

6. **Put the steps in the right order.** Few things are more irritating to a reader than trying to follow directions that skip back and forth. Careful planning, drafting, and revision can help you get the time sequence right.

7. **Be specific in the details and steps.** To make sure you have sufficient detail and clear steps, keep your reader in mind. Put yourself in the reader's place. Could you follow your own directions or understand your steps?

If you remember that a process explains, you will focus on being clear. Now that you know the purpose and strategies of writing a process paragraph, you can begin the prewriting step of writing one.

communication at work

Process is everywhere! For example, are you aware of your school's fire evacuation procedures? Here's the procedure used at Vancouver's Simon Fraser University (2007):

If You Discover a Fire in the Building

1. Immediately sound the fire alarm by activating the nearest fire alarm pull station.
2. Alert people in the immediate area.
3. Dial (9) 911 (Vancouver Fire Department):
   a. state your name
   b. state that a fire is in progress and give address
   c. provide information about the fire (i.e., what floor, how fast the fire is spreading, people trapped, etc.)
4. Leave the building using the nearest exit. DO NOT USE THE ELEVATOR.

EXERCISE 1

RECOGNIZING GOOD TOPIC SENTENCES FOR PROCESS PARAGRAPHS

If a sentence is a good topic sentence for a process paragraph, put *OK* on the line provided. If a sentence has a problem, label that sentence with one of these letters:

A This is an **announcement**; it makes no point.

B This sentence covers a topic that is **too big** for one paragraph.

NS This sentence describes a topic that does **not require steps**.

1. _____ There is a simple plan for finding the best deals on car insurance.
2. _____ How I learned to clean fish is the subject of this paragraph.
3. _____ There are several reasons for updating your home computer.
4. _____ The process of building a house is challenging.
5. _____ Selling your car for the best price means knowing how to clean it to look its best.
6. _____ This paper describes the method for refinishing an antique chair.
7. _____ Civil rights in Canada evolved in several stages.
8. _____ There are many things to remember when you enter college.
9. _____ If you learn just a few trade secrets, you can install your own hardwood floors.
10. _____ Munesh learned the right way to apply for a car loan.

EXERCISE 2

INCLUDING NECESSARY MATERIALS IN A PROCESS

Below are three possible topics for a process paragraph. For each topic, work with a partner or a group and list the items (materials, ingredients, tools, utensils, supplies) that the reader will have to gather before he or she begins the process. When you've finished the exercise, check your lists with another group to see if you've missed any items.

1. **topic:** making and packing a school lunch for a six-year-old
    needed items: _____
    _____
    _____

2. **topic:** cooking a hamburger on a barbecue
    needed items: _____
    _____
    _____

3. **topic:** preparing a package for mailing (the package contains a breakable item)
    needed items: _____
    _____
    _____

WRITING THE PROCESS PARAGRAPH IN STEPS

PREWRITING **GATHERING IDEAS: PROCESS**

The easiest way to start writing a process paragraph is to choose a small topic, one that you can cover well in one paragraph. Then you can gather ideas by listing or freewriting or both.

If you decided to write about how to find the right apartment, you might begin by freewriting.

Then you might check your freewriting, looking for details that have to do with the process of finding an apartment. You can underline those details, as in the example that follows.

> ### Freewriting for a Process Paragraph
>
> **Topic: Finding the Right Apartment**
>
> You have to <u>look around. Don't pick the first apartment you see.</u> Sean did that, and he wound up with a dump. <u>Look at a bunch.</u> But <u>not too many,</u> or you'll get confused. <u>The lease,</u> too. <u>Check it carefully. Do you pay the hydro? Do you want a one-bedroom? Friends can help</u> if they know of any nice apartments. I found my place that way. Maybe somebody you know lives in <u>a good neighbourhood.</u> A <u>convenient location can be more expensive.</u> But <u>can save you money on transportation.</u>

Next, you can put what you've underlined into a list, in correct time sequence:

before the search

do you want a one-bedroom?

friends can help

a good neighbourhood

convenient location can be more expensive

can save you money on transportation

during the search

look around

don't pick the first apartment you see

look at a bunch

but not too many

after the search

check the lease carefully

do you pay the hydro?

Check the list. Are some details missing? Yes. A reader might ask, "What other ways (besides asking friends) can help you find apartments? What else should you do before you search? When you're looking at apartments, what should you be looking for? What questions should you ask? After the search, how do you decide which apartment is best? And what, besides the hydro, should you check on the lease?" Answers to questions like these can give you the details needed to write a clear and interesting directional process paragraph.

Writing a Topic Sentence for a Process Paragraph

Freewriting and a list can now help you focus your paragraph by identifying the point of your process. You already know what the subject of your paragraph is: finding the right apartment. But what's the point? Is it easy to find the right apartment? Is it difficult? What does it take to find the right apartment?

Maybe a topic sentence could be

Finding the right apartment takes planning and careful investigation.

Once you have a topic sentence, you can think about adding details that explain your topic sentence and can begin the planning stage of writing.

EXERCISE **3**	**FINDING THE STEPS OF A PROCESS IN FREEWRITING**

Read the following freewriting, then reread it, looking for all the words, phrases, and sentences that have to do with steps. Underline all those items. Once you've underlined the freewriting, put what you've underlined into a list, in the correct time sequence.

How I Found a Great Gift for My Father: Freewriting

Birthdays are tough. How do you find the right gift? Especially for a parent. Usually, I give my dad a tie or a sweater, something very ordinary that he stashes in the back of his closet. This year, he was really surprised when he saw his present draped across the couch. It was a small blanket, called a "throw," with a pattern of hockey sweaters and team names. It began when I decided to get my father something he would really use. I started to observe his habits and interests. He gardened; he played cards with some friends. Hockey was his favourite sport on television. He always fell asleep watching it. He would curl up as if he were cold. Now I had some gift ideas. I went to the stores to see if there were any new gardening gadgets, accessories for card tables, or books on hockey. Nothing appealed to me. Finally, I found the perfect gift. I bought what I knew he would use and like.

_____

_____

_____

_____

_____

_____

_____

PLANNING   **DEVISING A PLAN: PROCESS**

Using the freewriting and topic sentence on finding the right apartment, you could make an outline. Then you could revise it, checking the topic sentence and list of details, improving them where you think they could be better. A revised outline of finding an apartment follows.

An Outline for a Process Paragraph

topic sentence: Finding the apartment you want takes planning and careful investigation.

details:

before the search

　Decide what you want.

　Ask yourself, "Do I want a one-bedroom?" and "What can I afford?"

　A convenient location can be more expensive.

　It can also save you money on transportation.

　Friends may know of available apartments.

　Maybe somebody you know lives in a good neighbourhood.

　Check the classified advertisements in the newspapers or online.

　Look around.

during the search

　Don't pick the first apartment you see.

　Look at several.

　But don't look at too many.

　Check the cleanliness, safety, plumbing, and appliances of each one.

　Ask the manager about the laundry room, additional storage, parking facilities, and maintenance policies.

after the search

Compare the two best places you saw.

Consider the price, location, and condition of the apartments.

Check the leases carefully.

Check the cost of monthly hydro.

Check the requirements for first and last months' rent deposits.

The following checklist may help you to revise an outline for your own process paragraph.

CHECKLIST · FOR REVISING A PROCESS OUTLINE

✓ Is my topic sentence focused on some point about the process?
✓ Does it cover the whole process?
✓ Do I have all the steps?
✓ Are they in the right order?
✓ Have I explained clearly?
✓ Do I need better details?

EXERCISE 4 · REVISING THE TOPIC SENTENCE IN A PROCESS OUTLINE

The following topic sentence doesn't cover all the steps of the process. Read the outline several times, then write a topic sentence that covers all the steps of the process and has a point.

topic sentence: If you want to save money at the supermarket, write a list at home.

details: First, leave a pencil and a piece of paper near your refrigerator.
Each time you use the last of some item, like milk, write that item on the page.
Before you go to the store, read what's written on the page and add it to the list.
Then rewrite the list, organizing it according to the layout of your store.
Put all the dairy products together on the list, for instance.
Put all the fresh fruits and vegetables together.
At the store, begin with the first items on your list.
Move purposefully through the aisles.
Keep your eyes on your list so that you don't see all kinds of goodies you don't need.
Pass by the gourmet items.
Keep going through each aisle, buying only what's on your list.
At the end of the last aisle, check what's in your cart against your list.

Get any item you forgot.
When you stand in the checkout line, avoid looking at the
overpriced and tempting snacks that fill the area.

revised topic sentence:

_____

_____

EXERCISE 5	REVISING THE ORDER OF STEPS IN A PROCESS OUTLINE

The steps in each of these outlines are out of order. Put numbers in the spaces
provided, indicating what step should be first, second, and so on.

1. **topic sentence:** Leaving a professional voice-mail message requires
   forethought and practice.
   details: _____ Be sure to state your name and the date.
   _____ Repeat your name, spell it, and give your phone number.
   _____ Explain the reason for your call, and provide an "action
   item": an action you would like the recipient to do, or
   question you would like answered.
   _____ Take a minute to determine the nature of the call.
   _____ Always repeat your phone number.
   _____ Ensure that you include an appropriate closing, such as
   "Thank you for your time" or "Have a good day."
   _____ When you hear the message's beep, open with a greeting,
   such as "Good morning."

2. **topic sentence:** Cody knows exactly how to persuade me to go to the
   movies.
   details: _____ He says, "The paper says there's a new movie opening
   today. We could go to that."
   _____ "It's supposed to be a really good movie," he adds.
   _____ Then he says, "If you go to the movies with me, I'll pay."
   _____ He starts by looking at the TV listings and sighing.
   _____ "There's nothing on television," he says, "so what will
   we do tonight?"
   _____ He looks through the newspaper and asks if I know
   about any new movies.
   _____ I say I don't know about any new movies.
   _____ Suddenly, going to the movies seems very attractive to me.

3. **topic sentence:** Ken has a perfect system for getting out of work early.
   details: _____ Ken's excuse always gets him out of work early because
   our boss thinks Ken has done so much extra work all day.
   _____ By the time our boss arrives, Ken looks as if he's hard at
   work.
   _____ He makes sure she notices him as soon as she arrives
   because he immediately asks her a question or strolls by
   her work area.

_____ Then, about an hour before his shift is over, he comes up with an excuse.

_____ He starts by getting to work earlier than our boss does.

_____ As he acts busy, he calls attention to himself by sighing or racing around.

_____ Ken acts busy all morning and most of the afternoon.

_____ His excuse can be a headache, or a dental appointment, or a sudden need to buy more photocopy paper or other office supplies.

| EXERCISE **6** | **LISTING ALL THE STEPS IN AN OUTLINE** |

Below are three topic sentences for process paragraphs. Write all the steps needed to complete an outline for each sentence. After you've listed all the steps, number them in the correct time order.

1. **topic sentence:** Anyone can create his or her own exercise plan.

   steps: _____

   _____

   _____

   _____

   _____

   _____

   _____

   _____

2. **topic sentence:** You can devise a plan for saving money on your credit card bills.

   steps: _____

   _____

   _____

   _____

   _____

   _____

   _____

   _____

3. **topic sentence:** There is a simple method for getting to work on time.

   steps: _____

   _____

   _____

   _____

   _____

   _____

   _____

DRAFTING AND REVISING: PROCESS

If you take the outline and write it in paragraph form, you'll have a first draft of the process paragraph. As you write the first draft, you can combine some of the short sentences from the outline. Then you can review your draft and revise it for organization, detail, clarity, grammar, style, and word choice.

Using the Same Grammatical Person

Remember that the *directional* process speaks directly to the reader, calling him or her *you*. Sentences in a directional process use the word *you*, or they imply *you*.

> **directional:** *You* need a good paintbrush to get started. Begin by making a plan. (*You* is implied in the second sentence.)

Remember that the *informational* process involves somebody doing the process. Sentences in an informational process use words like *I* or *we* or *he* or *she* or *they* or a person's name.

> **informational:** *Tomoko* needs a good paintbrush to get started. First, *I* can make a list.

One problem in writing a process paragraph is shifting from describing how somebody did something to telling the reader how to do an activity. When that shift happens, the two kinds of processes get mixed. That shift is called a **shift in person.** In grammar, the words *I* and *we* are considered to be in the first person; *you* is in the second person; and *he, she, it,* and *they* are in the third person.

If these words refer to one, they are called *singular*; if they refer to more than one, they are called *plural.* The following list may help.

INFOBOX	**A LIST OF PERSONS**

1st person singular: I
2nd person singular: you
3rd person singular: he, she, it, or a person's name

1st person plural: we
2nd person plural: you
3rd person plural: they, or the names of more than one person

In writing your process paragraph, decide whether your process will be directional or informational, and stay with that approach. Below are two examples of a shift in person. Look at them carefully and study how the shift is corrected.

Shift in person:

> After **I** preheat the oven to 350 degrees, **I** mix the egg whites and sugar with an electric mixer set at high speed. **Mix** until stiff peaks form. Then **I** put the mixture in small mounds on an ungreased cookie sheet.

("Mix until stiff peaks form" is a shift to the *you* person.)

Shift corrected:

> After **I** preheat the oven to 350 degrees, **I** mix the egg whites and sugar with an electric mixer set at high speed. **I** mix until stiff peaks form. Then **I** put the mixture in small mounds on an ungreased cookie sheet.

Shift in person:

> **A salesperson** has to be very tactful when customers try on clothes. **The salesperson** can't hint that a suit may be a size too small. **You** can insult a customer with a hint like that.

(The sentences shifted from *salesperson* to *you*.)

Shift corrected:

> **A salesperson** has to be very careful when customers try on clothes. **The salesperson** can't hint that a suit may be a size too small. **He** (or **she**) can insult a customer with a hint like that.

Using Transitions Effectively

As you revise your draft, you can add transitions. Transitions are particularly important in a process paragraph because you're trying to show the steps in a *specific sequence*, and you're trying to show the *connections* between steps. Good transitions will also keep your paragraph from sounding like a choppy, boring list.

Below is a list of some of the transitions you can use in writing a process paragraph. Make sure that you use transitional words and phrases only when it's logical to do so, and try not to overuse the same transitions in a paragraph.

INFOBOX   **TRANSITIONS FOR A PROCESS PARAGRAPH**

after, afterward, as, as he is . . ., as soon as . . ., as you are . . ., at last, at the same time, before, begin by, during, eventually, finally, first, second, third (etc.), first of all, gradually, in the beginning, immediately, initially, last, later, meanwhile, next, now, once, quickly, sometimes, soon, suddenly, the first step, the second step (etc.), then, to begin, to start, until, when, whenever, while, while I am . . .

When you write a process paragraph, you must pay particular attention to clarity. As you revise, keep thinking about your audience in order to make sure your steps are easy to follow. The following checklist can help you revise your draft.

CHECKLIST   **FOR REVISING A PROCESS PARAGRAPH**

✓ Does the topic sentence cover the whole paragraph?
✓ Does the topic sentence make a point about the process?
✓ Is any important step left out?
✓ Should any step be explained further?
✓ Are the steps in the right order?
✓ Should any sentences be combined?
✓ Have I used the same *person* throughout the paragraph to describe the process?
✓ Have I used transitions effectively?

| EXERCISE 7 | CORRECTING SHIFTS IN PERSON IN A PROCESS PARAGRAPH |

Below is a paragraph that shifts from an informational to a directional process in several places. Those places are underlined. Rewrite the underlined parts, directly above the underlining, so that the whole paragraph is an informational process.

Kathleen has an efficient system for paying her bills. As soon as a bill arrives in the mail, she stacks it in a tray marked "To Pay." Every weekend, she takes the bills out of the tray and pays them. She could wait and pay them all at the end of each month, as some people do, but she feels that by waiting <u>you</u> might miss a bill that is due sooner and have to pay a late penalty. Once she's paid all the bills, she writes "Paid" and the date on her bill stub. <u>File</u> that customer's stub in a file divided into sections like Hydro Bills, Rent, Telephone Bills, and Car Payments. Once a year, Kathleen surveys that file and discards stubs more than six months old. With her system, <u>your</u> unpaid bills are all in one place, and <u>you have</u> clear records of paid bills.

| EXERCISE 8 | REVISING TRANSITIONS IN A PROCESS PARAGRAPH |

The transitions in this paragraph could be better. Rewrite the underlined transitions, directly above each one, so that the transitions are smoother.

In a few simple steps, you can make a delicious ice cream sundae. <u>First</u>, gather a deep bowl or sundae glass, one large and one small spoon, ice cream, chocolate syrup, nuts, and a spray can of whipped cream. <u>Second</u>, use the large spoon to put mounds of ice cream into the glass or bowl. <u>Third</u>, cover the ice cream with the chocolate syrup. <u>Fourth</u>, sprinkle the ice cream with nuts. <u>Fifth</u>, spray the whipped cream to form a peak at the top of the ice cream. <u>Sixth</u>, dip the small spoon into the sundae and enjoy the treat.

| EXERCISE 9 | COMBINING SENTENCES IN A PROCESS PARAGRAPH |

The paragraph below contains some short, choppy sentences, which are underlined. Wherever you see two or more underlined sentences next to each other, combine them into one clear, smooth sentence. Write your revised version of the paragraph in the spaces above the lines.

Preparing a professional résumé need not be intimidating. First, reflect on your experiences and accomplishments. <u>Think of your education. Think of your work history.</u> Make a list. You now have to choose a résumé format—which one works best for you? <u>There is the reverse chronological format. There is also the skills-based format.</u> If you have a linear educational and work history, you may choose the reverse chronological format. In this format, you list your education and work history with the most recent first. If you have gaps in your education or work history, you might choose a skills-based format. <u>This is where you group your transferable skills together. You also group your technical skills together.</u> List details for each entry: What projects did you complete in school? What accomplishments did you have at work? Finally, list your volunteer experiences and other activities. Proofread for spelling, grammar, and formatting errors. Your résumé is your first introduction to a potential employer, so make sure you put your best foot forward!

The Draft

Below is a draft of the process paragraph on finding an apartment. The draft has more details than the outline. Some short sentences have been combined, and transitions have been added.

> ### A Draft of a Process Paragraph
>
> Finding the apartment you want takes planning and careful investigation. First of all, you must decide what you want. Ask yourself, "Do I want a one-bedroom?" and "Do I want a studio apartment?" Most important, ask yourself, "What can I afford?" A convenient location can be expensive; on the other hand, that location can save you money on transportation. Before you start looking for a place, do some research. Friends may know of available apartments. Be sure to check the classified advertisements in the newspapers and online. Once you begin your search, don't pick the first apartment you see. You should look at several places, but looking at too many can make your search confusing. Just be sure to check each apartment's cleanliness, safety, plumbing, and appliances. Then ask the manager about the laundry room, additional storage, parking facilities, and maintenance policies. After you've completed your search, compare the two best places you saw. Consider each one's price, location, and condition. Carefully check the leases, studying the cost of monthly hydro and the deposits for first and last month's rent.

PROOFREADING   **PROOFREADING AND POLISHING: PROCESS**

Following is the final version of the process paragraph on finding the apartment you want. You'll notice that it contains several changes from the previous draft.

- The sentence "friends may know of available apartments" has been changed to "friends may know of available apartments in desirable areas" to make the description more specific.

- The sentence that began "You should look" has been rewritten so that it follows the pattern of the preceding sentences. Three sentences in a row now include the parallel pattern of "Be sure," "don't pick," and "Look at."
- The second use of "be sure" has been changed to "remember" to avoid repetition.
- A new detail about what to check for in the leases has been added.
- A final sentence that relates to the topic of the paragraph has been added.

> ### A Final Version of a Process Paragraph (*changes from the draft are underlined*)
>
> Finding the apartment you want takes planning and careful investigation. First of all, you must decide what you want. Ask yourself, "Do I want a one-bedroom?" and "Do I want a studio apartment?" Most important, ask yourself, "What can I afford?" A convenient location can be expensive; on the other hand, that location can save you money on transportation. Before you start looking for a place, do some research. Friends may know of available apartments <u>in desirable areas.</u> Be sure to check the classified advertisements in the newspapers and online. Once you begin your search, don't pick the first apartment you see. <u>Look</u> at several places, but <u>be aware that</u> looking at too many can make your search confusing. Just <u>remember</u> to check each apartment's cleanliness, safety, plumbing, and appliances. Then ask the manager about the laundry room, additional storage, parking facilities, and maintenance policies. After you've completed your search, compare the two best places you saw. Consider each one's price, location, and condition. Carefully check the leases, studying the cost of monthly hydro, the deposits for first and last month's rent, <u>and the rules for tenants. When you've completed your comparison, you're ready to choose the apartment you want.</u>

Before you prepare the final copy of your process paragraph, check your latest draft for errors in spelling and punctuation, and for any errors made in typing or recopying.

EXERCISE 10

PROOFREADING TO PREPARE THE FINAL PARAGRAPH

Below are two process paragraphs with the kinds of errors that are easy to overlook when you prepare the final version of an assignment. Correct the errors, writing above the lines. There are eleven errors in the first paragraph and nine in the second paragraph.

    1. The best way to deal with cockroaches is to never give up. Let's say you get up in the nite for a glass of water. Suddenly, when you turn on the light, an enormous roach skitters across you're bear feet. Of course, the first thing you do is scream, as if a peeping Tom were at the window. Next, you begin to plan an extermination You grab a newspaper and swat at the insect just as the ugly bug slips between the sink and the kitchen counter. You've missed it. Immediately, you being a search for the can of insect spray that You keep for emergencies. Eventually you find it, and spray the entire kitchen. You spray so much that every roach within twenny mile should be dead. Unfortunately, you don't know if youv'e killed the roach that crossed your toes in the kitchen. Now is the time to perservere. Never go back to bed in defeat. Instead, stand guard in the kitchen until one big roach staggers out in to the open.

    2. Pretending to enjoy a dinner you hate can be accomplished if you follow several sneaky steps. First, don't shudder when your father announces he have spent allday making his famous turkey stew. Do not remind him that you have allways despised that recipe. Instead, say something like, "Oh, I remember that stew." It would be a little too phony to say how much you use to love it. When the stew is placed in front of you, begin by moving it around on the plate, meanwhile chewing on a role or salad so that you give the illusion of eating the main coarse. As you pretend to eat, look around you. Is there a hungry dog under the table. Help him out by providing him with a secret meal. If there is no dog, try concealing the stew under some other food on your plate. Put the meat under a potato skin or a lettuce leaf. If you have a paper napkin, consider wrapping it around some stew and concealing the package in your pocket. At the end of the meal, be sure to comment that you're fathers stew is as good as it ever was.

Lines of Detail: A Walk-Through Assignment

Your assignment is to write a paragraph on how to plan a special day. Follow these steps:

Step 1: Focus on one special day. If you want to, you can begin by using your own experience. Ask yourself such questions as these: "Have I ever planned a birthday party? A baby or wedding shower? A surprise party? A picnic? A reunion? A barbecue? A celebration of a religious holiday? Have I ever seen anyone else plan such a day? If so, how would I teach a reader about planning for such a day?"

Step 2: Once you've picked the day, freewrite. Write anything you can remember about the day and how you or someone else planned it.

Step 3: When you've completed the freewriting, read it. Underline all the details that refer to steps in planning that event. List the underlined details, in time order.

Step 4: Add to the list by brainstorming. Ask yourself questions that can lead to more details. For example, if an item on your list is "Send out invitations early," ask questions like "How early?" and "How do you decide whom to invite?"

Step 5: Survey your expanded list. Write a topic sentence that makes some point about your planning for this special day. To reach a point, think of questions like "What makes a plan successful?" or "If you're planning for a special day (birthday, barbecue, surprise party, etc.), what must you remember?"

Step 6: Use the topic sentence to prepare an outline. Make sure that the steps in the outline are in the correct time order.

Step 7: Write a first draft of the paragraph. In this first draft, add more details and combine short sentences.

Step 8: Revise your draft. Be careful to use smooth transitions, and check that you've included all the necessary steps.

Step 9: Prepare and proofread the final version of your paragraph.

Writing Your Own Process Paragraph

When you write on one of these topics, make sure to work through the stages of the writing process in preparing your paragraph.

1. Write a **directional or informational process** about one of these topics:

   packing a suitcase

   choosing a new mobile phone

   writing a paragraph

   preparing for a test

   losing weight

   composing a professional email

   operating a cash register

   breaking up with a boyfriend or girlfriend

   getting good tips while working as a restaurant server

   acquiring as many friends as possible on Facebook

   driving a stick shift

   getting up in the morning

   securing your mobile phone via password

   creating a website

   operating a forklift or backhoe

   changing the oil in a car

   changing a tire

   breaking a specific habit

   winning an online auction

   installing speakers in a car

2. Write about the wrong way to do something, or the wrong way you (or someone else) did it. You can use any of the topics in the list in question 1, or you can choose your own topic.

3. Imagine that a friend is about to register for classes at your college. This will be your friend's first semester at the college. Write a paragraph giving your friend clear directions for registering. Make sure to have an appropriate topic sentence.

4. Interview one of the counsellors at your college. Ask the counsellor to tell you the steps for applying for financial aid. Take notes or tape the interview. Get copies of any forms that are included in the application process. Ask questions about these forms.

   After the interview, write a paragraph explaining the process of applying for financial aid. Your explanation is directed at a Grade 12 student who has never applied for aid.

5. Interview someone whose cooking you admire. Ask that person to tell you the steps involved in making a certain dish. Take notes or tape the interview.

   After the interview, write a paragraph (*not* a recipe) explaining how to prepare the dish. Your paragraph will explain the process to someone who is a beginner at cooking.

WRITING FROM READING: PROCESS

How to Get a Reference Letter
Andrew Potter

Andrew Potter is a columnist for Maclean's *magazine. This article originally appeared in the magazine's 2007 University Rankings issue.*

Before you read this selection, consider these questions:

Have you ever asked for a reference letter? Why?

How do you decide whom to ask for a reference letter?

What do you think is the best way to get the best possible reference letter?

distressing: upsetting

With **distressing** regularity, anyone who has taught in a university for any length of time receives an email that goes something like this:

Dear Professor Smith,
You probably don't remember me, but I was a student in your Intro 101 class back in 200X. After working for a few years, I've decided I would like to go to graduate school, and was wondering if I could possibly trouble you for a reference letter. I got a 74 per cent in your class, and I have appended my résumé showing what I have been up to since I graduated. I know this is a shot in the dark, but you are almost the only professor I could even ask, and I could really use your help.

Sincerely yours,
"A" student

Reference letters are a necessary part of any application to graduate or professional school, along with a writing sample, statement of research interest, standardized test scores, and a transcript. The relative importance of each of these varies depending on the discipline and department, with grades and test scores mattering a great deal for admission to law and medicine, whereas humanities departments tend

ubiquitous: everywhere

to pay more attention to the writing sample. Yet backing it all up are the **ubiquitous** reference letters, testimonials written on the student's behalf speaking to his or her ability, character and personality.

meek: submissive

sheepish: embarrassed

Unfortunately, many students shoot themselves in the foot when it comes to getting reference letters, and those who write **meek** pleas like the one above are making two fundamental errors. The first is pretty simple to fix: don't be **sheepish** or apologetic. Writing reference letters for students is not a favour that professors grant to their students, it is one of their professional obligations. Crazy as it seems, professors want to get their best students into grad schools, and writing strong letters on their behalf is part of the job.

The second mistake is a bit harder to fix after the fact. The time to start making your case for a reference letter is not when you decide to go to graduate school. Rather, you need to start setting the stage for possible letters when you are still an undergrad, with your academic future still dimly imagined. This stage is built on three pillars: your course selection, your choice of professors, and your behaviour in class.

Start with course selection. It is hard for profs to get to know you in a class of 200 or 300 students, which is why you have to find at least a couple of courses, preferably in the upper years, that have a maximum enrolment of 30 students or so. Take these courses even if you aren't particularly interested in the topic, since the attention and recognition you will get from the professor will more than make up for dull content.

off-load: to get rid of by giving it to someone else

adjunct: someone or something of lesser rank

itinerant: travelling

Second of all, pay attention to who is teaching the class. At almost every university in Canada a great deal of instruction is being **off-loaded** to grad students, **adjunct** faculty and contract workers. They tend to be young and desperate, and consequently put a lot of effort into their teaching. But they are also **itinerant** workers, with very little status within the profession. When you go looking for reference letters a few years down the road it might be hard just finding them, since they could be literally anywhere in the world. And even when you do track them down, chances are that they will be either still working on contracts, or even out of the academic business altogether. In either case, any reference they give you will carry relatively little weight within the profession. So when selecting your courses, do a quick check in the department calendar and find out which instructors are permanent members of the faculty, and take as many of their classes as you can.

Finally, it is useful to keep one thing in mind: professors can only write you a good letter if they know who you are, what you are like, and how your mind works. It is very hard to write a strong letter for a student when all you can really say is that "so-and-so took my class and got a B+." So do all the readings and go to class. And when you are in class, ask a lot of questions. Then make a point of dropping by during the prof's office hours, and pepper him or her with comments about the lecture or the readings or the assignment. In short, be the annoying keener that everyone hates.

References aren't the most important part of your application, and it would take a truly outstanding letter to make up for miserable grades or an incompetent writing sample. But reference letters are a necessary part of your application, and they signal your acceptance into a community of scholars. If you are an undergraduate student

mercenary: acting just
for money or other
reward
with even the slightest thought that you might someday want to go on to graduate school, it is never too early to start working on getting those letters. Be as strategic and **mercenary** about it as possible—you have nothing to apologize for.

UNDERSTANDING "HOW TO GET A REFERENCE LETTER"

1. What are the two mistakes Potter claims students make when requesting reference letters?

2. Why does Potter suggest that it's important to consider who is teaching the course?

3. Why do you think it might be difficult for students to be "strategic and mercenary" about securing reference letters, as Potter suggests?

WRITING FROM READING "HOW TO GET A REFERENCE LETTER"

When you write on any of these topics, be sure to work through the stages of the writing process in preparing your process paragraph.

1. Andrew Potter encourages being an "annoying keener." However, there is a fine line between being memorable and being annoying. Write a humorous process paragraph that describes how to ensure you get a *negative* reference letter.

2. Reverse the roles: pretend *you* are the professor, and one of your students has asked you to write him or her a reference letter. Write a process paragraph describing how to write (a) a positive reference letter or (b) a negative reference letter.

3. Has anyone ever asked you for a favour? What if you didn't feel comfortable doing this favour? Write a paragraph outlining the steps you would take to decline without hurting the other person's feelings.

4. Many schools have very specific processes that candidates must follow when applying to their programs. Do some research and write a process paragraph detailing the steps a candidate must follow to apply.

CHAPTER 7
Comparison and Contrast

"Shadow owes its birth to light."

~ JOHN GAY

▼
JOHN GAY WAS AN
EIGHTEENTH-CENTURY
POET AND DRAMATIST.

WHAT IS COMPARISON? WHAT IS CONTRAST?

To **compare** means to point out *similarities*. To **contrast** means to point out *differences*. When you compare or contrast, you need to come to some conclusion. It's not enough to say, "These two things are similar" or "These two things are different." Your reader will be asking, "So what? What's your point?" For example, you may be pointing out the differences between eyeglasses and contact lenses in order to explain which is more convenient to wear:

> If you have an active lifestyle, you may choose to wear contact lenses rather than eyeglasses.

Or you may be explaining the similarities between two family members to show how people with similar personalities can clash:

> My cousin Bill and my brother Karram are both so stubborn, they can't get along.

Hints for Writing a Comparison or Contrast Paragraph

1. **Limit your topic.** When you write a comparison or contrast paragraph, you might think that the easiest topics to write about are broad ones with many similarities or differences. However, if you make your topic too large, you won't be able to cover it well, and your paragraph will be full of very general, boring statements.

   Here are some topics that are too large for a comparison or contrast paragraph: two countries, two periods in history, two kinds of addiction, two wars, two economic or political systems, two prime ministers.

2. **Avoid the obvious topic.** Some students may think it's easier to write about two things if the similarities or differences between them are obvious, but with an obvious topic you'll have nothing new to say, and you'll risk writing a boring paragraph.

   Here, for example, are two obvious topics: the differences between high school and college, and the similarities between desktops and laptops. If you're drawn to an obvious topic, *try a new angle* on the topic. Write about the unexpected, using the same topic. Write about the similarities between high school and college, or the differences between desktops and laptops. You may have to do more thinking before you come up with ideas, but your ideas may be more interesting to write about and to read.

3. **Make your point in the topic sentence of your comparison or contrast paragraph.** Indicate whether the paragraph is about similarities or differences in topic sentences like these:

   Because of its portability, a tablet is a better choice for a college student than a laptop.

   (The phrase "better choice" indicates differences.)

   My two botany teachers share a love of the environment and a passion for protecting it.

   (The word "share" indicates similarities.)

4. **Do not announce in the topic sentence.** The sentences below are announcements, not topic sentences.

   I will discuss why a tablet is a better choice for a college student than a laptop.

   This paper will explain the similarities between my two botany teachers.

5. **Make sure your topic sentence has a focus.** It should indicate similarities or differences; it should focus on the specific kind of comparison or contrast you will make.

not focused:	My old house is different from my new house.
focused:	My new home is bigger, brighter, and more comfortable than my old one.

6. **The topic sentence should cover both subjects to be compared or contrasted.**

only one subject:	The beach at Santa Lucia was dirty and crowded.
both subjects:	The beach at Santa Lucia was dirty and crowded, but the beach at Fisher Bay was clean and private.

Be careful. It's easy to get so carried away by the details of your paragraph that you forget to put both subjects into one sentence.

EXERCISE

1

IDENTIFYING SUITABLE TOPIC SENTENCES FOR A COMPARISON OR CONTRAST PARAGRAPH

Below is a list of possible topic sentences for a comparison or contrast paragraph. Some would make good topic sentences. The ones that wouldn't make good topic sentences have one or more of these problems: they are announcements, they don't indicate whether the paragraph will be about similarities or differences, they don't focus on the specific kind of comparison or contrast to be made, they cover subjects that are too big to write about in one paragraph, or they don't cover both subjects.

Mark the problem sentences with an *X*. If a sentence would make a good topic sentence for a comparison or contrast paragraph, mark it *OK*.

1. _____ I have two friends, Rick and Luke.
2. _____ My two close friends, Rick and Luke, are very similar.
3. _____ My two close friends, Rick and Luke, are alike in their athletic ability and obsession with sports.
4. _____ Canada and the United States are similar in their economic system, history, and culture.
5. _____ Laptops are better because they're more powerful and have more storage space.
6. _____ This paragraph will discuss the similarities between tea and Red Bull energy drink.
7. _____ Men and women are different in their physical, intellectual, and emotional makeup.
8. _____ On the one hand, there is community college, and then there is university.
9. _____ Mr. Sheridan is a more energetic and enthusiastic teacher than Mr. Smith.
10. _____ My second semester in college was a big improvement over my first.

Organizing Your Comparison or Contrast Paragraph

Whether you decide to write about similarities (to compare) or differences (to contrast), you'll have to decide how to organize your paragraph. You can choose between two patterns of organization: *subject-by-subject* and *point-by-point*.

Subject-by-Subject Organization In the subject-by-subject pattern, you support and explain your topic sentence by first writing all your details on one subject and then writing all your details on the other subject. If you choose a subject-by-subject pattern, make sure to discuss the points for your second subject *in the same order* as you did for the first subject. For example, if your first subject is an amusement park, you might cover (1) the price of admission, (2) the length of lines at rides, and (3) the quality of the rides. When you discuss the second subject, another amusement park, you should write about its prices, length of lines, and quality of rides in the same order.

Look carefully at the following outline and the comparison paragraph for a subject-by-subject pattern.

A Comparison Outline: Subject-by-Subject Pattern

topic sentence: Once I realized that my brother and my mother are very much alike in temperament, I understood why they don't get along.

details:

first subject, James—temper, unkind words, stubbornness

My brother James is a hot-tempered person.

It's easy for him to lose control of his temper.

When he does, he often says things he later regrets.

James is also very stubborn.

In an argument, he will never admit he's wrong.

Once we were arguing about baseball scores.

Even when I showed him the right score, printed in the paper, he wouldn't admit he was wrong.

He said that the newspaper had made a mistake.

James's stubbornness overtakes his common sense.

second subject, mother—temper, unkind words, stubbornness

James has inherited many of his character traits from our mother.

She has a quick temper, and anything can provoke it.

Once, she got angry because she had to wait too long at a traffic light.

She also has a tendency to use unkind words when she's angry.

She never backs down from a disagreement or concedes that she was wrong.

My mother even quit a job because she refused to admit she'd made a mistake in taking inventory.

Her pride can lead her into foolish acts.

After I realized how similar my brother and mother are, I understood how such inflexible people are likely to clash.

A Comparison Paragraph: Subject-by-Subject Pattern

first subject, James

Once I realized that my brother and my mother are very much alike in temperament, I understood why they don't get along. My brother James is a hot-tempered person. It's easy for him to lose control of his temper, and when he does, he often says things he regrets. James is also very stubborn. In an argument, he will never admit he's wrong. I remember one time when we were arguing about baseball scores. Even when I showed him the right score, printed in the newspaper, he wouldn't admit he was wrong. James insisted that the newspaper must have made a mistake in printing the score. As this example shows, sometimes James's stubbornness overtakes James's common sense. It took me a while to realize that my stubborn brother James has inherited many of his traits from our mother. Like James, she has a quick temper, and almost anything

second subject, mother

> can provoke it. She once got angry because she had to wait too long at a traffic light. She also shares James's habit of saying unkind things when she's angry. And just as James refuses to back down when he's wrong, my mother will never back down from a disagreement or concede that she's wrong. In fact, my mother once quit a job because she refused to admit she'd made a mistake in taking inventory. Her pride is as powerful as James's pride, and it can be just as foolish. After I realized how similar my mother and brother are, I understood how such inflexible people are likely to clash.

Look carefully at the paragraph in the subject-by-subject pattern, and you'll note that it

- begins with a topic sentence about both subjects—James and his mother;
- gives all the details about one subject—James; and
- then gives all the details about the second subject—his mother—in the same order.

Point-by-Point Organization In the point-by-point pattern, you support and explain your topic sentence by discussing each point of comparison or contrast, switching back and forth between your subjects. You explain one point for each subject, then explain another point for each subject, and so on.

Look carefully at the outline and the comparison paragraph that follows for the point-by-point pattern.

A Comparison Outline: Point-by-Point Pattern

topic sentence: Once I realized that my brother and my mother are very much alike in temperament, I understood why they don't get along.

details:

1st point, temper

My brother James is a hot-tempered person.

It's easy for him to lose control of his temper.

My mother has a quick temper, and anything can provoke it.

Once she got angry because she had to wait too long at a traffic light.

2nd point, unkind words

When my brother gets angry, he often says things he regrets.

My mother has a tendency to use unkind words when she's angry.

3rd point, stubbornness

James is very stubborn.

In an argument, he will never admit he's wrong.

Once we were arguing about baseball scores.

Even when I showed him the right score, printed in the paper, he wouldn't admit he was wrong.

(continued)

He said the newspaper had made a mistake.

James's stubbornness overtakes his common sense.

My mother will never back down from a disagreement or admit that she's wrong.

She even quit a job because she refused to admit she'd made a mistake in taking inventory.

She was foolish in her stubbornness.

After I realized how similar my mother and brother are, I understood how such inflexible people are likely to clash.

> ## A Comparison Paragraph: Point-by-Point Pattern

Once I realized that my brother and my mother are very much alike in temperament, I understood why they don't get along. My
1st point brother is a hot-tempered person, and it's easy for him to lose control of his temper. My mother shares James's quick temper, and anything can provoke her anger. Once, she got angry because she had to wait too long at a traffic light. When my brother gets angry,
2nd point he often says things he regrets. Similarly, my mother is known for the unkind things she's said in anger. James is a very stubborn
3rd point person. In an argument, he will never admit he's wrong. I can remember one argument we were having over baseball scores. Even when I showed him the right score, printed in the newspaper, he wouldn't admit he had been wrong. He simply insisted that the paper had made a mistake. At times like this, James's stubbornness overtakes his common sense. Like her son, my mother will never back down from an argument or admit she was wrong. She even quit a job because she refused to admit she'd made a mistake in taking inventory. In that case, her stubbornness was as foolish as James's. It took me a while to see the similarities between my brother and mother. Yet after I realized how similar these two people are, I understood how two inflexible people are likely to clash.

Look carefully at the paragraph in the point-by-point pattern, and you'll note that it

- begins with a topic sentence about both subjects—James and his mother;
- discusses how both James and his mother are alike in these points—their quick tempers, the unkind things they say in a temper, and their often foolish stubbornness; and
- switches back and forth between the two subjects.

Subject-by-subject and point-by-point patterns can be used for either a comparison or a contrast paragraph. But whatever pattern you choose, remember these hints:

1. **Make sure to use the same points to compare or contrast two subjects.** If you're contrasting two cars, you can't discuss the price and safety features

of one and the styling and speed of the other. You must discuss the price of both, or the safety features, or styling, or speed of both.

You don't have to list the points in your topic sentence, but you can include them, like this: "My old Celica turned out to be a cheaper, safer, and faster car than my boyfriend's new Dart."

2. **Make sure to give roughly equal space to both subjects.** This rule doesn't mean you must write the same number of words—or even sentences—on both subjects. It does mean you should be giving fairly equal attention to the details of both subjects.

Since you'll be writing about two subjects, this type of paragraph can involve more details than other paragraph formats. Thus, a comparison or contrast paragraph may be longer than twelve sentences.

3. **Consider using two paragraphs, one for each subject.** If your comparison or contrast becomes too lengthy, use one paragraph for all your details on one subject and then a second paragraph for all your details on the other subject.

Using Transitions Effectively for Comparison or Contrast

The transitions you use in a comparison or a contrast paragraph, as well as when to use them, depend on the answers to two questions:

1. Are you writing a comparison or a contrast paragraph?

   - When you choose to write a *comparison* paragraph, you use transition words, phrases, or sentences that point out *similarities*.
   - When you choose to write a *contrast* paragraph, you use transition words, phrases, or sentences that point out *differences*.

2. Are you organizing your paragraph in the point-by-point or subject-by-subject pattern?

   - When you choose to organize your paragraph in the *point-by-point pattern,* you need transitions *within each point* and *between points*.
   - When you choose to organize your paragraph in the *subject-by-subject pattern,* you need to place *most of your transitions* in the *second half* of the paragraph, to remind the reader of the points you made in the first half.

The Infobox lists some transitions you can use in writing comparison or contrast paragraphs. There are many others that may be appropriate for your ideas.

INFOBOX	TRANSITIONS FOR A COMPARISON OR A CONTRAST PARAGRAPH

To show similarities: additionally, again, also, and, as well as, both, each of, equally, furthermore, in addition, in the same way, just like, like, likewise, similarly, similar to, too, so

To show differences: although, but, conversely, different from, despite, even though, except, however, in contrast to, instead of, in spite of, nevertheless, on the other hand, otherwise, still, though, unlike, whereas, while, yet

Writing a comparison or contrast paragraph challenges you to make decisions: Will I compare or contrast? Will I use a point-by-point or a subject-by-subject pattern? These decisions will determine what kind of transitions you'll use and where you will use them.

| EXERCISE **2** | **WRITING APPROPRIATE TRANSITIONS FOR A COMPARISON OR CONTRAST PARAGRAPH** |

Below are pairs of sentences. First, decide whether each pair shows a comparison or a contrast. Then combine the two sentences into one, using an appropriate transition (either a word or phrase).

You may have to rewrite parts of the original sentences to create one smooth sentence. The first pair is done for you.

1. Dr. Cheung is a professor of art.

   Dr. Mbala is a professor of history.

   combined: Dr. Cheung is a professor of art while Dr. Mbala is a professor of
   history.

2. *Dr. Doolittle* featured animals that talked.

   In *Babe*, farm animals spoke.

   combined: _____

   _____

3. Small children are often afraid to leave their parents.

   Teenagers can't wait to get away from their parents.

   combined: _____

   _____

4. Urban living can be stressful and expensive.

   Living in the country can be economical and idyllic.

   combined: _____

   _____

5. Exercise can help you fight heart disease, lower your cholesterol levels, and relieve stress.

   A doctor can give you medicine for heart disease, high cholesterol, or stress.

   combined: _____

   _____

6. Ms. Colletti is outgoing and loves meeting new people.

   Mr. Colletti enjoys hosting dinner parties and organizing community events.

   combined: _____

   _____

7. Introduction to Philosophy was a challenging course that developed my skills in reasoning.

   College Writing, a tough course, taught me how to think and reason.

   combined: _____

   _____

8. Camping takes work and can be uncomfortable.
   Staying in a motel is easy and pleasant.
   combined: _____

   _____

9. Staying in a motel costs money.
   Camping requires expensive supplies.
   combined: _____

   _____

10. My co-workers at The Sports Store were friendly and supportive.
    The people I worked with at Bruno's Subs created a warm and helpful
    working environment.
    combined: _____

WRITING THE COMPARISON OR CONTRAST PARAGRAPH IN STEPS

PREWRITING   GATHERING IDEAS: COMPARISON OR CONTRAST

One way to get started on a comparison or a contrast paragraph is to list as many differences or similarities as you can on one topic. Then you can see whether you have more similarities (comparisons) or more differences (contrasts), and decide which approach to use. For example, if you're asked to compare or contrast two methods of transportation, you could begin with a list like this:

> **List for Two Methods of Transportation: Car and Public Transit**
>
> **similarities**
>
>   both use fuel
>
>   both can be convenient
>
> **differences**
>
> | Car | Public Transit |
> | --- | --- |
> | comfortable | crowded |
> | expensive | affordable |
> | bad for the environment | environmentally friendly |
> | uses gasoline | uses gasoline, electricity, biofuel |

Getting Points of Comparison or Contrast

Whether you compare or contrast, you're looking for points of comparison or contrast, items you can discuss about both subjects.

If you surveyed the list on the two methods of transportation and decided you wanted to contrast the two, you'd see that you already have these points of contrast:

environmental impact   cost   convenience   fuel

To write your paragraph, start with several points of comparison or contrast. As you work through the stages of writing, you may decide that you don't need all the points you've jotted down, but it's better to start with too many points than with too few.

EXERCISE

3

DEVELOPING POINTS OF COMPARISON OR CONTRAST

Do this exercise with a partner or a group. Below are some topics that could be used for a comparison or a contrast paragraph. Underneath each topic, write three points of comparison or contrast. Be prepared to share your answers. The first topic is done for you.

1. **topic:** Compare or contrast two television reality shows.
    points of comparison or contrast:

    a. the host

    b. the kinds of "challenges" participants face

    c. the prizes

2. **topic:** Compare or contrast a movie and its sequel.
    points of comparison or contrast:

    a. _____

    b. _____

    c. _____

3. **topic:** Compare or contrast two holidays.
    points of comparison or contrast:

    a. _____

    b. _____

    c. _____

4. **topic:** Compare or contrast two college courses.
    points of comparison or contrast:

    a. _____

    b. _____

    c. _____

5. **topic:** Compare or contrast two professional athletes.
    points of comparison or contrast:

    a. _____

    b. _____

    c. _____

EXERCISE 4

FINDING DIFFERENCES IN SUBJECTS THAT LOOK SIMILAR

Below are pairs of subjects that are very similar but do have some differences. List three differences for each pair.

1. **subject:** Burger King and McDonald's
   differences:

   a. _____

   b. _____

   c. _____

2. **subject:** Facebook and Twitter
   differences:

   a. _____

   b. _____

   c. _____

3. **subject:** external hard drives and USB drives
   differences:

   a. _____

   b. _____

   c. _____

4. **subject:** SUVs and minivans
   differences:

   a. _____

   b. _____

   c. _____

5. **subject:** motorcycles and motor scooters
   differences:

   a. _____

   b. _____

   c. _____

EXERCISE 5

FINDING SIMILARITIES IN SUBJECTS THAT LOOK DIFFERENT

Below are pairs of subjects that are different but have some similarities. List three similarities for each pair.

1. **subject:** attending college part-time and attending college full-time
   similarities:

   a. _____

   b. _____

   c. _____

2. **subject:** downloading a movie and going to a movie
   similarities:

   a. _____

   b. _____

   c. _____

3. **subject:** working the night shift and working daytime hours
   similarities:

   a. _____

   b. _____

   c. _____

4. **subject:** love and hate
   similarities:

   a. _____

   b. _____

   c. _____

5. **subject:** starting a new business and starting a new relationship
   similarities:

   a. _____

   b. _____

   c. _____

Adding Details to Your Points

Once you have some points, you can begin adding details. The details may lead you to more points. Even if they don't, the process will help you develop the ideas of your paragraph.

If you were to write about the differences in methods of transportation, for example, your new list with added details might look like this:

> ## List for a Contrast of Two Methods of Transportation
>
> | Car | Public Transit |
> | --- | --- |
> | significant environmental impact—emissions contribute to greenhouse effect | less impact on the environment because it transports more people |
> | certain driving habits increase fuel usage | reduces wear on roads and highways |
> | cost—costs lots of money to buy a car | cash fares for one trip are usually no more than $3.50 in Canada |
> | maintenance and upkeep of the car cost money every month | can purchase monthly pass |
> | convenience—you can go anywhere, any time | you often have to wait for the bus, street-car, or subway |
> | driver's comfort—climate control, music, seat | public transportation is often crowded, noisy, and uncomfortable |
> | fuel—usually gasoline, sometimes a hybrid of gasoline and electric | sometimes gasoline, often electricity or biofuel |

Reading the list about transportation, you might conclude that while a car may be more convenient and comfortable, public transit may still be preferable. Why? There are several hints within your list: for example, a car is more expensive and has more of a negative impact on the environment.

Now that you have a point, you can put it into a topic sentence. A topic sentence contrasting the methods of transportation could be

> In the ongoing car versus public transit debate, does convenience outweigh cost
>
> and the impact on the environment?

Once you have a possible topic sentence, you can begin working on the outline stage of your paragraph.

EXERCISE 6

WRITING TOPIC SENTENCES FOR COMPARISON OR CONTRAST

Below are lists of details. Some are for comparison paragraphs; some are for contrast paragraphs. Read each list carefully; then write a topic sentence for each list.

1. topic sentence: _____

   _____

   ### List of Details

living alone	**having a roommate**
advantages—privacy; no need to share; quiet; no conflicts	lots of space; cheaper; never lonely; always have support
disadvantages—more costly; no emotional support	conflicts may arise; different lifestyles

2. topic sentence: _____

_____

List of Details

traditional books	**digital books**
availability—the general public	those with access to the appropriate technology
cost—anywhere from free at the public library to $35 for a new hardcover release; value may increase with age	anywhere from free at the public library to $15 for a newly released downloaded book; likely no value for a digital book
longevity—can last indefinitely with proper care	likely deleted after reading in order to free up space for other books

3. topic sentence: _____

_____

List of Details

pick-up truck	**sport utility vehicle (e.g., Bronco, Explorer)**
seating—for two	seats four or five
room to carry things—large truck bed covered by canvas or permanently closed	large covered space behind seats, but not as big as pick-up's space
good for rough terrain, hunting and fishing, hauling and moving, construction work	good for country driving but also for suburban families with space for toys, baby strollers, car seats

4. topic sentence: _____

_____

List of Details

pick-up truck	**sport utility vehicle**
buyers—popular with young people, outdoor enthusiasts, farmers	people in their twenties, people who camp or fish
image—a rugged, solid, practical vehicle	fashionable, rugged, useful
accessories available—USB port, fancy speakers, air conditioning	luxurious interiors, USB port and speakers, air conditioning

communication at work

On the job, many employers turn to their experienced and specialized staff to help them make sound business decisions. For instance, your boss may tell you that your company is thinking of outsourcing its network security. Knowing that you're an expert in the field, she may ask you to prepare a report comparing and/or contrasting two competing vendors. What aspects do you think you would compare or contrast?

PLANNING DEVISING A PLAN: COMPARISON OR CONTRAST

Once you have a topic sentence, you can begin to draft an outline. Before you can write an outline, however, you have to make a decision: What pattern do you want to use in organizing your paragraph? Do you want to use the subject-by-subject or the point-by-point pattern?

The following box shows an outline of a contrast paragraph using a point-by-point pattern.

An Outline of a Contrast Paragraph: Point-by-Point Pattern

topic sentence: In the ongoing car versus public transit debate, does convenience outweigh cost and the impact on the environment?

details:

1st point: environmental impact

Emissions from cars contribute to the greenhouse effect.

Idling the engine, speeding, and other driving habits can increase fuel usage.

Larger vehicles such as SUVs use considerably more fuel than smaller cars.

The production of personal vehicles uses many resources, including petroleum.

Public transportation has a smaller impact on the environment because it can transport significantly more people than a car.

Fewer vehicles on the roads means less wear on roads and highways, which would need to be maintained and repaired less often.

The use of buses, subways, streetcars, and other means of public transportation can reduce traffic and pollution.

2nd point: cost

It can cost anywhere from hundreds to hundreds of thousands of dollars to purchase a car.

Maintenance and upkeep on a car cost money every month.

Insurance can be very expensive.

The price of gasoline keeps increasing.

Cash fares for one transit trip are usually no more than $3.50 in Canada.

Transit riders can save money by purchasing monthly passes.

Some transit passes allow riders unlimited rides in a certain time frame.

In some cities, one payment gives riders access to the whole system.

3rd point: convenience

Having access to a car means you can go anywhere, any time.

Everything can be adjusted to the driver's liking: climate control, music, the seat.

It's often much faster to drive than to take public transit, as there is no need to wait for a vehicle to arrive.

It's much easier to transport heavy items or to shop with a car.

Public transit is often crowded, noisy, and uncomfortable.

Public transit doesn't always run on schedule.

conclusion

Though costly, a car can certainly be convenient. However, is the convenience worth the cost to the environment?

Once you've drafted an outline, check it. Use the checklist below to help you review and revise your outline.

CHECKLIST   **FOR AN OUTLINE OF A COMPARISON OR A CONTRAST PARAGRAPH**

- ✓ Do I have enough details?
- ✓ Are all my details relevant?
- ✓ Have I covered all the points on both sides?
- ✓ If I'm using a subject-by-subject pattern, have I covered the points in the same order on both sides?
- ✓ Have I tried to cover too many points?
- ✓ Have I made my main idea clear?

Using this checklist as your guide, compare the outline with the prewriting list. You may notice some changes:

- The point on fuel has been omitted because there were some similarities between the two subjects; that is, both a car and some forms of public transportation use gasoline.
- A concluding sentence has been added to reinforce the main idea.

EXERCISE 7   **ADDING A POINT AND DETAILS TO A COMPARISON OR A CONTRAST OUTLINE**

The following outline is too short. Develop it by adding a point of contrast and details about both colleges.

topic sentence: Carson College is a friendlier place than Wellington College.

details: When a person enters Carson College, he or she sees groups of students who seem happy.
They're sprawled on the steps and on the lawns, looking as if they're having a good time.
They're laughing and talking to each other.
At Wellington College, everyone seems to be a stranger.
Students are isolated.
They lean against the wall or sit alone, reading intently or staring into space.
The buildings at Carson seem open and inviting.
There are many large glass windows in each classroom.
There are wide, airy corridors.
Many signs help newcomers find their way around.
Wellington College seems closed and forbidding.
It has dark, windowless classrooms.
The halls are narrow and dirty.
There are no signs or directions posted on the buildings.

Add a new point of contrast, with details about each college: _____

_____

_____

_____

_____

_____

EXERCISE **8**	**FINDING IRRELEVANT DETAILS IN A COMPARISON OR CONTRAST OUTLINE**

The following outline contains some irrelevant details. Cross out the details that don't fit.

topic sentence: My daughter's fourth birthday party and my high school graduation ceremony showed that people of all ages celebrate in similar ways.

details: Last week, my daughter Nina's friends dressed in their best for her birthday party.
The girls wore frilly or flowered dresses.
The boys sported new shirts and clean shoes.
I always loved to go barefoot when I was a child.
Years ago, my classmates and I were also elaborately dressed.
We were self-conscious in our graduation caps and gowns.
Some of us wore special hoods or coloured tassels.
The children at the party were eager for the fun to get started.
They wanted to play, but their parents had told them to behave.
Some children are too good to be true.
They misbehave at home but are angels in public.
The graduates were eager to get their diplomas.
They fidgeted in their chairs as the guest speaker droned on.
He was the president of a large corporation.
They looked behind them at their families and friends.
But they tried to behave because the vice-principal had warned them that she would be watching.
When Nina's four-year-old friends heard some music playing, they began to loosen up.
They started to jump around, dance, and giggle.
Soon, they were wild with happiness.
When the graduates had all received their diplomas, they let themselves go.
They jumped up, tossed their caps in the air, and hugged each other.
Their parents started taking photographs.
Soon, the graduates filled the air with laughter and shouts of victory.

EXERCISE
9

REVISING THE ORDER IN A COMPARISON OR A CONTRAST OUTLINE

Below is an outline written in a subject-by-subject pattern. Rewrite the second half of the outline so that the points in the second half follow the order of the first half. You don't have to change any sentences; just rearrange them.

topic sentence: Young people and old people are both victims of society's prejudices.

details: Some people think young people aren't capable of mature thinking.
They think the young are on drugs.
They think the young are alcoholics.
The young are considered parasites because they don't earn a great deal of money.
Many young people are in college or university and not working full-time.
Many young people rely on help from their parents.
The young are outcasts because their appearance is different.
The young wear trendy fashions.
They have strange haircuts.
People may think the young are punks.
The way young people look makes other people afraid.
Old people are also judged by their appearance.
They are wrinkled or scarred or frail looking.
People are afraid of growing old and looking like that.
So they are afraid of the old.
Some people think elderly people aren't capable of mature thinking.
They think the old are on too much medication to think straight.
They think the old are senile.
Some people consider the old to be parasites because elderly people don't earn a great deal of money.
Some of the elderly have small pensions.
Some have only old-age pensions.
The young and the old are often stereotyped.

Rewritten order: _____

_____

_____

_____

_____

_____

_____

_____

_____

DRAFTING AND REVISING

DRAFTING AND REVISING: COMPARISON OR CONTRAST

When you've revised your outline, you can write the first draft of the transportation paragraph. After making a first draft, you may want to combine more sentences, rearrange your points, fix your topic sentence, or add vivid detail. You may also need to add transitions.

The Draft

Here is a draft version of the paragraph on contrasting two methods of transportation. As you read it, notice the changes from the outline: sentences have been combined and transitions have been added.

> ### A Draft of a Contrast Paragraph, Point-by-Point Pattern (*transitions are underlined*)
>
> In the ongoing car versus public transit debate, does convenience outweigh cost and the impact on the environment? Emissions from cars contribute to the greenhouse effect. Idling the engine, speeding, and other driving habits can increase fuel usage. Larger vehicles such as SUVs use considerably more fuel than smaller cars. The production of personal vehicles uses many resources, including petroleum. Public transportation, <u>on the other hand,</u> has a lesser impact on the environment because it can transport significantly more people than a car. Fewer vehicles on the roads means less wear on roads and highways, which would need to be replaced and repaired less often. The use of buses, subways, streetcars, and other means of public transportation can reduce traffic and pollution. <u>Cost is an important factor when choosing between a car and public transit.</u> It can cost anywhere from hundreds to hundreds of thousands of dollars to purchase a car. Maintenance and upkeep on a car cost money every month. Insurance can be very expensive, and the price of gasoline keeps increasing. Using public transit is much more affordable. Cash fares for one transit trip are usually no more than $3.50 in Canada. Frequent transit riders can save money by purchasing monthly passes. Some transit passes allow riders unlimited rides in a certain time frame. In some cities, one payment gives riders access to the whole system. <u>Convenience is usually the deciding factor in the debate.</u> Having access to a car means you can go anywhere, any time. <u>In a car,</u> everything can be adjusted to the driver's liking: climate control, music, and the seat. Often it's much faster to drive than to take public transit, as there is no need to wait for a vehicle to arrive. It's much easier to transport heavy items or to shop with a car. <u>Conversely,</u> public transit can be crowded, noisy, and

(continued)

uncomfortable. Public transit doesn't always run on schedule, so it can be diffi-

cult to get to appointments on time. <u>Though</u> costly, a car certainly can be conven-

ient. <u>However,</u> is the convenience worth the cost to the environment?

The following checklist may help you revise your own draft:

CHECKLIST   **FOR REVISING THE DRAFT OF A COMPARISON OR A CONTRAST PARAGRAPH**

✓ Did I include a topic sentence that covers both subjects?
✓ Is the paragraph in a clear order?
✓ Does it stick to one pattern, either subject-by-subject or point-by-point?
✓ Are both subjects given roughly the same amount of space?
✓ Do all the details fit?
✓ Are the details specific and vivid?
✓ Do I need to combine any sentences?
✓ Are transitions used effectively?
✓ Have I made my point?

EXERCISE

10

REVISING THE DRAFT OF A COMPARISON OR A CONTRAST PARAGRAPH BY ADDING VIVID DETAILS

You can do this exercise alone, with a writing partner, or with a group. The following contrast paragraph lacks the vivid details that could make it interesting. Read it, then rewrite the underlined parts in the space above the underlining. Replace the original words with more vivid details.

    My new car is giving me the same problems that I had in my old car. My old car, a Honda Civic, cost at least a hundred dollars a month to keep on the road. I was constantly paying for some minor but expensive repairs. One month, the car needed <u>three things</u> repaired. In addition, my Honda was uncomfortable. The seats were <u>not good,</u> and I always had to <u>sit funny.</u> Another irritation with the Honda was its little quirks. For example, the radio <u>never worked right.</u> I'd hoped to put all those problems behind me when I bought my new Nissan Pathfinder, but my hopes were not fulfilled. Just like my old car, my new one costs me <u>a lot</u> to keep on the road. This time, the money doesn't go to repairs; it goes to filling the gas tank. I hadn't realized that the Pathfinder would use quite so much gas. And while the Pathfinder has <u>nice</u> seats, I'm still uncomfortable. I'm not used to sitting so high off the ground. Also, I'm not used to stepping so far down when I get out of the vehicle. Finally, the car shares a radio problem with my old one. The Nissan's radio worked right—for a while. Then someone broke off my antenna, and now the radio doesn't work at all. Thinking of all the similar flaws in my two cars, I have concluded that I must accept them and pray that they won't show up in my next car.

EXERCISE **11**	REVISING A DRAFT BY COMBINING SENTENCES

The paragraph below has many short, choppy sentences, which are underlined. Whenever you see two or more underlined sentences next to each other, combine them into one smooth, clear sentence. Write the new sentence above the underlined portions.

Both my mother and my older sister, Andrea, treat me like a little boy. First of all, they both criticize my eating habits. <u>My mother is disturbed when she sees me eating chocolate-chip cookies for breakfast. She's upset if I drink Sprite for breakfast.</u> She doesn't believe that I'm getting the proper nutrition. <u>Andrea eats only health food. She gets concerned about my diet. She gets upset when she sees me eating junk food like Whoppers or fried chicken nuggets.</u> My mother and Andrea also monitor my comings and goings. <u>If I'm late getting home from work, my mother asks questions. She wants to know if the traffic was bad. She wonders if I had an accident.</u> Similarly, Andrea is always asking why I'm leaving late for school or whether I'm skipping classes. Worst of all, these two women investigate and evaluate my friends, particularly my girlfriends. My mother will ask, "Whatever happened to that sweet girl you were seeing? I really liked her." My sister is blunter. She's likely to say, "You'll never find a finer girl than your last girlfriend. You should apologize to her." If she doesn't like a girl I'm seeing, Andrea says, "You can do better than that." Although these comments irritate me, I love my mother and Andrea. <u>I know that my mother and sister care about me. I just wish they would treat me like an adult.</u>

PROOFREADING

PROOFREADING AND POLISHING: COMPARISON OR CONTRAST

Contrast Paragraph: Point-by-Point Pattern

Following is the revised version of the paragraph contrasting two methods of transportation, using a point-by-point pattern. When you read it, you'll notice several changes:

- Additional detail from the Canadian Automobile Association regarding the estimated costs to own and operate a car have been included.
- Detail has been added regarding the cost of car insurance.

- Additional, specific details about the cost of cash fares in cities across Canada has been added.
- The statement regarding access to the entire transit system with one payment has been clarified.
- Detail about not having to wait in the cold or the rain has been added.

> ## A Final Version of a Contrast Paragraph, Point-by-Point Pattern (*changes from the draft are underlined*)

In the ongoing car versus public transit debate, does convenience outweigh cost and the impact on the environment? Emissions from cars contribute to the greenhouse effect. Idling the engine, speeding, and other driving habits can increase fuel usage. Larger vehicles such as SUVs use considerably more fuel than smaller cars. The production of personal vehicles uses many resources, including petroleum. Public transportation, on the other hand, has a lesser impact on the environment because it can transport significantly more people than a car. Fewer vehicles on the roads means less wear on roads and highways, which would need to be replaced and repaired less often. The use of buses, subways, streetcars, and other means of public transportation can reduce traffic and pollution. Cost is an important factor when choosing between a car and public transportation. It can cost anywhere from hundreds to hundreds of thousands of dollars to purchase a car. Maintenance and upkeep on a car cost money every month. Insurance can be very expensive <u>depending on your driving experience and where you live,</u> and the price of gasoline keeps increasing. <u>The Canadian Automobile Association estimates that in 2014 it cost over $9200 per year to own and operate a compact car in Canada.</u> Using public transport is much more affordable. Cash fares for one transit trip cost <u>$2.25 in Charlottetown, $3.20 in Edmonton, and $3.00 in Toronto.</u> Frequent transit riders can save money by purchasing monthly passes. Some passes allow riders unlimited rides in a certain time frame. In some cities, payment for one trip gives riders access to the whole system, <u>from one end to the other.</u> Convenience is usually the deciding factor in the debate. Having access to a car means you can go anywhere, any time. In a car, everything can be adjusted to the driver's liking: climate control, music, and the seat. Often it's much faster to drive than to take public transit, as there is no need to wait for a vehicle to arrive, <u>possibly in the cold or the rain.</u> It's much easier to transport heavy items or to shop with a car. Conversely, public transit can be crowded, noisy, and uncomfortable. Public transit doesn't always run on

schedule, so it can be difficult to get to appointments on time. Though costly, a
car certainly can be convenient. However, is the convenience worth the cost to
the environment?

Before you prepare the final copy of your comparison or contrast paragraph,
check your latest draft for errors in spelling and punctuation, and for any errors
made in typing or recopying.

The Same Contrast Paragraph: Subject-by-Subject

To show you what the same paragraph contrasting methods of transportation would
look like in a subject-by-subject pattern, the outline, draft, and final versions follow.

An Outline: Subject-by-Subject Pattern

topic sentence: In the ongoing car versus public transport debate, does
convenience outweigh cost and the impact on the environment?

details:

1st subject: car

Emissions from cars contribute to the greenhouse effect.

Idling the engine, speeding, and other driving habits can increase fuel
usage.

Larger vehicles such as SUVs use considerably more fuel than
smaller cars.

The production of personal vehicles uses many resources, including
petroleum.

It can cost anywhere from hundreds to hundreds of thousands of dollars
to purchase a car.

Maintenance and upkeep on a car cost money every month.

Insurance can be very expensive.

The price of gasoline keeps increasing.

Having access to a car means you can go anywhere, any time.

Everything can be adjusted to the driver's liking: climate control, music,
the seat.

Often it's much faster to drive than to take public transit, as there is no
waiting for a vehicle to arrive.

It's much easier to transport heavy items or to shop with a car.

2nd subject: public transit

Public transit has less impact on the environment because it can transport significantly more people than a car.

Fewer vehicles on the roads mean less wear on roads and highways, which
would be replaced and repaired less often.

(continued)

The use of buses, subways, streetcars, and other means of public transportation can reduce traffic and pollution.
Cash fares for one trip are usually no more than $3.50 in Canada.
Transit riders can save money by purchasing monthly passes.
Some passes allow riders unlimited rides in a certain time frame.
In some cities, one payment gives riders access to the whole system.
Public transit can be crowded, noisy, and uncomfortable.
Public transit doesn't always run on schedule, so it can be difficult to get to appointments on time.

A Draft: Subject-by-Subject Pattern (*transitions are underlined*)

In the ongoing car versus public transit debate, does convenience outweigh cost and the impact on the environment? Emissions from cars contribute to the greenhouse effect. Idling the engine, speeding, and other driving habits can increase fuel usage. Larger vehicles such as SUVs use considerably more fuel than smaller cars. The production of personal vehicles uses many resources, including petroleum. There are many expenses when it comes to owning and operating a car. It can cost anywhere from hundreds to hundreds of thousands of dollars to purchase a car. Maintenance and upkeep on a car cost money every month. Insurance can be very expensive, and the price of gasoline keeps increasing. However, owning a car can be very convenient. Having access to a car means you can go anywhere, any time. Everything can be adjusted to the driver's liking: climate control, music, the seat. Often it's much faster to drive than to take public transit, as there is no waiting for a vehicle to arrive. It's much easier to transport heavy items or to shop with a car. <u>Public transit, on the other hand, does have its benefits.</u> Public transportation has less impact on the environment because it can move significantly more people than a car. Fewer vehicles on the roads means less wear on roads and highways, which would need to be replaced and repaired less often. The use of buses, subways, streetcars, and other means of public transportation can reduce traffic and pollution. Cash fares for one trip are usually no more than $3.50 in Canada. Frequent transit riders can save money by purchasing monthly passes. Some passes allow riders unlimited rides in a certain time frame. In some cities, one payment gives riders access to the whole system. Public transit can be crowded, noisy, and uncomfortable—and it doesn't always run on schedule, so it can be difficult to get to appointments on time. Though costly, a car can certainly be convenient. However, is the convenience worth the cost to the environment?

> ## A Final Version: Subject-by-Subject Pattern (*changes from the draft are underlined*)

In the ongoing car versus public transit debate, does convenience outweigh cost and the impact on the environment? Emissions from cars contribute to the greenhouse effect. Idling the engine, speeding, and other driving habits can increase fuel usage. Larger vehicles such as SUVs use considerably more fuel than smaller cars. The production of personal vehicles uses many resources, including petroleum. There are many expenses when it comes to owning and operating a car: it can cost anywhere from hundreds to hundreds of thousands of dollars to purchase a car, and maintenance and upkeep on a car cost money every month. Insurance can be very expensive depending on your driving experience and where you live, and the price of gasoline keeps increasing. The Canadian Automobile Association estimates that in 2014, it cost over $9200 per year to own and operate a compact car in Canada. However, owning a car can be very convenient. Having access to a car means you can go anywhere, any time. Everything can be adjusted to the driver's liking: climate control, music, the seat. Often it's much faster to drive than to take public transit, as there is no waiting for a vehicle to arrive, possibly in the cold or the rain. It's much easier to transport heavy items or to shop with a car. Public transit, on the other hand, does have its benefits. Public transportation has a lesser impact on the environment because it can move significantly more people than a car. Fewer vehicles on the roads means less wear on roads and highways, which would need to be replaced and repaired less often. The use of buses, subways, streetcars, and other means of public transportation can reduce traffic and pollution. Cash fares for one trip cost $2.25 in Charlottetown, $3.00 in Toronto, and $3.20 in Edmonton. Transit riders can save money by purchasing monthly passes. Some passes allow riders unlimited rides in a certain time frame. In some cities, payment for one trip gives riders access to the whole system, from one end to the other. Public transit can be crowded, noisy, and uncomfortable—and it doesn't always run on schedule, so it can be difficult to get to appointments on time. Though costly, a car can certainly be convenient. However, is the convenience worth the cost to the environment?

| EXERCISE **12** | **PROOFREADING TO PREPARE THE FINAL VERSION** |

Below are two comparison paragraphs with the kinds of errors that are easy to overlook in a final copy of an assignment. Correct the errors, writing your corrections above the lines. There are thirteen errors in the first paragraph and nine errors in the second paragraph.

1. My nephew's stuffed dog and my portable MP3 player meet the same needs in both of us. Brendan, who is four, won't go anywhere without the ragged stufed dog he loves. To him, that dog represents security I have seen him cry so long and so hard that his parents had to turn the car around and drive fifty kilometres to pick up the dog they forgot. My MP3 player is my security, and I take it everywere. I even take it to the library when I study; I just plug in the earphones. When Brendan feels tense, he runs to grab his dog. One day Brendans mother was yelling at him, an his face got puckered up and red. Brendan ran out of the room and hid in the corner of the hallway. He was clutching his dog. While I dont clutch my MP3 player, I do turn to my mussic to relax whenever I felt anxious. Brendan uses his toy to excape the world. I seen him sit silent for half an hour, holding his dog and starring into space. He is involved in some fantasy with his puppy. Whenever I feel tense, I turn on my music. It soothes me and puts me in a world of my own. I guess adults and children have there own ways of coping with conflict, and they have their own toys, too!

2. The last two Thanksgivings I celebrated were as different as the people who invited me to them. Two years ago, my sister Teresa asked me to come to her house for Thanksgiving dinner. When I arrive, the first think I noticed was an elaborately set table with white linen napkins, china plates, and a centrepiece of fresh flowers and autumn leaves. When we sat down at the table, Teresa set the tone for the formal diner. She made sure that her two sons pulled out chairs for their two great ants, and she slowly passed around the platters of food while her husband carved the turkey. After dinner, Teresa, who likes to be organized. got everyone to sit queitly in the living room, where we chatted politely about past holidays. My sister Camille had a completely diffrent kind of Thanksgiving last year. Camille is a casual person, so I was not surprised to see that when I got to her house, the table was not even sit. Instead, three or four people were coming from the kitchen, loading the table with bowls and platters of food. A pile of plastic utensils and paper plates sat on top of some large paper napkins. In the middle of all this food was a centrepiece of a paper turkey. At dinner time, everyone piled food on a paper plate and sat somewhere in the living room, or den.

People kept coming and going, grabbing or offering more food. After dinner, Camile sat back and watched a hockey game while others played cards or napped. From one holiday to the next, I had witnessed how personalities reveal themselves in family holidays.

Lines of Detail: A Walk-Through Assignment

Write a paragraph that compares or contrasts any experience you've heard about with your own experience living it. For example, you could compare or contrast what you heard about starting college with your actual experience of starting college. You could compare or contrast what you heard about falling in love with your experience of falling in love, or what you heard about playing a sport with your own experience playing that sport. To write your paragraph, follow these steps:

Step 1: Choose the experience you'll write about, then list all the similarities and differences between the experience as you heard about it and the experience as you lived it.

Step 2: To decide whether to write a comparison or a contrast paragraph, survey your list to see which has more details, the similarities or the differences.

Step 3: Add details to your comparison or contrast list. Survey your list again, and group the details into points of comparison or contrast.

Step 4: Write a topic sentence that includes both subjects, focuses on comparison or contrast, and makes a point.

Step 5: Decide whether your paragraph will be in the subject-by-subject or point-by-point pattern. Write your outline in the pattern you chose.

Step 6: Write a draft of your paragraph. Revise your draft, checking the transitions, the order of the points, and the space given to each point. For each subject, check the relevance and vividness of the details. Combine any short, choppy sentences.

Step 7: Before you prepare the final copy of your paragraph, edit for word choice, spelling, punctuation, and transitions.

Writing Your Own Comparison or Contrast Paragraph

When you write on one of these topics, make sure to follow the stages of the writing process.

1. Contrast what your appearance (or your behaviour) makes others think of you and what you're like below the surface of your appearance (or behaviour). If your instructor agrees, you can ask a writing partner or a group to give you ideas on what your appearance or behaviour says about you.
2. Contrast something you did in the past with the way you do the same thing today. For example, you could contrast the two ways (past and present) of studying, shopping, treating your friends, spending your free time, driving a car, or getting along with a parent or child.

3. Compare or contrast any of the following:

two fashion designers	two newspapers	two movies
two cars	two websites	two TV shows
two stores	two family traditions	two jobs
two athletic teams	two birthdays	two classes

If your instructor agrees, you may want to brainstorm points of comparison or contrast with a writing partner or with a group.

4. Imagine that you're a reporter who specializes in helping consumers get the best for their money, and that you've been asked to rate two brands of the same supermarket item. Write a paragraph advising your readers which is the better buy. You can rate two brands of cola, yogurt, potato chips, toothpaste, ice cream, chocolate-chip cookies, or paper towels— any item you can get in a supermarket.

   Make sure to come up with *enough* points of contrast. You can't, for example, do a well-developed paragraph on just the taste of two cookies. You can also discuss texture, colour, smell, price, fat content, calories, number of chocolate chips, and so on. If your instructor agrees, you may want to brainstorm topics or points of contrast with a group as a way of beginning the writing process. Then work on your own on the outline, draft, and final version.

5. Contrast your taste in music, or dress, or ways of spending leisure time with that of another generation.

6. If you've ever shopped online for sales or bargains offered by your favourite store, or a store without outlets in your area, contrast this experience with shopping inside the store itself. Select one specific store for this assignment, but make sure to contrast the specific differences between the two shopping choices. You should include three points of contrast in your paragraph.

7. Interview a person of your age group who comes from a different part of the country. (Note: There may be quite a few people from different parts of Canada in your class.) Ask him or her about similarities or differences between his or her former home and this part of the country. You could ask about similarities or differences in dress, music, dating, nightlife, ways to spend leisure time, favourite entertainers, or anything else you like.

   After the interview, write a paragraph that shows how people of the same age group from different parts of the country have either different tastes in music, dress, and so on, or share the same tastes in music, dress, and so on. Whichever approach you choose, use details you collected in the interview.

WRITING FROM READING: COMPARISON AND CONTRAST

Hey, Canada's One Cool Country
Samantha Bennett

Samantha Bennett is a columnist at the Pittsburgh Post-Gazette *and vice-president of the National Society of Newspaper Columnists. This article was later published in the* Toronto Star.

Before you read this selection, consider these questions:

Compare Canada with its closest neighbour and largest trading partner, the United States. Consider each country's politics, social programs, and culture. How are they similar? How are they different?

Do you think the United States is becoming more or less progressive?

Would you ever leave a country if you disagreed with its social or international policies?

You live next door to a clean-cut, quiet guy. He never plays loud music or throws **raucous** parties. He doesn't gossip over the fence, just smiles politely and offers you some tomatoes. His lawn is cared-for, his house is **neat as a pin** and you get the feeling he doesn't always lock his front door. He wears Dockers. You hardly know he's there.

And then one day you discover that he has pot in his basement, spends his weekends at peace marches and that guy you've seen mowing the yard is his spouse.

Allow me to introduce Canada.

The Canadians are so quiet that you may have forgotten they're up there, but they've been busy doing some surprising things. It's like discovering that the mice you are dimly aware of in your attic have been building an espresso machine.

Did you realize, for example, that our reliable little tag-along brother never joined the **Coalition of the Willing**? Canada wasn't willing, as it turns out, to join the fun in Iraq. I can only assume American diner menus weren't angrily changed to include "**freedom bacon**" because nobody here eats the stuff anyway.

And then there's the wild drug situation: Canadian doctors are authorized to dispense medical marijuana. Parliament is considering legislation that would not exactly legalize marijuana possession, as you may have heard, but would reduce the penalty for possession of under 15 grams to a fine, like a speeding ticket. This is to allow law enforcement to concentrate resources on traffickers. If your garden is full of wasps, it's smarter to go for the nest rather than trying to swat every individual bug. Or, in the United States, **bong**.

Now, here's the part that I, as an American, can't understand. These poor benighted **pinkos** are doing everything wrong. They have a drug problem. Marijuana offences have doubled since 1991. And Canada has strict gun control laws, which mean that the criminals must all be heavily armed, the law-abiding civilians helpless and the government on the verge of a massive confiscation campaign. (The laws have been in place since the '70s, but I'm sure the government will get around to the confiscation eventually.) They don't even have a death penalty!

And yet, nationally, overall crime in Canada has been declining since 1991. Violent crimes fell 13 per cent in 2002. Of course, there are still crimes committed with guns—brought in from the United States, which has become the major illegal weapons supplier for all of North America—but my theory is that the surge in pot-smoking has rendered most criminals too relaxed to commit violent crimes. They're probably more focused on shoplifting boxes of **Ho-Hos** from convenience stores.

---

raucous: loud

neat as a pin: extremely tidy

Coalition of the Willing: term used by former US president George W. Bush to refer to countries that would assist the United States in the war in Iraq

freedom bacon: Canadian bacon. This is a reference to the reaction some American restaurateurs had to France's refusal to join the Coalition of the Willing: "french fries" were changed to "freedom fries" on their menus

bong: device used to smoke marijuana or other drugs

pinkos: slang; a term once used to describe a person with leftist political views

Ho-Hos: American snack, something like a small cake

And then there's the most reckless move of all. Just last month, Canada decided to allow and recognize same-sex marriages. Merciful moose, what can they be thinking? Will there be married Mounties (they always get their man!)? **Dudley Do-Right** was sweet on Nell, not Mel! We must be the only ones who really care about families. Not enough to make sure they all have health insurance, of course, but more than those libertines up north.

This sort of behaviour is a clear and present danger to all our stereotypes about Canada. It's supposed to be a cold, wholesome country of polite, beer-drinking hockey players, not founded by freedom fighters in a bloody revolution, but quietly assembled by loyalists and royalists more interested in order and good government than liberty and independence.

But if we are the rugged individualists, why do we spend so much of our time trying to get everyone to march in **lockstep**? And if Canadians are so reserved and moderate, why are they so progressive about letting people do what they want to?

Canadians are, as a nation, less religious than we are, according to polls. As a result, Canada's government isn't influenced by large, well-organized religious groups and thus has more in common with those of Scandinavia than those of the United States, or, say, Iran.

Canada signed the Kyoto global warming treaty, lets 19-year-olds drink, has more of its population living in urban areas and accepts more immigrants per capita than the United States.

These are all things we've been told will wreck our society. But I guess Canadians are different, because theirs seems oddly sound.

Like teenagers, we fiercely idolize individual freedom but really demand that everyone be the same. But the Canadians seem more adult—more secure. They aren't afraid of foreigners. They aren't afraid of homosexuality. Most of all, they're not afraid of each other.

I wonder if America will ever be that cool.

UNDERSTANDING "HEY, CANADA'S ONE COOL COUNTRY"

1. Does Bennett use the subject-by-subject or point-by-point form of contrast? Do you think this form is more or less effective than the other for this topic?

2. Bennett uses humour throughout the article. Do you think this makes her article more or less effective?

3. Canada has been described as being more moderate than the United States. Why do you think this might be?

Dudley Do-Right: a Canadian Mountie featured in a television cartoon

lockstep: a rigid process, often mindlessly followed

WRITING FROM READING "HEY, CANADA'S ONE COOL COUNTRY"

When you write on any of the following topics, make sure to work through the stages of the writing process in preparing your paragraph.

1. Have you noticed any similarities between Canada and your home country? Write a paragraph comparing or contrasting one element (e.g., importance of family; approach to health care, child care, welfare) of the two countries.

2. What are some of the most common misperceptions that Americans have of Canada and Canadians? That Canadians have of Americans? Write a paragraph in which you compare or contrast these misperceptions.

3. It has long been thought that weather can have an impact on behaviour; Shakespeare alluded to this in *Romeo and Juliet* when a character suggests that, because of the hot weather, a fight would break out. Do you think Canadians are often considered polite because of our cool weather? Write a paragraph in which you compare or contrast "weather behaviours."

MyWritingLab

Go to MyWritingLab to access a diagnostic test that creates your own personalized learning path supported by rich multimedia resources and a variety of animated tutorials, all aimed at helping you improve your writing. MyWritingLab also includes a complete eText version of the book that is fully searchable and accessible through your web browser or most mobile devices.

CHAPTER 8
Classification

"What is set down by order and division doth demonstrate that nothing is left out or omitted, but all is there."

~ SIR FRANCIS BACON

▼
SIR FRANCIS BACON WAS AN ENGLISH PHILOSOPHER, STATESMAN, SCIENTIST, JURIST, ORATOR, ESSAYIST, AND AUTHOR.

WHAT IS CLASSIFICATION?

When you **classify**, you divide something into different categories, and you do it according to some basis. For example, you may classify the people in your neighbourhood into three categories: those you know well, those you know slightly, and those you don't know at all. Although you may not be aware of it, you've chosen a basis for this classification; that is, you're classifying the people in your neighbourhood according to *how well you know them*.

Hints for Writing a Classification Paragraph

1. **Divide your subject into three or more categories.** If you're thinking about classifying neighbourhoods, for instance, you might think about dividing them into residential and commercial neighbourhoods. Your basis for classification would be the zoning of neighbourhoods. But you would need at least one more zoning category—industrial neighbourhoods. Using at least three categories helps you to be reasonably complete in your classification.

2. **Choose one basis for classification and stick with it.** If you're classifying neighbourhoods on the basis of zoning, you can't divide them into residential, commercial, and expensive. Two of the categories relate to zoning, but "expensive" does not.

In the following examples, notice how one item doesn't fit its classification and has been crossed out:

anglers

anglers who fish every day

weekend anglers

~~anglers who own their own boat~~

anglers who fish once a year

(If you're classifying anglers on the basis of how often they fish, "anglers who own their own boat" doesn't fit.)

tests

essay tests

objective tests

~~math tests~~

combination essay and objective tests

(If you're classifying tests on the basis of the type of questions they ask, "math tests" doesn't fit because it describes the subject being tested.)

3. **Be creative in your classification.** While it's easy to classify drivers according to their age, your paragraph will be more interesting if you choose another basis of comparison, such as how drivers react to a very slow driver in front of them.

4. **Have a reason for your classification.** You may be classifying to help a reader understand a topic or to help a reader choose something. You may be trying to prove a point, to criticize, or to praise.

A classification paragraph must have a unifying reason behind it, and the details for each category should be as descriptive and specific as possible. Determining your audience and deciding why you're classifying can help you stay focused and make your paragraph more interesting.

EXERCISE 1	FINDING A BASIS FOR CLASSIFYING

Write three bases for classifying each of the following topics. The first topic is done for you.

1. **topic to classify:** jobs
   You can classify jobs on the basis of

   a. *what kind of education is required* _____

   b. *which industry they're in* _____

   c. *how much they pay* _____

2. **topic to classify:** cars
    You can classify cars on the basis of

    a. _____

    b. _____

    c. _____

3. **topic to classify:** children
    You can classify children on the basis of

    a. _____

    b. _____

    c. _____

4. **topic to classify:** books
    You can classify books on the basis of

    a. _____

    b. _____

    c. _____

EXERCISE

2

IDENTIFYING WHAT DOESN'T FIT THE CLASSIFICATION

In each list below, one item doesn't fit because it's not classified on the same basis as the others in the list. First, determine the basis for the classification. Then, cross out the one item on each list that doesn't fit.

1. **topic:** parties

    basis for classification: _____

    list: anniversary parties
           birthday parties
           small parties
           retirement parties

2. **topic:** liars

    basis for classification: _____

    list: constant liars
           frequent liars
           occasional liars
           vicious liars

3. **topic:** jewellery

    basis for classification: _____

    list: earrings
           diamond
           necklace
           bracelet

4. **topic:** sleepers

   basis for classification: _____

   list: late sleepers
   people who snore
   people who toss and turn
   people who talk in their sleep

5. **topic:** police

   basis for classification: _____

   list: captain
   detective
   officer of the year
   constable

EXERCISE 3

FINDING CATEGORIES THAT FIT ONE BASIS FOR CLASSIFICATION

In the lines under each topic, write three categories that fit the basis of classification that is given. The first one is done for you.

1. **topic:** cartoons on television

   basis for classification: when they're shown

   categories:

   a. *Saturday morning cartoons* _____

   b. *weekly cartoon series shown in the evening* _____

   c. *cartoons that are holiday specials* _____

2. **topic:** doctors

   basis for classification: their specialty

   categories:

   a. _____

   b. _____

   c. _____

3. **topic:** computers

   basis for classification: price

   categories:

   a. _____

   b. _____

   c. _____

4. **topic:** music

    basis for classification: genre

    categories:

    a. _____

    b. _____

    c. _____

5. **topic:** vacations

    basis for classification: how long they are

    categories:

    a. _____

    b. _____

    c. _____

communication at work

> In today's competitive marketplace, companies are constantly striving to keep their employees' skills up to date. To this end, most corporations have invested sometimes large portions of their budgets in—and entire departments to—training and development. Many corporations have classified their training initiatives on the basis of how the learning is delivered: through elearning, in a classroom, in a virtual classroom, or through blended learning, a combination of methods. In what other ways is classification used in the workplace?

WRITING THE CLASSIFICATION PARAGRAPH IN STEPS

 GATHERING IDEAS: CLASSIFICATION

First, pick a topic for your classification. The next step is to choose some basis for your classification.

Brainstorming a Basis for Classification

Sometimes, the easiest way to choose one basis is to brainstorm about different types related to your topic and see where your brainstorming leads you. For example, if you were to write a paragraph classifying phone calls, you could begin by listing anything about phone calls that occurs to you:

Phone Calls

sales calls at dinnertime	people talk too long
short calls	calls I hate getting
calls in middle of night	wrong number
long-distance calls	waiting for a call

The next step is to survey your list. See where it's leading you. The list of phone calls includes a few *unpleasant phone calls*:

> sales calls at dinnertime
>
> wrong number
>
> calls in middle of night

Maybe you can label these "Calls I Don't Want," and that will lead you toward a basis for classification. You might think about calls you *don't* want and calls you *do* want. You think further and realize that you want or don't want certain calls because of their effect on you. You decide to use the effect of the calls on you as the basis for classification. Remember, however, that you need at least three categories. If you stick with this basis for classification, you can come up with three categories:

> Calls that please me
>
> Calls that irritate me
>
> Calls that frighten me

You can then gather details about your three categories by brainstorming:

Added Details for Three Categories

Calls that please me

from boyfriend

good friends

catch-up calls—someone I haven't talked to for a while

make me feel close

Calls that irritate me

sales calls at dinnertime

wrong numbers

calls that irritate or interrupt

invade privacy

Calls that frighten me

emergency call in middle of night

"let's break up" call from boyfriend

change my life, indicate some bad change

Matching the Points within the Categories

As you begin thinking about details for each of your categories, try to write about the same points in each category. For instance, in the list of phone calls, each category includes some details about who made the call.

> Calls that please me—from good friends, my boyfriend
>
> Calls that irritate me—from salespeople, unknown callers
>
> Calls that frighten me—from the emergency room, my boyfriend

Each category also includes some details about why you react to them in a specific way:

> Calls that please me—make me feel close
>
> Calls that irritate me—invade privacy
>
> Calls that frighten me—indicate some bad change

You achieve unity by covering the same points for each category.

Writing a Topic Sentence for a Classification Paragraph

The topic sentence for a classification paragraph should do two things:

1. It should mention what you are classifying.
2. It should indicate the basis for your classification by stating the basis or listing your categories, or both.

Consider the details on phone calls. To write a topic sentence about the details, you

1. mention what you are classifying: phone calls; and
2. indicate the basis for classifying by (a) stating the basis (whether I want to get the calls), or (b) listing the categories (calls that please me, calls that irritate me, and calls that frighten me). You may also state both the basis and the categories in the topic sentence.

Following these guidelines, you can write a topic sentence like this:

> I can classify phone calls according to their effect on me.

or

> Phone calls can be grouped into the ones that please me, the ones that irritate me, and the ones that frighten me.

Both of these topic sentences state what you're classifying and give some indication of the basis for the classification. Once you have a topic sentence, you're ready to begin the outline stage of writing the classification paragraph.

EXERCISE 4

CREATING QUESTIONS TO GET DETAILS FOR A CLASSIFICATION PARAGRAPH

Do this exercise with a partner or group. Each of the following lists includes a topic, the basis for classifying that topic, and three categories. For each list, think of three questions you could ask to get more details about the types. The first list is done for you.

1. **topic:** moviegoers

   basis for classification: how they behave during the movie

   categories: the quiet moviegoers, the irritating moviegoers, the obnoxious moviegoers

questions you can ask:

a. *Does each type use a cellphone?* _____

b. *Does each type talk during the movie?* _____

c. *Does each type come and go during the movie?* _____

2. **topic:** sports fans at a game

   basis for classification: how much they like the sport

   categories: fanatics, ordinary fans, bored observers

   questions you can ask:

   a. _____

   b. _____

   c. _____

3. **topic:** people in line at the supermarket

   basis for classification: their reason for shopping

   categories: the convenience-food singles, the responsible parents, the healthy dieters

   questions you can ask:

   a. _____

   b. _____

   c. _____

4. **topic:** cellphone users

   basis for classification: the features of their phones

   categories: those who use cellphones with internet access, those who use cellphones with cameras and camcorders, those who use basic cellphones

   questions you can ask:

   a. _____

   b. _____

   c. _____

5. **topic:** college students

   basis for classification: what they carry in their backpacks

   categories: those who carry the bare essentials, those who carry a few extras, those who carry more than they need

   questions you can ask:

   a. _____

   b. _____

   c. _____

| EXERCISE 5 | WRITING TOPIC SENTENCES FOR A CLASSIFICATION PARAGRAPH |

Review the topics, bases for classification, and categories in Exercise 4. Then, using that material, write a good topic sentence for each topic.

Topic Sentences

for topic 1: _____

_____

_____

for topic 2: _____

_____

_____

for topic 3: _____

_____

_____

for topic 4: _____

_____

_____

for topic 5: _____

_____

_____

PLANNING   DEVISING A PLAN: CLASSIFICATION

Effective Order in Classifying

After you have a topic sentence and a list of details, you can create an outline. Think about which category you want to write about first, second, and so forth. The order of your categories will depend on what you're writing about. For example, if you're classifying ways to meet people, you can save the best one for last. If you're classifying three habits that are bad for your health, you can save the worst one for last.

If you list your categories in the topic sentence, list them in the same order that you will explain them in the paragraph.

Below is an outline for a paragraph classifying phone calls. The prewriting has been put into categories. The underlined sentences have been added to clearly define each category before the details are given.

An Outline for a Classification Paragraph

topic sentence: Phone calls can be grouped into the ones that please me, the ones that irritate me, and the ones that frighten me.

category 1 details

There are some calls that please me.

They make me feel close to someone.

I like calls from my boyfriend, especially when he calls just to say he's thinking of me.

I like to hear from good friends.

I like catch-up calls.

These are calls from people I haven't talked to in a while.

category 2 details

There are some calls that irritate me.

These calls invade my privacy.

Sales calls always come at dinnertime.

They offer me newspaper subscriptions or "free" vacations.

I get at least four wrong-number calls each week.

All these intrusive calls irritate me, and I have to interrupt whatever it is I'm doing to answer them.

category 3 details

There are some calls that frighten me.

They're the calls that tell me about some bad change in my life.

I once got a call in the middle of the night.

It was from a hospital emergency room.

The nurse said my brother had been in an accident.

I once got a call from a boyfriend.

He said he wanted to break up.

You can use the following checklist to help you revise your own classification outline.

CHECKLIST | **FOR REVISING THE CLASSIFICATION OUTLINE**

✓ Do I have a consistent basis for classifying?

✓ Does my topic sentence mention what I'm classifying and indicate the basis for classification?

✓ Do I have enough to say about each category in my classification?

✓ Are the categories presented in the most effective order?

✓ Am I using clear and specific detail?

With a revised outline, you can begin writing your draft.

EXERCISE **6**	**RECOGNIZING THE BASIS FOR CLASSIFICATION WITHIN THE TOPIC SENTENCE**

The topic sentences below don't state a basis for classification, but you can recognize the basis nevertheless. After you've read each topic sentence, write the basis for classification on the line provided. The first one is done for you.

1. **topic sentence:** Neighbours can be classified into complete strangers, acquaintances, and buddies.

   basis for classification: *how well you know them*

2. **topic sentence:** At the Thai restaurant, you can order three kinds of hot sauce: hot sauce for beginners, hot sauce for the adventurous, and hot sauce for fire eaters.

   basis for classification: _____

3. **topic sentence:** When it comes to photographs of yourself, there are three types: the ones that make you look good, the ones that make you look fat, and the ones that make you look ridiculous.

   basis for classification: _____

4. **topic sentence:** On any airplane, there are some passengers who bring one small piece of luggage, others who bring a couple of large pieces, and still others who bring enough luggage to fill the trunk of a car.

   basis for classification: _____

5. **topic sentence:** Internet users can be grouped into those who rely on it for news, those who use it for research, and those who use it for entertainment.

   basis for classification: _____

EXERCISE **7**	**ADDING DETAILS TO A CLASSIFICATION OUTLINE**

Do this exercise with a partner or group. In this outline, add details where the blank lines indicate. Match the points covered in the other categories.

   topic sentence: My jobs can be categorized into pleasant jobs, acceptable jobs, and unbearable jobs.

   details: My first job was a pleasant job.
   I worked at a small coffee shop.
   I worked behind the pastry counter.
   Business was steady but never hectic.
   The staff was friendly and helpful to new employees.
   The customers were regulars who enjoyed visiting the café.
   Another job was an acceptable job.
   I worked in the library at college.

I worked at the book checkout and return counter.
Sometimes, there was no one in the library, and the job
     was boring.

_____

My last job was an unbearable job.
I worked at a movie theatre.
I sold tickets.

_____

_____

There were very few staff members, so it was lonely.

DRAFTING AND REVISING

DRAFTING AND REVISING: CLASSIFICATION

You can transform your outline into a first draft of a paragraph by writing the topic sentence and the details in paragraph form. As you write, you can begin combining some of the short sentences, adding details, and inserting transitions.

Transitions in Classification

Various transitions can be used in a classification paragraph. The transitions you select will depend on what you're classifying and the basis you choose for classifying. For example, if you're classifying roses according to how pretty they are, you can use transitions like "One lovely kind of rose . . ."; "Another, more beautiful kind . . ."; and "The most beautiful kind . . . ." In other classifications, you can use transitions like "The first type . . ."; "Another type . . ."; and "The final type . . . ." In revising your classification paragraph, use the transitions that most clearly connect your ideas.

As you write your own paragraph, you may want to refer to a "kind" or a "type." For variety, try other words like "class," "category," "group," "species," "form," or "version," if it's logical to do so.

After you have a draft of your paragraph, you can revise and review it. The checklist below may help you with your revisions.

✓

CHECKLIST | **FOR REVISING THE DRAFT OF A CLASSIFICATION PARAGRAPH**

✓ Does my topic sentence include what I'm classifying?

✓ Does it indicate the basis of my classification?

✓ Should any of my sentences be combined?

✓ Do my transitions clearly connect my ideas?

✓ Should I add more details to any of the categories?

✓ Are the categories presented in the most effective order?

Below is a revised draft of the classification paragraph on phone calls with these changes from the outline:

- An introduction has been added, preceding the topic sentence, to make the paragraph smoother.
- Some sentences have been combined.
- Some details have been added.
- Transitions have been added.
- A final sentence has been added, so that the paragraph makes a stronger point.

> ### A Draft of a Classification Paragraph
>
> I get many phone calls, but they fit into three types. Phone calls can be grouped into the ones that please me, the ones that irritate me, and the ones that frighten me. There are some calls that please me because they make me feel close to someone. I like calls from my boyfriend, especially when he calls just to say he's thinking of me. I like to hear from my good friends. I like catch-up calls, the calls from people I haven't talked to in a while that fill me in on what friends have been doing. There are also calls that irritate me because they invade my privacy. Sales calls, offering me newspaper subscriptions and "free" vacations, always come at dinnertime. In addition, I get at least four wrong-number calls each week. All these calls irritate me, and I have to interrupt what I'm doing to answer them. The more serious calls are the ones that frighten me. They're the calls that tell me about some bad change in my life. Once, in the middle of the night, a call from a hospital emergency room told me that my brother had been in an accident. Another time, a boyfriend called to tell me he wanted to break up. When I get bad news by phone, I realize that the telephone can bring frightening calls as well as friendly or irritating ones.

EXERCISE 8	COMBINING SENTENCES FOR A BETTER CLASSIFICATION PARAGRAPH

The following paragraph has some short sentences that would be more effective if they were combined. Combine each pair of underlined sentences into one sentence. Write the new sentence in the space above the old ones.

In the dog world, there are yipper-yappers, authoritative barkers, and boom-box barkers. <u>Yipper-yappers have a short, high-pitched bark. Their bark sounds like hysterical nagging.</u> Yipping dogs are usually small dogs like miniature poodles or terriers. <u>The fiercely emotional quality of their bark is frightening. I'm not too afraid of these dogs.</u> I know they can only get to my ankles if they attack. There's also a moderate kind of dog. It's the authoritative barker. This type of dog has a deep bark; it signifies that the dog means business. Boxers, collies, and other medium-size dogs possess this commanding voice. <u>They demand my respect. I'm afraid of them. Their low, growling bark and their size make me afraid.</u> The third kind of dog has a boom-box bark. <u>Its bark is very loud. It can be heard from blocks away.</u> Dogs that sound like this are usually the enormous ones like Great Danes or German shepherds. These dogs strike fear into my heart. They sound intimidating, and they have large bodies and giant teeth. <u>People say you can't judge a book by its cover. You can tell quite a bit about a dog by its bark.</u>

EXERCISE 9

IDENTIFYING TRANSITIONS IN A CLASSIFICATION PARAGRAPH

Underline all the transitions in the following paragraph. The transitions may be words or groups of words.

At the supermarket where I work as a cashier, I classify my customers according to how they relate to me. First, there are those who are polite and kind. After I say, "Hello, how are you today?" they usually say, "Fine." Some make a funny comment about the weather or the traffic. This type of customer often makes pleasant conversation while I ring up the groceries. Another class of customer doesn't talk at all. As far as this kind is concerned, I don't exist. This kind simply stares right through me or, even worse, talks on a cellphone as I ring up and bag the groceries. Recently, I've seen customers glued to their phones throughout their time at the checkout counter, not even acknowledging me when I announce the total or hand them their change. The final and most dreaded type of customer is the angry customer. This kind is angry at me, at the other customers, and possibly at the whole world. Members of this group argue about the price of every item, complain about how long it takes to ring them up, and criticize the way I pack their groceries. They always leave shaking their heads in disgust. Dealing with these varieties of customers each day, I'm grateful that most people fit into the first category, the good-natured, pleasant group.

PROOFREADING ## PROOFREADING AND POLISHING: CLASSIFICATION

Following is the final version of the classification paragraph on phone calls. If you compare the draft and final versions, you'll notice these changes:

- The first sentence has been rewritten so that it's less choppy, and a transition word, "My," has been added to the second sentence in order to link it to the first.

■ Some words have been eliminated and sentences rewritten so that they're not too wordy.

■ The word choice has been refined: "someone" has been changed to "a person I care about" and "bad change" has been replaced by "crisis" in order to make the details more precise, and "irritate" has been changed to "annoy" to avoid repetition.

> ### A Final Version of a Classification Paragraph
>
> I get many phone calls, but most of them fall into one of three types. <u>My</u> phone calls can be grouped into the ones that please me, the ones that irritate me, and the ones that frighten me. There are some calls I want to receive because they make me feel close to <u>a person I care about.</u> I like calls from my boyfriend, especially when he calls just to say he's thinking of me. I like to hear from my good friends. I like catch-up calls from friends I haven't talked to in a while. There are also calls I don't want because they invade my privacy. Sales calls, offering me newspaper subscriptions and "free" vacations, always come at dinnertime. In addition, I get at least four wrong-number calls each week. All these calls <u>annoy</u> me, and I have to interrupt what I'm doing to answer them. The more serious calls are the ones <u>I really don't want to receive.</u> They're the calls that tell me about some <u>crisis</u> in my life. <u>I once got a midnight call from a hospital emergency room, informing me that my brother had been in an accident.</u> Another time, a boyfriend called to tell me he wanted to break up. When I get bad news by phone, I realize that the telephone can bring frightening calls as well as friendly or irritating ones.

Before you prepare the final version of your own classification paragraph, check your latest draft for errors in spelling and punctuation, and for any errors made in typing or recopying.

EXERCISE 10   PROOFREADING TO PREPARE THE FINAL VERSION

Here are two classification paragraphs with the kinds of errors that are easy to overlook when you prepare the final version of an assignment. Correct the errors, writing above the lines. The first paragraph has thirteen errors; the second has thirteen errors.

1. My experince in school has shown me their are three kinds of pencils, and they are the pencils that work great, the pencils that barely work, and the pencils that dont work at all. The pencil's that work are the ones that are perfectly sharpened to a razor-fine point and have huge, clean

erasers at the end. These pencils produce a dark, clear line when I write with them unfortunatly, I never do write with them. Great pencils are the ones I always come accross, all over the house, when i'm looking for something else. The pencils I usually rite with are the damaged pencils. They work, but not well. They need sharpening, or their erasers are worn so far down that using them leaves rips across the page. Sometimes these pencils leave a faded, weak line on the paper. Sometimes the line is so thick it look like a crayon. The third kind of pencl is the worst of all. Pencils in this group just don't work. They have no point. Or if they have a point, it brakes off as soon as I write. They have no eraser. The pencils are so chewed and mutilated they might have been previously owned by woodpeckers. Non-working pencils are the ones I bring to class on test days. I just do'nt seem to have much luck with pencils.

2. Sleepers fall into three categories and they are the light sleeper, the average sleepers, and the heavy sleepers. Light sleepers have a hard time falling asleep and staying asleep. My mother is a light sleeper, and she cant fall asleep unless the room is totaly quite and completely dark. She have a sleep mask and earplugs to help her get to sleep. Even after she falls asleep, she does not sleep soundly. She swears she can hear me tiptoe acrost the living room when she is wearing her earplugs in bed. She wakes up and reads, raids the refridgerator, or turns on the television at least twice each night. Unlike my mother, I am a average sleeper. I fall asleep fairly easily, unless I have a problem on my mind. Even if I toss and turn until I get to sleep, I tend to sleep through the night. Loud noises like car alarms or sirens can wake me, but I am usually deep in sleep until my clock radio blasts me awake. My roommate is a much deeper sleeper then I am. He falls into the class of sleeper who can fall asleep in an instant. He can climb into bed and be unconscience in a minute. I may come in late, slam the door, and bump into a chair, but my roommate won't wake up. A car wreck outside the window doesn't disturb him. He sleeps trough the alarm clock, every morning until I shake him into awareness. He has a gift for sleeping that I wish he could share with my mother.

Lines of Detail: A Walk-Through Assignment

Write a paragraph that classifies bosses on the basis of how they treat their employees. To write the paragraph, follow these steps:

Step 1: List all the details you can remember about bosses you have worked for or known.

Step 2: Survey your list. Then list three categories of bosses, based on how they treat their employees.

Step 3: Now that you have three categories, study your list again, looking for matching points for all three categories. For example, all three categories could be described by this matching point: where the boss works.

Step 4: Write a topic sentence that (a) names what you're classifying, and (b) states the basis for classification or names all three categories.

Step 5: Write an outline. Check that your outline defines each category, uses matching points for each category, and puts the categories in an effective order.

Step 6: Write a draft of the classification paragraph. Check the draft, revising it until it has specific detail, smooth transitions, and effective word choice.

Step 7: Before you prepare the final copy of your paragraph, check your last draft for any errors in punctuation, spelling, word choice, or mechanics.

Writing Your Own Classification Paragraph

When you write on any of these topics, make sure to work through the stages of the writing process in preparing your classification paragraph.

1. Write a classification paragraph on any of the following topics. If your instructor agrees, brainstorm with a partner or with a group to come up with (1) a basis for your classification, (2) categories related to the basis, and (3) points you can make to give details about each of the categories.

horror movies	cars	MP3 players
romantic movies	hockey players	scams
children	fans at a concert	excuses
parents	fans at a sports event	cellphone applications
students	neighbours	dogs
teachers	restaurants	fears
drivers	dates	weddings
salespeople		

2. Adapt one of the topics in question 1 by making your topic smaller. You can classify Chinese restaurants, for example, instead of restaurants, or sports cars instead of cars. Then write a classification paragraph that helps your reader make a choice about your topic.

3. Following are some topics. Each one already has a basis for classification. Write a classification paragraph on one of these topics. If your instructor agrees, work with a partner or with a group to brainstorm categories, matching points, and details for the categories.

Classify . . .

1. exams on the basis of how difficult they are.
2. weekends on the basis of how busy they are.
3. assignments on the basis of how difficult they are.
4. breakfasts on the basis of how healthy they are.
5. snowboarders (or people who engage in some other sport) on the basis of how experienced they are.
6. singers on the basis of the kind of audience they appeal to.
7. parties on the basis of how much fun they are.
8. television commercials on the basis of what time of day or night they're broadcast.
9. radio stations on the basis of what kind of music they play.
10. urban legends on the basis of how illogical they are.

WRITING FROM READING: CLASSIFICATION

Colour-Coding a Corporate Culture
Janet McFarland

Janet McFarland is a journalist who writes about issues concerning the corporate world. Born in Saskatchewan, she has written for the Winnipeg Free Press *and the* Financial Post. *She currently writes for* The Globe and Mail.

Before you read this essay, consider these questions:

Have you ever had to work as part of a team, either at work or at school? Did any disagreements or conflicts arise?

Do you think personality plays a part in disagreement or conflict?

If you were better able to understand someone's personality and preferred working style, do you think you'd be better able to manage conflict?

Do you have more of a "red" personality, or are you more predominantly "green"?

If you are a corporate director, chances are your dominant personality type is red—and new research suggests this can have implications for the way you make decisions.

Two co-founders of Vancouver leadership consulting firm Concentrix Solutions Inc. have compiled personality profile test results from more than 300 directors they have instructed at the director education program run by the Institute of Corporate Directors.

The profiles identify the dominant personality traits of participants in four colour-coded categories, based on a testing system designed by Insights Learning & Development Ltd. of Dundee, Scotland.

preponderance: an amount greater than others

A **preponderance** of directors—41 percent—have a dominant "red energy," a bold personality type defined as action-oriented, tough-minded and decisive. The next largest group, 25 percent, are dominantly "blue," defined as questioning, analytical and detail-oriented.

That leaves just one-third of directors in the more people-oriented yellow and green categories—directors who are more dominantly team players, good listeners, creative, **mediators** or persuaders. Of that one-third, just 14 percent are predominantly "green"—relationship-focused people who sit back, listen carefully, mediate compromises and consider the interests of all stakeholders.

mediators: people who encourage compromise

Wendy Sage-Hayward, co-founder of Concentrix, says directors' personality types are far more concentrated in the "red" category than is the societal norm, adding that the implications of this orientation are key for the way boards make decisions.

If a majority of a board's directors are dominantly "red" and have a tendency to prefer quick and bold decisions, for example, it is valuable to understand what is missing in the decision-making equation.

"The whole point is to try to create awareness of what the dynamic is in the boardroom," she says. "And how do you compensate for some of the energies that might be overbearing or dominating in the decision-making process?"

Co-founder Laura Greig says many successful leaders who are "red" types may have communications issues and not realize it. One of the biggest pitfalls, for example, is that these directors may be active talkers but poor listeners—more keen to contribute opinions than listen to understand others' views. "When you've got that much red energy in the room, they're all waiting for their turn to talk and they're cutting in. They're having lots of discussion, but they're talking over top of each other."

Ms. Greig says better decisions are made when the broadest array of perspectives are considered and not just those of the most dominant people at the table. "That's where companies get into trouble," she says. "A lot of the examples you've seen in the past where things go wrong is when people are not asking the questions and they're not challenging—they're **deferring**."

deferring: yielding to another's opinion

Bob Garnett, who sits on the board of Coast Capital Savings Credit Union, has undergone the profile test twice, and says it is a practical tool for improving communications with other directors.

"If you understand their basic makeup and how they like to look at things, it helps you understand where they're coming from," he says.

Mr. Garnett, a classic "red and blue" entrepreneur who owns two courier companies, says most of his board members are in the same categories as him, and that only one director has a lot of green in his personality. Knowing more about colleagues' **hard-wiring** allows the board to watch out for possible gaps and avoid misunderstandings, he says.

hard-wiring: ingrained tendencies

The profiling has also helped him in his business career. He says one of his business partners is predominantly yellow and green—a complete opposite—but they have come to understand the differences in their communication styles.

"It allows you to say, 'He's not upset with me or he's not opposing what I'm saying—he's coming at it from a different perspective,'" he notes.

One goal of the profiling is to give practical advice and strategies to different types of directors.

For example, assertive people are coached to practise techniques such as asking questions about others' comments, rather than leaping to offer opinions. Ms. Greig says she advises people to try to "get curious" about others' opinions, including views they might reject immediately.

"That sparks a different way of interacting with them. It makes you wonder what they see that I don't see, or how did they get to that conclusion."

Everyone has aspects of all personality styles, but most people have one or two that are dominant, Ms. Greig and Ms. Sage-Hayward stress, and leaders can come from any place in the circle. Their success comes from the ability to make modifications and use less dominant tendencies when needed, even if they feel less natural.

The two teamed up eight years ago to provide leadership development consulting, quickly branching from executives and management teams to boards of directors.

While there are many personality tests available for use, they say they favour the colour-coded personality profiles because the testing is quick and easy for subjects to complete, and the results are simple to understand and remember. They also believe it has a good validity rate, with subjects routinely saying they feel their profiles are accurate.

advocate: support, speak in favour of

functional competency: how well a person works on a practical, day-to-day level

They do not, however, **advocate** that companies or boards recruit new directors using the model, arguing it offers no insight into **functional competency** or ability.

It does, however, help directors become more tolerant of other styles and understand how they contribute to good decision making. Many people have a tendency to find their opposite types annoying, but this can be reduced by understanding the differences.

"It's interesting to watch people move from an irritation or a dismissiveness to not only a tolerance for [their opposite type] but even an appreciation of it," Ms. Greig says.

The Boardroom Rainbow

Personality profiles of more than 300 corporate directors show a preponderance of people who are action-oriented or analytical, and a minority of people whose personality type is primarily people-focused or creative. Board advisers say this can have an impact on the way decisions are made.

* * * * *

Red: 41%

Reds are extroverted and competitive.

On a good day: They are demanding, determined and action-oriented, good at seeing the end goals at the start of a task. They want to get the job done efficiently and quickly.

On a bad day: They are aggressive, poor listeners, impatient of others' less-purposeful styles, and make decisions without considering all sides.

* * * * *

Blue: 25%

Blues are thoughtful and objective.

On a good day: They are precise, organized, detail-oriented, and good at maintaining focus. They want to get the job done logically and right.

On a bad day: They are cold and introverted, delaying decision making because they want to work through all the details.

* * * * *

Yellow: 20%

Yellows are sociable and creative.

On a good day: They are innovative and persuasive, creating friendly and stimulating environments and excelling at big-picture thinking. They want to get the job done as a team working together.

On a bad day: They are excitable, unfocused or too hasty, branching off on **tangents** during conversations.

* * * * *

tangent: off-topic
thought or action

Green: 14%

Greens are caring and encouraging.

On a good day: They are patient, relationship-oriented, good at mediating and building consensus, and can concentrate on one task for long periods of time. They want to get the job done harmoniously.

On a bad day: They are docile, plodding, stubborn, or too concerned with the "process" of decision making.

UNDERSTANDING "COLOUR-CODING A CORPORATE CULTURE"

1. What are some advantages to identifying and understanding your co-workers' colour profiles?

2. According to the article, what two colour profiles represent two-thirds of corporate directors?

3. Consider what kind of personality the "red" type seems to indicate. What might the decision process look like in a team that is predominantly red?

4. Out of the many personality tests available, why do some organizations prefer the colour-coded versions?

5. For what, according to the article, should the colour-coding model not be used? Why not?

WRITING FROM READING "COLOUR-CODING A CORPORATE CULTURE"

When you write on any of the following topics, make sure to work through the stages of the writing process.

1. Consider a place in which you've worked, and your co-workers there. Did you notice different working styles—for instance, efficient, laid-back, or goal-oriented styles? Write a paragraph in which you classify different working styles.

2. Much research has been done on the conflict, and resolution of such conflict, in team environments. Consider a time when you had to work as part of a team—either at work, school, or in your leisure activities—and a conflict arose. Did different personalities emerge? Did one team member, for example, try to act as peacemaker? Another as instigator? Write a paragraph in which you discuss the different conflict-management styles you observed.

3. Consider the different jobs you've held, and the bosses you've had. Management styles, like communication styles, can vary greatly. Did your boss give you a task and then expect you to complete it on your own? Did he or she work on a project collaboratively with you? Write a paragraph in which you discuss the different management styles you've experienced.

MyWritingLab

Go to MyWritingLab to access a diagnostic test that creates your own personalized learning path supported by rich multimedia resources and a variety of animated tutorials, all aimed at helping you improve your writing. MyWritingLab also includes a complete eText version of the book that is fully searchable and accessible through your web browser or most mobile devices.

CHAPTER 9
Cause and Effect

LEARNING OBJECTIVES

After you have read this chapter and completed its exercises and assignments, you should be able to

- choose an appropriate topic for a cause or effect paragraph
- write an appropriate topic sentence for a cause or effect paragraph
- provide clear and specific causes or effects in a paragraph
- use appropriate transitions in a cause or effect paragraph
- draft and edit your cause or effect paragraph

"Life is a perpetual instruction in cause and effect."

~ RALPH WALDO EMERSON

RALPH WALDO EMERSON WAS A NINETEENTH-CENTURY POET AND ESSAYIST. HE WAS ALSO CONSIDERED ONE OF THE GREATEST ORATORS (SPEECHMAKERS) OF HIS TIME.

WHAT IS CAUSE AND EFFECT?

Almost every day, you consider the causes or effects of events so that you can make choices and take action. In writing a paragraph, when you explain the *reasons* for something, you're writing about **causes**. When you write about the *results* of something, you're writing about **effects**. Often in writing, you consider both the causes and effects of a decision, an event, a change in your life, or a change in society, but in this chapter you'll be asked to concentrate on *either* causes (reasons) *or* effects (results).

Hints for Writing a Cause or Effect Paragraph

1. **Choose a topic that you can handle in one paragraph.** A topic you can handle in one paragraph is one that (a) is not too large and (b) doesn't require research.

   Some topics are so large that you probably can't cover them in one paragraph. Topics that are too large include ones like

   Why People Get Angry
   Effects of Unemployment on My Family

Other topics require you to research the facts and to include the opinions of experts. They would be good topics for a research paper, but not for a one-paragraph assignment. Topics that require research include ones like

The Causes of Divorce
The Effects of Television Viewing on Children

When you write a cause or effect paragraph, choose a topic you can write about by using what you already know. That is, make your topic smaller and more personal. Topics that use what you already know are ones like

Why Children Love Video Games
The Causes of My Divorce
What Enlistment in the Armed Forces Did for My Sister
How Alcoholics Anonymous Changed My Life

2. **Try to have at least three causes or effects in your paragraph.** Make sure you consider immediate and remote causes or immediate and remote effects. Think about your topic and gather as many causes or effects as you can *before* you start drafting your paragraph.

   An event usually has more than one cause. Think beyond the obvious, the *immediate cause*, to more *remote causes*. For example, the immediate cause of your car accident might be the other driver who hit the rear end of your car. But more remote causes might include the weather conditions or the condition of the road.

   Situations can have more than one result, too. If you take Algebra I for the second time and you pass the course with a C, an *immediate result* is that you fulfill the requirements for graduation. But there may be other, more *remote results*. Your success in algebra may help to change your attitude toward mathematics courses. Or your success may build your confidence in your ability to handle college work. Or your success may lead you to sign up for another course taught by the same instructor.

3. **Make your causes and effects clear and specific.** If you're writing about why Facebook is popular, don't write "Facebook is popular because everybody is on it" or "Facebook is popular because it's a trend." If you write either of these statements, you're really saying, "Facebook is popular because it's popular."

   Think further. Don't people get back in touch with friends they haven't seen in years? What about the applications and groups? By giving specific details that explain, illustrate, or describe a cause or effect, you help the reader understand your point.

4. **Write a topic sentence that indicates whether your paragraph is about causes or effects.** You shouldn't announce, but you can *indicate*.

   not this: The effects of my winning the scholarship are going to be discussed. (an announcement)
   but this: Winning the scholarship changed my plans for college. (indicates that effects will be discussed)

   You can *list* a short version of all your causes or effects in your topic sentence, like this:

   The popularity of foreign cars has forced North American carmakers to change their products, close manufacturing plants, and create a whole new line of hybrid cars.

You can *hint* at your points by summarizing them, like this:

> The popularity of foreign cars has challenged and even threatened their competition, but it has also created new business opportunities.

Or you can use words that *signal* causes or effects.

words that signal causes: reasons, why, because, motives, intentions
words that signal effects: results, impact, consequences, changed, threatened, improved

---

EXERCISE 1

SELECTING A SUITABLE TOPIC FOR A CAUSE OR EFFECT PARAGRAPH

Below is a list of topics. Some topics are suitable for a cause or effect paragraph. Some are too large to handle in one paragraph, some would require research, and some are both too large and would require research. Put *OK* next to any topic that is suitable, and an *X* next to any topic that is not.

Topics—Suitable and Not Suitable

1. _____ Why Dinosaurs Appeal to Children
2. _____ The Effects of Smoking Cigarettes
3. _____ Reasons I Attend College Part-Time
4. _____ Why Kids Love Soccer
5. _____ The Impact of Technology on Education
6. _____ The Causes of Drug Abuse
7. _____ The Effects of Obesity on Our Society
8. _____ How My Favourite Teacher Changed My Perceptions about Math
9. _____ Why Marriages Fail
10. _____ The Causes of Anorexia

EXERCISE 2

RECOGNIZING CAUSE AND EFFECT IN TOPIC SENTENCES

In the following list, if the topic sentence is for a "cause" paragraph, put a *C* next to it. If the topic sentence is for an "effect" paragraph, put an *E* next to it.

Topic Sentences for Cause or Effect Paragraphs

1. _____ Taking on shift work at the shop had interesting consequences on my part-time studies.
2. _____ I decided to pierce my eyebrow out of a desire to look different, to do something exciting, and to shock my parents.
3. _____ Jack has several motives for proposing marriage.
4. _____ Until I actually owned one, I never knew how a tablet could change a person's work habits.
5. _____ The television's remote control device has created conflicts in my marriage.
6. _____ Children enjoy horror movies because the movies allow them to deal with their fears in a non-threatening way.
7. _____ People buy clothes with designer labels to impress others, to feel successful, and to feel accepted into a high social class.

8. _____ The birth of my little sister had an unexpected impact on my life.
9. _____ I am beginning to understand why my mother was a strict disciplinarian.
10. _____ Our digital footprints have had an impact on our privacy.

WRITING THE CAUSE OR EFFECT PARAGRAPH IN STEPS

 PREWRITING GATHERING IDEAS: CAUSE OR EFFECT

Once you've picked a topic, the next—and very important—step is getting ideas. Because this paragraph will contain only causes or effects and details about them, you must have enough causes or effects to write a developed paragraph.

Freewriting on a Topic

One way to get ideas is to freewrite on your topic. Because causes and effects are clearly connected, you can begin by freewriting about both and then choose one—causes or effects—later.

If you were thinking about writing a cause or effect paragraph on owning a car, you could begin by freewriting something like this:

> ### Freewriting on Owning a Car
>
> A car of my own. Why? I needed it. Couldn't get a part-time job without one. Because I couldn't get to work. Needed it to get to school. Of course, I could have taken the bus to school. But I didn't want to. Feel like an adult when you have a car of your own. Freedom to come and go. I was the last of my friends to have a car. Couldn't wait. An old Camaro. But I fixed it up nicely. Costs a lot to maintain. Car payments, car loan. Car insurance.

Now you can review the freewriting and make separate lists of causes and effects you wrote down:

Causes (Reasons)

needed to get a part-time job

needed to get to school

my friends had cars

Effects (Results)

feel like an adult

freedom to come and go

costs a lot to maintain

car payments

car loan

car insurance

Because you have more details on the effects of owning a car, you decide to write an effects paragraph.

Your list of effects can be used in a couple of ways. You can add to it if you think of ideas as you're reviewing your list. As well, you can begin to group ideas in your list. Grouping helps you see how many effects and details you have; you can then add to these. Below is a grouping of the list of effects.

Effects of Getting My Own Car

first effect:	I had to pay for the car and related expenses.
details:	costs a lot to maintain
	car payments
	car loan
	car insurance
second effect:	I had the freedom to come and go.
details:	none
third effect:	I felt like an adult.
details:	none

Will these effects work in a paragraph? One way to decide is to try to add details to the effects that have no details. Now ask questions to get the details.

second effect: I had the freedom to come and go.

> **What do you mean?**
> Well, I didn't have to beg my father for his truck anymore.
> I didn't have to get rides from friends. I could go to the city when I wanted. I could ride around just for fun.

third effect: I felt like an adult.

> **What do you mean, "like an adult"?**
> Adults can go where they want, when they want.
> They drive themselves.

If you look carefully at the answers to the questions above, you'll find that the second and third effects are really *the same*. By adding details to both effects, you'll find that both are saying that owning a car gives you the adult freedom to come and go.

So the list needs another effect of owning a car. What else happened? How else did things change when you got your car? You might answer,

> I worried about someone hitting my car.
> I worried about bad drivers.
> I wanted to avoid the scratches you get in parking lots.

With answers like these, your third effect could be

> I became a more careful driver.

Now that you have three effects and some details, you can rewrite your list. You can add details as you rewrite.

List of Effects of Getting My Own Car

first effect:	I had to pay for the car and related expenses.
details:	costs a lot to maintain
	car payments
	car loan
	car insurance

second effect:	I had the adult freedom to come and go.
details:	didn't have to beg my father for his truck
	didn't have to get rides from friends
	could go to the city when I wanted
	could ride around for fun
third effect:	I became a more careful driver.
details:	worried about someone hitting the car
	worried about bad drivers
	wanted to avoid the scratches cars get in parking lots

Designing a Topic Sentence

With at least three effects and some details for each effect, you can create a topic sentence. The topic sentence for this paragraph should indicate that the subject is the *effects* of getting a car. You can summarize all three effects in your topic sentence, or you can just hint at them. A possible topic sentence for the paragraph can be

> Owning my own car cost me money, gave me freedom, and made me more careful about how I drive.

or

> Once I got a car of my own, I realized the good and bad sides of ownership.

With a topic sentence and a fairly extensive list of details, you're ready to begin the outline step in preparing your paragraph.

EXERCISE 3

DESIGNING QUESTIONS FOR A CAUSE OR EFFECT PARAGRAPH

Below are four topics for cause or effect paragraphs. For each topic, write five questions that could lead you to ideas on the topic. (The first one is completed for you.) After you've written five questions for each topic, give your list to a member of your writing group. Ask him or her to add one question to each topic and then to pass the exercise on to the next member of the group. Repeat the process so that each group member adds to the lists of all the other members.

Later, if your instructor agrees, you can answer the questions (and add more questions and answers) as a way to begin writing a cause or effect paragraph.

1. **topic:** the effects of camera phones on crime

   questions that can lead to ideas and details:

   a. Are unsuspecting people photographed and blackmailed?

   b. Can the cameras be used to photograph confidential documents?

   c. Are the cameras used by peeping Toms?

   d. Can criminals use the camera phones to photograph banks?

   e. Can citizens photograph a crime in progress?

   additional questions: Can citizens photograph a suspect or perpetrator? Can police use the cameras in surveillance?

2. **topic:** why college students work part- or full-time
    questions that can lead to ideas and details:

    a. _____

    b. _____

    c. _____

    d. _____

    e. _____

    additional questions: _____

    _____

    _____

    _____

3. **topic:** the effects of portable technology (e.g., tablets, laptops, wireless
    internet access, smartphones) on family life
    questions that can lead to ideas and details:

    a. _____

    b. _____

    c. _____

    d. _____

    e. _____

    additional questions: _____

    _____

    _____

    _____

4. **topic:** why Canadians are eating more meals away from home
    questions that could lead to ideas and details:

    a. _____

    b. _____

    c. _____

    d. _____

    e. _____

    additional questions: _____

    _____

    _____

    _____

    _____

5. **topic:** the effects of high gas prices on drivers
   questions that could lead to ideas and details:

   a. _____

   b. _____

   c. _____

   d. _____

   e. _____

   additional questions: _____

   _____

   _____

   _____

   _____

EXERCISE **4**	**CREATING CAUSES OR EFFECTS FOR TOPIC SENTENCES**

For each of the following topic sentences, create three causes or effects, depending on what the topic sentence requires. The first one is completed for you.

1. **topic sentence:** Text messaging has both improved and complicated my life.

   a. <u>I always know what my friends are doing.</u>

   b. <u>Last month, I received and sent over 300 messages, and my bill was for $500.</u>

   c. <u>I feel as though I might miss an important message, so I never turn off my phone.</u>

2. **topic sentence:** Households may have unhealthy diets for a number of reasons.

   a. _____

   _____

   b. _____

   _____

   c. _____

   _____

3. **topic sentence:** There are several reasons why students may choose not to speak in class.

   a. _____

   _____

   b. _____

   _____

   c. _____

   _____

4. **topic sentence:** Credit cards can have negative effects on those who use them.

a. _____

_____

b. _____

_____

c. _____

_____

5. **topic sentence:** Taking too many college courses at one time can have serious consequences.

a. _____

_____

b. _____

_____

c. _____

_____

communication at work

Canada has recognized the importance of skilled immigrants to its economic growth. According to a 2012 TD economics report, "There is widespread consensus that immigration has the potential to deliver substantial economic and social benefits to receiving countries. Newcomers complement the skills of the domestic labour force, bring new investment and innovative practices, help to open trade routes with their countries of origin and enhance cultural diversity." What are some other effects of provincial and federal government policies?

 DEVISING A PLAN: CAUSE OR EFFECT

With a topic sentence and a list of causes (or effects) and details, you can draft an outline of your paragraph. Once you have a rough outline, you can work on revising it. You may want to add to it, take out certain ideas, rewrite the topic sentence, or change the order of the ideas. The checklist here may help you revise your outline.

✓ **CHECKLIST**   **FOR REVISING THE OUTLINE OF A CAUSE OR EFFECT PARAGRAPH**

✓ Does my topic sentence make my point?

✓ Does it indicate whether my paragraph is about causes or effects?

✓ Does the topic sentence fit the rest of the outline?

✓ Have I included enough causes or effects to make my point?

✓ Have I included enough details?

✓ Should I eliminate any ideas?

✓ Is the order of my causes or effects clear and logical?

The Order of Causes or Effects

Looking at a draft outline can help you decide on the best order for your reasons (causes) or results (effects). There is no single rule for organizing reasons or results. Instead, you should think about the ideas you're presenting and decide on the most logical and effective order.

For example, if you're writing about some immediate and some long-range effects, you might want to discuss the effects in a **time order**. You might begin with the immediate effect, then discuss what happens later, and end with what happens last of all. If you're discussing three or four effects that aren't in any particular time order, you might save the most important effect for last, for an **emphatic order**. If one cause leads to another, then use the **logical order** of discussing the causes.

Compare the following outline on owning a car to the previous list of effects. Notice that the carefree side of owning a car comes first, and the cares of owning a car, the expense and the worry, come later. The topic sentence follows the same order.

> ### An Outline for an Effects Paragraph
>
> **topic sentence:** Owning my own car gave me freedom, cost me money, and made me careful about how I drive.
>
> **effect 1:** I had the adult freedom to come and go.
> **details:** I didn't have to beg my father for his truck.
> I didn't have to get rides from my friends.
> I could go to the city when I wanted.
> I could ride around for fun.
>
> **effect 2:** I had to pay for the car and related expenses.
> **details:** A car costs a lot to maintain.
> I had car payments.
> I had a car loan to pay.
> I had car insurance.
>
> **effect 3:** I became a more careful driver.
> **details:** I worried about someone hitting the car.
> I worried about bad drivers.
> I wanted to avoid the scratches cars can get in a parking lot.

Once you have a revised outline of your cause or effect paragraph, you're ready to begin your draft.

EXERCISE 5

WRITING TOPIC SENTENCES FOR CAUSE OR EFFECT OUTLINES

Below are two outlines. They have no topic sentences. Read the outlines carefully, several times. Then write a topic sentence for each.

1. topic sentence: _____

   _____

   _____

details: When I don't get enough sleep, I get irritable.
Little things, like my friend's wise remarks, make me angry.
At work, I'm not as patient as I usually am when a customer complains.
Lack of sleep also slows me down.
When I'm tired, I can't think as fast.
For instance, it takes me ten minutes to find a number in the phone listings when I can usually find one in a minute.
When I'm tired, I'm slower in restocking the shelves at the store where I work.
Worst of all, I make more mistakes when I'm tired.
Last Monday, I was so tired I locked myself out of my car.
And a sleepless night can cause me to ring up a sale the wrong way.
Then I have to spend hours trying to fix my mistake before my boss catches it.

2. topic sentence: _____
_____
_____
_____

details: Denise wasn't really interested in the things I like to do.
She hated sports.
She always complained when we went to football games together.
Denise was not much fun to be with.
Whenever we were together, we wound up fighting over some trivial thing.
For example, we once spent a whole evening arguing about what movie we should see.
My main reason for breaking up was Denise's lack of trust in me.
Denise couldn't believe I cared about her unless I showed her, every minute.
She made me call her at least three times a day.
She needed to know where I was at all times.
She was jealous of the time I spent away from her.

EXERCISE 6

REVISING THE ORDER OF CAUSES OR EFFECTS

Below are topic sentences and lists of causes or effects. Reorder each list according to the directions given at the end of the list. Put *1* by the item that would come first, *2* by the next one, and so forth.

1. topic sentence: My brother went on a diet for several reasons.

_____ He couldn't exercise for as long as he was used to.

_____ His clothes were too tight.

_____ A doctor told him his weight was raising his cholesterol to a dangerous level.

Use this order: From least important to most important (emphatic order).

2. **topic sentence:** Cellphones have had a serious impact on driving.

    _____　Some areas are banning the use of cellphones by drivers.

    _____　Many accidents have involved distracted drivers texting on their cellphones.

    _____　People began to use cellphones while they drove because the phones were so convenient.

    Use this order: Time order.

3. **topic sentence:** Losing my job had negative and positive effects on me.

    _____　I was in a state of shock because I had no idea I'd be laid off.

    _____　I eventually realized that the job had been a dead-end one and that I could do better.

    _____　I went from shock to a feeling of failure.

    Use this order: The order indicated by the topic sentence, from bad to good.

EXERCISE **7**	**DEVELOPING AN OUTLINE**

The outlines below need one more cause or effect and details related to that cause or effect. Fill in the missing parts.

1. **topic sentence:** A promotion at work can be both rewarding and frightening.

    effect 1: Moving up is a sign that others respect a person's work.

    details: My father was thrilled to be promoted to assistant manager. His boss had told him that the promotion was a reward for good work.
    It also signalled his boss's faith in him.

    effect 2: In addition, a promotion is a chance to use more of one's talents and skills.

    details: I was delighted to move up in the shipping company I worked for.
    I knew I would no longer be locked into the same dull, daily routine.
    Instead, I could make some of my own decisions.

    effect 3: _____

    _____

    _____

    details (at least two sentences): _____

    _____

    _____

    _____

2. **topic sentence:** People give many reasons for running red lights.

    cause 1:   Some claim it was safe to do so.

    details: They say they were all alone on a deserted road.
               They say there was no traffic coming or going.
               Therefore, they say, they didn't need to stop.

    cause 2:   Many drivers swear they didn't see the light.

    details: Some swear they were distracted by their children misbehaving in the car.
               Others blame the dog; they say it jumped on them.
               A few say they were changing the radio station and didn't look up in time.

    cause 3: _____

_____

_____

    details (at least three sentences): _____

_____

_____

_____

DRAFTING AND REVISING

DRAFTING AND REVISING: CAUSE OR EFFECT

Once you have an outline in good order, with a sufficient number of causes or effects and a fair number of details, you can write a first draft of the paragraph. When the first draft is complete, you can read and reread it, deciding how you'd like to improve it. The checklist here may help you revise.

✓ **CHECKLIST**   **FOR REVISING THE DRAFT OF A CAUSE OR EFFECT PARAGRAPH**

   ✓   Does my topic sentence indicate cause or effect?

   ✓   Does it fit the rest of the paragraph?

   ✓   Do I have enough causes or effects to make my point?

   ✓   Do I have enough details for each cause or effect?

   ✓   Are my causes or effects explained clearly?

   ✓   Is there a clear connection between my points?

   ✓   Do I need to combine sentences?

   ✓   Do I need an opening or closing sentence?

Linking Ideas in Cause or Effect

When you write about how one event or situation causes another, or about how one result leads to another, you have to be clear in showing the connections between events, situations, or effects.

One way to be clear is to rely on transitions. Some transitions are particularly helpful in writing cause or effect paragraphs.

INFOBOX   **TRANSITIONS FOR A CAUSE OR EFFECT PARAGRAPH**

For cause paragraphs: because, due to, for, for this reason, since

For effect paragraphs: as a result, consequently, hence, in consequence, so, then, therefore, thus

---

Making the Links Clear

Using the right transition word isn't always enough. Sometimes you have to write the missing link in your line of thinking so that the reader can understand your point. To write the missing link means writing phrases, clauses, or sentences that help the reader follow your reasoning.

> **not this:**   Many parents are working outside the home. Consequently, takeout and convenience foods are popular.

> **but this:**   Many parents are working outside the home and have less time to cook. Consequently, takeout and convenience foods, which are located near the entrance of most grocery stores, are popular.

The hard part of making clear links between ideas is that you have to put yourself in your reader's place. Remember that your reader can't read your mind, only your paper. Connections between ideas may be clear to you, but you must spell them out on the page.

Revising the Draft

Below is a draft of the paragraph on owning a car. When you read it, you'll notice many changes from the outline stage:

- The details on "car payments" and "a car loan" said the same thing, so the repetition has been cut out.
- Some details about the costs of maintaining a car and about parking have been added.
- The order of the details about the costs of a car has been changed. Now, paying for a car comes first, maintaining it comes after.
- Sentences have been combined.
- Transitions have been added.

> A Draft of an Effects Paragraph (*transitions are underlined*)
>
> Owning my own car gave me freedom, cost me money, and made me more careful about how I drive. <u>First of all,</u> my car gave me the adult freedom to come and go. I didn't have to beg my father for his truck or get rides from my friends anymore.

(continued)

I could go to the city or even ride around for fun when I wanted. <u>On the negative side,</u> I had to pay for the car and related expenses. I had to pay for the car loan. I also paid for car insurance. <u>A car costs a lot to maintain, too.</u> I paid for oil changes, tune-ups, tires, belts, and filters. <u>With so much of my money put into my car,</u> I became a more careful driver. I worried about someone hitting the car and watched out for bad drivers. <u>In addition,</u> I wanted to avoid the scratches a car can get in a parking lot, so I always parked far away from other cars.

EXERCISE 8

MAKING THE CONNECTIONS CLEAR

Below are ideas that are connected, but the connection is not clearly explained. Rewrite each pair of ideas, making the connection clear.

1. I never wrote a research paper in high school. Therefore, I did poorly in Canadian economic history in college.

   rewritten: _____

   _____

   (Hint: Did your Canadian economic history class require a research paper? Did you know how to write one?)

2. Young teens see musicians and actors with elaborate tattoos. The young teens want to get tattoos.

   rewritten: _____

   _____

   _____

   (Hint: Do the young teens want to look like their favourite musicians and actors?)

3. I drank three cups of coffee last night. Consequently, I couldn't sleep.

   rewritten: _____

   _____

   (Hint: Do you usually or rarely drink coffee at night? What substance in the coffee kept you awake?)

4. Some cities are facing massive traffic jams on the highways. As a result, the cities have created carpool-only lanes.

   rewritten: _____

   _____

   (Hint: Are the carpool-only lanes designed to encourage drivers to share rides? What makes the lanes attractive?)

5. Pine Tree College was nearer to home than Lake College. As a result, I went to Pine Tree College.

   rewritten: _____

   _____

   _____

(Hint: Did you want a college close to home? Did you want to save money by attending college and living at home? Did you want a shorter trip to school?)

| EXERCISE 9 | REVISING A PARAGRAPH BY ADDING DETAILS |

Each of the following paragraphs is missing details. Add details—at least two sentences—to each paragraph using the blank lines.

1. Becoming a parent has made me a happier, more cautious, and more ambitious person. I had never believed the friends who told me that parenthood would change my life, but they were right. First of all, parenthood has brought the joy of watching my child grow and change every day. I am constantly amazed when I realize that I'm a part of this little person. My happiness is mixed with caution because I'm protective of my child. I now listen to the weather report every day because I don't want my child to catch cold in the snow or sniffle in the rain. I scan every room in my apartment to clear it of the stray pencil or china coffee mug that my baby might pick up. Being a parent has made me more careful than I've ever been, and also more ambitious.

   _____

   _____

   _____

   _____

Now that I have a child, I feel that I've been reborn as a more fulfilled, careful, and motivated person.

2. The school board had good reasons for closing Maple Heights Secondary School. First, the school was extremely overcrowded. Maple Heights Secondary was designed to hold 2000 students; last year, it had 4500. Expanding it to accommodate a population that continues to grow would be more expensive than building a new school. The school wasn't only too small; it was also in the wrong place. When it opened thirty-five years ago, Maple Heights was surrounded by neighbourhoods with families, but shortly after, the

neighbourhood changed. Today, the school is surrounded by empty lots and decaying warehouses. Maple Heights hasn't kept up with the changing times in another respect. It lacks the modern technology a good school needs.

_____

_____

_____

_____

Although it's always difficult to see a secondary school close, Maple Heights is too crowded, poorly located, and outdated to save.

EXERCISE 10 — REVISING A DRAFT BY COMBINING SENTENCES

Combine the underlined sentences in the following paragraph. Write your combinations in the space above the original sentences.

The latest television commercial is designed to make viewers think that freedom, excitement, and nature come with the car. First of all, the ad starts with a tired executive. The executive rips off his tie and leaps into his convertible. As he speeds out of the city, the viewers get a sense of freedom. The freedom is connected to a sense of excitement. The car zips past slower cars. Loud rock 'n' roll plays on the soundtrack. The car races around curves and conquers dangerous corners. Soon, viewers see the ultimate effect of owning the convertible. The car brings the executive to the middle of a green area. There is a gorgeous lake. Everything is unspoiled. The rock 'n' roll music fades away, and the only sounds heard are bird calls and gentle breezes. Truly, this commercial says, a new car can change viewers' lives. This ad isn't really for a car; instead, it sells a dream of excitement and escape.

PROOFREADING

PROOFREADING AND POLISHING: CAUSE OR EFFECT

Following is the final version of the paragraph on owning a car. When you contrast the final version with the draft, you'll notice several changes:

- An introductory sentence has been added.
- Some sentences have been combined.
- Transitions have been revised.
- Some words have been changed so that the language is more precise.

Changes in style, word choice, sentence variety, and transitions can all be made before you decide on the final version of your paragraph. You may also want to add an opening or closing to your paragraph.

> A Final Version of an Effects Paragraph (*changes from the draft are underlined*)

<u>When I bought my first car, I wasn't prepared for all the changes it made in my life.</u> Owning my own car gave me freedom, cost me money, and made me careful about how I drive. First of all, my car gave me the adult freedom to come and go. I didn't have to beg my father for his truck or get rides from my friends anymore. I could go to the city or even ride around for fun when I wanted. On the negative side, I had to pay for the car and related expenses. <u>I had to pay for both the car loan and car insurance.</u> A car costs <u>money</u> to maintain, too. I paid for oil changes, tune-ups, tires, belts, and filters. With so much of my money put into my car, I became a more careful driver. I worried about someone hitting the car and watched out for bad drivers. <u>To avoid dangers in the parking lot,</u> I always parked far away from other cars, <u>keeping my car safe from scratches.</u>

Before you prepare the final copy of your paragraph, check your latest draft for errors in spelling and punctuation, and for any errors made in typing or recopying.

EXERCISE 11

PROOFREADING TO PREPARE THE FINAL VERSION

Below are one cause paragraph and one effect paragraph with the kinds of errors that are easy to overlook when you prepare the final version of an assignment. Correct the errors, writing above the lines. There are nine errors in the first paragraph and eight errors in the second paragraph.

1. I signed up for an Introduction to Computers class this semster so that I could get some useful skills. One reason I took the Course is that, I want to be able to use my son's computer. He is ten years old and knows all about email and the Internet, but I don't know anything. At thirty, I should be able to keep up with my son. I also want to know some thing my son doesn't know, and that is how to do word processing. Now that I am in college, I have many written assinments that would be much easier if I knew word processing. A basic knowledge of computers would also be a important asset in my future. Right now I am in a low-paying job, but I think I get a better job if I had some computer skills. I know that banks, stores, schools, buisnesses, and hospitals all want to hire people who know how to use technolgy. I believe learning computer skills will help me at home, at school, and at work.

2.   A major traffic jam can have a number of affects. Of coarse, the tie-up directly affects those caught in it and the drivers forced to find alternite routes. These people experience frustration and even rage as they realize they will be late for work, school, or other responsibility. When they finally excape the traffic snarl they take their nasty moods with them. They should consider themselves lucky to get out with no damage but lost time. Others has more to complain about. They get caught in the overheating cars or minor accidents that occur when traffic cannot move. these poor drivers have to deal with tow trucks, repair services, and even insurance agents. While most people think of a traffic jam's effects on drivers, not many think of it's effect on law enforcement. The local or provincial police must not only find the cause of the gridlock but also deal with impatient drivers. While some search for the source of the traffic snarl. Other officers direct the masses of cars to merge or take a detour. A traffic jam calls for patience in every direction.

Lines of Detail: A Walk-Through Assignment

Write a paragraph on this topic: "Why Canadians Are Eating More Meals Away from Home." To write your paragraph, follow these steps:

Step 1:   Go back to Exercise 3, topic 4 of this chapter (on page 216). Topic 4 is the same topic as this assignment. If you've done that exercise, you've already written five or more questions that can lead you to ideas and details. If you haven't done the exercise, do topic 4 now.

Step 2:   Use the answers to your questions to prepare a list of ideas and details. Put the items on your list into groups of reasons and related details. Add to the groups until you have at least three reasons (and related details) why Canadians are eating more meals away from home.

Step 3:   Write a topic sentence that fits your reasons.

Step 4:   Write an outline. Check that your outline has sufficient details and that you've put the reasons in the best order.

Step 5:   Write a rough draft of your paragraph. Revise it until you have enough specific details to explain each reason, and the links between your ideas are smooth and clear. Check whether any sentences should be combined and whether your paragraph could use an opening sentence or a concluding one.

Step 6:   Before you prepare the final copy of your paragraph, check your latest draft for word choice, punctuation, transitions, and spelling.

Writing Your Own Cause or Effect Paragraph

When you write on any of the following topics, make sure to work through the stages of the writing process.

1. Write a cause paragraph on one of the following topics. Create the topic by filling in the blanks.

Why I Chose _____

Why I Stopped _____

Why I Enjoy _____

Why I Started _____

Why I Hate _____

Why I Bought _____

Why I Decided _____

2. Write a one-paragraph letter of complaint to the manufacturers of a product you bought or to the company that owns a hotel, restaurant, airline, or some other service you used. In your letter, write at least three reasons why you (1) want your money refunded or (2) want the product replaced. Be clear and specific about your reasons. Make sure your letter has a topic sentence.

    If your instructor agrees, read a draft of your letter to a writing partner and ask your partner to pretend to be the manufacturer or the head of the company. Ask your partner to point out where your ideas aren't clear or convincing and where you make your point effectively.

3. Think of a current fad or trend. The fad can be a popular style of clothing, a kind of movie, a type of music, a sport, a pastime, an actor, an athlete, a gadget, an invention, or an appliance. Write a paragraph on the causes of this fad or trend or the effects of it.

    If your instructor agrees, begin by brainstorming with a group. Create a list of three or four fads or trends. Then create a list of questions to ask (and answer) about each fad or trend. If you're going to write about causes, for example, you might ask questions like

What changes in society have encouraged this trend?

Have changes in the economy helped to make it popular?

Does it appeal to a specific age group? Why?

Does it meet any hidden emotional needs? For instance, is it a way to gain status, or to feel safe, or powerful?

If you're going to write about effects, you might ask questions like

Will this trend last?

Has it affected competitors?

Is it spreading?

Is the fad changing business, education, or the family?

Has it improved daily life?

WRITING FROM READING: CAUSE AND EFFECT

Saving the Planet One Swamp at a Time
David Suzuki

David Suzuki is arguably Canada's most famous and well-respected environmental educator. He has worked in the media as a journalist and broadcaster, and in 1990 founded the David Suzuki

Foundation, a non-profit organization dedicated to examining public policy and educating the public about environmental issues.

Before you read this selection, consider these questions:

Do you have a special memory of nature?

Aside from the obvious environmental impacts, what other impacts might global warming have?

Currently, what efforts do you and your family make to reduce your impact on the environment?

indelible: cannot be removed; permanent

Do you have a swamp? I don't mean literally. I mean a special place where, at some point, you really connected with nature—a place that made an **indelible** imprint on your mind, the smell, the sound, the feel of which has stayed with you forever.

Maybe yours was a family cabin at the lake. Or a special river where you canoed with your grandfather. Or a tree you climbed in your backyard. Mine actually was a swamp near my home in London, Ont. I spent hours there, looking for frogs and birds, and wading through the **brackish** water, searching for new life. Afterward, I would lie on my back in the tall grass, drying off, breathing the humid air, staring up at the sky, and wondering about it all. How vast it all seemed and how **puny** I felt in comparison.

brackish: slightly salty

puny: very small

Back then, I would never have imagined human beings could significantly alter something as huge as the planet's atmosphere. It was beyond comprehension. Sure, when I was very young, I remember smoke fogs from wood and coal burning in Vancouver, where I was born, that settled in on the city and made it difficult to see across the street. But a good wind would eventually clear the smoke. That's the way it always was. Nature took care of our waste, cleansing our air and water and making them pure again.

What I didn't know as a boy was that my swamp and the sky above me were not actually separate things at all. Our atmosphere, our oceans, our lakes, soils and all living things are intricately connected. Making a major change to any one thing in this zone of life, our biosphere, will have profound repercussions throughout the entire system. It can actually affect how our natural services function. That's why global warming is such a big deal.

In Canada, it's tempting to shrug off global warming as something that will make life in our cold country more pleasant. Vineyards in Winnipeg, farms in the Arctic. But the reality is not so simple. And decidedly less fun.

By burning vast quantities of fossil fuels like coal, oil and gas, and by cutting down massive forested areas, humans have released enough greenhouse gases and reduced the absorptive capacity of nature enough to fundamentally alter our atmosphere. There is now 32 per cent more carbon dioxide, the main greenhouse gas, in our atmosphere today than there was before the industrial revolution.

The trouble with greenhouse gases like carbon dioxide is that they trap heat, much like a blanket, and hold it near the planet's surface. If we didn't have any of these gases, heat from the sun would shine onto the planet and then radiate back into space, and our planet would be either too hot or too cold. Over millions of years, our Earth has created the perfect conditions for life, with just the right amount of greenhouse gases to ensure that it is never too hot or too cold. Without this stable climate, human civilization would likely never have developed to where we are today. We depend on it.

But all the extra carbon dioxide and other gases we keep adding to the air are disrupting the stable climate that has been so very important to us. I say "disrupting" because it is really a more accurate description of what happens. Adding heat to the atmosphere also means adding energy that can **manifest** itself in unusual ways—more frequent or extreme storms, for example.

manifest: show, display

In other words, global warming does not equate to a modest, pleasant warming. Rather, it means higher global temperatures overall, which translates to a host of other, often unforeseen, problems. This year, the headlines have been full of these issues: falling water tables, retreating lakeshores, acidification of oceans, shrinking ice caps and glaciers, expanded ranges for invasive species, and more. Even noxious weeds like poison ivy are expected to blossom in a carbon-dioxide enriched atmosphere.

Air quality in urban areas will also be affected. Smog is created from a chemical interaction in the atmosphere between automobile and smokestack pollution, and heat and sunlight. More heat and more sunlight will mean more smog. Resulting new **infrastructure** needs and increasing health care costs add up quickly. Already, the Ontario Medical Association says air pollution costs the province more than $1 billion in hospital charges and lost workdays. That will only get worse as our climate warms.

infrastructure: the basic foundation of a system or organization

But enough about the risks—most people are aware of them by now. Scary stories have been all over the news for the past six months. In fact, it seems like results of yet another study are published practically every day confirming something bad about global warming. It's getting to the point where I worry people will be tempted to just throw up their hands and say "I give up!" Yet that would be a huge mistake, because it's not too late to avoid what scientists call "dangerous warming." Yes, some warming has already occurred and more will come, but we can still avoid the **brunt** of a disrupted climate by taking action now.

brunt: the main burden

Sir Nicholas Stern, former chief economist with the World Bank, has estimated that to pay for all the changes necessary to avoid dangerous warming, it will cost the global economy about 1 per cent of the world's annual GDP. That's not insignificant. But what's astounding is what it will cost us if we carry on with business as usual: up to 20 per cent of the global economy per year, which could lead to a worldwide depression.

So taking action now is far and away the most **prudent** financial course. We simply cannot afford to wait. A recent statement by the scientific academies of 13 countries put it this way: "The problem is not yet insoluble, but becomes more difficult with each passing day."

prudent: reasonable, practical

Tackling the problem sufficiently will involve all sectors of society, from governments to businesses and individuals. It means having firm national targets and timelines that will spur innovation and provide certainty and a level playing field for industry.

It means giving individuals options so they can more easily pick the most sustainable choice. And it means leadership at all levels to break us away from the status quo and put us on a new path.

Individuals can learn about reducing their own footprint at dozens of environmental websites or they can take the initiative and:

Leave the car at home and sometimes walk, bike, or take transit.

Switch all their light bulbs to modern energy-efficient CFLs.

Buy fuel-efficient vehicles.

Choose more local foods.

Use a programmable thermostat.

Buy Energy Star appliances.

Weather-strip their homes.

Encourage friends or political leaders to take action.

I could go on and on.

Many people are already doing these things, but to really solve global warming we need our leaders to take it seriously, too. Because right now, Canada is still falling behind. And our world, which once seemed so vast and limitless, is actually far smaller and more interconnected than we could ever have imagined.

UNDERSTANDING "SAVING THE PLANET ONE SWAMP AT A TIME"

1. According to the article, what are two causes of global warming?

2. List at least three effects of global warming, according to Suzuki's article. Are any of these surprising or new to you?

3. Suzuki has listed some ways in which individuals can help the environment. What do you, your family, and your friends do to minimize your impact on the environment? What else might you consider doing? What would it take for you to consider doing more?

WRITING FROM READING "SAVING THE PLANET ONE SWAMP AT A TIME"

When you write on any of the following topics, make sure to work through the stages of the writing process.

1. Environmentalists have often encouraged the public to "think globally, act locally." What do you think this means? Write a paragraph in which you discuss some of the effects of doing this.

2. Suzuki mentions fond memories of a swamp he visited in childhood as one of the reasons he is so environmentally aware today. Think of some of the issues you feel strongly about: What are your reasons for feeling that way? Write a paragraph in which you discuss the causes of your passion.

3. It has been said that global warming will affect the poor more than the wealthy. Do you agree or disagree? Write a paragraph on the effects of global warming on the poor.

4. Do you think global warming affects countries differently? Write a paragraph in which you explore how global warming uniquely affects Canada or another country.

CHAPTER 10
Argument

"When I'm getting ready to reason with a man, I spend one-third of my time thinking about myself and what I am going to say— and two-thirds thinking about him and what he is going to say."

~ ABRAHAM LINCOLN

▼

KNOWN FOR HIS POWERFUL SPEECHES, ABRAHAM LINCOLN WAS THE SIXTEENTH PRESIDENT OF THE UNITED STATES AND BROUGHT AN END TO SLAVERY IN HIS COUNTRY.

WHAT IS ARGUMENT?

A written **argument** is an attempt to *persuade* a reader to think or act in a certain way. When you write an argument paragraph, your goal is to get people to see your point, to agree with it, and perhaps to act on it.

In an argument paragraph, you take a stand. Then you support your stand with reasons. In addition, you give details for each reason. Your goal is to persuade your reader by making a point that has convincing reasons and details.

Hints for Writing an Argument Paragraph

1. **Pick a topic you can handle.** Your topic should be small enough to be covered in one paragraph. For instance, you can't argue effectively for world peace in just one paragraph.
2. **Pick a topic you can handle based on your own experience and observation.** Such topics as drug legalization, gun control, capital punishment, or air pollution require extensive research into facts, figures, and expert opinions to make a complete argument. These are topics you can write

about convincingly in a longer research paper, but for a one-paragraph argument, choose a topic based on what you've experienced yourself.

| not this topic: | Pollution |
| but this topic: | How Pollution Has Affected My Health |

3. **Do two things in your topic sentence: Name the subject of your argument, and take a stand.** The following topic sentences do both:

subject	takes a stand
The college	cafeteria should serve more healthy snacks.

subject	takes a stand
High school athletes who fail a course	should not be allowed to play on a school team.

You should take a stand, but *don't announce it*:

| not this: | This paragraph will explain why Medicine Hat needs a teen centre. |
| but this: | Medicine Hat should open a teen centre. (A topic sentence with a subject and a stand.) |

4. **Consider your audience.** Consider why these people should support your points. How will they be likely to object? How will you get around these objections? For instance, you might want to argue, to the residents of your community, that the intersection of Hawthorne Road and Sheridan Street needs a traffic light. Would anyone object?

At first you might think, "No. Why would anyone object? The intersection is dangerous. There's too much traffic there. People risk major accidents while getting across the intersection." But if you think further about your audience, which is the people in your community, you might identify these objections: Some town residents may not want to pay for a traffic signal. Some drivers may not want to spend extra time waiting for a light to change.

There are several ways to handle objections. First, you can *refute* an objection. To refute it means to prove it isn't valid. For instance, if someone says that a light wouldn't do any good, you might say that a new light has already worked in a nearby neighbourhood.

Sometimes, it's best to admit that the other side has a point. You have to *concede* that point. For instance, traffic lights do cost money. And waiting for a light to change does take time.

Sometimes, you can *turn an objection into an advantage*. When you acknowledge the objection and yet use it to make your own point, you show that you've intelligently considered both sides of the argument. This is what Abraham Lincoln meant in the accompanying quotation. For instance, you might say that the cost of a traffic signal at the intersection is well worth it because that light will buy safety for all the drivers who try to cross Hawthorne Road and Sheridan Street. Or you might say that waiting a few moments for the light to change is better than waiting many minutes for an opening in the heavy traffic of the intersection.

5. **Be specific, clear, and logical in your reasons.** As always, think before you write. Think about your point and your audience. Try to come up with at least three reasons for your position.

Be careful that your reasons do not overlap. For instance, you might write the following:

topic sentence: College students should get discounts on transit passes.

audience: chair of the Transit Commission

reasons: 1. Given their limited budgets, many college students can't afford to pay as much as adults who work full-time.
2. The cost of passes is high for most students.
3. More people taking public transit reduces emissions.

Notice that reasons 1 and 2 overlap; they are really part of the same reason.

Be careful not to argue in a circle. For instance, if you say, "One reason for having an afterschool program at Riverside Elementary School is that we need one there," you've just said, "We need an afterschool program because we need an afterschool program."

Finally, be specific in stating your reasons.

not this: One reason to start a bus service to and from the college is to help people.

but this: A bus service to and from the college would encourage students to leave their cars at home and use travel time to study.

| EXERCISE **1** | RECOGNIZING GOOD TOPIC SENTENCES IN AN ARGUMENT PARAGRAPH |

Some of the following topic sentences are appropriate for an argument paragraph. Some are for topics that are too large for one paragraph or require research. Others are announcements or don't take a stand. Put *OK* next to the sentences that would work well in an argument paragraph.

1. _____ People should try to cure their own addictions.
2. _____ Graffiti is a much-maligned art form.
3. _____ We must ban offshore oil drilling in Canadian waters.
4. _____ Junk food should be banned at all elementary schools.
5. _____ We need stricter penalties for young offenders.
6. _____ Something should be done about victims' rights.
7. _____ The city should incorporate bicycle lanes on all major streets.
8. _____ Tolls on provincial highways are a good way to ease pollution.
9. _____ The reasons to ban bottled water will be the subject of this essay.
10. _____ College students deserve more financial aid.

EXERCISE **2**	**RECOGNIZING AND HANDLING OBJECTIONS**

Below are topic sentences of arguments. Working with a group, list two possible objections to each argument that might come from the specific audience identified. Then think of ways to handle each objection, either by refuting it, conceding it, or trying to turn it to your advantage. On the lines provided, write the actual sentence(s) you would use in a paragraph.

1. **topic sentence:** The college library, which is currently open until 10:00 p.m., should be open until midnight every night.

   audience: the deans, the vice-president, the president of the college

   possible objections from this audience:

   a. _____

   b. _____

   answering objections:

   a. _____

   b. _____

2. **topic sentence:** During the summer, the municipal government should keep public schools open for community programs.

   audience: the schools' local communities

   possible objections from this audience:

   a. _____

   b. _____

   answering objections:

   a. _____

   b. _____

3. **topic sentence:** Broadleaf Public School should ban junk-food vending machines in its hallways.

   audience: principal of Broadleaf Public School, trustees, superintendents

   possible objections from this audience:

   a. _____

   b. _____

   answering objections:

   a. _____

   b. _____

4.   **topic sentence:** The Downtown Doughnut Shop should stop serving coffee in styrofoam cups.

audience: the owners of the Downtown Doughnut Shop

possible objections from this audience:

a. _____

b. _____

answering objections:

a. _____

b. _____

5.   **topic sentence:** Local daycare centres should be required, by law, to provide one adult supervisor for every two children under the age of one year.

audience: the owners of the Happy Child Daycare Centre, which currently has one adult supervisor for every three children under the age of one year

possible objections from this audience:

a. _____

b. _____

answering objections:

a. _____

b. _____

WRITING THE ARGUMENT PARAGRAPH IN STEPS

PREWRITING   ### GATHERING IDEAS: ARGUMENT

Imagine that your instructor has given you this assignment:

> Write a one-paragraph letter to the editor of your college newspaper. Argue for something at your college that needs to be changed.

One way to begin is to brainstorm for some specific point you can write about.

> Are there services at the college that should be improved?
>
> Is there a way that the college could be more engaged with the community?
>
> Are there college facilities that could be improved or renovated?
>
> What could be done to improve the student experience?

By answering these questions, you may come up with one topic, and then you can list ideas about it.

> **topic:**   Reducing the College's Environmental Impact
>
> **ideas:**   recycling and reducing the use of paper
>
>   automated lighting and heating

green roof

solar panels

entire college community could participate

use of local food in the cafeteria

You can consider your audience and possible objections:

audience: the college community: students, faculty, staff, and administrators

possible objections from this audience: Would cost money.
More important things to spend money on.

answering objections: Over time, the college would save more money than it initially spends. The college community would feel a greater connection with the neighbouring community.

Grouping Your Ideas

Once you have a list, you can start grouping the ideas in your list. Some of the objections you wrote down may actually lead you to reasons that support your argument. That is, by answering objections, you may come up with reasons that support your point. Below is a list with a point to argue, three supporting reasons, and some details about reducing the college's environmental impact.

> ### A List for an Argument Paragraph
>
> **point:** The college should transform the campus roof to a green roof.
>
> **reason:** A green roof would reduce heating and cooling costs.
>
> **details:** Such a roof would insulate the building from the summer's heat. This roof would also retain heat better in the winter.
>
> **reason:** A green roof would reduce the college's environmental impact.
>
> **details:** Such a roof would absorb heat in the summer, reflecting less back into the atmosphere.
> This roof would absorb carbon dioxide, a contributor to the greenhouse effect, and release oxygen.
>
> **reason:** Students and staff could enjoy the green space in their free time.
>
> **details:** Students could meet and socialize with friends in the fresh air.
> Staff could eat their lunch in a natural setting.

With three reasons and some details for each, you can draft a topic sentence. Remember that your topic sentence for an argument should (1) name your subject and (2) take a stand. Here is a topic sentence that does both:

subject — takes a stand

The college — should transform the campus roof to a green roof.

Now that you have a topic sentence, you're ready to move on to the outline stage of preparing an argument paragraph.

EXERCISE 3	DISTINGUISHING BETWEEN REASONS AND DETAILS

Each list below has three reasons and details for each reason. Write *reason 1*, *reason 2*, or *reason 3* next to the reasons on each list. Then write *detail for 1*, *detail for 2*, or *detail for 3* next to the items that give details about each reason. There may be more than one sentence of details connected to one reason.

1. **topic sentence:** The city needs to pick up garbage at my apartment complex three times, not twice, a week.

_____ Garbage spills out past the dumpster.

_____ People throw their garbage on top of already loaded dumpsters; the bags fall and split open.

_____ Garbage that piles up, uncovered, is a health hazard.

_____ Too much garbage accumulates when the schedule allows for only two pickups.

_____ Flies buzz over the garbage, a sign of dangerous contamination that can spread.

_____ The roaches from the garbage area move into the apartments, carrying disease.

_____ Garbage piles make people lose pride in their neighbourhood.

_____ Apartment residents are starting to litter the parking lot because they've lost respect for their homes.

_____ One long-time resident is thinking of moving to a better neighbourhood.

2. **topic sentence:** Children under ten years of age should not be permitted in the Mountain Mall unless they're accompanied by an adult.

_____ It's not safe for children to be alone in the mall.

_____ Unsupervised children cause trouble for mall merchants.

_____ Children left alone in the mall aren't always happy with their freedom.

_____ I saw one nine-year-old boy roam the mall for hours, looking forlorn.

_____ Sometimes pairs of sad young girls wait by the food court for an hour, until a parent, who is late, remembers to pick them up.

_____ Once I saw two seven-year-old boys walk back and forth in front of my store for half an hour, with nothing to do.

_____	Children have been kidnapped in malls.
_____	If a child gets sick at the mall, will he or she know what to do?
_____	Bored children run through stores, chasing each other.
_____	I saw one child shoplifting.

EXERCISE 4

FINDING REASONS TO SUPPORT AN ARGUMENT

Give three reasons that support the point that is made. In each case, the readers of your local newspaper will be the audience for an argument paragraph.

1. **point:** The province should ban all telephone sales calls between the hours of 5:00 p.m. and 8:00 p.m.

   reasons:

   a. _____

   b. _____

   c. _____

2. **point:** Our city must ban the use of office lighting after work hours.

   reasons:

   a. _____

   b. _____

   c. _____

3. **point:** Cellphones should be banned in classrooms.

   reasons:

   a. _____

   b. _____

   c. _____

4. **point:** Public education should start with preschool, at age three.

   reasons:

   a. _____

   b. _____

   c. _____

PLANNING   DEVISING A PLAN: ARGUMENT

With a topic sentence and a list of reasons and details, you can draft an outline. Then you can review it, making whatever changes you think it needs. The following checklist may help you review and revise your outline.

✓ **CHECKLIST**   **FOR REVISING AN ARGUMENT OUTLINE**

✓ Does my topic sentence make my point? Does it state a subject and take a stand?

✓ Have I considered the objections to my argument so that I'm arguing intelligently?

✓ Do I have all the reasons I need to make my point?

✓ Do any reasons overlap?

✓ Are my reasons specific?

✓ Do I have enough details for each reason?

✓ Are my reasons in the best order?

communication at work

Argument and conflict are inevitable whenever you have to work with other people; different personalities, work experiences, and styles, combined with the stress of our daily lives, can make for an explosive environment. In recognition of this, most corporations today have devoted numerous programs and workshops to training their employees to deal with conflict. Although there are a number of theories on how to deal with conflict, many have the same premise as your argument paragraph: clearly, objectively stated details in support of your argument, along with an acknowledgment of the other person's point of view, will often give you a win–win situation.

The Order of Reasons in an Argument

When you're giving several reasons, it's a good idea to keep the most convincing or most important reason for last. Saving the best for last is called using **emphatic order**. For example, you might have these three reasons to tear down an abandoned building in your neighbourhood: (1) the building is ugly, (2) drug dealers are using the building, and (3) the building is infested with rats. The most important reason, the drug dealing, should be used last, for an emphatic order.

Below is an outline on transforming the college roof to a green roof. When you look at the outline, you'll notice several changes from the previous list:

- Since lessening the college's negative environmental impact is the most important, it's put as the last detail.
- Some details have been added.
- A sentence has been added at the end of the outline. It explains why the green roof is a good idea even to people who will never use it themselves. It's a way of answering these people's objections.

> ## An Outline for an Argument Paragraph
>
> **topic sentence:**   The college should transform the campus roof to a green roof.
>
> **reason:**   A green roof would reduce heating and cooling costs.
>
> **details:**   Such a roof would insulate the building from the summer's heat, thus reducing cooling costs.
>
>   This roof would also insulate in the winter, allowing the building to retain heat and reducing heating costs.
>
> **reason:**   Students and staff could enjoy the green space in their free time.
>
> **details:**   Students could meet and socialize with friends in the fresh air.
>
>   Staff could eat their lunches in a natural setting, reducing stress.
>
> **reason:**   A green roof would reduce the college's environmental impact.
>
> **details:**   Such a roof would absorb heat in the summer, reflecting less back into the atmosphere.
>
>   This roof would absorb carbon dioxide, a contributor to the greenhouse effect, and release oxygen.
>
> **final idea:**   With its environmental advantages, a green roof would benefit not only the college community but also the surrounding neighbourhood.

EXERCISE 5

WORKING WITH THE ORDER OF REASONS IN AN ARGUMENT OUTLINE

Below are topic sentences and lists of reasons. For each list, put a star or asterisk in the blank beside the reason that is the most significant—the reason you would save for last in an argument paragraph.

1. **topic sentence:** Manufacturers of vitamins should stop the double packaging of their products.

   reason 1: _____ Putting a small bottle into a big box is deceptive, making buyers think they're getting more for their money.

   reason 2: _____ Consumers with arthritis find it difficult to open two packages.

   reason 3: _____ Double packaging wastes valuable natural resources.

2. **topic sentence:** Our city should not sell public space, such as benches and garbage cans, to advertisers.

   reason 1: _____ Advertising is ugly.

   reason 2: _____ The city shouldn't be able to decide on the use of public space without asking the public's opinion.

   reason 3: _____ There is already too much advertising in the city.

3. **topic sentence:** The province's highway speed limit should not be raised.

    reason 1: _____ A slower speed limit has been shown to save lives.

    reason 2: _____ One hundred kilometres an hour is the ideal speed limit to maximize fuel efficiency.

    reason 3: _____ The current speed limit maintains the ideal traffic flow.

4. **topic sentence:** Seven-year-olds should be given a small allowance to spend as they wish.

    reason 1: _____ Seven-year-olds see other children their age with spending money.

    reason 2: _____ Children need to learn to handle money responsibly.

    reason 3: _____ Learning to make change develops math skills.

| EXERCISE **6** | RECOGNIZING REASONS THAT OVERLAP |

Below are topic sentences and lists of reasons. In each list, two reasons overlap. Put an X beside the two reasons that overlap.

1. **topic sentence:** The college cafeteria should serve more locally grown food.

    a. _____ The college would be supporting small, independent farmers.

    b. _____ Fresher products contain more nutrients.

    c. _____ Spending money within the province supports local jobs and the local economy.

    d. _____ Students would be willing to pay more for fresher, healthier meals.

2. **topic sentence:** Advertising should be banned from all Saturday morning children's TV programs.

    a. _____ Young children are too innocent to know the way advertising works.

    b. _____ Much advertising is for unhealthy food, like sugary cereals and junk food.

    c. _____ Advertising manipulates unsuspecting children.

    d. _____ A lot of commercials push expensive toys that many parents can't afford.

3. **topic sentence:** Our college needs a larger, lighted sign at the entrance.

    a. _____ Some residents of our town have never heard of our college, so a large sign would be good publicity.

    b. _____ Visitors to the college have a hard time finding it.

    c. _____ Students who are preoccupied sometimes drive right past the entrance to their college at night.

    d. _____ A better sign would make people more aware of the college.

EXERCISE 7	IDENTIFYING A REASON THAT IS NOT SPECIFIC

In each of the following lists, put an *X* beside the reason that is not specific.

1. **topic sentence:** The college library should ban access to social networking sites on its computers.

   a. _____ Students who need to use the library's computers for research often can't find an available computer.

   b. _____ Students who access social networking sites often use the computer for hours.

   c. _____ Computers are frequently infected by viruses from the sites.

   d. _____ There aren't enough computers in the library.

2. **topic sentence:** Canadian college students should learn a foreign language.

   a. _____ Countries that compete with us economically, like Japan and Germany, have a competitive edge because their children routinely learn English.

   b. _____ It's often easier for a person to get a good job when he or she speaks two or more languages.

   c. _____ Learning a new language broadens a person's horizons.

   d. _____ Most Canadians have to interact with immigrants or visitors who don't speak English or French.

3. **topic sentence:** Our school should renovate the fitness centre in the college gym.

   a. _____ The lack of light in the fitness area discourages students from going.

   b. _____ An improved fitness centre would benefit students.

   c. _____ Because it's so small, only a handful of students can attend fitness classes.

   d. _____ The school could show its commitment to students' health and well-being.

EXERCISE 8	ADDING DETAILS TO AN OUTLINE

Below is part of an outline. It includes a topic sentence and three reasons. Add at least two sentences of detail to each reason. Your details may be examples or descriptions.

topic sentence: The staff at Bargain Supermarket should enforce the "9 Items or Fewer" rule at the express checkout lane.

reason: Customers who follow the rule suffer because of people who don't obey the rule.

detail: _____

_____

detail: _____

_____

reason: Not enforcing the rule can create unpleasant confrontations among
          customers.

detail: _____

_____

detail: _____

_____

reason: If it doesn't enforce the rule, Bargain Supermarket may lose customers.

detail: _____

_____

detail: _____

_____

DRAFTING AND REVISING

DRAFTING AND REVISING: ARGUMENT

Once you're satisfied with your outline, you can write the first draft of your paragraph. When you have completed it, you can begin revising the draft so that your argument is as clear, smooth, and convincing as it can be. The checklist below may help you with your revisions.

✓ **CHECKLIST** | **FOR REVISING THE DRAFT OF AN ARGUMENT PARAGRAPH**

  ✓ Do any of my sentences need combining?

  ✓ Have I left out a serious or obvious reason?

  ✓ Should I change the order of my reasons?

  ✓ Do I have enough details?

  ✓ Are my details specific?

  ✓ Do I need to explain the problem or issue I'm writing about?

  ✓ Do I need to link my ideas more clearly?

  ✓ Do I need a final sentence to stress my point?

Checking Your Reasons

Make sure that your argument has covered all the serious or obvious reasons. Sometimes, writers get so caught up in drafting their ideas that they forget to mention something very basic to the argument. For instance, if you were arguing for a leash law for your community, you might give the reason that off-lead dogs running free can hurt people, scare children, and damage property. But don't forget to mention another serious reason to keep dogs on leashes: Dogs that are not restrained can get hurt or killed by vehicles.

One way to see whether you've left out a serious or obvious reason is to ask a friend or classmate to read your draft and react to your argument. Another technique is to put your draft aside for an hour or two and then read it as if you were a reader, not the writer.

Explaining the Problem or the Issue

Sometimes, your argument discusses a problem so obvious to your audience that you don't need to explain it. But there are also times when you need to explain a problem or issue so that your audience can understand your point. If you tell readers of your local paper about teenage vandalism at Central High School, you probably need to explain what kind of vandalism has occurred there and how often. It's usually smart to convince readers of the seriousness of a situation by explaining it a little; that way, they'll be more persuaded by your argument.

Transitions That Emphasize

In writing an argument paragraph, you can use different transitions, depending on how you present your point. But no matter how you present your reasons, you'll probably want to *emphasize* one of them. The Infobox here shows some transitions that can be used for emphasis.

INFOBOX	TRANSITIONS TO USE FOR EMPHASIS

above all, especially, finally, mainly, most important, most of all, most significant, primarily

For example, by saying "*Most important,* broken windows at Central High School are a safety problem," you put the emphasis for your audience on this one idea.

A Draft

Below is a draft of the argument paragraph on the green roof. When you read it, you'll notice these changes from the outline:

- A description of the problem has been added.
- Details have been added.
- Short sentences have been combined.
- Transitions, including two sentences of transition, have been added. "Most importantly"—a transition that shows emphasis—has been included.

A Draft of an Argument Paragraph (*transitions are underlined*)

As a member of the neighbouring community, our college has an obligation to reduce its environmental impact as much as possible. The college should transform the campus roof to a green roof. A green roof would reduce heating and cooling costs. Such a roof would insulate the building from the summer's heat, thus reducing cooling costs. This roof would <u>also</u> insulate in the winter, allowing the building to retain heat. Cost savings <u>aren't the only reason</u> to transform the roof. The college community would benefit. Students and staff could enjoy the green space in their free time. Students could meet and socialize with friends in the fresh air; they could

(continued)

also meet for group projects or brainstorming sessions. Staff could eat their lunches in a natural setting, reducing stress. Perhaps *most importantly,* a green roof would reduce the college's environmental impact. Such a roof would absorb heat in the summer, reflecting less back into the atmosphere. This roof would absorb carbon dioxide, a contributor to the greenhouse effect, and release oxygen. *In addition,* it would create a habitat for insects and animals. With its environmental benefits, a green roof would benefit not only the college community, but also the surrounding neighbourhood.

EXERCISE **9**	**ADDING AN EXPLANATION OF THE PROBLEM TO AN ARGUMENT PARAGRAPH**

This paragraph could use an explanation of the problem before the argument is stated. Write a short explanation of the problem in the lines provided.

_____

_____

_____

Directional and exit signs on Lake Highway must be designed with larger lettering. Larger lettering would help a significant number of our residents. Lake Valley has many older residents whose vision is not perfect. Signs in large letters would make driving easier for those who are currently straining to see the right exit, only to find it as they pass it. Another group that would appreciate bigger lettering is visitors to the area. Many of them are struggling to find their way to a motel, restaurant, or store they've never seen, and they're not sure where to turn. Better signs would reduce their confusion and make their visit more pleasant. Most of all, larger lettering would result in safer driving. If signs were larger, drivers would see them sooner. Thus, they could change lanes sooner and more safely as they merged into the correct lane or got to an exit ramp. Many of the accidents caused by drivers suddenly switching lanes would be avoided. Better signs would then lead to safer, smoother driving.

EXERCISE **10**	**RECOGNIZING TRANSITIONS IN AN ARGUMENT PARAGRAPH**

Underline all the transitions—words, phrases, or sentences—in the following paragraph. Put a double line under any transitions that emphasize.

At the start of each workday, millions head to their jobs with good intentions. However, many start the day already tired and stressed and therefore unable to make their best efforts. They are living proof that workers in Canada need four weeks' annual paid vacation. Employees need more time off because they're facing more stress in the workplace. Many are working longer hours; some hold a second job to supplement their income. Bosses demand more productivity and new skills. Employees face further stress at home, too. When both parents work outside the home, they strain to find time for their children and their household duties. When one parent works, the family may face economic hardship due to the loss of income of the stay-at-home parent. Single parents struggle to cope alone. Those without partners or children may seem lucky, but they, too, fight to pay the bills and find time for a personal life. More vacation time would de-stress these workers, but most of all, it would also benefit employers. Exhausted, burned-out workers can't give their best when they're struggling just to get through the day. In contrast, people who have sufficient time to rest return to work with renewed energy. Thus, everyone—employees and employers—would profit from more vacation for workers.

EXERCISE **11**	**REVISING A DRAFT BY COMBINING SENTENCES**

In the following paragraph, combine each cluster of underlined sentences into one clear, smooth sentence. Write your combinations in the space above the original sentences.

At Ashley Apartments, there are large clusters of residents' mailboxes. They appear in front of each building. Each cluster has a couple of dozen individual mailboxes, each opened by a resident's key. The system works well. The mailboxes have one problem. These mailboxes need to be repaired immediately. They create a bad image for the apartments. They have crumbling plaster. They have rotten wood. Few people looking for an apartment and seeing the mailboxes would decide to rent at Ashley Apartments. The current renters are also affected by the sagging, chipped boxes. These residents lose respect for the apartment complex. This disrespect can be seen in the increase of litter. It can also be seen in the garbage bags. They're casually tossed beside the dumpsters, not inside them. The most significant reason to repair the mailboxes is a safety issue. The boxes are made of wood, plaster, and metal. As they begin to fall apart, they expose rough wooden boards and sharp metal edges. Children play in the parking lots. The parking lots are next to the mailboxes. One day soon, a child may run right into one of these wooden boards or sharp edges. Clearly, it is time to fix the situation.

EXERCISE 12

ADDING A FINAL SENTENCE TO AN ARGUMENT PARAGRAPH

The following paragraph would benefit from a final sentence to sum up the reasons or to reinforce the topic sentence. Add that final sentence in the space provided.

I am twenty years old, and I live with my parents while I work and attend college. Living at home, I'm comfortable and save money, but I'm in constant conflict with my parents. Parents of grown children who live at home should remember that these children are adults. Attempting to monitor grown children as if they were still in high school doesn't work. My parents continually ask me, "Where are you going? When will you be back?" They want to know when I plan to study or how I'm spending my money. The more questions they fire at me, the less I tell them. Questioning doesn't achieve its goal, and trying to control an adult child doesn't work, either. I've heard the warning, "You're still living under our roof, and as long as you do, you must follow our rules." This is a logical point, but most of the time I'm not under their roof. I'm at my job, at school, or with friends, so my folks must learn to trust me, not control me. The most significant reason why parents should respect their children's adult status is that respect leads to cooperation. I'm always happy when my parents praise one of my decisions—a decision made without their nagging. When they don't push me, I'm more likely to make choices they would approve of.

_____

_____

_____

PROOFREADING

PROOFREADING AND POLISHING: ARGUMENT

Below is the final version of the argument paragraph on the green roof. When you read the final version, you'll notice some changes from the draft:

- Some words have been changed to improve the details.
- Shorter sentences have been combined.

> **A Final Version of an Argument Paragraph (*changes from the draft are underlined*)**
>
> As a member of the neighbouring community, our college has an obligation to reduce its environmental impact as much as possible. The college should transform the campus roof to a green roof, and thereby reduce its heating and cooling costs.

Such a roof would insulate the building from the summer's heat, thus reducing cooling <u>costs; it would also</u> insulate in the winter, allowing the building to retain heat. <u>But</u> cost savings aren't the only reason to transform the <u>roof: The</u> college community would benefit<u>, too.</u> Students and staff could enjoy the green space in their free time. Students could meet and socialize with friends in the fresh air; they could also meet for group projects or brainstorming sessions. Staff could eat their lunches in a natural setting, reducing stress. Perhaps most importantly, a green roof would reduce the college's environmental impact. Such a roof would absorb heat in the summer, reflecting less back into the atmosphere. This roof would <u>also</u> absorb carbon dioxide, a contributor to the greenhouse effect, and release oxygen. In addition, it would create a habitat for insects and animals; <u>some courses could even do field work there.</u> With its environmental benefits, a green roof would benefit not only the college community, but also the surrounding neighbourhood.

Before you prepare the final copy of your argument paragraph, check your latest draft for errors in spelling and punctuation, and look for any errors made in typing or recopying.

EXERCISE 13

PROOFREADING TO PREPARE THE FINAL VERSION

Below are two paragraphs with the kinds of errors that are easy to overlook when you prepare the final version of an assignment. Correct the errors, writing above the lines. There are nine errors in the first paragraph and ten errors in the second paragraph.

1. Our college should create more student meeting areas on campus. Currently, the only places on campus for students to meet and socializing are the cafeteria and the library. However, these places are designated for other purposes—the cafeteria, for eating, and the library, for studying and doing research. It is usually so busy in the cafeteria that it is difficult to conversation, and quiet is needed in the library. Because the college does not have a dormitory, most students commuting to and from classes. A long commute home means that students often would prefer to leave immediately after class instead of meeting of campus to relax. More student meeting areas on campus would mean more revenue for the campus cafeteria and stores. Students would feel more connected to their college and find it more easier to make friends. It would be easier to work on group assignments and projects, some may argue

that there is no space to create student gathering places, or that it would cost too much to convert existing spaces. However, the morale and sense of college community such gathering places would create in the student body, would be well worth the cost. In fact, students may be willing to contribute a small, additional amount toward the creation of these spaces. Many student councils of other post-secondary institutions have collect such fees. An additional $5 per year from every student would go a long way to creating a welcoming, open space on campus.

2.   My local Cable Television Service, Friendly Cable Company, needs to live up to the terms of its contract with subscribers. For one thing, Friendly Cable Company promises fast service, but their response is slow. When I call the company I have to go through an entire menu of sales offers, before I get to press number five for cable service. Than I am placed on hold for as long as twenty minutes. When I finally reach a service representative, I am given a service appointment that is three days later. Friendly Cable isn't very fast, and it isn't too friendly, either. Once I asked to speak to the Manager. The representative said I couldn't speak to the manager, but I could leave my number, and the manager would get back to me. The manager never cal me. Most importantly, the Friendly Caple Company contract provides cable television in return for money. The contract says that if I don't pay my cable bill, I don't get to watch cable television. I always pay my bill, but I do'nt get functioning cable television. Twice in this month alone, my cable has been out. I think Friendly Cable owes me some money for the times when I didn't get my money's worth. I like watching cable television, but I wish my cable service did it's job.

Lines of Detail: A Walk-Through Assignment

Write a one-paragraph letter to the editor of your local newspaper. Argue for some change you want for your community. You could argue for a traffic light, turn signal, or stop sign at a specific intersection. Or you could argue for bike paths in certain places, a recycling program, more bus service, or for any other specific change you feel is needed. To write your paragraph, follow these steps:

Step 1:   Begin by listing all the reasons and details you can about your topic. Survey your list and consider any possible objections. Answer the objections as well as you can, and see if the objections can lead you to more reasons.

Step 2: Group your reasons, listing the details that fit under each reason. Add details where they are needed and check to see if any reasons overlap.

Step 3: Survey the reasons and details, and draft a topic sentence. Make sure that your topic sentence states the subject and takes a stand.

Step 4: Write an outline. Then revise it, checking that you have enough reasons to make your point. Also check that your reasons are specific and in an effective order. Make sure that you have sufficient details for each reason. Check that your outline includes answers to any significant objections.

Step 5: Write a draft of your argument. Revise the draft until it includes any necessary explanations of the problem being argued, all serious or obvious reasons, and sufficient specific details. Also check that the most important reason is stated last. Add all the transitions that are needed to link your reasons and details.

Step 6: Before you prepare the final copy of your paragraph, decide whether you need a final sentence to stress your point and whether your transitions are smooth and logical. Refine your word choice. Then check for errors in spelling, punctuation, and grammar.

Writing Your Own Argument Paragraph

When you write on any of the following topics, make sure to work through the stages of the writing process in preparing your argument paragraph.

1. Write a paragraph for readers of your local newspaper, arguing for one of the following:

   a. a ban on all advertising of alcohol
   b. mandatory jail terms for those convicted of impaired driving
   c. the inclusion of more locally grown, organic food in grocery stores
   d. secondary school guidance counsellors to encourage students to enter the trades, as an alternative to university

2. In a paragraph, argue one of the following topics to the audience specified. If your instructor agrees, brainstorm your topic with a group before you start writing. Ask the group to "play audience," reacting to your reasons, raising objections, and asking questions.

   a. early-morning classes should be abolished at your college
      audience. the dean of Academic Affairs
   b. attendance in college classes should be optional
      audience. the instructors at your college
   c. college students should be forgiven a portion of their student loans
      audience. your MP (member of Parliament)
   d. your college should provide a free daycare facility for students with children
      audience. the president of your college
   e. businesses should hire more student interns
      audience. the president of a company (name it) that you'd like to work for

3. Write a paragraph for or against any of the following topics. Your audience for the argument is your classmates and your instructor.

For or Against

a. privatized health care
b. do-it-yourself projects
c. inviting doctors trained in other countries to practise in Canada
d. passing a law that requires all businesses to disclose what pollution they create and the extent of their emissions
e. having a public, online rating system for health-care professionals
f. funding for religion-based schooling
g. banning cellphones in the classroom
h. increasing the maximum speed limit on Canada's highways
i. big-box stores
j. imported produce
k. reality TV
l. a minimum percentage of Canadian content on all Canadian radio and television stations
m. online dating services
n. lowering the age limit for young offenders

WRITING FROM READING: ARGUMENT

Have We Forgotten the Trojan Horse?

Charles Gordon

Charles Gordon is a columnist for the Ottawa Citizen *and* Maclean's *magazine.*

Before you read this selection, consider these questions:

Have you noticed an increase in advertising in public spaces?

Does advertising affect your purchase decisions?

How important are brand-name products to you?

Do you shop exclusively at specific stores? Do you buy only certain brands?

The commercialization of just about everything began the day the Berlin Wall came down. That event represented the triumph of capitalism over communism, which no one will dispute, and the right of corporations to do anything they please, which hardly anyone seems to dispute either.

At least not yet. The free market is in. Regulation is out. Taxation is discredited. Government spending is passé. And what corporations do, provided it is within the letter of the law, is OK, even putting advertising on boxes of Girl Guide cookies.

Is nothing **sacred**? The *Globe and Mail* felt **constrained** to comment. Here is its editorial: "The Girl Guides of Canada are going to solicit advertising sponsors for their cookies. Sigh." Although the Guides founder "would probably have harrumphed herself into a coronary over it, advertising isn't immoral," the *Globe* continues, "we are a culture as much defined by what we buy as what we believe. And thinking creatively, it is just possible that, in addition to badges in pet-keeping, fishing and canoe

sacred: treated with utmost respect; safeguarded by reverence or tradition

constrained: forced

safety, future Girl Guides could receive awards for demonstrating mastery in the fine art of product placement. Still. Sigh."

dilemma: state of
indecision between two
alternatives

Could there be a better illustration of our modern **dilemma**? The *Globe,* as demonstrated by all the sighing, clearly knows that something is not quite right. But it cannot bring itself to say so, because "advertising isn't immoral" and because the Girl Guides are responding to market forces that are, by definition, good. Still. Sigh. This is not the only example of cherished institutions entering into partnerships with the corporate world. There is the well-publicized relationship between the Royal Canadian Mounted Police and Walt Disney. There is the Walt Disney Co.'s involvement with Canada Post, which issued a series of stamps featuring a Disney character.

More recently, there is a peculiar relationship between a doughnut company, the Canadian armed forces and the minister of national defence, as illustrated by a Tim Hortons commercial aired during the Super Bowl game. It shows the minister's limousine pulling up beside a Canadian Forces ship and several cases of Tim Hortons coffee being unloaded from the trunk for the coffee-hungry crew. This is likely to become a trend. Explained a Forces public affairs officer: "Next time I want to put out a brochure on a navy ship, I'm going to track down some company that's willing to put its logo on the back and cover the costs."

No money seems to have changed hands here, but are we, the Canadian public, ready for the idea of our armed forces being sponsored? Well, we know how strapped the armed forces are, and how much demands are already being placed on the taxpayer. If a corporation wants to help out, where's the harm? That's the conventional logic. Still, sigh.

Further examples are all around. Some are almost too familiar, particularly in the world of sports, where corporations are able to attach their names to anything that moves, not to mention skis, skates or drives. We take for granted the advertising on the boards in hockey arenas, or on the uniforms worn by tennis players and race car drivers. Rare now is the tournament, stadium or big game that does not have some corporation's name on it. And now Girl Guide cookies. Next: the northern lights.

Can we do anything but sigh at this corporate invasion of our public and private spaces? Well, sigh. To legislate bans would be in violation of many fundamental human rights. And that's assuming that the political will to take such action existed, which it doesn't.

The answer lies, as it usually does, with us as individuals. If we protest and make a noise, things can happen. The Nike corporation came to Ottawa last year to offer a free gymnasium floor, then withdrew its offer when city councillors asked questions

Third World: developing
nations of Africa, Asia,
and Latin America; the
more acceptable term
today is Global South

about the corporation's record in the **Third World**.

Continuing attempts by corporations to get their names into schools have also met with resistance. The most recent example involves a school being offered a satellite dish and television monitors in classrooms, on which students are shown 12-minute news broadcasts that include two to 2½ minutes of commercials.

It is funding cuts, of course, that increase the appeal of such proposals. The school (or the city, or the hospital, or the team) gets some equipment it would not otherwise be able to afford, virtually free. Only on rare occasions does someone dare to suggest that virtually free is too high a price. But, in the case of the schools, that has happened in the past, with groups of parents and educators being able to convince departments of education to look gift horses in the mouth. That could work again, and it wouldn't hurt either to do some serious **lobbying** against funding cuts.

lobbying: seeking to influence legislators on behalf of a particular cause

More direct approaches can work, too. Corporations are sensitive about their public image (otherwise, why spend vast sums to be just above the elbow on the left sleeve of a race car driver's jacket?), and will respond to letters of protest. A smart corporation president is like a smart politician—able to recognize when the mail, be it snail or e-, represents a segment of public opinion that it would be risky to offend. The president of a company thinking of putting the company logo on either the vanilla crème or the chocolate mint would certainly think again after receiving some personal letters urging him or her to take another advertising approach.

If we want to stop the commercialization of everything, if we want corporations to keep their names to themselves, then we have to let them know. A sigh is just a sigh.

UNDERSTANDING "HAVE WE FORGOTTEN THE TROJAN HORSE?"

1. Charles Gordon cites several examples of public or private organizations teaming up with corporations. List three examples here:

   _____ and _____

   _____ and _____

   _____ and _____

2. Why does "conventional logic" see no harm in this trend toward free corporate advertising for public and private organizations?

   _____

   _____

   _____

   _____

3. What does a school or a team gain from allowing corporate advertising in its classrooms or on its uniforms?

   _____

   _____

   _____

   _____

4. The title of Charles Gordon's article refers to the Trojan horse. In classical Greek mythology, the Greek army hid soldiers inside a large, hollow horse made of wood. They presented the horse to their enemies, the Trojans (residents of Troy). Thinking the horse was a gift for their goddess, the Trojans brought it inside their city walls. The soldiers inside the wooden horse then broke out and opened the city gates for the Greek army. The Greeks burned the city of Troy and defeated the Trojans.

According to Gordon, how is the "commercialization of just about everything" like a Trojan horse?

_____

_____

_____

_____

_____

WRITING FROM READING "HAVE WE FORGOTTEN THE TROJAN HORSE?"

1. Write a one-paragraph summary of Charles Gordon's article. Focus on the point of his argument and the details he uses to support his point.

2. Write an argument that agrees or disagrees with any of the statements below. You can support your argument with reasons or specific examples. Your audience is your classmates and your instructor.

   Advertising is misleading and makes people buy what they don't need.

   Schools should form partnerships with corporations to ensure that up-to-date technology is provided for today's students.

   Governments should increase funding to education, health, and sports.

WRITING FROM READING: ARGUMENT

Assimilation, Pluralism, and "Cultural Navigation": Multiculturalism in Canadian Schools

Hiren Mistry

Hiren Mistry is a Toronto educator and author whose activist and research interests focus on pluralism in education.

Before you read this selection, consider these questions:

In your everyday life, how many different people do you meet? What ages? What races? What cultural backgrounds?

How many times have you heard someone say in reference to newcomers to Canada, "Why don't they just go back to where they came from?"

What makes Canada different from the United States? From the United Kingdom? From European countries? From other Commonwealth countries?

pedagogical gurus: influential speakers or writers on the science of teaching

proverbial: well-known, notorious

Arguably, Canadian public high schools are giant cultural laboratories: Canada's multicultural future is tested, experimented with, and reproduced here. Teachers, administrators and **pedagogical gurus** are the **proverbial** lab technicians of this cultural experiment. The "test subjects" are the students who fill Canadian classrooms from all over the globe. The formula? This is where opinions differ in the lab. A larger,

camp: group of
supporters
advocates: promotes a
particular cause or policy

paradigms: typical
examples or patterns;
models of thought

more historically established **camp advocates** a policy of assimilation, while a smaller, growing camp asserts a policy of pluralism. A world of difference separates these two **paradigms**. I would equally argue that the failure or success of our nation is also caught up in the differences between these two approaches to dealing with multicul-turalism in our schools. After all, what is tested and reproduced in our schools will leave a mark on the future of Canada. We would, therefore, do well to examine our choices carefully before we experiment any further.

assimilation: absorption
into a larger group,
making all alike

Assimilation is the paradigm of choice amongst a significant number of established and therefore powerful educators in this country. They argue that participation in Canadian public life should foster a sense of common national heritage, regardless of where one emigrates from. For these educators, this nationalist ethic is first fostered in the classroom; hence their belief that the celebration of "traditional" Canadian values should be given priority in the curricular, as well as extracurricular, life of our schools. Flag Day, Remembrance Day, and Thanksgiving, for instance, should be given prece-dence over school-wide celebrations of Ramadan or the establishment of multicultural councils. Assemblies and curriculum in support of Black History or Asian Heritage Month would be seen as equally distracting. While advocates of assimilation would agree that cultural diversity is a fact of Canadian life, they would be quick to point out that Canadian students, and their families, have all the freedom to celebrate and practise their cultural ancestry in the privacy of their *own homes*. However, they believe it is the moral duty of all Canadians to separate their *public* and *private* cultural obligations.

implicit: understood,
but not directly
expressed

For assimilationists, their argument for the promotion of common Canadian val-ues and identity underlies a not-so-**implicit** fear of difference. For one, they believe a focus on cultural diversity in schools will weaken Canada's already fragile identity. Secondly, they claim that, by encouraging students to explore the cultural ancestry of their peers, or even themselves, schools will culturally *ghettoize*. Rather than learning how to get along, they believe students would end up becoming more self-interested, racist, and prone to establishing gangs and **instigating** violence. As an extension to this argument, they claim that, in a world of increasing international tension between competing cultural and religious groups, nationalist conflicts and historical **vendettas** would be played out in the halls of Canadian high schools.

instigating: causing,
encouraging

vendettas: bitter,
prolonged feuds
involving the seeking of
vengeance

While I do not doubt that the above concerns are very real in the minds of those educa-tors advocating a multicultural policy of assimilation, I hesitate to take their alarm too seri-ously. Their arguments for assimilation—and against pluralism—are founded equally on their fear of change (and the loss of cultural **hegemony**), as well as on a **naive** understanding of culture. The consequences of their blind spots are too critical to ignore, for all Canadians.

hegemony: predominance

naive: innocent, childlike

pluralist: approach in
which minority groups
maintain their cultural
traditions as part of the
broader society

Advocates of a **pluralist** approach to multiculturalism envision an environment where the global connections of our Canadian students are actively engaged and thor-oughly integrated into all facets of curricular and extracurricular school life. Their argument is, quite simply, that the cultural composition of Canada has irreversibly changed. If a casual look at a typical urban classroom won't silence doubters, then the 2001 Canadian census statistics for Toronto, Montreal, and Vancouver would quickly put any doubts to rest. In the 1990s, 73 percent of all new immigrants settled in these three cities, of which nearly 77 percent were of South Asian, African, South American and Chinese descent.[1] More significantly, Canada wide, immigrants from these regions grew by over 24 percent from 1991 to 2001, and there is no sign that this is a receding trend. Pluralists, therefore, see it as the obligation of the education system to *prepare* students for the future, rather than enchant them with romantic notions of cultural **homogeneity**. Assimilation might have been a *possible* response (though still morally questionable) to multiculturalism, when ethnic minorities in fact lived up (or rather down) to this **demographic** classification. However, in urban communities, such as in Brampton, Ontario, where more than 40 percent of the population is of non-European and American descent, assimilation is no longer a viable option. New immigrants do not leave their ancestral customs and beliefs at the border when they enter Canada or Canadian schools. Indeed, they take their culture with them and import it into their Canadian lives: publicly and privately. Unless Canadian students, therefore, know how to interact with their multicultural peers in public space, we need to be concerned about the outcome of their ignorance once their lives move beyond the classroom.

Pluralists, however, do not advocate an "either–or" scenario of cultural loyalties. Why can't nationalist heritage of Canadian identity be fostered at the same time as the multicultural heritages of our students? Our brains are **cognitively** equipped to deal with such cultural diversity, for our brains are no more necessarily monocultural than they are monolingual. Just as one with the **requisite** exposure to a second language gains enough competence to become bilingual, it also follows that those who gain exposure to and competence in more than one culture will become moderately, if not successfully, bicultural. "Having such a capacity is no more a threat to one's personal integrity than bilingualism is a cause for brain damage."[2] There is no need for Canada's national heritage to be at odds with the ancestral cultures of Canadian students. They needn't cancel each other out. All that is required is exposure to and engagement with culture.

The consequences for not engaging in this bold, yet practical, experiment are **manifold**. If Canadian schools continue to respond to the presence of diversity through assimilation, they will see their worst fears come true. Students who do not see their world views recognized in their school environment will seek other ways, outside of the school environment, to reinforce their personal and cultural integrity. This is doubly reinforced when ESL students, in particular, find little academic success after receiving minimal language training before mainstreaming to regular academic courses. The polarization between cultural groups and the mainstream of Canadian schools—and the fallout of ignorance, fear, and prejudice—has a source closer to home than most Canadian educators would like to think.

However, all is not "doom and gloom." The choice is clear. If Canadian educators take seriously the challenge to foster the "cultural intelligence" of their students and adopt a pluralist pedagogy to prepare them to engage the multicultural world beyond their classroom walls, Canada can proudly live up to its reputation for being

homogeneity: sameness, uniformity

demographic: a particular sector of a population, according to statistics on age, ethnicity, and so on

cognitively: mentally, perceptually

requisite: necessary, required

manifold: many and various

1.   Cf. "Canada 2nd to Australia in foreign-born residents: census," Tue., 21 Jan. 2003 (http://cbc.ca/stories/2003/01/21/census_immigrants030121).

2.   Roger Ballard, "Race, Culture and Ethnicity," CASAS Occasional Papers, University of Manchester, 2002, p. 25.

purveyors: promoters

a global model of multiculturalism. If not, the seeds of ignorance, fear, and bigotry—which **purveyors** of multiculturalism most wish to avoid—will most certainly be sown. And, unfortunately, Canadian educators will have only themselves to blame.

UNDERSTANDING "ASSIMILATION, PLURALISM, AND 'CULTURAL NAVIGATION': MULTICULTURALISM IN CANADIAN SCHOOLS"

1. According to the author, Hiren Mistry, what are the two paradigms used to study the multicultural future of Canada?

   _____

   _____

   _____

2. Assimilationists argue that promotion of cultural diversity may "ghettoize" Canada's high schools. What consequences do they fear?

   _____

   _____

   _____

3. Why does Mistry believe that "assimilation is no longer a viable option" for modern-day Canada?

   _____

   _____

   _____

4. The article "Assimilation, Pluralism, and 'Cultural Navigation': Multiculturalism in Canadian Schools" includes two endnotes, marked with numbers [1] and [2]. What purposes do these endnotes serve?

   _____

   _____

   _____

5. In your opinion, does multiculturalism mean "your culture *or* my culture" or "your culture *and* my culture"? Give three reasons for your view.

   _____

   _____

   _____

WRITING FROM READING "ASSIMILATION, PLURALISM, AND 'CULTURAL NAVIGATION': MULTICULTURALISM IN CANADIAN SCHOOLS"

1. Mistry asserts that Canadian students of all backgrounds need to "know how to interact with their multicultural peers in public space." Interview your classmates to find out what their experiences have been. Do they consider themselves part of the dominant Canadian culture? Part of their traditional culture? Part of both cultures? Do they get along with some

cultural groups more easily than others? Why or why not? Then write a paragraph arguing *one* of the following views:

    a. Most young people in Canada today accept and understand other cultures on a day-to-day basis.

    b. Many young people in Canada today feel that they don't belong and that they're misunderstood, owing to their cultural backgrounds.

2. According to the 2001 Canadian census statistics Mistry cites, the rate of immigration from South Asia, Africa, South America, and China increased by almost 25 percent during the 1990s. What do you think are the Canadian values that appealed to these immigrants and influenced their choice to settle here? How do you think these rates may have changed in subsequent years?

3. Each pair of topic sentences below offers opposing views on multiculturalism in Canada. Choose one position *only* and provide reasons and details to support it. (To expand your ability to debate effectively, try arguing the point of view that you don't personally agree with.) Your audience is your classmates and your instructor.

    a. Learning more about other cultures in school results in better relations in society.

       or

       Learning more about other cultures in school will do little to change the attitudes children learn at home.

    b. People from all over the world immigrate to Canada to take advantage of economic opportunities, not to become part of Canadian society.

       or

       People from all over the world choose Canada as their home in order to build a new life that blends both traditional and Canadian values.

    c. Public schools should remain non-denominational and provide a secular education only.

       or

       Celebrating cultural and religious differences in public schools excludes no one and acknowledges recent changes in Canadian society.

4. In the late 1960s, Canada promoted a policy of bilingualism and biculturalism that reflected the history of English and French Canada. This federal policy ensured that English- and French-speaking Canadians had separate but equal rights and privileges. Has this separation of cultures helped or hurt Canada? Should this policy be extended now to other language groups and cultures? Support your argument with reasons or predictions. Your audience is your instructor and your classmates.

MyWritingLab

Go to MyWritingLab to access a diagnostic test that creates your own personalized learning path supported by rich multimedia resources and a variety of animated tutorials, all aimed at helping you improve your writing. MyWritingLab also includes a complete eText version of the book that is fully searchable and accessible through your web browser or most mobile devices.

CHAPTER 11
Writing an Essay

"Nobody trips over mountains. It is the small pebble that causes you to stumble. Pass all the pebbles in your path and you will find you have crossed the mountain."

~ AUTHOR UNKNOWN

WHAT IS AN ESSAY?

You write an essay when you have more to say than can be covered in just one paragraph. An essay can be one paragraph, but in this book we take it to mean a written work of more than one paragraph. An essay has a main point, called a **thesis**, which is supported by subpoints. The subpoints are the **topic sentences**. Each paragraph in the **body**, or main part, of the essay has a topic sentence. In fact, every paragraph in the body of an essay is like the paragraphs you've already written, because each one makes a point and then supports it.

COMPARING THE SINGLE PARAGRAPH AND THE ESSAY

Read the paragraph and the essay that follow, both about Bob, the writer's brother. You'll notice many similarities.

A Single Paragraph

I think I'm lucky to have a brother who is two years older than I am. For one thing, my brother Bob fought all the typical child–parent battles, and I was the real winner. Bob was the one who made my parents understand that seventeen-year-olds shouldn't have an 11:00 p.m. curfew on weekends. He fought for his rights. By the time I turned seventeen, my parents had accepted the later curfew, and I didn't have to fight for it. Bob also paved the way for me at school. He was such a great athlete that I benefited from his reputation. When I tried out for the basketball team, I had an advantage before I hit the court. I was Bob Cruz's younger brother, so the coach thought I had to be pretty good. At home and at school, my big brother was a big help to me.

An Essay

Some people complain about being the youngest child or the middle child in the family. These people believe that older children get all the attention and grab all the power. I'm the younger brother in my family, and I disagree with the complainers. I think I'm lucky to have a brother who is two years older than I am.

For one thing, my brother Bob fought all the typical child–parent battles, and I was the real winner. Bob was the one who made my parents understand that seventeen-year-olds shouldn't have an 11:00 p.m. curfew on weekends. He fought for his rights, and the fighting wasn't easy. I remember months of arguments between Bob and my parents as Bob tried to explain that not all teens on the street at 11:30 are punks or criminals. Bob was the one who suffered from being grounded or who lost the use of my father's car. By the time I turned seventeen, my parents had accepted the later curfew, and I didn't have to fight for it.

Bob also paved the way for me at school. Because he was so popular with the other students and the teachers, he created a positive image of what the boys in our family were like. When I started school, I walked into a place where people were ready to like me, just as they liked Bob. I remember the first day of class when the teachers read the new class rolls. When they got to my name, they asked, "Are you Bob Cruz's brother?" When I said yes, they smiled. Bob's success opened doors for me in school sports, too. He was such a great athlete that I benefited from his reputation. When I tried out for the basketball team, I had an advantage before I hit the court. I was Bob Cruz's younger brother, so the coach thought I had to be pretty good.

I had many battles to fight as I grew up. Like all children, I had to struggle to gain independence and respect. In my struggles at home and at school, my big brother was a big help to me.

If you read the two sample selections carefully, you noticed that they make the same main point, and they support that point with two subpoints.

main point: I think I'm lucky to have a brother who is two years older than I am.

subpoints: 1. My brother Bob fought all the typical child–parent battles, and I was the real winner.
2. Bob also paved the way at school.

You'll notice that the essay is longer because it has more details and examples to support the points.

ORGANIZING AN ESSAY

When you write an essay of more than one paragraph, the thesis is the *focus* of your entire essay; it's the major point of your essay. The other important points that are part of the thesis are in topic sentences.

thesis: Working as a salesperson has changed my character.
topic sentence: I've had to learn patience.
topic sentence: I've developed the ability to listen.
topic sentence: I've become more tactful.

Notice that the thesis expresses a bigger idea than the topic sentences following it, and that it's supported by the topic sentences. The essay has an introduction, a body, and a conclusion.

1. **Introduction:** The first paragraph is usually the introduction. The thesis most often goes here.
2. **Body:** This central part of the essay is the part in which you support your main point (the thesis). Each paragraph in the body of the essay has its own topic sentence.
3. **Conclusion:** Usually one paragraph long, the conclusion reminds the reader of the thesis.

WRITING THE THESIS

There are several characteristics of a thesis:

1. It is expressed in a sentence. A thesis is *not* the same as the topic of the essay, or as the title of the essay:

    topic: quitting smoking
    title: Why I Quit Smoking
    thesis: I quit smoking because I was concerned for my health, and I wanted to prove to myself that I could break the habit.

2. A thesis *does not announce*; it makes a point about the subject:

    announcement: This essay will explain the reasons why young adults should watch what they eat.

    thesis: Young adults should watch what they eat so that they can live healthy lives today and prevent future health problems.

3. A thesis *is not too broad.* Some ideas are just too big to cover well in an essay. A thesis that tries to cover too much can lead to a superficial or boring essay.

> **thesis too broad:** People should work on solving their interpersonal communication problems.
>
> **acceptable thesis:** As an immigrant, I had a hard time understanding that many Canadians thought my imperfect English meant I was uneducated.

4. A thesis *is not too narrow.* Sometimes, students start with a thesis that looks good because it seems specific and precise. Later, when they try to support such a thesis, they can't find anything to say.

> **thesis too narrow:** My sister pays forty dollars a week for a special formula for her baby.
>
> **acceptable thesis:** My sister had no idea what it would cost to care for a baby.

Hints for Writing a Thesis

1. Your thesis can *mention the specific subpoints* of your essay. For example, your thesis might be

> I hated *No Country for Old Men* because the film is extremely violent and it glorifies criminals.

With this thesis, you have indicated the two subpoints of your essay: *No Country for Old Men* is extremely violent; *No Country for Old Men* glorifies criminals.

2. Or your thesis can make a point without mentioning the specific subpoints of your essay. For example, you can write a thesis like the following:

> I hated *No Country for Old Men* because of the way it makes the unspeakable into entertainment.

With this thesis, you can still use the subpoints stating that the movie was extremely violent and glorified criminals. You just don't have to mention all your subpoints in the thesis. Make sure to check with your instructor about the type of thesis you should use.

| **EXERCISE 1** | **RECOGNIZING GOOD THESIS SENTENCES** |

Below is a list of thesis statements. Some are acceptable, but others are too broad or too narrow. Some are announcements; others are topics, not sentences. Put a *G* next to the good thesis sentences.

1. _____ Why oat bran is an important part of a healthy diet will be discussed in the following essay.
2. _____ My family was a small family unit.
3. _____ The environment is a major concern of people in today's society.
4. _____ How to install speakers in a car.

5. _____ Canadians should be concerned about the invasions of their digital privacy.

6. _____ Being an only child has its advantages.

7. _____ Canadian senators should be elected, not appointed.

8. _____ A crisis in the banking industry.

9. _____ Newfoundland and Labrador is Canada's youngest province.

10. _____ The advantages of buying a North American car.

EXERCISE 2

SELECTING A GOOD THESIS SENTENCE

In each pair of thesis statements below, put a *G* next to the good thesis sentence.

1. a. _____ Road rage incidents and people under stress.

   b. _____ People under stress are more likely to be involved in incidents of road rage.

2. a. _____ Drinking bottled water is a popular but expensive habit.

   b. _____ Pollution of the oceans, rivers, and lakes of the world is threatening to change life as we know it.

3. a. _____ The challenges of being a foreign student will be discussed in this essay.

   b. _____ Foreign students face academic, social, and financial challenges.

4. a. _____ The need for a better highway system in northwestern Ontario.

   b. _____ The province needs to expand and restructure its highway system in northwestern Ontario.

5. a. _____ I failed my third sociology test last Friday.

   b. _____ Sociology has too many strange terms, boring statistics, and complicated studies for me to remember.

6. a. _____ The old house needs basic repairs in several areas.

   b. _____ Where the old house needs basic repair work is the subject of this paper.

7. a. _____ The differences between a foster child and an adopted child in the provincial legal system.

   b. _____ In the provincial legal system, there are three significant differences between a foster child and an adopted child.

8. a. _____ Becoming a vegan benefits one's health, one's community, and the environment.

   b. _____ Why everyone should be vegan.

9. a. _____ Gold jewellery and its quality.

    b. _____ There are three signs that a piece of jewellery is real gold.

10. a. _____ Child abuse is a problem in families of every social class.

    b. _____ The local child abuse hotline is helping to save lives.

EXERCISE 3

WRITING A THESIS THAT RELATES TO THE SUBPOINTS

Below are lists of subpoints that could be explained in an essay. Write a thesis for each list. Remember that there are two ways to write a thesis: You can write a thesis that includes the subpoints, or you can write one that makes a point without listing the subpoints. As an example, the first one is done for you, using both kinds of thesis statements.

1. **one kind of thesis:** Cities that demonstrate a commitment to urban planning see less urban sprawl within their boundaries.

    another kind of thesis: Cities that are committed to mixed-use practices, to green space, and to defensible space see less urban sprawl within their boundaries.

    subpoints:

    a. Paris, for instance, has increased densification by including a mixture of residential, commercial, and work space in parts of the city.

    b. Central Park, designed in 1858, was envisioned as an oasis for New York's citizens.

    c. The use of cobblestone streets, leafy trees, and the like is termed defensible space, meaning the use of strategies to decrease crime in an area.

2. **thesis:** _____

    _____

    subpoints:

    a. Employers look for workers who are prepared to work hard.

    b. Employers will hire people with the right training.

    c. Employers want workers who have a positive attitude.

3. **thesis:** _____

    _____

    subpoints:

    a. Neighbours will often collect your mail when you're out of town.

    b. In an emergency, neighbours can lend you the tools you need.

   4. thesis: _____

   _____

   subpoints:

   a. Neighbours will often collect your mail when you're out of town.

   b. In an emergency, neighbours can lend you the tools you need.

   c. Neighbours can be nosy and critical.

   d. Neighbours can invade your living space.

   5. thesis: _____

   _____

   subpoints:

   a. There is an application that will give the local weather forecast.

   b. Another application will give the name of a song playing on the radio.

   c. One popular application will give the user the names of all the constellations in the sky above.

WRITING THE ESSAY IN STEPS

In an essay, you follow the same steps you learned in writing a paragraph—prewriting, planning, drafting and revising, and proofreading and polishing—but you adapt them to the longer essay form.

PREWRITING   ### GATHERING IDEAS: AN ESSAY

The prewriting stage often begins with *narrowing a topic*. Your instructor may give you a large topic so that within it you can find something smaller you'd like to write about.

Some students think that because they have several paragraphs to write, they'd better pick a large topic, one that will give them enough to say. But large topics can lead to boring, shallow, general essays. A smaller topic can challenge you to find the specific, concrete examples and details that make an essay interesting and effective.

If your instructor asked you to write about college, for instance, you might *freewrite* some ideas as you narrow the topic:

> Narrowing the Topic of College
>
> What college means to me—too big, and it could be boring
>
> College vs. high school—everyone might choose this topic
>
> College students—too big
>
> College students who have jobs—better!
>
> Problems of working and going to college—okay!

In your freewriting, you can consider your *purpose*—to write an essay about some aspect of college—and *audience*—your instructor and your classmates. Your narrowed topic will appeal to this audience because many students hold jobs and instructors are familiar with the problems of working students.

Listing Ideas

Once you have a narrow topic, you can use whatever process works for you. You can brainstorm by writing a series of questions and answers about your topic, you can freewrite about the topic, you can list ideas about the topic, or you can do any combination of these processes.

Below is a sample listing of ideas about the problems of working and going to college.

Problems of Working and Going to College

early classes

too tired to pay attention

tried to study at work

got caught

got reprimanded

slept in class

constantly racing around

no sleep

little time to do homework

weekends only time to study

no social life

apartment a mess

missed work for make-up test

got behind in school

need salary for tuition

rude to customers

girlfriend ready to kill me

Clustering the Ideas

By clustering the items on the list, you'll find it easier to see the connections between them. The following items have been clustered (grouped) under a subtitle.

Problems of Working and Going to College: Ideas in Clusters

Problems at School	Problems at Work
early classes	tried to study at work
too tired to pay attention	got caught
slept in class	got reprimanded
little time to do homework	missed work for make-up test
got behind in school	rude to customers

(continued)

Problems Away from of Work and School

weekends only time to study

no social life

apartment a mess

girlfriend ready to kill me

When you surveyed the clusters, you probably noticed that some of the ideas from the original list were left out. These ideas—about racing around, not getting enough sleep, and needing tuition money—could fit into more than one place and might not fit anywhere. You might come back to them later.

When you name each cluster by giving it a subtitle, you move toward a focus for each body paragraph of your essay. By beginning to focus the body paragraphs, you start thinking about the main point, the thesis of your essay. Concentrating on the thesis and on focused paragraphs helps you *unify* your essay.

Reread the clustered ideas. When you do so, you'll notice that each cluster is about problems at a different place. You can incorporate that concept into a thesis with a sentence like this:

> Students who work while they attend college face problems at school, at work, and at home.

Once you have a thesis and a list of details, you can begin working on the outline of your essay.

EXERCISE 4

NARROWING TOPICS

Working with a partner or with a group, narrow these topics so that the new topics are related, but smaller, and suitable for short essays that are between four and six paragraphs. The first topic is narrowed for you.

1. **topic:** summer vacation

   smaller, related topics:

   a. a car trip with children _____

   b. Disney World: not a vacation paradise _____

   c. my vacation job _____

2. **topic:** driving

   smaller, related topics:

   a. _____

   b. _____

   c. _____

3. **topic:** sports
   smaller, related topics:
   a. _____
   b. _____
   c. _____

4. **topic:** the environment
   smaller, related topics:
   a. _____
   b. _____
   c. _____

5. **topic:** money
   smaller, related topics:
   a. _____
   b. _____
   c. _____

6. **topic:** urban living
   smaller, related topics:
   a. _____
   b. _____
   c. _____

EXERCISE 5

CLUSTERING RELATED IDEAS

Below are two topics, each with a list of ideas. Mark all the related items on the list with the same number (*1, 2,* or *3*). Some items might not get a number. When you've finished marking the list, write a title for each number that explains the cluster of ideas.

1. **topic:** giving a speech
   _____ audience may be large
   _____ begin by thinking of a good topic
   _____ right before you speak, take a deep breath
   _____ make eye contact with your audience as you speak
   _____ make a list of what you want to say
   _____ organize your list onto note cards
   _____ relax as you get up to speak
   _____ speak slowly
   _____ as you wait to speak, remember that all speakers are nervous
   _____ stand confidently

The ideas marked 1 can be titled _____

The ideas marked 2 can be titled _____

The ideas marked 3 can be titled _____

2. **topic:** why a new job is stressful

_____ boss may be bad tempered

_____ you may feel all your co-workers are watching you

_____ you don't know anyone who works there

_____ you think you can't learn the new routines

_____ a different computer program is challenging

_____ you may be given very little autonomy

_____ the salary may be low

_____ you may think that all the co-workers are gossiping about you

_____ you may be afraid that you won't get the work done quickly enough

_____ the boss may have strong dislikes

The ideas marked 1 can be titled _____

The ideas marked 2 can be titled _____

The ideas marked 3 can be titled _____

PLANNING **DEVISING A PLAN: AN ESSAY**

In the next stage of writing your essay, draft an outline. Use the thesis to focus your ideas. There are many kinds of outlines, but all are used to help a writer organize ideas. When you use a **formal outline,** you show the difference between a main idea and its supporting details by *indenting* the supporting details. In a formal outline, Roman numerals (I, II, III, and so on) and capital letters are used. Each Roman numeral represents a paragraph, and the letters beneath the numeral represent supporting details.

> **The Structure of a Formal Outline**
>
> | | |
> |---|---|
> | **first paragraph** | I. Thesis |
> | **second paragraph** | II. Topic sentence |
> | | A. |
> | | B. |
> | **details** | C. |
> | | D. |
> | | E. |
> | **third paragraph** | III. Topic sentence |
> | | A. |
> | | B. |
> | **details** | C. |
> | | D. |
> | | E. |

fourth paragraph	IV. Topic sentence
	⌐ A.
	B.
details	C.
	D.
	⌐ E.
fifth paragraph	V. Conclusion

Hints for Outlining

Developing a good, clear outline now can save you hours of confused, disorganized writing later. The extra time you spend to make sure your outline has sufficient details and that *each paragraph stays on one point* will pay off in the long run.

1. **Check the topic sentences:** Keep in mind that each topic sentence in each body paragraph should support the thesis sentence. If a topic sentence isn't carefully connected to the thesis, the structure of the essay will be confusing. Here's a thesis with a list of topic sentences; the topic sentence that doesn't fit is crossed out.

thesis:	I	A home-cooked dinner can be a rewarding experience for both the cook and the guests.
topic sentences:	II	Preparing a meal is a satisfying activity.
	III	It's a pleasure for the cook to see guests enjoy the meal.
	IV	~~Many recipes are handed down through generations.~~
	V	Dinner guests are flattered when someone cooks for them.
conclusion:	VI	Dining at home is a treat for everyone at the table.

   Since the thesis of this outline is about the pleasure of dining at home, for the cook and the guests, topic sentence IV doesn't fit: it isn't about the joy of cooking *or* about being a dinner guest. It takes the essay off track. A careful check of the links between the thesis and the topic sentences will help keep your essay focused.

2. **Include some details:** Some writers believe that they don't need many details in the outline. They feel they can fill in the details later, when they actually write the essay. Even though some writers do manage to add details later, others who are in a hurry or who run out of ideas can have problems.

   Imagine, for example, that a writer has included very few details in an outline, like this:

   I A burglary makes the victim feel unsafe.
      A. The person has lost property.
      B. The person's home territory has been invaded.

The paragraph created from this outline might be too short and lack specific details, like this:

> A burglary makes the victim feel unsafe. First of all, the victim has lost property. Second, a person's home territory has been invaded.

If you have difficulty thinking of ideas when you write, try to tackle the problem in the outline. The more details you put into your outline, the more detailed and effective your draft essay will be. For example, suppose the same outline on the burglary topic had more details, like this:

II A burglary makes the victim feel unsafe.

more details about burglary itself:

A. The person has lost property.
B. The property could be worth hundreds of dollars.
C. The victim can lose a television or camera or laptop.
D. The burglars may take cash.
E. Worse, items with personal value, like family jewellery or heirlooms, can be stolen.

more details about safety concerns:

F. Even worse, a person's territory has been invaded.
G. People who thought they were safe now know that they're not.
H. The fear is that the invasion can happen again.

You will probably agree that the paragraph will be more detailed, too.

3. **Stay on one point:** It's a good idea to check the outline of each body paragraph to see whether each paragraph stays on one point. Compare each topic sentence, which is at the top of the list for the paragraph, against the details indented under it. Staying on one point gives each paragraph unity.

Below is the outline for a paragraph that has problems staying on one point. See if you can spot the problem areas.

III Sonya is a generous person.

A. I remember how freely she gave her time when our club had a car wash.
B. She's always willing to share her lecture notes with me.
C. Sonya gives 10 percent of her salary to her church.
D. She's a member of Big Sisters and spends every Saturday with a disadvantaged child.
E. She can read people's minds when they're in trouble.
F. She knows what they're feeling.

The topic sentence of this paragraph is about generosity. But sentences E and F talk about Sonya's insight, not her generosity.

When you have a problem staying on one point, you can solve the problem in one of two ways:

a. Eliminate details that don't fit your main point.

or

b. Change the topic sentence so that it relates to all the ideas in the paragraph.

For example, you could cut out sentences E and F about Sonya's insight, getting rid of the details that don't fit. Or you could change the topic sentence in the paragraph so that it relates to all the ideas in the paragraph: "Sonya is a generous and insightful person."

Revisiting the Prewriting Stage

Writing an outline can help you identify underdeveloped places in your plan—places where your paragraphs need more details. You can develop these details in two ways:

1. Go back to the writing you did in the prewriting stage. Check whether items on a list or ideas from freewriting can lead you to more details for your outline.
2. Brainstorm for more details using a question-and-answer approach. For example, if the outline includes "My apartment is a mess," you might ask, "Why? How messy?" Or if the outline includes "I have no social life," you might ask, "What do you mean? Parties? Clubs?"

The time you spend writing and revising your outline will make it easier for you to write an essay that is well developed, unified, and coherently structured. The following checklist may help you revise.

 **CHECKLIST** | **FOR REVISING THE OUTLINE OF AN ESSAY**

✓ **Unity:** Do the thesis and topic sentences all lead to the same point? Does each paragraph make one, and only one, point? Do the details in each paragraph support the topic sentence? Does the conclusion unify the essay?

✓ **Support:** Do the body paragraphs have enough supporting details?

✓ **Coherence:** Are the paragraphs in the most effective order? Are the details in each paragraph arranged in the most effective order?

A sentence outline on the problems of working and going to college follows. It includes the thesis in the first paragraph. The topic sentences have been created from the titles of the ideas clustered earlier. The details have been drawn from ideas in the clusters and from further brainstorming. The conclusion has just one sentence that unifies the essay.

 An Outline for an Essay

paragraph 1

> **introduction**
>
> I   Thesis: *Students who work while going to college face problems at school, at work, and at home.*

paragraph 2

> **topic sentence**
>
> II   *Trying to juggle job and school responsibilities creates problems at school.*

details

    A. Early classes are difficult.

    B. I'm too tired to pay attention.

    C. Once I slept in class.

    D. I have little time to do homework.

    E. I get behind in school assignments.

paragraph 3

    topic sentence

    III Work can suffer when workers attend college.

    details

    A. I tried to study at work.

    B. I got caught by my boss.

    C. I was reprimanded.

    D. Sometimes I come to work very tired.

    E. When I don't have enough sleep, I can be rude to customers.

    F. Rudeness gets me in trouble.

    G. Another time, I had to cut work to take a make-up test.

paragraph 4

    topic sentence

    IV Working students also suffer outside of classes and the workplace.

    details

    A. I work nights during the week.

    B. The weekends are the only time I can study.

    C. My apartment is a mess since I have no time to clean it.

    D. Worse, my girlfriend is ready to kill me because I have no social life.

    E. We never even go to the movies anymore.

    F. When she comes over, I'm busy studying.

paragraph 5   conclusion

    V I've learned that working students have to be very organized to cope with their responsibilities at college, work, and home.

EXERCISE 6

COMPLETING AN OUTLINE FOR AN ESSAY

Following is part of an outline that has a thesis and topic sentences, but no details. Add the details and write in complete sentences. Write one sentence for each capital letter. Be sure that the details are connected to the topic sentence.

    I thesis: Video cameras have several beneficial uses in today's society.

II People use their video cameras to record memorable family events.

A. _____

B. _____

C. _____

D. _____

E. _____

III Video cameras are being used to prevent or detect crimes.

A. _____

B. _____

C. _____

D. _____

E. _____

IV Video cameras have given ordinary people an opportunity to feel what it's like to be a director or an actor.

A. _____

B. _____

C. _____

D. _____

E. _____

V The video camera has changed the way people celebrate family rituals, has contributed to the prevention and detection of crime, and has made ordinary people into directors and performers.

EXERCISE 7   FOCUSING AN OUTLINE FOR AN ESSAY

The following outline has a thesis and details, but it has no topic sentences for the body paragraphs. Write the topic sentences.

I thesis: After my last meal at Don's Diner, I swore I'd never eat there again.

II _____

_____

A. My friend and I were kept waiting for a table for half an hour.

B. During that time, several tables were empty, but no one bothered to clear the dirty dishes.

C. We just stood in the entrance, waiting.

D. Then, when we were seated, the server was surly.

    E. It took fifteen minutes to get a menu.

    F. The plates of food were slammed down on the table.

    G. The orders were mixed up.

III _____

    _____

    A. The hamburger was full of gristle.

    B. Toasting the hamburger bun couldn't hide the fact that it was stale.

    C. The french fries were cold and as hard as cardboard.

    D. The iced-tea powder was floating on top of the glass.

    E. The lettuce had brown edges.

    F. Ketchup was caked all over the outside of the ketchup bottle.

IV I never want to repeat the experience I had at Don's Diner.

DRAFTING AND REVISING: AN ESSAY

When you're satisfied with your outline, you can begin drafting and revising the essay. Start by writing a first draft, making sure that it includes an introduction, body paragraphs, and a conclusion.

WRITING THE INTRODUCTION

Where Does the Thesis Go?

The thesis should appear in the **introduction** of the essay, in the first paragraph. But usually it is not the first sentence. Preceding the thesis statement, write three or more sentences of introduction. Generally, the thesis is the *last sentence* in the introductory paragraph.

Why put the thesis at the end of the first paragraph? First, writing several sentences before you express your main idea gives you a chance to lead into it gradually and smoothly without immediately confronting the reader with it. This method will help you build interest and gain the reader's attention.

Second, if your thesis is at the end of the introduction, it states the main point of the essay just before that point is supported in the body paragraphs. Putting the thesis at the end of the introduction is like inserting an arrow that points to the supporting ideas in the essay.

Hints for Writing the Introduction

There are a number of ways to write an introduction.

    1. You can begin with some general statements that gradually lead to your thesis:

      general statements   Students face all kinds of problems when they start college. Some students struggle with a lack of basic math skills; others have never learned to write a term paper. Students who were stars in high school have to cope with being just another student number at a large institution. Students with small children have to find a way to be good parents and good students, too. Although all these problems are common, I found an even more typical conflict. <u>My biggest problem in college was learning to organize my time.</u>

thesis at end

2. **You can begin with a quote** that smoothly leads to your thesis. The quote can be from someone famous, or it can be an old saying. It can be something your mother always told you, a slogan from an advertisement, or the words of a song.

quote

Everybody has heard the old saying "time flies," but I never really thought about that statement until I started college. I expected college to challenge me with demanding course work. I expected it to excite me with the range of people I would meet. I even thought it might amuse me with the fun and intrigue of dating and romance. But I never expected college to exhaust me. I was surprised to discover that <u>my biggest problem in college was learning to organize my time.</u>

thesis at end

(Note: You can add transitional words or phrases to your thesis, as in the sample above.)

3. **You can tell a story** as a way of leading into your thesis. Try opening with the story of something that happened to you or to someone you know, or a story that you read about or heard on the news.

story

My friend Phyllis is two years older than I am, and so she started college before I did. When Phyllis came home from college for the Thanksgiving weekend, I called her with a huge list of activities she and I could enjoy. I was really surprised when Phyllis told me she planned to spend most of the weekend sleeping. I didn't understand her when she told me she was worn out. When I started college myself, I understood her perfectly. Phyllis was a victim of that old college ailment: not knowing how to handle time. I developed the same disease. <u>My biggest problem in college was learning to organize my time.</u>

thesis at end

4. **You can explain why this topic is worth writing about.** Explaining could mean giving some background on the topic, or it could mean discussing why the topic is an important one.

explain

I don't remember a word of what was said during my first-year orientation, and I wish I did. I'm sure somebody somewhere warned me about the problems I'd face in college. I'm sure somebody talked about getting organized. Unfortunately, I didn't listen, and I had

thesis at end

to learn the hard way. I hope other students will listen and learn and be spared my hard lesson and my main problem. <u>My biggest problem in college was learning to organize my time.</u>

5. **You can use one or more questions to lead into your thesis.** Try opening with a question or questions that will be answered by your thesis. Or you can open with a question or questions that catch the reader's attention and move toward your thesis.

question

Have you ever stayed up all night to study for an exam, then fallen asleep at dawn and slept right through the time of the exam? If you have, then you were probably the same kind of college student I was. I was the student who always ran into class three minutes late, the one who begged for an extension on the term paper, the one who pleaded with the teacher to postpone the test. I just could not get things done on schedule. <u>My biggest problem in college was learning to organize my time.</u>

thesis at end

6. **You can open with a contradiction of your main point** as a way of attracting the reader's interest and leading to your thesis. The contrast between your opening and your thesis creates interest.

contradiction

People who knew me in my first year probably felt really sorry for me. They saw a girl with dark circles under her bloodshot eyes, a girl who was always racing from one place to another. Those people probably thought I was exhausted from overwork. But they were wrong. My problem in college was definitely not too much work; it was the way I handled my work. <u>My biggest problem in college was learning to organize my time.</u>

thesis at end

EXERCISE 8 — WRITING AN INTRODUCTION

Below are five thesis sentences. Pick one. Then write an introductory paragraph on the lines provided. Your last sentence should be the thesis sentence. If your instructor agrees, read your introduction to others in the class who wrote an introduction for the same thesis, or read your introduction to the entire class.

Thesis Sentences

1. Young girls are becoming dangerously preoccupied with their weight.
2. Our city should invest more in public transit.
3. People are often surprised at the occupational hazards of my job.
4. One family member has been my greatest role model.
5. People should be more careful in protecting their personal information online.

Write an introduction: _____

_____

_____

_____

_____

_____

_____

_____

_____

_____

WRITING THE BODY OF THE ESSAY

In the body of the essay, the paragraphs *explain, support,* and *develop* your thesis. In this part of the essay, each paragraph has its own topic sentence, which does two things:

1. It focuses the sentences in the paragraph.
2. It makes a point connected to the thesis.

The thesis and the topic sentences are ideas that need to be supported by details, explanations, and examples. You can visualize the connections among the parts of an essay like this:

Introduction with Thesis

Body
$\left\{ \begin{array}{l} \text{Topic Sentence} \\ \quad \text{Details} \\ \text{Topic Sentence} \\ \quad \text{Details} \\ \text{Topic Sentence} \\ \quad \text{Details} \end{array} \right.$

Conclusion

When you write topic sentences, you can help organize your essay by referring to the following checklist.

✓

CHECKLIST **FOR TOPIC SENTENCES OF AN ESSAY**

✓ Does the topic sentence give the point of the paragraph?

✓ Does the topic sentence connect to the thesis of the essay?

How Long Are the Body Paragraphs?

Remember that the body paragraphs of an essay are the place where you explain and develop your thesis. These paragraphs should be long enough to explain, not just list, your points. To do this well, try to make your body paragraphs *at least seven sentences* long. As you develop your writing skills, you may find that you can support your ideas in fewer than seven sentences.

Developing the Body Paragraphs

You can write well-developed body paragraphs by following the same steps you used in writing single paragraphs for the earlier assignments in this text. By working through the stages of gathering ideas, outlining, drafting, revising, editing, and proofreading, you can create clear, effective paragraphs.

To focus and develop the body paragraphs, ask the questions in the following checklist as you revise.

CHECKLIST   FOR DEVELOPING BODY PARAGRAPHS IN AN ESSAY

✓ Does the topic sentence cover everything in the paragraph?

✓ Do I have enough details to explain the topic sentence?

✓ Do all the details in the paragraph support, develop, or illustrate the topic sentence?

EXERCISE 9   CREATING TOPIC SENTENCES

Below are thesis sentences. For each thesis, write topic sentences (as many as are indicated by the numbered blanks). The first one is done for you.

1. **thesis:** These days, parents are over-programming their children.

    topic sentence 1: _Often, children have activities planned for every day of the week._

    topic sentence 2: _Unstructured time is important for children's emotional well-being._

    topic sentence 3: _Doctors have said that some children are as stressed as adults._

2. **thesis:** Professor Thompson is willing to help his students both in class and during his office hours.

    topic sentence 1: _____

    _____

    topic sentence 2: _____

    _____

3. **thesis:** It's easy to recognize the student who's at college just to have a good time.

   topic sentence 1: _____

   _____

   topic sentence 2: _____

   _____

   topic sentence 3: _____

   _____

4. **thesis:** The ideal roommate has several characteristics.

   topic sentence 1: _____

   _____

   topic sentence 2: _____

   _____

   topic sentence 3: _____

   _____

5. **thesis:** Moving to a new town has its good and bad points.

   topic sentence 1: _____

   _____

   topic sentence 2: _____

   _____

   topic sentence 3: _____

   _____

   topic sentence 4: _____

   _____

WRITING THE CONCLUSION

The last paragraph in the essay is the **conclusion**. It doesn't have to be as long as a body paragraph, but it should be long enough to tie the essay together and remind the reader of the thesis. You can use any of these strategies in writing the conclusion:

1. **You can restate the thesis, in new words.** Go back to the first paragraph of your essay and reread it. For example, this could be the first paragraph of an essay:

introduction

thesis at end

> Even when I was a child, I didn't like being told what to do. I wanted to be my own boss. When I grew up, I figured that the best way to be my own boss was to own my own business. I thought that being in charge would be easy. I now know how difficult being an independent business person can be. <u>Independent business owners have to be smart, highly motivated, and hard-working.</u>

The thesis, underlined above, is the sentence that you can restate in your conclusion. Your task is to *make the point again but to use different words.* Then work that restatement into a short paragraph, like this:

restating the thesis

> People who own their own business have to be harder on themselves than any employer would ever be. Their success is their own responsibility; they can't blame company policy or rules because they set the policy and make the rules. <u>If the business is to succeed, their intelligence, drive, and effort are essential.</u>

2. **You can make a judgment, evaluation, or recommendation.** Instead of simply restating your point, you can end by making some comment on the issue you've described or the problem you've illustrated. If you were looking for another way to end the essay on owning one's own business, for example, you could end with a recommendation.

ending with a recommendation

> People often dream of owning their own business. Dreaming is easy, but the reality is tough. <u>Those who want to succeed in their own venture should find a role model.</u> Studying a role model would teach them that know-how, ambition, and constant effort lead to success.

3. **You can conclude your essay by framing it.** Try tying your essay together neatly by using something from your introduction as a way of concluding. When you take an example, a question, or even a quote from your first paragraph and refer to it in your last paragraph, you are "framing" the essay.

frame
frame

frame

> Children <u>who don't like to take directions</u> may think that <u>being their own boss will be easy.</u> Adults who try to start a business soon discover that they must be totally self-directed; that is, they must be strong enough to <u>keep learning,</u> to <u>keep pushing forward,</u> and to <u>keep working.</u>

EXERCISE 10	CHOOSING A BETTER WAY TO RESTATE THE THESIS

Below are five clusters. Each cluster consists of a thesis sentence and two sentences that try to restate the thesis. Each restated sentence could be used as part of the conclusion to an essay. Put *B* next to the sentence in each pair that is a better restatement. Remember that the better choice repeats the same idea as the thesis but doesn't rely on too many of the same words.

1. **thesis:** Students choosing a college major should consider their abilities, their interests, and their financial goals.

   restatement 1: _____ Before they choose a major, students should think about what they do well, what they like to do, and what they want to earn.

   restatement 2: _____ Abilities, interests, and financial goals are things students choosing a major should consider.

2. **thesis:** One of the best ways to meet people is to take a college class.

   restatement 1: _____ Taking a class in college is one of the best ways to meet people.

   restatement 2: _____ College classes can make strangers into friends.

3. **thesis:** The three frosh-week activities I enjoyed the most were the scavenger hunt, the club night, and the boat cruise.

   restatement 1: _____ Frosh-week organizers obviously know what activities will help students make new friends.

   restatement 2: _____ The scavenger hunt, club night, and boat cruise were my favourite frosh-week activities.

4. **thesis:** My first job taught me the importance of being on time.

   restatement 1: _____ At my first job, I learned how important it is to be on time.

   restatement 2: _____ Punctuality was the key lesson of my first job.

5. **thesis:** Saving even a small amount of money each month is better than not saving at all.

   restatement 1: _____ Saving a little money every month can be better than not saving at all.

   restatement 2: _____ No matter how small it is, setting aside a small amount of money in a savings account each month is better than living paycheque to paycheque.

Revising the Draft

Once you have a rough draft of your essay, you can begin revising it. The following checklist may help you make the necessary changes in your draft.

✓ CHECKLIST   FOR REVISING THE DRAFT OF AN ESSAY

✓ Does the essay have a clear, unifying thesis?

✓ Does the thesis make a point?

✓ Does each body paragraph have a topic sentence?

✓ Is each body paragraph focused on its topic sentence?

✓ Are the body paragraphs roughly the same size?

✓ Do any of the sentences need to be combined?

✓ Do any of the words need to be changed?

✓ Do the ideas seem to be smoothly linked?

✓ Does the introduction catch the reader's interest?

✓ Is there a definite conclusion?

✓ Does the conclusion remind the reader of the thesis?

Transitions within Paragraphs

In an essay, you can use two kinds of transitions: those within a paragraph and those between paragraphs.

Transitions that link ideas *within a paragraph* are the same kinds you've used previously. Your choice of words, phrases, or even sentences depends on the type of connection you want to make. Here's a list of some common transitions and the kind of connection they express.

INFOBOX   COMMON TRANSITIONS WITHIN A PARAGRAPH

To join two ideas: again, also, and, another, besides, furthermore, in addition, likewise, moreover, similarly

To show a contrast or a different opinion: but, however, in contrast, instead, nevertheless, on the contrary, on the other hand, otherwise, or, still, yet

To show a cause-and-effect connection: accordingly, as a result, because, consequently, for, so, therefore, thus

To give an example: for example, for instance, in the case of, like, such as, to illustrate

To show time: after, at the same time, before, finally, first, meanwhile, next, recently, shortly, soon, subsequently, then, until

Transitions between Paragraphs

When you write something that's more than one paragraph long, you need transitions that link each paragraph to the others. There are several effective ways to link paragraphs and to remind the reader of your main idea and of how the smaller points connect to it. *Restatement* and *repetition* are two ways to link:

1. **Restate an idea** from the preceding paragraph at the start of a new paragraph. Look closely at the following two paragraphs and notice how the second paragraph repeats an idea from the first paragraph and provides a link.

If people were more patient, driving would be less of an ordeal. If, for instance, the driver behind me didn't honk his horn as soon as the traffic light turned green, both he and I would probably have lower blood pressure. He wouldn't be irritating himself by pushing so hard. And I wouldn't be reacting by slowing down, trying to irritate him even more, and getting angry at him. When I get impatient in heavy traffic, I just make a bad situation worse. Hurrying doesn't get me to my destination any faster; it just stresses me out.

transition
restating an idea

<u>The impatient driver doesn't get anywhere;</u> neither does the impatient customer at a restaurant. Impatience at restaurants doesn't pay. I work as a host at a restaurant, and I know that the customer who moans and complains about waiting for a table won't get one any faster than the person who makes the best of the wait. In fact, if a customer is too aggressive or obnoxious, the restaurant staff may actually slow down the process of getting that customer a table.

2. **Use synonyms and repetition** as a way of reminding the reader of an important point. For example, in the following two paragraphs, notice how certain repeated words, phrases, and synonyms all remind the reader of a point about facing fear. The repeated words and synonyms are underlined.

Some people just <u>avoid</u> whatever they <u>fear</u>. I have an uncle who is <u>afraid</u> to fly. Whenever he has to go on a trip, he does anything he can to <u>avoid</u> getting on an airplane. He'll drive for days, travel by train, take a bus trip. Because he's so <u>terrified</u> of flying, he lives with <u>constant anxiety</u> that someday he may have to actually do it. He's always thinking of the one emergency that could force him to <u>confront what he most dreads</u>. Instead of <u>dealing directly with his fear</u>, he lets it <u>haunt</u> him.

Other people are even worse than my uncle. He won't <u>attack his fear</u> of something external. But there are those who won't <u>deal with their fear</u> of themselves. My friend Sam is a good example of this kind of person. Sam has a serious drinking problem. All Sam's friends know that he's an alcoholic. But Sam <u>won't admit</u> his addiction. I think he's <u>afraid to face</u> that part of himself. So he denies his problem, saying he can stop drinking any time he wants to. Of course, until Sam has the courage to <u>admit what he's most afraid of</u>—his alcoholism—he won't be able to change.

A Draft Essay

Following is a draft of the essay on working and going to college. As you read it, you'll notice many changes from the outline:

- An introduction has been added, phrased in the first person, "I," to unify the essay.
- Transitions have been added within and between paragraphs.

- General statements have been replaced by more specific ones.
- Word choice has been improved.
- A conclusion has been added. Some of the ideas added to the conclusion come from the original list about the topic of work and school. They are ideas that didn't fit in the body paragraphs but are useful in the conclusion.

A Draft of an Essay (*thesis and topic sentences are underlined*)

I work thirty hours a week at the front desk of a motel in Riverside. When I first signed up for college classes, I figured college would be fairly easy to fit into my schedule. After all, college students aren't in class all day, as high school students are. So I thought the twelve hours a week I'd spend in class wouldn't be too much of a load. But I was in for a big surprise. <u>My first semester at college showed me that students who work while getting an education face problems at school, at work, and at home.</u>

<u>First of all, trying to juggle job and school responsibilities creates problems at school.</u> Early-morning classes, for example, are particularly difficult for me. Because I work every weeknight from six to midnight, I don't get home until 1:00 a.m., and I can't fall asleep until 2:00 a.m. or later. I'm too tired to pay attention in my 8:00 a.m. class. Once, I even fell asleep in that class. My work hours create other conflicts. They cut into my study time, so I have little time to do all the assigned reading and papers. I get behind in these assignments, and I never seem to have enough time to catch up. Consequently, my grades are not as good as they could be.

Because I both work and go to school, I have problems doing well at school. But <u>work can also suffer when workers attend college.</u> Students shouldn't bring school into the workplace. One night, I tried to study at work, but my boss caught me reading my biology textbook at the front desk. I was reprimanded, and now my boss doesn't trust me. Sometimes, I come to work very tired. When I don't get enough sleep, I can be rude to motel guests who give me a hard time. Then the rudeness can get me into trouble. I remember one particular guest who reported me because I was sarcastic to her. She'd spent half an hour complaining about her bill, and I'd been too tired to be patient. Once again, my boss reprimanded me. Another time, school interfered with my job when I had to cut work to take a make-up test. I know my boss was unhappy with me then, too.

As a working student, I run into trouble on the job and at college. <u>Working students also suffer outside of college and the workplace.</u> Since I work nights during the week, the weekends are the only time I can study. Because I have to use my weekends to do schoolwork, I can't do other things. My apartment is a mess since I have no time to clean it. Worse, my girlfriend is ready to kill me because I have no social life. We never even go to the movies anymore. When she comes over, I'm busy studying.

With responsibilities in all three areas of my life, I face a cycle of stress. I'm constantly racing around, and I can't break the cycle. I want a college education, and I must have a job to pay my tuition. The only way I can succeed is to learn to manage my time. <u>I've learned that working students have to be very organized in order to cope with their responsibilities at college, at work, and at home.</u>

EXERCISE 11	IDENTIFYING THE MAIN POINTS IN THE DRAFT OF AN ESSAY

Below is the draft of a five-paragraph essay. Read it, then reread it and underline the thesis, as well as the topic sentences in each body paragraph and in the conclusion.

Until this year, I had never considered spending my free time helping others in my community. Volunteer work, I thought, was something retired folks and rich people did to fill their days. Just by chance, I became a volunteer for the public library's Classic Connection, which arranges read-a-thons and special programs for elementary school children. Although I don't receive a salary, working with some perceptive and entertaining Grade 3 students has been very rewarding in other ways.

Currently, I meet with my small group of four girls and three boys each Saturday morning from ten to eleven o'clock, and they've actually taught me more than I ever thought possible. I usually assign the children various passages in an illustrated children's classic like *The Little Prince,* and I help them with the difficult words as they read aloud. When I occasionally read to them, they follow right along, but when it's their turn, they happily go off track. I've learned that each child has a mind of his or her own, and I now have much more respect for daycare workers and elementary school teachers who must teach, entertain, and discipline thirty rowdy children all day long. I'm tired after just one hour with only seven children.

I've also learned the value of careful planning. I arrive at each session with a tape recorder and have them record a sound effect related to the story we'll be reading. At certain points during the session, we stop to hear the sound effects. They love to hear themselves and seem more focused on reading when I use this method. When I'm well prepared, I feel more relaxed and the sessions go smoothly.

I've enjoyed making several new friends and contacts through Classic Connection. I've become friendly with the parents of the kids in my reading group, and one of the fathers has offered me a well-paying job at his printing business.

He even mentioned that he could be flexible about my schedule. I asked him if he could help me put a collection together of the group's most outrageous original stories, and he said he'd be glad to do it in *his* free time. I've thus learned that the spirit of volunteerism is indeed contagious.

I plan to keep volunteering for Classic Connection's programs and look forward to a new group that should be starting soon. I don't know if I'm ready to graduate to an older group. After all, Grade 3 students still have much to teach me.

EXERCISE 12 ADDING TRANSITIONS TO AN ESSAY

The following essay needs transitions. Write the transitions on the blank lines, using the type of transition—word, phrase, or sentence—that is indicated.

When I finished high school, I was determined to go to college. What I hadn't decided was *where* I would go. Most of my friends were planning to leave home to attend college. They wanted to be responsible for themselves and to be free of their parents' supervision. Like my friends, I thought of going away. But I finally decided to go to a college near my home. I chose a college near home for several reasons.

_____ [add a phrase], I can save money by attending a community college near home. _____ [add a word] I'm still living at home, I don't have to pay for room and board at a college residence or pay rent for an apartment off campus. I don't have to pay for the transportation costs of visits home. My friends who are away at school tell me about all the money they're spending on the things I get at home for free. These friends are paying for things like doing their laundry and hooking up their cable TV.

_____ [add a phrase], my college expenses are basically just tuition, fees, and books. I think I have a better deal than my friends who went away to college.

_____

_____ [add a sentence]. By attending college near home, I've kept a secure home base. I think it would be very hard for me to handle a new school, a new town, a new set of classmates, and a new place to live all at the same time. I've narrowed my challenges to a new school and new classmates. _____ [add a word] I come home after a stressful day at college, I still have Mom and Dad's home cooking and sympathy to console me. I still sleep in my own comfortable—and comforting—room. Students who go away to school may have more freedom, _____ [add a word] I have more security.

_____

_____ [add a sentence]. My decision to stay home for college gave me a secure job base as well. For the past year, I've had a job I like very much. My boss is very fair, and she has come to value my work enough to let me set my own work schedule. _____ [add a word or phrase], she lets me plan my work schedule around my class schedule. If I had moved away to attend college, I would have had to find a new job. _____ [add a word or phrase], I would have had a hard time finding a boss as understanding as the one I have now.

There are many good reasons to go to a college away from home. _____ [add a word or phrase], there are probably as many good reasons to go to one near home. I know that I'm happy with my decision. It has paid off financially and has helped me maintain a secure place to live and to work.

EXERCISE 13

RECOGNIZING SYNONYMS AND REPETITION USED TO LINK IDEAS IN AN ESSAY

In the following essay, underline all the synonyms and repetition (of words or phrases) that help remind the reader of the thesis sentence. (To help you, the thesis is underlined.)

Our local TV news often features stories of extraordinary acts of courage. A firefighter, for example, rushes into a burning building to save an old man. Or a mother risks her own life to save her child from traffic. These are once-in-a-lifetime acts of courage, and they are indeed admirable. But <u>there is another, quiet kind of courage demonstrated all around us, every day.</u>

This kind of courage can be the fortitude of the person who has a terminal illness but who still carries on with living. I knew a person like that. He was the father of four. When he found out he had a year to live, he didn't waste much time in misery and despair. Instead, he used every moment to prepare his family for the time when he would no longer be there. He made financial arrangements. He spent time with his children to show them how much he loved them. His bravery in the face of death wasn't unusual. Every day, there is someone who hears bad news from a doctor and quietly goes on. But because such people are so quiet in their courage, they're not given much credit.

Another example of quiet, everyday courage can be seen in people with the guts to try new and frightening things. The older person who decides to go to college, for instance, must feel very afraid. But he or she faces that fear and enters the classroom. And any student, of any age, who chooses the course that's supposed to be hard or the teacher who's supposed to be tough shows a certain courage. Equally brave are the people who switch careers in middle age because they haven't found satisfaction in the workplace. It's frightening to start over at mid-life, especially when starting over means trading job security and money for uncertainty and a lower starting salary. Yet many people make that trade, demonstrating real fortitude.

Sometimes, we think that heroes are people who make the news. Granted, there are heroes splashed loudly across the papers and acclaimed on TV. Yet there are other, equally brave people who never make the news. They're the ones whose lives show a less dramatic form of courage. They're the ones who are all around us, and who deserve our admiration and respect.

PROOFREADING PROOFREADING AND POLISHING: AN ESSAY

When you're satisfied with the final draft of your essay, you can begin preparing a good copy. Your essay will need a title. Try to think of a short title that is connected to your thesis. Since the title is the reader's first contact with your essay, an imaginative title can create a good first impression. If you can't think of anything clever, try using a key phrase from your essay.

The title is placed at the top of your essay, about 2.5 centimetres above the first paragraph. Always capitalize the first and last words of the title and all other words *except* articles (e.g., *the, an, a*) and short prepositions (e.g., *of, in, with*). Do not underline or put quotation marks around your title.

The Final Version of an Essay

Below is the final version of the essay on working and going to college. When you compare it with the draft, you'll notice some changes:

- A title has been added.
- In the first paragraph, the words "I thought" have been added to make it clear that the statement is the writer's opinion.
- One topic sentence, in paragraph two, has been revised so that it includes the word "students" and the meaning is more precise.
- Words have been changed to sharpen the meaning.
- Transitions have been added.

A Final Version of an Essay (*changes from the draft are underlined*)

Problems of the Working College Student

I work thirty hours a week at the front desk of a motel in Riverside. When I first <u>registered</u> for college classes, I figured college would be fairly easy to fit into my schedule. After all, <u>I thought,</u> college students aren't in class all day, as high school students are. So I <u>assumed that</u> the twelve hours a week I'd spend in class wouldn't be too much of a load. But I was in for a big surprise. My first semester at college showed me that students who work while getting an education face problems at school, at work, and at home.

First of all, <u>students who try</u> to juggle job and school responsibilities <u>find trouble at school.</u> Early-morning classes, for example, are particularly difficult for me. Because I work every weeknight from six to midnight, I don't get home until 1:00 a.m., and I can't fall asleep until 2:00 a.m. or later. <u>Consequently,</u> I'm too tired to pay attention in my 8:00 a.m. class. Once, I even fell asleep in that class. My work hours create other conflicts. They cut into my study time, so I have little time to do all the assigned reading and papers. I get behind in these assignments, and I never seem to have enough time to catch up. <u>As a result,</u> my grades are not as good as they could be.

Because I both work and go to school, I have problems doing well at school. But work can also suffer when workers attend college. Students shouldn't bring school into the workplace. <u>I've been guilty of this practice and have paid the price.</u> One night, I tried to study at work, but my boss caught me reading my biology textbook at the front desk. I was reprimanded, and now my boss doesn't trust me. Sometimes, I come to work very tired, <u>creating another problem.</u> When I don't get enough sleep, I can be rude to motel guests who give me a hard time. Then the rudeness can get me into trouble. I remember one particular guest who reported me because I was sarcastic to her. She'd spent half an hour complaining about her bill, and I'd been too tired to be patient. Once again, my boss reprimanded me. Another time, school interfered with my job when I had to cut work to take a make-up test. I know my boss was unhappy with me then, too.

As a working student, I run into trouble on the job and at college. <u>But</u> working students also suffer outside of classes and the workplace. <u>My schedule illustrates the conflicts of trying to juggle too many duties.</u> Since I work nights during the week, the weekends are the only time I can study. Because I have to use my

(continued)

weekends to do schoolwork, I can't do other things. My apartment is a mess since I have no time to clean it. Worse, my girlfriend is ready to kill me because I have no social life. We never even go to the movies anymore. When she comes over, I'm busy studying.

With responsibilities in all three areas of my life, I face a cycle of stress. I'm constantly racing around, and I can't break the cycle. I want a college education, and I must have a job to pay my tuition. The only way I can succeed is to learn to manage my time. <u>In my first semester at college, I've realized</u> that working students have to be very organized in order to cope with their responsibilities at college, at work, and at home.

Before you prepare the final copy of your essay, check your latest draft for errors in spelling and punctuation, and for any errors made in typing or recopying.

communication at work

Can't think why you might be asked to write anything as complex as an essay in the line of work you're planning? Think again. Technical reports, business cases, marketing descriptions, and the like may all be part of the job. For instance, if you're a computer technician, your employer may ask you to write a report comparing one operating system with another and recommending which should be implemented at your company. Or you may be asked to submit a written proposal outlining why your company would be the best one to supply a given service. The Toronto Zoo, for example, once issued a request for proposal (RFP) for the installation of a new skylight:

> You are invited to submit a written proposal, to the Purchasing & Supply of the Toronto Zoo, to provide Architectural/Engineering Design Services for the proposed Skylight Glazing Replacement and Exhibit Refurbishment at the African Rainforest Pavilion. Services to include review of existing facility and services, design, analysis with other consultants, and conformance of design to project budget, review and evaluation of tenders, and review during the construction of the project.

This kind of project demands focused writing and a clearly defined structure—skills that you practise when you write essays.

EXERCISE 14

PROOFREADING TO PREPARE THE FINAL VERSION

Below are two essays with the kinds of errors that are easy to overlook when you prepare the final version of an assignment. Correct the errors, writing above the lines. There are fifteen errors in the first essay and twenty in the second.

Three Myths about Young People

Today, when a person says the word "teenager" or refers to "college kids," that person may be speaking with a little sneer. Young people have acquired a bad reputation. Some of that repution may be deserved, but some of it may not be.

Young people are often judged according to myths—beliefs that are not true. Older people should not believe in three common myth's about the young.

We are always hearing that young people are irresponsable but their are many teens and people in their early twenties who disprove this statement. In every town, there are young people who hold full-time jobs and support a family. There are even more young people who work and go to school. All of my friends have been working since Grde 11. The fact that not one of them has ever been fired from a job implies they must be pretty good workers. Furthermore, young people today are almost forced to be responsible they must learn to work and pay for their clothes and college tuition.

Another foolish belief is that all young people take drugs. Hollywood encourages this myth by often including a drug-crazed teenager in its films. And when television broadcasts a public service announcement about drugs, the drug user shown is often a young person. In reality, many young people have chosen not to take drugs. For every teen with a problem of abuse, there is probally another teen who has never taken drugs or who has conquered a drug problem. In my high scool, an anonymous student poll showed that more than half of the students had never experimented with drugs.

Some older adults label young people as irresponsible and addicted. Even more people are likely to say that the young are apathetic, but such critics are wrong. The young are criticized for not carring about political or social issues, for being unconscience of the problems we all face. yet high school and college students are the ones who are out there, cleaning up the litter on the highways or beaches, whenever there is a local clean-up campaign. During the holidays, every school and college collects food, clothing, and toys for the needy students organize these drives, and students distributes these items. On many weekends, young people are out walking and cycling, collecting for charity.

Granted, there are apathetic, addicted, and irresponsible young people. But a whole group should not be judged by the actions of a few. Each young person deserve to be treated as an individual, not as an example of a myth.

Everyday Pleasures

As I hurry through each day, I focus on the demands and difficulties that face me. I thinks about diving in rush hour; or studying for a quizz. I rarely stop to consider the many moments of enjoyment that fill each day. These simple pleasures compensate for all life's stressful moments.

Even as I get ready for the day ahead, I enjoy the sootheing comfort of a hot shower. The stream of hot waters soothes my aching muscles. I adjust the shower head so that warm needles of water masage my back. The rising steam surrounds me. I fill my body restoring itself and I never want to leave. Yet when

I face the cold air outside the shower, drying off with the soft bath towels leaves me feeling clean and new

When I return home, my dogs greeting allways makes me smile. I hear him bark as I turn the key in the lock. Then he sees me and wriggles his entire body with joy. I feel a wet nose against my hand and look into two, deep brown eyes. He seems to be smiling at me. To my dog, my return means a long walk, some fun with a ball, and a good dinner. My dog's happiness makes me happy.

The evening has its own enjoyments. My couch is deep and wide with many pillows, perfect for laying in front of the television. I stretch out and turn on a movie, my dog at my feet. The movie is silly, but it does'nt matter. I burrow into the pillows. Soon my dog and me are both asleep on the couch.

As I face the irritations of my day, I forget the moments of pleasure, comfort, and happiness that I expereince. Because they are routine and ordinary, they are easy to forget, However stopping to remember these times makes me appreciate the good I have in my life.

Lines of Detail: A Walk-Through Assignment

Think of two careers that you believe would be right for you. They don't have to be careers for which you're studying or preparing now—they can be the kind of work you'd choose if you had unlimited funds along with the time to study, train, or otherwise prepare.

Step 1: Begin with some investigation. For example, seek out an expert in your college's career centre; look into what training and education as well as what mental, psychological, and physical abilities are required; talk to someone currently working in this field or to a student who is preparing for it; and conduct research online and in the college or local public library.

Step 2: As you investigate, take notes. Keep in mind that your purpose is to discover what to expect if you were to work toward earning the qualifications for employment in this field.

Step 3:   Survey your notes. Try to focus on a point you can make about the two possible careers. Do they both require the same type of personality? What are the rewards of each? What are the drawbacks? What is the current job market like for those in each field?

The answers to such questions can help you focus on a thesis.

Step 4:   Once you have a thesis, you can begin to cluster the details you've gathered.

Step 5:   Once you have clustered these details, draft an outline. Revise your draft outline until it's unified, expresses the ideas in a clear order, and has enough supporting details.

Step 6:   Write a draft of your essay. Revise the draft, checking it for balanced paragraphs, relevant and specific details, a strong conclusion, and smooth transitions.

Step 7:   Before you prepare the final version of your essay, check for spelling, word choice, and punctuation errors. Also, give your essay a title.

Writing Your Own Essay

When you write on any of these topics, make sure to work through the stages of the writing process in preparing your essay.

1. Take any paragraph you've written for this class and develop it into an essay of four or five paragraphs. If your instructor agrees, read the paragraph to a partner or group, and ask your listener(s) to suggest points within the paragraph that could be developed into paragraphs of their own.

2. Write an essay using one of the following thesis statements:

   If I won a million dollars, I know what I would do with it.

   Most families waste our natural resources every day, simply by going through their daily routines.

   Television coverage of hockey [or basketball, or tennis, or any other sport you choose] could be improved by a few changes.

   The one place I'll never visit again is _____, because _____.

   All bad romances share certain characteristics.

   If I could be someone else, I'd like to be _____ for several reasons.

3. Write an essay on people's earliest childhood memories. Interview three classmates to gather details and to focus your essay. Ask each one to tell you about the earliest memory he or she has of childhood. Before you begin interviewing, make a list of questions, like these: What is your earliest memory? How old were you at the time of that recollection? What were you doing? Do you remember other people or events in that scene? If so, what were the others doing? Were you indoors? Outdoors? Is this a pleasant memory? Why do you think this memory has stayed with you?

Use the details collected during the interviews to write a five-paragraph essay with a thesis sentence like one of the following:

Childhood memories vary a great deal from person to person.

The childhood memories of different people are surprisingly similar.

Although some people's first memories are painful, others remember a happy time.

Some people claim to remember events from their infancy, but others can't remember anything before their third [or fourth, or fifth, etc.] birthday.

4. Freewrite for ten minutes on the two best days of your life. After you've completed the freewriting, review it. Do the two days have much in common? Or were they very different? Write a four-paragraph essay based on their similarities or differences, with a thesis like one of these:

The two best days of my life were both _____. [Focus on similarities.]

While one of the best days of my life was _____, the other great day was _____. [Fill in with differences.]

5. Write an essay on one of the following topics:

Three Careers for Me	The Three Worst Jobs
Three Workplace Hazards	Three Workplace Friends
Three Lucky People	Three Wishes
Three Family Traditions	Three Decisions for Me

6. Narrow one of the following topics and then write an essay on it:

nature	dreams	crime	music	celebrities
fears	family	lies	health	romance
habits	books	money	animals	travel
students	teachers	games	secrets	fashion

WRITING FROM READING: THE ESSAY

When Immigration Goes Awry
Daniel Stoffman

Daniel Stoffman's work has appeared in such publications as The Walrus *magazine and* The Globe and Mail. *He also co-wrote the bestseller* Boom, Bust and Echo.

Before you read this selection, consider these questions:

What are some of the most challenging issues—political, social, and economic—facing Canada today?

How well does this essay, written in 2006, reflect the current situation in Canada?

What are some of the challenges new immigrants face when settling in Canada?

What challenges do major urban centres face that smaller towns do not?

affluent: well-off

It's 2020 and, in Toronto, the days when everyone used the public health-care system are gone. So is the time when a majority of **affluent**, middle-class parents sent their kids to public schools. In 2020, vast tracts of suburban slums occupy what used to be good farmland on the city's outskirts.

Traffic congestion and air pollution are unbearable. Toronto's reputation as one of North America's most livable cities is a distant memory. It's now known as the "Sao Paulo of the north."

dystopian: bleak, nightmarish

This **dystopian** vision of the future of Canada's largest city is hardly far-fetched. Toronto is already suffering severe growing pains, the result of the federal government's insistence on maintaining the world's largest per capita annual immigration intake—around 250,000 people a year of whom about 43 percent come to Toronto. That's more than 100,000 newcomers year after year after year.

infrastructure: facilities and systems that serve a community

It is impossible for any city to maintain its social and physical **infrastructure** in the face of such relentless population growth.

By 2020, Greater Toronto's population will have ballooned from 5 million to 7 million, or even more if immigration levels are raised higher still.

Every year Mercer Human Resource Consulting ranks world cities according to their livability. Vancouver always places at or near the top of the list while the other big Canadian cities are among the top 30. Most of the top-ranked cities are relatively small—places like Copenhagen (500,000) and Zurich (340,000).

agglomeration: a jumbled mass or collection

amenity: any feature that provides comfort, convenience, or pleasure

megalopolis: very large city

None of the world's vast urban **agglomerations** of 10 million or more, such as Sao Paulo and Seoul, are rated by Mercer as desirable places to live. Smaller big cities are more livable because their residents can enjoy the **amenities** of urban life without the congestion, crime, and pollution associated with sprawling **megalopolises**.

irreparable: cannot be repaired

jurisdiction: authority

Canada's livable cities are an unsung national asset. One of the things that make them special is the presence of immigrants from all over the world who have contributed new energy and cultural diversity. But, in immigration as in everything else, too much of a good thing isn't better. Ottawa's policy of mass immigration, for which no reasonable explanation has ever been offered, risks doing **irreparable** damage to our cities. This policy of rapid urban growth is being implemented by Ottawa even though it has no **jurisdiction** over urban affairs and even though the policy has never been stated explicitly.

Yet the impact is already evident.

Highway 401 across Toronto has become the busiest road in North America, the city can't find a place to put its garbage, and its public schools can't afford to provide the English instruction newly arrived children need. In Vancouver, meanwhile, controversy rages over the British Columbia government's plan to expand the Port Mann bridge that links the rapidly growing Fraser Valley suburbs to the city.

Amazingly, the local politicians who have to cope with the results never suggest that perhaps the immigration intake might be lowered from time to time as was standard practice until the late 1980s. To listen to their silence, one would think the relentless influx of huge numbers of new residents was a natural phenomenon like the weather rather than a deliberate federal policy that easily could be changed.

disingenuous: insincere

Ottawa might claim it is not to blame for unmanageable urban growth because it just lets the immigrants in, it doesn't tell them where to go. But this would be **disingenuous**, because Ottawa knows Toronto gets almost half of all immigrants while Vancouver gets 18 percent and Montreal 12 percent. Many of those who settle elsewhere at first also eventually wind up in one of the three biggest cities.

dispersion: spreading out

Attempts at **dispersion** are doomed because immigrants want to live where previous cohorts of the same ethnicity are already established. They also want to live in cities for the same reason Canadian-born people do—they are more likely to find jobs there.

The country most comparable to Canada is Australia. Like Canada, it is an English-speaking Commonwealth nation settled in relatively recent history. Like Canada, it has an organized immigration program and has used immigration effectively to enhance population growth and increase the **vigour** and diversity of its major cities.

vigour: vitality

Australia's current net migration rate (immigration minus emigration per 1,000 of population) is 3.85. Canada's is 5.85. Before the Progressive Conservative government of Brian Mulroney increased immigration levels and made them permanent during the latter part of the 1980s, a policy continued by the Liberals under Jean Chrétien, Canada had an intake similar, on a per-capita basis, to Australia's.

There is no reason why Canada should have far more immigration than any other country. Canada's existing population is younger than those of most other developed countries and its ratio of working age people to retired ones is higher. If Canada reverted to its traditional, more moderate, immigration program, it could continue to enjoy the benefits of immigration while sparing its cities the problems of unmanageable growth. Immigrants would benefit too. Their economic performance has been in free fall over the past 15 years.

Previously the number of new immigrants varied according to labour market needs. Sometimes it would be cut to give the newly arrived a chance to be absorbed successfully into the economy without intense competition from more new arrivals. Not any more.

An endless stream of newcomers arrives in the big cities with few options but to work in poorly paid jobs such as cleaning houses and driving taxis. Wages of these jobs are thus kept low and the occupants of them have little chance to get ahead.

Previously, poverty levels among immigrants were about the same as those of the Canadian-born. Now they are much worse. According to a report by the Canadian Council on Social Development, whereas the poverty level of those who arrived before 1986 was 19.7 percent, or slightly lower than that of the Canadian-born, the poverty level of those who came after 1991 was an alarming 52.1 percent, while that of people born in Canada remained unchanged at around 20 percent.

entrenched: firmly fixed

gentrification: revitalization of an older neighbourhood that often results in the displacement of lower-income residents by new higher-income residents

If this trend is not reversed, Toronto and Vancouver will by 2020 be home to an **entrenched** underclass living in slums. Because of **gentrification** and rising property values in the central cities, these slums will be located in the suburbs, requiring long commutes for those fortunate enough to have employment.

shrewdly: showing astute powers of judgment; cleverly

Fan Yang, a reader of the *Toronto Star*, **shrewdly** analyzed the impact of federal immigration policy in a letter to the newspaper in 2003. He accused the federal government of "dumping more cheaply acquired labour into the domestic labour pool, regardless of whether there is a healthy demand. Businesses welcome that enthusiastically as they bear no direct cost of unemployed immigrants and only garner the rewards of lower labour costs."

Even skilled workers are doing poorly. According to the 2001 census, male immigrants with a university degree who came to Ontario in the late 1990s were earning after six to 10 years in Canada only 54 percent of what native-born Canadians with similar qualifications in that province earned.

Remarkably, immigrant labour market performance has declined during a time of increasing shortages of skilled workers. But, as the above data suggest, just bringing in huge numbers of people doesn't solve skills shortages. Mexico has a worse skills shortage than Canada yet it has no shortage of people. The trick is to match immigrants to jobs and our current immigration program doesn't do that well.

reinvent the wheel: duplicate a basic, already established method

emulate: try to equal or excel

Luckily, Canada doesn't need to **reinvent the wheel**. It merely needs to **emulate** the solutions that Australia's more successful immigration program has already found, such as requiring the credentials of skilled immigrants to be approved before they come and imposing strict requirements for language skills.

cohort: group of people having the same statistical characteristics; e.g., age

interminable: tediously long

In addition to creating poverty, mismanaged immigration is weakening our public health-care and education systems. By 2020, the huge baby boomer **cohort** of Canadians will be entering its stage of heaviest reliance on the health-care system. The boomers will not tolerate **interminable** waits for hip replacements and cancer treatment.

As if the challenge of caring for impatient boomers weren't enough, the presence of millions of new immigrants will intensify the demands on the system. Many of the newcomers will be old because Canada is the most generous country in allowing immigrants to sponsor elderly parents and grandparents.

There is no chance that our health-care system can survive in its current form given the demands on it from these demographic changes. As a result, by 2020 a full-fledged, parallel, private health-care system will be in operation in the major immigrant-receiving cities which are also where most of the boomers live. Private health care will be relied upon not just by the wealthy but by much of the middle class as well.

A similar transformation will occur in education. A report last January conducted for the Elementary Teachers of Toronto said teachers were spending the equivalent of one day a week trying to make up for the lack of English as a second language support for their immigrant students.

"The more time the regular classroom teacher is having to devote to ESL students . . . detracts from the level of service we want for all of our students," union president Martin Long told *The Globe and Mail*.

rash: reckless, hasty

In other words, the lack of support for ESL students is hurting all students. This is certainly not the fault of the immigrant children. It is the fault of **rash** and ill-conceived federal policy. As a result, by 2020 most middle-class families will have abandoned the public system. This will be an unfortunate development because the public schools are where immigrants and Canadian-born children get to know each other. They are an important force for social cohesion.

plausible: believable; workable

A seemingly **plausible** argument for boosting the population of at least one Canadian city to 10 million or more would be that the truly great cities of the world are very big. But London and Paris grew to their current size gradually over hundreds of years and their greatness is the result of the wealth of the empires of which they were the capitals.

You don't build London and Paris by adding millions of bodies over a short period of time. That's how you build Mumbai and Mexico City.

Ontario's environment commissioner, Gord Miller, issued a warning last year about what the future holds for Toronto given current trends:

"The environmental impacts of this magnitude of growth . . . will compromise the quality of our lifestyle to a stage where it will be unrecognizable," he said. "We already have trouble dealing with our waste right now . . . What about another 4 million tonnes a year? What about another 4 million cars?"

The new [federal] Conservative government's immigration minister, Monte Solberg, told a House of Commons committee in May that he was concerned about the "huge burden" high immigration levels place on our major cities. He thus became the first immigration minister in at least two decades to show any sensitivity to the impact of immigration policy on the urban environment.

ostrichlike: refusal to acknowledge reality

Now it's the turn of local officials to abandon their **ostrichlike** refusal even to mention immigration when discussing urban growth. Perhaps they fear being branded "anti-immigrant" if they do.

trump: surpass; gain an advantage over

But Pierre Trudeau, in his last year as prime minister, cut immigration by 25 percent and no one called him anti-immigrant. In that case, good management **trumped** politics. It's an example the Conservative government would do well to follow.

UNDERSTANDING "WHEN IMMIGRATION GOES AWRY"

1. According to the article, why do "vast urban centres" often not make the list of the most desirable places to live?

2. Given the way Stoffman envisions the year 2020, do you think Canadian immigration policy should change? How?

3. Keeping in mind that this essay was written in 2006, in what ways might current policies differ from, or remain the same as, those that Stoffman outlines?

4. What does Stoffman suggest as a possible solution to the situation? What do you think of this solution?

WRITING FROM READING "WHEN IMMIGRATION GOES AWRY"

1. Canada's cultural diversity has often been described as a "mosaic," whereas in the United States it has been called a "melting pot." What do you think these terms mean? Write an essay in which you argue for or against either a mosaic or a melting pot.

2. Immigrants often settle in areas where there are higher concentrations of people who speak their language and share their customs. However, some critics have said that this prevents immigrants from learning a new language, learning about their new country, and meeting other citizens. Write an essay in which you agree or disagree with this position.

3. Are you a recent immigrant to Canada? If so have your experiences been primarily positive or negative? Write an essay advising friends and family "back home" either to immigrate to Canada or stay home.

4. It has been suggested that the Canadian government provide incentives (e.g., financial bonuses, housing) to new immigrants to encourage them to settle in less populated areas. What do you think of this suggestion? Can you think of any other solutions to the problem of increased stress on our cities' infrastructure? Write an essay in which you explore some other options.

MyWritingLab

Go to MyWritingLab to access a diagnostic test that creates your own personalized learning path supported by rich multimedia resources and a variety of animated tutorials, all aimed at helping you improve your writing. MyWritingLab also includes a complete eText version of the book that is fully searchable and accessible through your web browser or most mobile devices.

CHAPTER 12
The Research Process

LEARNING OBJECTIVES

After you have read this chapter and completed its exercises, you should be able to

- recognize how the integration of research can strengthen an essay
- locate both print and electronic information at the library and online
- evaluate print and online sources for validity
- integrate and acknowledge sources in an essay
- document research in MLA and APA formats
- avoid plagiarism in an essay using proper attribution and documentation

> *"Research is formalized curiosity. It is poking and prying with a purpose."*
>
> ~ ZORA NEALE HURSTON

▼

ZORA NEALE HURSTON WAS AN AFRICAN-AMERICAN WRITER BEST KNOWN FOR HER NOVEL *THEIR EYES WERE WATCHING GOD* AND FOR HER USE OF REGIONAL DIALECTS IN HER WRITING.

RESEARCH IN DAILY LIFE

During your college experience, you will no doubt use research techniques in your coursework as well as in your daily life. Even if you haven't yet written a formal paper involving research, you've probably already employed various research techniques to solve problems or make crucial decisions. For example, deciding what college to attend and learning about financial-aid opportunities may have involved contacting professionals and taking careful notes. Similarly, if you're also a parent and have investigated community daycare options or family insurance plans, you'll be well aware of the importance of thorough research. Asking key questions and organizing your findings are research skills that can serve you well in college and in life.

USING RESEARCH TO STRENGTHEN ESSAYS

Many of the writing assignments you've completed thus far have probably been based on your own experiences, observations, or opinions. By writing regularly, you now know the importance of purpose, audience, organization, supporting details, and revision in producing a polished final version of an essay. Such an appreciation of the basics of effective writing also enables you to recognize how essays can be strengthened through research. This chapter introduces you to the research process and explains how a student writer can strengthen his or her original essay by smoothly incorporating supporting material from outside sources.

AN EXAMPLE OF AN ESSAY WITHOUT RESEARCH

The following outline and short essay about dog-rescue groups are based solely on the writer's own experience and knowledge about dog-rescue operations. The writer's thesis is that such groups perform a humane service by rescuing homeless dogs and carefully matching potential adopters with suitable pets. (Later, you will see how the writer smoothly incorporates information from five sources into an outline, draft, and final version of the essay.)

An Outline without Research

Here's the outline of an essay without research. You may notice that it's in the same form as the outlines you viewed in Chapter 11, "Writing an Essay."

An Outline for an Essay without Research

I. Dog-rescue organizations perform a humane service by saving homeless dogs and matching responsible adopters with a devoted new family member.

II. Dog-rescue volunteers play several roles.
   A. Some volunteers are *spotters* who look for specific breeds at local shelters.
   B. Experienced rescue volunteers may become coordinators and arrange assistance from various sources.
   C. Volunteers work with national organizations such as Save-A-Pet, which maintains a database of adoptable dogs from rescue groups throughout Canada and the United States.
   D. Volunteers assist at dog-rescue adoption days hosted by shelters and pet supply chains such as Pet Valu and PetSmart.

III. Rescue groups provide important information and benefits for prospective adopters.
   A. By viewing a rescue group's website, potential adopters can read about a dog's age, temperament, adoption fee, and any special medical conditions.
   B. If a potential adopter doesn't find a suitable dog, he or she can still complete an online application.
   C. On an application, a potential adopter can list his or her preferences for the age, sex, and size of the dog.
   D. Although some dogs are puppies rescued from abusive situations, most are adult dogs already socialized and housebroken.

IV. Careful screening often results in a successful adoption.
   A. Rescue groups routinely conduct home visits to check the living conditions and the neighbourhood.
   B. The applicant must have access to veterinary care.

> C. The applicant must agree to return the dog to the rescue organization if he or she can no longer care for the animal.
>
> D. A foster parent can fully inform the adoptive parent about potential adjustment problems.
>
> E. Careful attention to such details leads to a winning adoption process.
>
> V. Rescue groups not only provide care for homeless dogs, but they also remind us of the joy made possible by compassionate adoption.

An Essay without Research

The following essay, written from the outline you've just reviewed, contains no research from outside sources; it is based solely on the writer's own knowledge and experience. As you read it, you'll notice how the points in the outline have been developed through the use of specific details, effective sentence combining, and key transitions. You may also notice that some of the original words and phrases in the outline have been changed for better style.

> ### The Humane Work of Dog-Rescue Groups
>
> Although Canada and the United States are generally regarded as countries that love and pamper their pets, animal shelters are often filled to capacity with dogs that have been abandoned, abused, or surrendered by their owners. Sadly, some shelters routinely euthanize healthy dogs if no one claims or adopts them after a grace period ranging from just days to a few weeks. Fortunately, however, many shelters work closely with dog-rescue organizations that find loving, temporary homes where foster parents can provide care and, if necessary, rehabilitation. Staffed by dedicated volunteers, rescue groups perform a humane service by saving homeless dogs and enabling responsible adopters to gain a devoted new family member.
>
> From rescuing retired greyhounds to saving mini "mutts," dog-rescue volunteers play several roles. For example, they often serve as *spotters* at local shelters, looking for specific dogs that can be fostered by individuals who specialize in specific breeds, such as boxers and golden retrievers. Experienced volunteers may become coordinators who arrange for assistance from a variety of sources, including local veterinarians, groomers, transporters, and website designers. Many rescue groups work closely with organizations like Save-A-Pet, whose website publishes a comprehensive list of adoptable rescue dogs throughout Canada and the United States. On weekends, rescue volunteers can be seen helping out during adoption days sponsored by shelters and retailers, such as Pet Valu and PetSmart.
>
> Rescue groups provide both crucial information and welcome benefits for potential adopters. When one becomes interested in a specific dog on a rescue group's website, he or she can read about the animal's medical needs, age,

temperament, and adoption fee. Even if he or she doesn't spot a suitable dog but remains interested in adopting one from rescue, he or she can fill out an application and list preferences regarding a dog's age, sex, and size. Although rescue groups occasionally receive puppies and young dogs that have been picked up during police raids of abusive puppy mills and backyard breeders, the majority of dogs available for adoption are older ones. Any pet owner who has experienced the aggravation of sleepless nights and numerous housetraining "accidents" can appreciate the benefits of adopting an older, socialized, house-broken dog.

Although the adoption process may take several weeks, or even months, to find the best match, careful screening improves the chances for a successful adoption. Rescue groups routinely conduct home visits of prospective dog owners to see whether both the living conditions and the neighbourhood will be suitable for the dog's size, temperament, and exercise needs. In addition, the applicant must have access to veterinary care and agree to return the dog to the rescue organization if he or she can no longer properly care for it. A foster parent can fully inform the adoptive parent about a dog's potential adjustment problems because the animal's behaviour has been observed over a period of weeks—if not months—in a home setting. Careful attention to such details leads to a winning adoption process.

However a dog finds its way to a rescue group—by an owner surrender, a good Samaritan, or even by a police raid of an illegal breeding operation—it will have an opportunity to live out the rest of its life free from harm and neglect. Not only do rescue groups provide care for homeless dogs, but they also remind us of the joy made possible by compassion, commitment, and unconditional love.

FINDING RESEARCH TO STRENGTHEN ESSAYS

Adding documented research to your essay will strengthen your argument. Supporting your thesis with facts; statistics; and quotations from formal surveys, reports, and respected sources will demonstrate your commitment to the topic and help convince your reader of your argument.

Developing a Research Question

Research is an integral part of the writing process: Sometimes, you may not be able to focus a topic into a thesis statement until you decide how you feel about the topic, and this requires research. However, conducting research on a very broad topic will yield far too much information to help you decide how you feel about it. In fact, it may make you more confused.

Focus your research by developing a research question. To do this, consider your topic, and brainstorm a list of questions you would like answered about that topic. For instance, imagine you're interested in whether or not students should be permitted to use social media such as Facebook and Twitter in schools. You may ask . . .

■ Are social media sites too much of a distraction from students' studies?
■ Do social media encourage collaboration?
■ Is Twitter killing the English language?

You may then decide that you're interested in the effects of social media on college students' studies. Your research question, one you could use to drive your research, would be

What effects do social media have on college students' studies?

EXERCISE 1	DEVELOPING A TOPIC INTO A RESEARCH QUESTION

For each of the topics provided, brainstorm a list of questions and then develop a focused research question.

1. **topic:** Generation Y

   brainstorming questions:

   _____

   _____

   _____

   _____

   research question:

   _____

   _____

2. **topic:** distance education

   brainstorming questions:

   _____

   _____

   _____

   _____

   research question:

   _____

   _____

3. **topic:** airport security

   brainstorming questions:

   _____

   _____

   _____

   _____

   research question:

   _____

   _____

4. **topic:** mobile banking

   brainstorming questions:

   _____

   _____

   _____

   research question:

   _____

   _____

5. **topic:** the future of publishing

   brainstorming questions:

   _____

   _____

   _____

   research question:

   _____

   _____

Locating Material in Your Library

The Library Catalogue If you decide to use research to strengthen an essay, you can take advantage of a number of options. Your public or college library probably has an online catalogue system that lists all of the library's books and major holdings, both in print and digital. You can search the catalogue by a key word related to your subject, or, if you already have information about authors who write on your subject, you can search by an author's last name or the title of an author's book. An online catalogue can provide you with a list of sources, the call number of each source (the number that will help you find the book on the library shelves), and information regarding the availability of the source. The catalogue can tell you which location has a copy of the book you want. Ebooks are becoming an increasingly popular option at most libraries, and can be "borrowed" for varying periods. These ebooks often require special software to be read on different devices, so check with your library to ensure you have the correct software loaded on your device. Libraries offer numerous options for assistance—make sure to take advantage of any help menu the system provides as well as any orientation offered at your library. Many college libraries also provide an email function where you can ask questions of a librarian as well as a live online chat feature that allows you to seek assistance from a librarian during college library hours.

Popular Periodical Indexes Libraries commonly subscribe to several index services that provide access to complete articles (called "full-text" articles) from periodicals (magazines, journals, and newspapers). Some of the most widely used periodical indexes are EBSCOhost, InfoTrac, LexisNexis, NewsBank, ProQuest, and WilsonWeb. The periodical index can be an invaluable research tool; it offers the most current research and commentary, and can be searched by date, subject, or type. For instance, you can limit your search results to Canadian newspapers only, or to academic journals published after 2014. Additionally, most library databases can be accessed remotely twenty-four hours a day, seven days a week from any computer with internet access, allowing many students to conduct their research and download ebooks from home. Check with your college or community library to activate remote access with your library card.

Using the Periodical Index Because most college library indexes contain dozens of databases and can therefore yield thousands of results in a search, it's important to conduct your research in the periodical index with a focused, targeted search. When searching the periodical index, try to select the most effective key words and phrases. To choose key words and phrases, consider your research question: What are the most important words or phrases?

Consider the research question from page 308: "What effects do social media have on college students' studies?" Note in the following chart how research results change depending on the key words and phrases used.

Key Words/Phrases Entered	Number of Results	Nature of Articles
effects, social, media	over 2000	articles on socialization among the elderly, government funding for social programs
effects, "social media"	over 70	articles on the use of social media in university admissions, its effect on adolescents, its power to drive social change

Of course, you could narrow your search further by selecting only full-text articles, Canadian content, or articles published after a certain year—or by adding or modifying your key words and phrases.

Note how the inclusion of quotation marks limits the number of results. Using words or phrases in quotation marks yields articles with words or phrases exactly as they appear in the quotation marks.

EXERCISE 2

GENERATING KEY WORDS AND PHRASES FOR A DATABASE SEARCH

Take the research questions you developed in Exercise 1 and write some key words and phrases you could use to conduct a targeted periodical index search on each topic. Remember to use quotation marks around words that you want to appear in the article exactly as you phrase them.

1. **topic:** Generation Y
   key words/phrases:

   _____

   _____

2. **topic:** distance education
   key words/phrases:

   _____

   _____

3. **topic:** airport security
   key words/phrases:

   _____

   _____

4. **topic:** mobile banking
   key words/phrases:

   _____

   _____

5. **topic:** the future of publishing
   key words/phrases:

   _____

   _____

Always preview articles carefully to see whether they contain useful information for your research essay. Scan articles online, and save, email, or print copies of the articles that may be helpful in supporting your essay. If you print your articles, make sure the printouts include the information you'll need to document them (usually the author's name; the publication date, including month and day, if applicable; the name of the magazine, journal, or newspaper; the name of the database; and the date you read the article). Also make sure to ask your instructor whether he or she will require copies of the articles you used in your essay.

Internet Search Engines You're probably very familiar with searching the internet to obtain information. Your browser gives you access to institutions, organizations, and publications as well as libraries around the world. Unfortunately, the highly changeable nature of the internet means that some links posted on websites may be unavailable. Outdated information may also remain posted on a website indefinitely, so students need to be cautious about using statistics or expert opinions that are several years old.

Checking for Validity of Sources

The writer of the dog-rescue essay decided to strengthen his paper by adding material from outside sources. The instructor required students to incorporate information from at least one print publication (magazine, newspaper, or book) and two valid electronic (online) sources. While a traditional research paper involves a more comprehensive use of outside sources and a lengthier planning and research process, a short essay can often be enhanced by adding relevant material from experts. Regardless of the scope of any research assignment, the sources used must be valid.

Generally, material located through the periodical index will come from valid sources. Articles published in newspapers, magazines, and academic journals have been professionally reviewed and edited. However, information found through a general internet search can be less reliable; many websites haven't had their information fact-checked or edited, and are often a repository for a poster's opinions. This kind of information would not be sufficiently reliable to support an academic essay.

Evaluating Internet Sources It's been said that trying to find information on the internet is like "sipping from a fire hydrant," meaning that there's just too much information to assess. Observing the domain names of websites can help you filter out the more valuable websites. Domain names are the two or three letters at the end of a URL, and often indicate the nature of the sponsoring organization. Common domain names include the following:

.com (company)	.org (non-profit organization).
.edu (educational institution)	.ca (Canadian organization)
.net (network)	.gov (US government)

Information from educational or governmental websites is generally considered to be reliable and valid; nonetheless, make sure to assess all the information you read on any website carefully. Check the author's credentials, such as educational background and professional experience, and other significant connections. In addition, try to locate any information about the background of the company or individuals responsible for a website.

The student writing the dog-rescue essay began his internet search by typing the key phrase "dog rescue organizations" into the Google search function. This initial search resulted in a list of several hundred potential sources. After confirming the validity of his sources with his instructor, he was able to narrow his list to several dozen suitable sources.

Keeping in mind that it's essential to check websites for accuracy and validity, the student tried to find expert testimony from a veterinarian or background information from a non-profit organization such as the Canadian Federation of Humane Societies. Because the veterinarian and the non-profit group are experienced and have no financial ties to the selling of dogs, their information is more valid than opinions from a pet shop owner, who makes money selling pets, or from a chat room popular with pet owners, who may know very little about dog-rescue groups.

Likewise, when reading a brochure advertising quick or foolproof dog-training programs, the student realized that this source wouldn't be as reliable as an article from a magazine endorsed by the Canadian Society for the Prevention of Cruelty to Animals (CSPCA). Remember that your college probably offers library orientations that include suggestions for determining the validity of a website's information and of a print source's reliability.

If you have any doubt about a source's validity, check with your instructor or seek advice from a librarian. At the very least, check whether an article lists the title or credentials of the author. If you've found an unsigned article, check whether the organization responsible for the material lists its history and/or purpose. Also check for the publication date of the article, the original place of publication, the tone of the article (e.g., Does it avoid slang? Does it appear serious?), and the proper use of statistics and expert opinion. Using valid sources will lend credibility to your work.

EXERCISE **3**	**EVALUATING WEBSITES FOR RELIABILITY**
	In groups, take the topics you used in Exercises 1 and 2 and conduct an internet search on each; try to find at least five sites for each topic. Discuss whether you think each site would be a reliable source of information, and why.

INCORPORATING AND ACKNOWLEDGING YOUR SOURCES

Gathering and Organizing Sources

Once you've previewed your potential sources and selected the ones best suited for your topic, you'll need printouts of any online article (or at least the necessary pages) for highlighting and note taking. If you're using a book or a magazine in its original form, you'll need to photocopy the relevant pages. To keep track of all the sources you're using, staple or paper-clip the pages of each source and label each one clearly.

If you've narrowed your search to several sources (e.g., three magazine articles, two newspaper articles, one book), you could organize them alphabetically by the authors' last names. If an article doesn't list its author, use the first major word of the title in place of the author's last name. Then you can label your sources as Source #1, Source #2, and so forth. This type of labelling will be useful later as you develop an outline that includes references to your sources.

Your instructor may want to see a preliminary list of your potential sources, and he or she may also require that your notes from sources be written on note cards. Other instructors may encourage you to use your computer for note taking. Make sure to follow your instructor's specific guidelines and directions.

Taking Notes and Acknowledging Your Sources

When you take notes from one of your sources and use the information in your paper, you must acknowledge the source. This acknowledgment is called **documentation** because you're documenting, or giving credit to, the author and the work that provided the information. When you provide documentation within a research essay, you're using what's called **internal citation**. ("Citation" means "giving credit," and "internal" means "inside" or "within" the paper.) At the end of your essay, list all the sources you cited within the paper. This list is called the **Works Cited** in MLA and the **References** in APA (see below for more information on MLA and APA). The list of works cited is on a separate page from the rest of the essay, and it is the last numbered page of the document.

Avoiding Plagiarism Plagiarism occurs when you use a source's words or ideas and fail to give proper credit to the author and/or source of the work. Even if you **paraphrase** (state someone else's ideas in your own wording; see Chapter 2), you must give credit to the original source.

Whether you summarize material from an outside source, quote directly from it, or even paraphrase from it, you must acknowledge the source. Failure to do so is a form of academic theft. Depending on departmental or college policy, the penalties for plagiarism can be severe, ranging from receiving a failing grade on the plagiarized paper or failing a course to expulsion. Some departments now use special software programs to check all student papers for plagiarism, and it is simply not worth the risk to submit research assignments without proper documentation.

What to Acknowledge When in doubt, remember that it's always safer to give credit to a source. That said, you must document

- any material that you summarize or paraphrase;
- anything you write that may use the same sentence structure or writing style as the original document;
- any material you copy directly from another source; and
- any facts or statistics that aren't *common knowledge*.

Common Knowledge Common knowledge is information that the general public would be expected to know and that can be found in multiple sources. Such information would be difficult to attribute to a single source, and so it does not need to be documented. Examples of common knowledge include the following:

- Sir John A. Macdonald was Canada's first prime minister.
- The five Great Lakes are Lake Huron, Lake Ontario, Lake Michigan, Lake Erie, and Lake Superior.
- Carbon emissions contribute to global warming.
- Biodiesel is an alternative fuel source for automobiles.
- Microsoft Windows is the most common operating system in use today.

EXERCISE **4**	**DETERMINING WHICH SOURCES TO DOCUMENT**

Review the statements below, and determine which would *not* be considered common knowledge, and therefore would need to be documented.

1. Nunavut is Canada's newest territory.
2. Nunavut officially separated from the Northwest Territories on April 1, 1999.
3. In Inuktitut, one of the languages spoken in Nunavut, *Nunavut* means "our land."
4. Nunavut is one of the least populated areas in Canada.
5. Jordin John Kudluk Tootoo, a forward with the New Jersey Devils, is the first Inuk to play in the National Hockey League.

communication at work

In 2006 an instance of plagiarism was reported in the publishing world. Harvard undergraduate Kaavya Viswanathan was accused of plagiarizing passages from two books by Megan F. McCafferty, among others. All editions of her book "How Opal Mehta Got Kissed, Got Wild and Got a Life" were subsequently withdrawn and her publishing deal with Little, Brown and Co. was cancelled. Discuss the two passages, Why is Viswanathan's considered plagiarized? Of what other professional examples of plagiarism are you aware? What were the consequences? The passage from McCafferty's novel is as follows:

> Marcus then leaned across me to open the passenger-side door. He was invading my personal space, as I had learned in Psych class, and I instinctively sank back into the seat. That just made him move in closer. I was practically one with the leather at this point, and unless I hopped into the backseat, there was nowhere else for me to go.

The passage in Viswanathan's novel reads,

> Sean stood up and stepped toward me, ostensibly to show me the book. He was definitely invading my personal space, as I had learned in a Human Evolution class last summer, and I instinctively backed up till my legs hit the chair I had been sitting in. That just made him move in closer, until the grommets in the leather embossed the backs of my knees, and he finally tilted the book toward me.

Revised passage:

_____

_____

_____

_____

_____

Options for Acknowledging Your Sources

The Modern Language Association (MLA) system of documentation is used in English and the humanities. Psychology and social sciences use the American Psychological Association (APA) system of documentation. Make sure to follow your instructor's directions regarding documentation requirements for your research assignments. There are many handbooks available that contain both MLA and APA styles of documentation, and many writing courses require that students purchase a handbook. You may want to check with your instructor to see which handbook is used in your program.

Over the next several pages, you'll see how MLA and APA documentation is used for summarizing, paraphrasing, and directly quoting information from sources. You'll also see how books, periodicals, and electronic sources should be listed on a Works Cited or References page that conforms to MLA or APA guidelines.

Internal ("In-Text") Citation: MLA and APA Format

When using internal citation, you have several options for incorporating and giving credit to the source of your information; this is called **attribution**. Without this, your essay will be considered plagiarized. If you use a combination of techniques, your paper will read more smoothly. The following examples of summarizing, directly quoting, paraphrasing, and combining a direct quote and paraphrasing will provide you with sufficient documentation options as you draft your essay. (For more information on how to summarize and paraphrase, refer to Chapter 2, "Writing from Reading.") Notice that authors, years, and page numbers (depending on the system) appear in parentheses; this form is called **parenthetical documentation**.

A Summary of an Entire Book

Leigh and Geyer's *One at a Time: A Week in an American Animal Shelter* describes the fate of seventy-five animals who passed through a local shelter in Northern California over a seven-day period.

The book *One at a Time: A Week in an American Animal Shelter* describes the fate of seventy-five animals who passed through a local shelter in Northern California over a seven-day period (Leigh & Geyer, 2003).

Note: No page numbers are included in the in-text citation because the *entire* work is summarized. In MLA style, when you refer to a whole work, include the author's name in the text rather than in a parenthetical reference. MLA now accepts italics for titles if the formatting is clear. (You can ask your instructor whether you should use underlining or italics when using MLA format.) In APA format, the title of the book is in italics, and major words are capitalized (i.e., not conjunctions, articles, and short prepositions of three letters or fewer) as well as proper nouns and the first letter in the title and subtitle. APA in-text citation uses an ampersand (&) and a comma before the year of publication.

A Direct Quotation

According to Leigh and Geyer, "The safest and most reliable identification is provided by a combination of an ID tag, which is easily visible, and a microchip, which is permanent" (2).

According to Leigh and Geyer (2003), "The safest and most reliable identification is provided by a combination of an ID tag, which is easily visible, and a microchip, which is permanent" (p. 2).

Note: If you introduce the author in the sentence that quotes from his or her work, you don't have to include the author's name in parentheses at the end of the quoted material. APA citations include the year of publication, and "p." to represent the page from which the quotation was taken. Notice that the period for the sentence goes after the final parenthesis. When multiple authors are referred to in the sentence, write out *and* instead of using the ampersand as in in-text citations.

A Paraphrase

MLA

> A clearly marked ID tag, along with a permanent microchip, provides an animal with the best and safest means of identification (Leigh and Geyer 2).

APA

> A clearly marked ID tag, along with a permanent microchip, provides an animal with the best and safest means of identification (Leigh & Geyer, 2003, p. 2).

A Source Quoted in Another Author's Work

MLA

> Kathy Nicklas-Varraso, author of *What to Expect from Breed Rescue*, notes that adopters will "most often get an adult whose chewing phase, housebreaking phase, and general puppy wildness are gone" (qtd. in Mohr).

APA

> Kathy Nicklas-Varraso, author of *What to Expect From Breed Rescue*, notes that adopters will "most often get an adult whose chewing phase, housebreaking phase, and general puppy wildness are gone" (as cited in Mohr, n.d.).

Note: Nicklas-Varraso is the author being quoted; her comment was found in an online magazine article by Mohr. Mohr is the source that the student writer found. Therefore, Mohr is the source cited in parentheses. No page numbers are cited when the article comes from an online magazine. No date was associated with the article, so APA uses "n.d." instead of a year.

EXERCISE 5

INCORPORATING AND ACKNOWLEDGING YOUR SOURCES

In pairs, choose one topic from Exercise 2. Using the key words and phrases you generated for that topic, conduct a search for articles in the periodical index. Print and read the article.

Group member #1: Write a summary of the article, including the appropriate in-text citation.

Summary:

_____

_____

_____

_____

_____

_____

_____

Group member #2: Highlight an important section of the article. Paraphrase it, including the appropriate in-text citation.

Paraphrase:

_____

_____

_____

_____

_____

_____

_____

A Combination of a Direct Quotation and a Paraphrase

MLA

Leigh and Geyer emphasize that the best means of identification for an animal is "provided by a combination of an ID tag, which is easily visible, and a microchip, which is permanent" (2).

APA

Leigh and Geyer (2003) emphasize that the best means of identification for an animal is "provided by a combination of an ID tag, which is easily visible, and a microchip, which is permanent" (p. 2).

A Source with an Unknown Author

MLA

As the article "The Rules of Local Zoning Boards" notes, many counties prohibit businesses from operating out of garages in residential communities (C1).

APA

As the article "The Rules of Local Zoning Boards" notes, many counties prohibit businesses from operating out of garages in residential communities (2004, p. C1).

or

MLA

Many counties prohibit businesses from operating out of garages in residential communities ("Rules" C1).

APA

Many counties prohibit businesses from operating out of garages in residential communities ("Rules," 2004, p. C1).

Note: In MLA and APA formats, if no author is provided for a source, you can introduce the full title of the work in the sentence or place an abbreviation of the title in parentheses at the end of the information being cited. When your source is a newspaper article, as in the examples above, give the section of the newspaper and the page number, as in C1, which stands for section C, page 1. In MLA format, article titles are placed within quotation marks; publication titles such as books or periodicals are italicized or underlined. Similarly, in APA format, article titles are in quotation marks; however, publication titles are in italics rather than underlined, and the year is included in the citation.

Signal Phrases

In some of the above examples, **signal phrases** are used to introduce quoted or paraphrased material. Signal phrases such as "Leigh and Geyer emphasize," "According to Leigh and Geyer," "Kathy Nicklas-Varraso notes," and "As the article 'The Rules of Local Zoning Boards' notes" enable you to lead smoothly into documented information. Here are some of the more commonly used signal phrases, using *Smith* as the author:

According to Smith,   Smith reports that
As Smith notes,   Smith claims that
Smith suggests that   Smith points out that
Smith emphasizes that   Smith contends that

Works Cited and References List: MLA and APA Format

The **Works Cited** (MLA) and **References** (APA) list of sources contain only the works you cited in your paper. This alphabetized list starts on a separately numbered page after the essay itself. The following sample entries represent some of the most commonly used sources. Entries should be *double-spaced*, and the second and subsequent lines of each entry should be *indented five spaces*. Double-spacing should also be used between each entry.

MLA style specifies the medium of the work (print, Web, CD-ROM, DVD, email, etc.).

BOOKS

Book by One Author

MLA

MacDonald, Cheryl Emily. *Pets to Remember*. Canmore: Altitude Publishing, 2006. Print.

APA

MacDonald, C. E. (2006). *Pets to remember*. Canmore: Altitude Publishing.

Note: Canmore is the place of publication, Altitude Publishing is the publisher, and 2006 is the year of publication. Short forms of the publisher's name should be used, so "Inc.," "Co.," and "Press" can be omitted. Note that book titles in APA format are in sentence case; that is, only proper names and the first letter of the title and subtitle are capitalized. In MLA style, book titles may be italicized or underlined; in APA, they are italicized.

Book by Two Authors

MLA

Leigh, Diane, and Marilee Geyer. *One at a Time: A Week in an American Animal Shelter*. Santa Cruz: No Voice Unheard, 2003. Print.

APA

Leigh, D., & Geyer, M. (2003). *One at a time: A week in an American animal shelter*. Santa Cruz: No Voice Unheard.

Note: In MLA format, when two or three authors are listed, the name of the first author is listed last name first, and the other authors are listed in regular order. If there are more than three authors, the name of the first author is listed last name first and followed by the Latin phrase *et al.*, which means "and others." Note that et al. is not italicized, and a period is placed after "al." but not after "et."

In APA format, when up to and including seven authors are named, list all the authors, using an ampersand (&) before the final author's name. If more than seven authors are named, list the first six, insert an ellipsis, and end with the last author's name.

Short Work in an Anthology

MLA

Belloc, Hillaire. "Letter from Canada." *The Very Richness of That Past: Canada through the Eyes of Foreign Writers*. Ed. Greg Gatenby. Toronto: Vintage Canada, 1995. 49–53. Print.

Belloc, H. (1995). Letter from Canada. In G. Gatenby (Ed.), *The very richness of that past: Canada through the eyes of foreign writers* (pp. 49–53). Toronto: Vintage Canada.

Note: An anthology is a book-length collection of short works such as articles, essays, poems, or short stories. It usually has at least one editor who compiles and organizes all the short works, which are written by different authors. When you're citing from an anthology in MLA format, begin with the author of the short work and its title; then provide the name of the anthology and its editor. Continue with the place of publication, the publisher, and the year of publication. At the end of the entry, list the page numbers of the short work and the medium of publication. The formatting of the entry in APA format is slightly different, including the order of information and the capitalization.

Introduction or Preface in a Book

Carruthers, Peter J. Preface. *Toronto: An Illustrated History of Its First 12,000 Years.* Ed. Ronald F. Williamson. Toronto: James Lorimer & Company, 2008. 7–9. Print.

Carruthers, P. J. (2008). Preface. In R. F. Williamson (Ed.), *Toronto: An illustrated history of its first 12,000 years* (pp. 7–9). Toronto: James Lorimer & Company.

Note: Sometimes, a book will contain an introduction, preface, or foreword written by someone other than the author or editor of the book. When citing from such introductory material in MLA, begin with the author of this material, followed by the word *Introduction* (or *Preface* or *Foreword*) not enclosed in quotation marks or italicized or underlined, the name of the book (italicized), the author or editor of the book, place of publication, publisher, date of publication, page numbers of the introduction, which often will be in small Roman numerals, and medium of publication. For APA format, remember that only the proper nouns and first letter of the title and subtitle are capitalized.

Dictionary or Encyclopedia

"Luxate." *Nelson Canadian Dictionary of the English Language.* 2nd ed. Toronto: ITP Nelson, 1997. Print.

Note: If the dictionary contains more than one entry for "Luxate," this should be specified—e.g., "Luxate." Entry 2.

Luxate. (1997). In Harkness, J., Friend, D., Keefer, J., Liebman, D., & Sutherland, F. (Eds.). *Nelson Canadian dictionary of the English language* (p. 811, 2nd ed.). Toronto: ITP Nelson.

Note: If the dictionary or encyclopedia is commonly used, omit the place of publication and the publisher, but include the edition number and date.

PERIODICALS

Periodicals are newspapers, magazines, and scholarly journals.

Newspaper Article

MLA

Weidner, Johanna. "A Great Outing for Fido: Dog Park Visits." *Guelph Mercury* 19 Jan. 2008: C2. Print.

APA   Weidner, J. (2008, January 19). A great outing for Fido: Dog park visits. *Guelph Mercury*, p. C2.

Note: In MLA Works Cited listings, all months except May, June, and July are abbreviated. Months are not abbreviated in APA format. C2 refers to the section (C) and page number (2) of the article. Note that all key words in periodical titles are capitalized in both MLA and APA formats.

Newspaper Editorial

MLA   "Reality Check, of a Sort." Editorial. *Edmonton Journal* 10 June 2008: A16. Print.

APA   Reality check, of a sort [Editorial]. (2008, June 10). *Edmonton Journal*, p. A16.

Note: Newspaper editorials do not list an author.

Magazine Article (from a Monthly or Bimonthly Publication)

MLA   Weder, Adele. "A Nip and Tuck." *Canadian Architect* Apr. 2008: 32–36. Print.

APA   Weder, A. (2008, April). A nip and tuck. *Canadian Architect*, 32–36.

Note: "32–36" refers to the page numbers of the magazine where the article is found.

Magazine Article (from a Weekly Publication)

MLA   Taylor, Peter Shawn. "Licensed to Whup Ass." *Maclean's* 16 June 2008: 20–21. Print.

APA   Taylor, P. S. (2008, June 16). Licensed to whup ass. *Maclean's*, 20–21.

Journal Article

MLA   Kirby, Dale. "Change and Challenge: Ontario's Collaborative Baccalaureate Nursing Programs." *Canadian Journal of Higher Education* 37.2 (1 Jan. 2007): 29–48. Print.

APA   Kirby, D. (2007, January 1). Change and challenge: Ontario's collaborative baccalaureate nursing programs. *Canadian Journal of Higher Education, 37*(2), 29–48.

Note: The number 37 is the volume number, 2 is the issue number, and 2007 is the year of publication. In APA, the volume number is italicized but not the issue number.

ELECTRONIC SOURCES

Electronic sources can include professional websites, online periodicals, works from subscription services (such as NewsBank), and even emails.

When you list a website as one of your sources, include as many of the following items as you can find on the site (the order will vary depending on whether you're using MLA or APA):

1. Author or group author's name
2. Title of the site or item
3. Date of publication or date of latest update

4. Company or organization that sponsors the website (if it's different from the group author)
5. Date you accessed the website
6. URL or DOI (for APA). Note that MLA doesn't cite the URL. Instead, include the title of the overall website or database, italicized, and the medium of publication (web).

Note: DOI stands for "digital object identifier," a system that assigns unique identifiers to digital objects such as files and webpages; these identifiers make information easier to locate. DOIs are recognized internationally and are permanent, unlike URLs, which can become inactive or change.

Entire Website

Home page. Canadian Federation of Humane Societies. n.d. Web. 13 June 2008.

(In text): The Canadian Federation of Humane Societies provides information about protecting your pets in hot summer weather (http://cfhs.ca).

Note: In this example, the sponsoring organization—the Canadian Federation of Humane Societies—is also the group author of the site, so it is not repeated. In MLA, include the date of posting or *n.d.* if no date is available. Occasionally, the URL address will appear on its own line because word processing programs won't split the site's address when slashes are used. You shouldn't allow your word processing program to hyphenate a URL, because the hyphen could be mistaken as part of the web address. In APA, if you're citing an entire website, give the address in the text of your essay rather than including it in the reference list.

Article or Short Work from a Website

Mohr, Lori. "Adopting from a Breed Rescue Group." *AnimalForum.com.* Arrow Web Design Inc., 2005. Web. 13 June 2014.

APA

Mohr, L. (n.d.). Adopting from a breed rescue group. *AnimalForum.com.* Retrieved from http://www.animalforum.com/dbreedrescue.htm

Note: In this example, the name of the author is known; often, however, the name might not be given. If the name of the author isn't given, use the name of the sponsoring organization (e.g., Animal Forum) instead. Include a publication date, if possible, and don't forget to include the date you accessed the article (e.g., June 13, 2014). Page numbers aren't listed for online articles because different printers will affect the page numbering of the printed article. However, the exception to this rule is that if an article is contained within a PDF file, the page numbers can be listed because the numbers will be consistent regardless of the system used. Notice that in MLA format you specify "web" between the publication date (if any) and the access date, and do not include the URL; in APA format, there is no final period after the URL or DOI.

Article from an Online Magazine

MLA

Woolf, Norma Bennett. "Getting Involved in Purebred Rescue." *Dog Owner's Guide.* Canis Major Publications, 18 May 2005. Web. 20 June 2014.

Woolf, N. B. (2005, May 18). Getting involved in purebred rescue. *Dog Owner's Guide.* Retrieved from http://www.canismajor.com/dog/rescinv.html

Email

Stuckey, Rachel. "Information for Project Meeting." Message to the author. 28 May 2014. Email.

(In text): Rachel Stuckey (personal communication, May 28, 2014) proposed solutions for the editorial queries in the author's text.

Note: In APA format, emails should not be included in the References list. However, do provide an in-text citation (see above).

OTHER SOURCES: NON-PRINT

Personal Interview

Sauer, Lara. Personal interview. 6 June 2014.

Note: For APA documentation, personal correspondence such as an interview is documented only in the text (see in "Email" above).

Radio or Television Program

"Parents Again." *W5.* Narr. Sandie Rinaldo. CTV. CTVglobemedia. 16 Feb. 2008. Television.

Fox, M. (Producer). (2008, February 16). Parents again [Television broadcast]. In Fox (Producer), *W5.* Toronto: CTVglobemedia.

Note: In this listing, "Narr." refers to the narrator of the program, and "CTV" refers to the network. The date is the date of the broadcast. Note the different information required for APA citations.

Finally, a word about citation machines. In the course of your research, you may notice that many periodical databases such as EBSCO and PROQUEST offer features that help you format your citations; these features are called **citation machines**. While convenient, many citation machines can make errors in their formatting—they can omit italics, misplace the publication date, etc. So it's crucial that, if you use citation machines, you proofread your citations before you submit your essay.

EXERCISE

6

WRITING REFERENCE ENTRIES

For each of the following sources, write its citation in either MLA or APA format; ask your instructor which format you should use.

An article entitled "Employment patterns of postsecondary students." This article was modified September 29, 2010, and was published on the Statistics Canada website, http://www.statcan.gc.ca/daily-quotidien/100929/dq100929c-eng.htm. No author was indicated.

citation: _____

_____

An article entitled "A sudden bounty of stories close to home; Edmonton the setting for three new novels." This article was published February 20, 2011, on page B5 in the *Edmonton Journal*. It was written by Richard Helm. You accessed this article from the newspaper.

citation: _____

_____

An article entitled "A sudden bounty of stories close to home; Edmonton the setting for three new novels." This article was published February 20, 2011, on page B5 in the *Edmonton Journal*. It was written by Richard Helm. You accessed this article from the newspaper's website, http://www.edmontonjournal.com.

citation: _____

_____

An article entitled "A sudden bounty of stories close to home; Edmonton the setting for three new novels." This article was published February 20, 2011, on page B5 in the *Edmonton Journal*. It was written by Richard Helm, and its DOI is 2273536211. You accessed this article from the Canadian Newsstand database.

citation: _____

_____

A book entitled *Theoretical Basis for Nursing*. This book was written in 2011 by Melanie McEwen and is the third edition of the book. It was published in Philadelphia by Wolters Kluwer/Lippincott Williams & Wilkins.

citation: _____

_____

Incorporating Research into Your Outline

After you've compiled all your notes from your sources, you need to determine what information you will use and where it best fits into your essay. The best way to do this is to work with your original outline before you draft a research version of your essay. Here again is the outline for the dog-rescue essay, but it's a bit different from the outline on pages 305 and 306. This version now includes references to sources; key information from these sources will be the research that strengthens the essay.

Notice that the headings "Introduction" and "Conclusion" have been added to the outline. In this version, the writer wanted to include some relevant research in both the introductory and concluding paragraphs as well as in the body paragraphs, so he expanded the outline. By placing research references in the outline, the student writer will know where the new information will be included when he prepares the drafts and final version of the research essay.

Note: The references to the added research appear in bold print so that you can compare this outline with the previous one without research on pages 305 and 306.

An Outline for an Essay with Research

I.   Introduction

    A.   Every year, more than 100,000 dogs and cats are euthanized at animal shelters and pounds across Canada. **See MacDonald, source #2.**

    B.   Some shelters euthanize animals routinely. **See Leigh and Geyer, source #1.**

    C.   Some shelters work with rescue groups.

           Thesis Statement: Dog-rescue organizations perform a humane service by saving homeless dogs and matching responsible adopters with a devoted new family member.

II.   Dog-rescue volunteers play several roles.

    A.   Some volunteers are *spotters* who look for specific breeds at local shelters.

    B.   Experienced rescue volunteers may become coordinators and arrange assistance from various sources. **See Woolf, source #5.**

    C.   Volunteers work with national organizations such as Save-A-Pet, which maintains a database of adoptable dogs from rescue groups throughout Canada and the United States.

    D   Volunteers assist at dog-rescue *adoption days* hosted by pet supply chains such as Pet Valu and PetSmart.

III.   Rescue groups provide important information and benefits for prospective adopters.

    A.   By viewing a rescue group's website, potential adopters can read about a dog's age, temperament, adoption fee, and any special medical conditions.

    B.   If a potential adopter doesn't find a suitable dog, he or she can still complete an online application.

    C.   On an application, a potential adopter can list his or her preferences for the age, sex, and size of the dog.

    D.   Although some dogs are puppies rescued from abusive situations, most are adult dogs already socialized and housebroken. **See Nicklas-Varraso in Mohr, source #3.**

IV.   Careful screening often results in a successful adoption.

    A   Rescue groups routinely conduct home visits to check the living conditions and the neighbourhood.

    B.   The applicant must have access to veterinary care.

    C.   The applicant must agree to return the dog to the rescue organization if he or she can no longer care for the animal.

    D.   A foster parent can fully inform the adoptive parent about potential adjustment problems.

    E.   Careful attention to such details leads to a winning adoption process.

V.   Conclusion

    A.   Rescue groups provide an opportunity for a dog to live out the rest of its life free from harm and neglect.

    B   We should "embrace non-lethal strategies" to show we are a humane society. **See Toronto Humane Society, source #4.**

Concluding Statement: Rescue groups not only provide care for homeless dogs, but they also remind us of the joy made possible by compassionate adoption.

A Draft of an Essay with Research

The following is a rough version of the original essay on dog-rescue groups; it has been strengthened with some material from outside sources. (The material is underlined so that you can spot it easily.) The marginal annotations will alert you to (1) places where the information is directly quoted or paraphrased, and (2) places where revisions are necessary to achieve a better style. Note that this essay is being prepared using MLA documentation.

The Humane Work of Dog-Rescue Groups

Although Canada and the United States are generally regarded as countries that love and pamper their pets, animal shelters are often filled to capacity with dogs that have been abandoned, abused, or surrendered by their owners. According to Shelagh MacDonald (2004), every year, more than 100,000 dogs and cats are euthanized at animal shelters and pounds across Canada. Sadly, some shelters routinely euthanize healthy animals if no one claims or adopts them after a grace period ranging from just days to a few weeks. Dogs such as these have only "about a fifty percent chance of getting out alive" (Leigh and Geyer viii). Fortunately, however, many shelters work closely with dog-rescue organizations that find loving, temporary homes where foster parents can provide care and, if necessary, rehabilitation. Staffed by dedicated volunteers, rescue groups perform a humane service by saving homeless dogs and enabling responsible adopters to gain a devoted new family member.

From rescuing retired greyhounds to saving mini "mutts," dog-rescue volunteers play several roles. For example, they often serve as *spotters* at local shelters, looking for specific dogs that can be fostered by individuals who specialize in specific breeds, such as boxers and golden retrievers. Experienced volunteers may become coordinators who arrange for assistance from a variety of sources, including local veterinarians, groomers, transporters, and website designers. Norma Bennett Woolf writes for the online magazine Dog Owner's Guide. Woolf states, "There's always room for more foster homes, fund-raisers, dog spotters, kennels, public relations workers, and trainers." Many rescue groups work closely with national organizations, such as Save-A-Pet, whose website publishes a comprehensive list of adoptable rescue dogs throughout Canada and the United States. On weekends, rescue volunteers can be seen helping out during adoption days sponsored by shelters and retailers, such as Pet Valu and PetSmart.

statistic and paraphrased statement from website, author given

direct quotation from the preface of a book with two authors

direct quotation from an online magazine; sentence combining needed; magazine title should be italicized in final version

Rescue groups provide both crucial information and welcome benefits for potential adopters. When one becomes interested in a specific dog on a rescue group's website, he or she can read about the animal's medical needs, age, temperament, and adoption fee. Even if he or she doesn't spot a suitable dog but remains interested in adopting one from rescue, he or she can fill out an application and list preferences regarding a dog's age, sex, and size. Although rescue groups occasionally receive puppies and young dogs that have been picked up during police raids of abusive puppy mills and backyard breeders, the majority of dogs available for adoption are older ones. Kathy Nicklas-Varraso wrote <u>What to Expect from Breed Rescue. This writer says, "You'll most often get an adult whose chewing phase, housebreaking phase, and general puppy wildness are gone" (qtd. in Mohr)</u>. Any pet owner who has experienced the agitation of sleepless nights and numerous housetraining "accidents" can appreciate the benefits of adopting an older, socialized, housebroken dog.

a source quoted in another author's work; title needs to be italicized; needs to be more smoothly blended

Although the adoption process may take several weeks or even months to find the best match, careful screening improves the chances for a successful adoption. Rescue groups routinely conduct home visits of prospective dog owners to see whether both the living conditions and the neighbourhood will be suitable for the dog's size, temperament, and exercise needs. In addition, the applicant must have access to veterinary care and agree to return the dog to the rescue organization if he or she can no longer properly care for it. A foster parent can fully inform the adoptive parent about a dog's potential adjustment problems because the animal's behaviour has been observed over a period of weeks—if not months—in a home setting. <u>Nicklas-Varraso states, "Borderline pets are offered for adoption within strict guidelines, such as no other pets or fenced yards only"</u> (qtd. in Mohr). Careful attention to such details leads to a winning adoption process.

direct quotation; needs a transition

However a dog finds its way to a rescue group—by an owner surrender, a good Samaritan, or even by a police raid of an illegal breeding operation—it will have an opportunity to live out the rest of its life free from harm and neglect. <u>"The injured receive veterinary care, and abandoned animals are given a safe haven 24 hours a day, 365 days a year" (Toronto Humane Society, para. 3)</u>. Not only do rescue groups provide care for homeless dogs, but they also remind us of the joy made possible by compassion, commitment, and unconditional love.

direct quotation from a website; no author, no publication date

Note: A Works Cited page will be included in the final version of this essay.

PREPARING THE FINAL VERSION OF AN ESSAY WITH RESEARCH

Making Final Changes and Refinements

The final version of the research essay includes the refinements suggested in the margins of the previous draft. You'll notice that the final essay reflects proper MLA documentation and page numbering format. Other improvements relate to the style of the essay. Changes from the previous draft include the following:

- The title has been changed to be more descriptive and appealing.
- Information from sources has been more smoothly blended by combining sentences and using signal phrases.
- An awkward repetition of "he or she" has been changed to the more specific term "a potential adopter" in the third paragraph.
- The word "humane" has been added in the last paragraph to reinforce the idea of compassionate care for animals.
- To conform to MLA format, the writer has placed his name, his instructor's name, the course title, and the date in the upper left-hand corner of the first page.
- Again following MLA guidelines, the writer has placed his last name and page number in the upper right-hand corner of each page of the essay.
- A Works Cited page, in proper MLA format, is included and appears as the last page of the essay.

Roberts 1

Jason Roberts

Professor Alvarez

English 100

8 December 2014

Crusading for Canines: Dog-Rescue

Groups and Winning Adoptions

Although Canada and the United States are generally regarded as countries that love and pamper their pets, animal shelters are often filled to capacity with dogs that have been abandoned, abused, or surrendered by their owners. According to Shelagh MacDonald (2004), every year, more than 100,000 dogs and cats are euthanized at animal shelters and pounds across Canada. Sadly, some shelters routinely euthanize healthy animals if no one claims or adopts them after a grace period ranging from just days to a few weeks. Dogs such as these have only "about a fifty percent chance of getting out alive" (Leigh and Geyer viii). Fortunately, however, many shelters work closely

with dog-rescue organizations that find loving, temporary homes where foster

parents can provide care and, if necessary, rehabilitation. Staffed by dedicated

volunteers, rescue groups perform a humane service by saving homeless dogs

and enabling responsible adopters to gain a devoted new family member.

From rescuing retired greyhounds to saving mini "mutts," dog-rescue

volunteers play several roles. For example, they often serve as *spotters* at local

shelters, looking for specific dogs that can be fostered by individuals who spe-

cialize in specific breeds, such as boxers and golden retrievers. Experienced vol-

unteers may become coordinators who arrange for assistance from a variety of

sources, including local veterinarians, groomers, transporters, and website

designers. As Norma Bennett Woolf suggests in the online magazine *Dog Own-*

er's Guide, "There's always room for more foster homes, fund-raisers, dog-spot-

ters, kennels, public relations workers, and trainers." Many rescue groups work

closely with national organizations, such as Save-A-Pet, whose website publishes

a comprehensive list of adoptable rescue dogs throughout Canada and the United

States. On weekends, rescue volunteers can be seen helping out during adoption

days sponsored by shelters and retailers, such as Pet Valu and PetSmart.

Rescue groups provide both crucial information and welcome benefits

for potential adopters. When a person becomes interested in a specific dog on

a rescue group's website, he or she can read about the animal's medical

needs, age, temperament, and adoption fee. Even if a potential adopter doesn't

spot a suitable dog but remains interested in adopting one from rescue, he or

she can fill out an application and list preferences regarding a dog's age, sex,

and size. Although rescue groups occasionally receive puppies and young dogs

that have been picked up during police raids of abusive puppy mills and

backyard breeders, the majority of dogs available for adoption are older ones.

Roberts 3

Kathy Nicklas-Varraso, author of *What to Expect from Breed Rescue*, notes that adopters will "most often get an adult whose chewing phase, housebreaking phase, and general puppy wildness are gone" (qtd. in Mohr). Any pet owner who has experienced the agitation of sleepless nights and numerous housetraining "accidents" can appreciate the benefits of adopting an older, socialized, and housebroken dog.

Although the adoption process may take several weeks or even months to find the best match, careful screening improves the chances for a successful adoption. Rescue groups routinely conduct home visits of prospective dog owners to see whether both the living conditions and the neighbourhood will be suitable for the dog's size, temperament, and exercise needs. In addition, the applicant must have access to veterinary care and agree to return the dog to the rescue organization if he or she can no longer properly care for it. A foster parent can fully inform the adoptive parent about a dog's potential adjustment problems because the animal's behaviour has been observed over a period of weeks—if not months—in a home setting. Nicklas-Varraso stresses that the "borderline pets are offered for adoption within strict guidelines, such as no other pets or fenced yards only" (qtd. in Mohr). Careful attention to such details leads to a winning adoption process.

However a dog finds its way to a rescue group—by an owner surrender, a good Samaritan, or even by a police raid of an illegal breeding operation—it will have an opportunity to live out the rest of its life free from harm and neglect. "The injured receive veterinary care, and abandoned animals are given a safe haven 24 hours a day, 365 days a year" (Toronto Humane Society, para. 3). Not only do rescue groups provide humane care for homeless dogs, but they also remind us of the joy made possible by compassion, commitment, and unconditional love.

Works Cited

Leigh, Diane, and Marilee Geyer. *One at a Time: A Week in an American Animal Shelter.* Santa Cruz: No Voice Unheard, 2003. Print.

MacDonald, Shelagh. "Can We Save Them All?" In *Animal Welfare in Focus.* Spring 2004. Canadian Federation of Humane Societies, 25 June 2008. Web. 14 Oct. 2014.

Mohr, Lori. "Adopting from a Breed Rescue Group." *AnimalForum.com.* Arrow Web Design Inc., 2005. Web. 13 June 2014.

Toronto Humane Society. *About the Toronto Humane Society.* 25 June 2008. Web. 12 Oct. 2014.

Woolf, Norma Bennett. "Getting Involved in Purebred Rescue." *Dog Owner's Guide.* Canis Major Publications, 18 May 2005. Web. 20 June 2014.

MyWritingLab

Go to MyWritingLab to access a diagnostic test that creates your own personalized learning path supported by rich multimedia resources and a variety of animated tutorials, all aimed at helping you improve your writing. MyWritingLab also includes a complete eText version of the book that is fully searchable and accessible through your web browser or most mobile devices.

GRAMMAR FOR WRITERS

The Bottom Line

INTRODUCTION

Overview

In this part of the book you'll be working with "the bottom line," the basics of grammar that you need to be a clear writer. If you're willing to memorize certain rules and work through various activities, you'll be able to apply grammatical rules automatically as you write.

Using "Grammar for Writers"

Because this portion of the textbook is divided into several self-contained sections, it does not have to be read in sequence. Your instructor may suggest you review specific rules and examples, or you may be assigned various segments as either a class or a group. Several approaches are possible, so you can regard this section as a user-friendly grammar handbook for quick reference. Mastering the practical parts of grammar will improve your writing; you'll feel more confident because you'll know the bottom line.

Contents

CHAPTER 13
The Simple Sentence

Identifying the crucial parts of a sentence is the first step in many writing decisions: how to punctuate, how to avoid sentence fragments, how to make sure that subjects and verbs "agree" (match). But in order to move forward to these decisions first requires a few steps backward—to basics.

RECOGNIZING A SENTENCE

Let's start with a few basic definitions. A basic unit of language is a **word**.

> **examples:** city, government, park

A group of words that relate to each other can be a **phrase**.

> **examples:** shiny sports car; welcoming, inclusive environment; in the bright sun

When a group of words contains a **subject** and a complete **predicate** (the verb, plus objects and phrases modifying the verb), it's called a **clause**. When the clause makes sense on its own, it's called a **sentence**, or an independent clause.

If you want to check whether you've written a complete sentence and not just a group of words that relate to each other, you first have to check for a subject and a verb. It's often easier to locate the verbs first.

RECOGNIZING VERBS

Verbs are words that express some kind of action or being. Verbs about the five senses—sight, touch, smell, taste, and sound—are part of the group called **being verbs**. Look at these examples of verbs as they work in sentences:

action verbs:

Students **register** for classes online and in person.

Machines **perform** repetitive tasks.

being verbs:

Mahatma Gandhi **is** India's greatest hero.

The customer **seems** dissatisfied.

The soup **smells** delicious.

EXERCISE 1	RECOGNIZING VERBS

Underline the verbs in each of the following sentences.

1. Rush-hour traffic frustrates commuters.
2. Yesterday, a minor accident snarled streets for hours.
3. Drivers become stressed.
4. Buses are packed with workers and students.
5. The process repeats itself in the afternoon.
6. City councillors discuss solutions.
7. They urge citizens to carpool.
8. More people work from home.
9. Some workers share a job.
10. We need better public transit.

More about Verbs

The verb in a sentence can be more than one word. First of all, there can be **helping verbs** in front of the main verb, which is the action or being verb. Here's a list of some frequently used helping verbs: *am, are, can, could, do, have, is, may, might, must, shall, should, was, were, will, would.*

> Everyone **was watching** the World Cup Finals. (The helping verb is **was**.)
>
> The school **should have notified** the parents. (The helping verbs are **should** and **have**.)
>
> The president **can select** his assistants. (The helping verb is **can**.)
>
> Leroy **will graduate** in May. (The helping verb is **will**.)

Helping verbs can make the verb in a sentence more than one word long. But a sentence can also have more than one main verb:

> Andrew **planned** and **practised** his speech.
>
> I **stumbled** over the rug, **grabbed** a chair, and **fell** on my face.

EXERCISE 2	WRITING SENTENCES WITH HELPING VERBS

Complete this exercise with a partner or with a group. First, ask one person to add at least one helping verb to the verb given. Then work together to write two sentences using the main verb and the helping verb(s). Appoint one spokesperson for your group to read all your sentences to the class. Notice how many combinations of main verbs and helping verbs you hear.

The first one is done as a sample.

1. **verb:** called

   verb with helping verb(s): has called

   sentence 1: Sam has called me twice this week.

   sentence 2: He has called her a hero.

2. verb: moving

  verb with helping verb(s): _____

  sentence 1: _____

  sentence 2: _____

3. verb: studying

  verb with helping verb(s): _____

  sentence 1: _____

  sentence 2: _____

4. verb: laughed

  verb with helping verb(s): _____

  sentence 1: _____

  sentence 2: _____

5. verb: spoken

  verb with helping verb(s): _____

  sentence 1: _____

  sentence 2: _____

RECOGNIZING SUBJECTS

After you learn to recognize verbs, it's easy to find the subjects of sentences because subjects and verbs are linked. If the verb is an action verb, for example, the subject will be the word or words that answer the question "Who or what is doing that action?"

The truck stalled on the highway.

Step 1: Identify the verb: *stalled*

Step 2: Ask, "Who or what stalled?"

Step 3: The answer is the subject: The **truck** stalled on the highway. The *truck* is the subject.

If your verb expresses being, the same steps apply to finding the subject.

Deon is my best friend.

Step 1: Identify the verb: *is*

Step 2: Ask, "Who or what is my best friend?"

Step 3: The answer is the subject: **Deon** is my best friend. *Deon* is the subject.

Just as there can be more than one word to make up a verb, there can be more than one subject.

examples: **Rob** and **John-David** planned the surprise party.

              The premier and **his aide** took questions after the session.

EXERCISE 3	RECOGNIZING SUBJECTS IN SENTENCES

Underline the subjects in the following sentences.

1. Job candidates should prepare carefully for job interviews.
2. Dressing professionally is a good idea.
3. It is important to arrive on time for an interview.
4. You should bring extra copies of your résumé to the interview.
5. A solid handshake makes a good impression.
6. Interviewers will ask a series of questions to determine your suitability.
7. The strongest candidates will answer questions with detailed responses.
8. Hiring managers and employers agree that candidates should research the company prior to the interview.
9. Getting the job means giving the right impression.
10. The job search process can be very rewarding.

More about Recognizing Subjects and Verbs

When you look for the subject of a sentence, look for the core word or words; don't include descriptive words around the subject. The idea is to look for the subject, not for the words that describe it.

> The dark blue **dress** looked lovely on Anita.

> Dirty **streets** and grimy **houses** destroy a neighbourhood.

The simple subjects of the above sentences are the core words *dress, streets,* and *houses,* not the descriptive words *dark blue, dirty,* and *grimy.*

Prepositions and Prepositional Phrases

Prepositions are usually small words that often signal a kind of position or possession, as shown in the Infobox here.

INFOBOX	SOME COMMON PREPOSITIONS				
about	around	between	in	on	under
above	at	beyond	inside	onto	until
across	before	by	into	over	up
after	behind	during	like	since	upon
against	below	except	near	through	with
along	beneath	for	of	to	within
among	beside	from	off	toward	without

A prepositional phrase is made up of a preposition and its object. Following are some prepositional phrases. In each one, the first word is the preposition; the other words are the object of the preposition.

Prepositional Phrases

about the movie	of mice and men
around the corner	off the record
between two lanes	on the mark
during recess	up the wall
near my house	with my sister and brother

There's an old memory trick to help you remember prepositions. Think of a chair. Now, think of a series of words you can put *in front of* the word *chair*:

around the chair	**with** the chair
by the chair	**to** the chair
behind the chair	**near** the chair
between the chairs	**under** the chair
of the chair	**on** the chair
off the chair	**from** the chair

These words are prepositions.

You need to know about prepositions because they can help you identify the subject of a sentence. Here's an important grammar rule about prepositions:

Nothing in a prepositional phrase can ever be the subject of the sentence.

Prepositional phrases describe people, places, or things. They may describe the subject of a sentence, but they *never include* the subject. Whenever you're looking for the subject of a sentence, begin by putting parentheses around all the prepositional phrases.

> The community college (in the centre) (of the city) is well known (for its trades programs).

Notice that the prepositional phrases are in parentheses. Since *nothing* in them can be the subject, once you've eliminated the prepositional phrases you can follow the steps to find the subject of the sentence:

> What's the verb? *is*
>
> Who or what is known for its trades programs? **The college**.
>
> *College* is the subject of the sentence.

By marking off the prepositional phrases, you're left with the *core* of the sentence. There is less to look at.

> (Behind the park), a **carousel** (with gilded horses) delighted children (from all the neighbourhoods).
>
> subject: **carousel**

> The **firm** (with flex hours) was named Company (of the Year).
>
> subject: **firm**

EXERCISE **4**	**RECOGNIZING PREPOSITIONAL PHRASES, SUBJECTS, AND VERBS**

Put parentheses around all the prepositional phrases in the following sentences. Then underline the subject and verb, putting *S* above the subject and *V* above the verb.

1. In an effort to encourage collaboration, many corporations have changed to an open-office format.

2. Many workers may share office space through the use of cubicles.

3. You can hear every word of your co-workers' conversations.

4. During lunch hour, the enticing smells of your co-workers' lunches can be distracting.

5. However, people may speak to each other more often.

6. Closed doors may deter people from speaking to each other.

7. In fact, some people will use any available workspace.

8. The traditional office is becoming obsolete in the modern workplace.

9. Many workers share office space on alternate work days.

10. In twenty years, the format of the office will surely have changed again.

EXERCISE 5 · WRITING SENTENCES WITH PREPOSITIONAL PHRASES

Complete this exercise with a partner. First, add one prepositional phrase to the core sentence given. Then ask your partner to add a second prepositional phrase to the same sentence. For the next sentence, let your partner add the first phrase; you add the second. Keep reversing the process throughout the exercise. When you've completed the exercise, be ready to read to the class the sentences with two prepositional phrases. The first one has been done for you as an example.

Hint: Make sure you're adding *only* a prepositional phrase (preposition plus its object) rather than a new clause. For example, if in question 1 you write, "After the sun set, rain fell on the mountains," you will have added a new subject (*sun*) and a new verb (*set*) instead of just a prepositional phrase.

1. core sentence: Rain fell.

   add one prepositional phrase: _Rain fell on the mountains._

   add another prepositional phrase: _After dark, rain fell on the mountains._

2. core sentence: The university was closed.

   add one prepositional phrase: _____

   add another prepositional phrase: _____

3. core sentence: The canoe drifted.

   add one prepositional phrase: _____

   add another prepositional phrase: _____

4. core sentence: Parents must struggle.

   add one prepositional phrase: _____

   add another prepositional phrase: _____

5. core sentence: Raj chopped the onions.

   add one prepositional phrase: _____

   add another prepositional phrase: _____

WORD ORDER

When we speak, we often use a very simple word order: first the subject, then the verb. For example, someone would say, "I am going to the store." *I* is the subject that begins the sentence; *am going* is the verb that comes after the subject.

But not all sentences are in such a simple word order. Prepositional phrases, for example, can change the word order.

sentence: Among the contestants was an older man.

Step 1: Mark off the prepositional phrase(s) with parentheses:

(Among the contestants) was an older man.

Remember that nothing in a prepositional phrase can be the subject of a sentence.

Step 2: Find the verb: *was*
Step 3: Who or what was? An older **man** was. The subject of the sentence is *man.*

After you change the word order of this sentence, you can see the subject (*S*) and verb (*V*) more easily.

                                  S   V
An older **man was** among the contestants.

EXERCISE 6

FINDING PREPOSITIONAL PHRASES, SUBJECTS, AND VERBS IN A COMPLICATED WORD ORDER

Put parentheses around the prepositional phrases in the sentences below. Then underline the subjects and verbs, putting *S* above each subject and *V* above each verb.

1. Down the street from my apartment is a house with award-winning architecture.
2. Behind the counter is a cash register.
3. Inside the student union are video games and vending machines.
4. Among the workers lay a long and deep-seated resentment.
5. Above the rooftops of the houses sits a blanket of smog.
6. From the back of the alley came a loud scream.
7. Between the houses was a fence with a clinging vine of red flowers.
8. On my laptop are stored all my work documents and family photos.
9. Among my fondest memories is a recollection of family dinners at my grandparents' house.
10. With the economic downturn came a rise in unemployment.

More about Word Order

The expected word order of subject first, then verb changes when a sentence starts with *There is/are, There was/were, Here is/are, Here was/were.* In such cases, look for the subject after the verb.

           V   S   S

There **are** a **bakery** and a **pharmacy** down the street.

        V   S

Here **is** the **man** with the answers.

If it helps you understand this pattern, change the word order:

   S   S   V

A **bakery** and a **pharmacy are** there, down the street.

   S   V

The **man** with the answers **is** here.

Also note that even when the subject comes after the verb, the verb has to "match" the subject. For instance, if the subject refers to more than one thing, the verb must also refer to more than one thing.

There **are** a **bakery** and a **pharmacy** down the street.

(Two things, a bakery and a pharmacy, *are* down the street.)

Word Order in Questions

Questions may have a different word order. The main verb and the helping verb may not be next to each other.

question: Do you like pizza?

subject: you

verbs: *do, like*

If it helps you understand this concept, think about answering the question. If someone accused you of not liking pizza, you might say, "I *do like* it." You'd use two words as verbs.

question: Will he think about it?

subject: he

verbs: will, think

question: Is Maria telling the truth?

subject: Maria

verbs: is, telling

EXERCISE 7

RECOGNIZING SUBJECTS AND VERBS IN A COMPLICATED WORD ORDER: A COMPREHENSIVE EXERCISE

Underline the subjects and verbs and put an *S* above the subjects and *V* above the verbs.

1. Have you ever taken a personality inventory?

2. Upon your hiring, you may be asked to take a personality inventory by your employer.

3. Some of the more popular personality inventories include Myers-Briggs, True Colors, and Facet 5.

4. There are an even number of questions in the Myers-Briggs.

5. There are numerous companies conducting personality inventories.

6. Among other findings, you will discover how to communicate with other personality types.

7. Personality inventories can often show you how to approach conflict among different personalities.

8. What is your conflict avoidance style?

9. From your Myers-Briggs results, you can determine whether you are introverted or extroverted.

10. From numerous sites online, you, too, can discover your personality type.

Words That Can't Be Verbs

Some words look like they're part of the verb in a sentence, but they're not verbs. Such words include adverbs (words like *always, ever, nearly, never, not, often, rarely*) that are placed close to the verb, or between the helping verb and main verb, but are not verbs.

When you're looking for verbs in a sentence, be careful to eliminate words like *often* and *not*.

> He will not listen to me. (The verbs are **will listen.**)
>
> Althea can often find a bargain. (The verbs are **can find.**)

Be careful with contractions:

> They haven't raced in years. (The verbs are **have raced.** *Not* is not a part of the verb, even in contractions.)
>
> Don't you come from Alberta? (The verbs are **do come**.)
>
> Won't he ever learn? (The verbs are **will learn. Won't** is a contraction for **will not.**)

Recognizing Main Verbs

If you're checking to see whether a word is a main verb, try the *pronoun test*. Combine your word with this simple list of pronouns: *I, you, he, she, it, we, they*.

A main verb is a word, such as *drive* or *noticed*, that can be combined with the words on this list. Now try the pronoun test.

> For the word *drive*: I drive, you drive, he drives, she drives, it drives, we drive, they drive
> For the word *noticed*: I noticed, you noticed, he noticed, she noticed, it noticed, we noticed, they noticed

But words like *never* can't be used, alone, with the pronouns:

> ~~I never, you never, he never, she never, it never, we never, they never~~ (Never did what?)

Never is not a verb. *Not* isn't a verb either, as the pronoun test indicates:

> ~~I not, you not, he not, she not, it not, we not, you not, they not~~

Verb Forms That Can't Be Main Verbs

There are forms of verbs that can't be main verbs by themselves, either. The *-ing* form of a verb, by itself, cannot be the main verb, as the pronoun test shows.

For the word ***voting***: ~~I voting, you voting, he voting, she voting, we voting, they voting~~

If you see the *-ing* form of a verb by itself, correct the sentence by adding a helping verb.

Danny ~~riding~~ his motorcycle. (*Riding, by itself, cannot be a main verb.*)

correction: Danny **was riding** his motorcycle.

Another verb form, called an **infinitive**, also cannot be a main verb. An infinitive is the form of the verb that has *to* placed in front of it.

INFOBOX	SOME SAMPLE INFINITIVES		
	to care	to play	to stumble
	to feel	to reject	to view
	to need	to repeat	to vote

Try the pronoun test and you'll see that infinitives can't be main verbs:

For the infinitive ***to vote***: ~~I to vote, you to vote, he to vote, she to vote, we to vote, they to vote~~

So if you see an infinitive being used as a verb, correct the sentence by adding a main verb.

We ~~to vote~~ in the election tomorrow. (*There's no verb, just an infinitive.*)

correction: We **are going** to vote in the election tomorrow. (*Now there's a verb.*)

The infinitives and the *-ing* forms of verbs just don't work as main verbs. You must put a verb with them to make a correct sentence.

EXERCISE 8	CORRECTING PROBLEMS WITH *-ING* OR INFINITIVE VERB FORMS

Most—but not all—of the following sentences are faulty; an *-ing* form of a verb or an infinitive may be taking the place of a main verb. Rewrite the sentences that have errors. Write *C* beside sentences that are correct as written.

1. Everyone in the Human Resources department to visit the Mini-Golfing range on Friday.

   rewritten: _____

   _____

2. My husband paying no attention to the feud between his sisters.

   rewritten: _____

   _____

3. The tuner car ahead of me speeding out of control and into the median.

   rewritten: _____

   _____

4. Sylvia learned to care about her health after her bout with pneumonia.

   rewritten: _____

   _____

5. Among his other goals, Jason to hike the entire Bruce Trail.

   rewritten: _____

   _____

6. After all the discussion and deliberation, the committee taking a very conservative position on the question of tenants' rights.

   rewritten: _____

   _____

7. One of the most famous experts in the field of forensic science to speak to my criminal justice class tomorrow.

   rewritten: _____

   _____

8. My manager being away from work for almost a month.

   rewritten: _____

   _____

9. Ever since the accident, I have been picking tiny pieces of glass out of the carpet.

   rewritten: _____

   _____

10. In her lectures, the nutritionist emphasizing the importance of fibre in our diet.

    rewritten: _____

    _____

EXERCISE 9

FINDING SUBJECTS AND VERBS: A COMPREHENSIVE EXERCISE

Underline the subjects and verbs in these sentences, putting *S* above the subjects and *V* above the verbs.

1. Have you ever visited the Parliament Buildings in Ottawa?

2. I, along with my husband and son, am going to go to the St. John's Ice Caps game on Sunday.

3. At the centre of campus is a large grassy field.

4. Robert needs to improve his grades.

5. Won't you consider my suggestion?

6. Hiring managers often consider internal candidates before external candidates.

7. I'll never again play outdoor sports without sunscreen.

8. There are many reasons to examine our current electoral process.

9. Jackie should have been thinking about her future employment prospects.

10. There are a Mazda, a Chrysler, and a Volkswagen in the used-car lot.

11. Lakeesha paid the bills and picked up her son from daycare.

12. Within the fenced yard is a lovely garden of tropical plants.

13. He and my father looked tired and dirty.

14. My classmates have had many amazing life experiences.

15. Swimming is easy on the joints.

EXERCISE 10

CREATE YOUR OWN TEXT

Complete this activity with two partners. Below is a list of rules you've just studied. Each member of the group should write one example for each rule. When your group has completed three examples for each rule, trade your completed exercise with another group, and check their examples while they check yours.

The first rule has been done for you, as a sample.

Rule 1: The verb in a sentence can express some kind of action.

examples: **a.** <u>Lara drives to work every day.</u>

b. <u>Last week my brother quit his job.</u>

c. <u>My little sister dyed her hands with henna.</u>

Rule 2: The verb in a sentence can represent some state of being or the perceptions of one of the five senses.

examples: **a.** _____

b. _____

c. _____

Rule 3: The verb in a sentence can consist of more than one word.

examples: **a.** _____

b. _____

c. _____

Rule 4: There can be more than one subject of a sentence.

examples: **a.** _____

b. _____

c. _____

Rule 5:   If you take out the prepositional phrases, it's easier to identify the subject of a sentence, because nothing in a prepositional phrase can be the subject of a sentence.

examples: (For examples, write sentences with at least one prepositional phrase in them; put parentheses around the prepositional phrases.)

a. _____

b. _____

c. _____

Rule 6:   Not all sentences have the simple word order of subject first, then verb.

examples: (Give examples of a more complicated word order.)

a. _____

b. _____

c. _____

Rule 7:   Words like *not, never, often, always,* and *ever* are not verbs.

examples: (Write sentences using those words, but underline the correct verb.)

a. _____

b. _____

c. _____

Rule 8:   An *-ing* verb form by itself or an infinitive (*to* preceding the verb) cannot be a main verb.

examples: (Write sentences with *-ing* verb forms or infinitives, but underline the main verb.)

a. _____

b. _____

c. _____

EXERCISE

11

RECOGNIZING SUBJECTS AND VERBS IN A PARAGRAPH

Underline the subjects and verbs in the paragraph and put an *S* above each subject and a *V* above each verb.

Recent developments in technology have caused some people to predict the death of print-based publishing. The internet has forced publishers to offer their material online at a reduced cost, or for free. Reading material can also be scanned and shared through email or file-sharing websites. Kindle, Kobo, and other ereaders have captured a portion of the market. An ereader can hold many books at once, in a conveniently small package. Publishing can be done online, without the benefit of an editor or publishing house. Any author can publish his or her own book. In schools, students are now more demanding of their textbooks. They want accessibility, portability, and value from their textbooks. Many publishers have acknowledged technology's impact, and have responded. Custom textbooks and etexts are some of the material available to students today. Behind the advances, however, lies an important question for the publishing industry. Do printed newspapers, magazines, and books still have a place in society?

CHAPTER 14
The Compound Sentence:
Coordination

A group of words containing a subject and a complete predicate is called a clause. When that group makes sense on its own, it is called a sentence, or an **independent clause**.

A sentence that has *one independent clause* is called a **simple sentence**. If you rely too heavily on a pattern of simple sentences, you risk writing paragraphs like

> Frederick Banting was born on November 14, 1891, in Alliston, Ontario. He attended the University of Toronto. He studied to be a doctor. He fought in World War I. Later, he practised medicine and taught. Banting was especially interested in diabetes. He discovered the hormone insulin. He and his colleagues won the Nobel Prize for medicine. He and his colleagues changed the lives of diabetics.

Here is a better version:

> Frederick Banting was born on November 14, 1891, in Alliston, Ontario. He attended the University of Toronto, studying to be a doctor. After he fought in World War I, he practised medicine and taught. Banting, who was especially interested in diabetes, discovered the hormone insulin. He and his colleagues won the Nobel Prize for medicine and changed the lives of diabetics.

OPTIONS FOR COMBINING SIMPLE SENTENCES

Good writing involves sentence variety. This means mixing a simple sentence with a more complicated one, or a short sentence with a long one. Sentence variety is easier to achieve if you can combine short, related sentences into one.

Some students avoid such combining because they're not sure how to do it. They don't know how to punctuate the new combinations. It's true that punctuation involves memorizing a few rules, but once you know those rules you'll be able to use them automatically and write with more confidence. Here are three options for combining simple sentences, followed by the punctuation rules you need to use in each case.

OPTION 1: USING A COMMA WITH A COORDINATING CONJUNCTION

You can combine two simple sentences with a **comma** and a coordinating conjunction. The coordinating conjunctions are *for, and, nor, but, or, yet,* and *so.* You'll need to memorize these seven coordinating conjunctions so that you can make a decision about punctuating your combined sentences.

An easy way to remember them is to think of the acronym *FANBOYS*: For, And, Nor, But, Or, Yet, So.

To coordinate means to join equals. When you join two simple sentences with a comma and a coordinating conjunction (CC), each half of the combination remains an independent clause, with its own subject (S) and verb (V).

Here are two simple sentences:

S   V   S   V
He cooked the dinner. **She washed** the dishes.

Here are the two simple sentences combined with a comma and the word *and*, a coordinating conjunction (CC):

S   V   , CC S   V
He cooked the dinner, **and she washed** the dishes.

The combined sentences keep the form they had as separate sentences; that is, they are still both independent clauses, with a subject and a verb and with the ability to stand alone.

The word that joins them is the **coordinating conjunction**. It's used to join *equals*. Look at some more examples. These examples use a variety of coordinating conjunctions to join two simple sentences:

sentences combined with *but*:
S   V   , CC S V
I rushed to the bank, **but I was** too late.

sentences combined with *or*:
S   V   , CC S   V
She can email Jim, **or she can call** him.

sentences combined with *nor*:
S   V   , CC   V S V
I didn't like the book, **nor did I like** the movie based on the book. (Notice what happens to the word order when you use *nor*.)

sentences combined with *for*:
S   V   , CC S   V
Sam worried about the job interview, **for he saw** many qualified applicants in the waiting room.

sentences combined with *yet*:
S   V   , CC S   V
Leo tried to please his manager, **yet she** never **seemed** appreciative of his efforts.

sentences combined with *so*:
S V   , CC S V
I was the first in line for the concert tickets, **so I got** the best seats in the stadium.

WHERE DOES THE COMMA GO?

Notice that the comma comes *before* the coordinating conjunction (*for, and, nor, but, or, yet, so*). It comes before the new idea—the second independent clause. It goes where the first independent clause ends. Try this punctuation check: after you've placed the comma, look at the combined sentences. For example,

> She joined the armed forces, and she travelled overseas.

Now split it into two sentences at the comma:

> She joined the armed forces. And she travelled overseas.

(The split makes sense.)

If you put the comma in the wrong place, after the coordinating conjunction, your split sentences would be

> She joined the armed forces and. She travelled overseas.

(The split doesn't make sense.)

This test helps you see whether the comma has been placed correctly—*where the first independent clause ends.* (Notice that you can begin a sentence with *and*. You can also begin a sentence with the other coordinating conjunctions—*for, nor, but, or, yet,* and *so*—as long as you're writing a complete sentence.)

If the subject is the *same* in the two simple sentences, you could write them either as two independent clauses joined by a coordinating conjunction *or* as a simple sentence with one subject and two verbs:

> **She joined** the armed forces, **and she travelled** overseas.

or

> **She joined** the armed forces **and travelled** overseas.

(In this case you don't need a comma.)

Caution: Do *not* put a comma every time you use the words *for, and, nor, but, or, yet,* and *so*; use it only when the coordinating conjunction joins independent clauses. Don't use a comma when the coordinating conjunction joins two words:

> blue and gold   tired but happy   hot or cold

Don't use a comma when the coordinating conjunction joins two phrases:

> on the chair or under the table
>
> in the water and by the shore
>
> with a smile but without an apology

The comma is used when the coordinating conjunction joins two independent clauses. Another way to say the same rule is to say that the comma is used when the coordinating conjunction joins two simple sentences.

Placing the Comma by Using S–V Patterns

An independent clause, or simple sentence, follows this basic pattern:

> S V
>
> **He ran.**

S   S V

He and **I ran**.

S   V   V

He ran and **swam**.

S   S V   V

He and **I ran** and **swam**.

Study all four patterns for the simple sentence, and you'll notice that you can draw a line separating the subjects on one side and the verbs on the other:

S	V
SS	V
S	VV
SS	VV

Whether the simple sentence has one or more subjects and one or more verbs, the pattern is subject(s) followed by verb(s)—or sometimes verbs followed by subject(s), when the sentence is in inverted word order.

When you combine two simple sentences, the pattern changes:

S   V   S V

two simple sentences: He swam. I ran.

S   V   S V

two simple sentences combined: He swam, but **I ran**.

In the new pattern, *SVSV*, you can't draw a line separating all the subjects on one side and all the verbs on the other. This new pattern is called a **compound sentence**: two simple sentences, or independent clauses, joined into one.

Recognizing the *SVSV* pattern will help you place the comma for compound sentences. Here's another way to remember this rule. When you have this pattern,

SV   SV

use a comma in front of the coordinating conjunction. Do not use a comma in front of the coordinating conjunctions with these patterns:

S	V
SS	V
S	VV
SS	VV

For example, use a comma for this pattern:

S   V   S V

Jane followed directions, but **I rushed** ahead.

but do not use a comma for this pattern:

S   V   V

Carol cleans her kitchen every week but never **wipes** the top of the refrigerator.

You've just studied one way to combine simple sentences. If you're going to take advantage of this method, you need to memorize the seven coordinating conjunctions—*for, and, nor, but, or, yet, so*—so that your use of them, with the correct punctuation, will become automatic.

EXERCISE 1	RECOGNIZING COMPOUND SENTENCES AND ADDING COMMAS

Add commas only where they're needed in the following sentences. Do not add words.

1. Terry Fox is considered one of Canada's greatest heroes and he was the youngest person ever to be awarded the Order of Canada.
2. Fox was a star basketball player in British Columbia but developed cancer in his leg when he was eighteen.
3. His right leg was amputated above the knee yet he still maintained a positive outlook and took up golf.
4. Fox underwent months of chemotherapy but he was still inspired by other cancer patients.
5. He realized the importance of cancer research and decided to try to raise money for it.
6. Terry Fox began his Marathon of Hope in Newfoundland and started his run across Canada.
7. He had hoped to raise one dollar from every Canadian for he believed that not enough money was spent on cancer research.
8. Terry Fox managed to run as far as Thunder Bay, Ontario, and had run more than 5000 kilometres before the cancer returned.
9. He had raised $1.7 million when he was forced to quit but people were so inspired by his courage that a telethon in his name raised over $10 million a week later.
10. Terry Fox runs are now held all over the world and more than half a billion dollars has been raised in his name.

EXERCISE 2	MORE ON RECOGNIZING COMPOUND SENTENCES AND ADDING COMMAS

Add commas only where they're needed in the following sentences. Do not add words.

1. Tommy Douglas was a Saskatchewan premier and the first leader of the NDP in Canada.
2. He was born in Scotland but his family moved to Canada when he was a young boy.
3. Douglas developed complications in his leg and some doctors believed it should be amputated.
4. One doctor believed he could save Douglas's leg and offered to do the procedure for free.
5. The experience convinced Douglas that health care should be free and this influenced his politics years later.
6. Douglas became premier of Saskatchewan in 1944 and passed legislation that allowed public service unions.
7. Canada's economy was doing well so Saskatchewan's government was slowly able to pay down its debt.

8. The strength of the province's economy at this time paved the way for Douglas to introduce universal health-care legislation in 1961.

9. Canada's system of universal health care has been hailed internationally and was featured in Michael Moore's movie *Sicko*.

10. Universal health care has contributed much to Canada's success as a nation yet many people take it for granted.

OPTION 2: USING A SEMICOLON BETWEEN TWO SIMPLE SENTENCES

Sometimes, you want to combine two simple sentences (independent clauses), but you don't want to use a coordinating conjunction. If you want to join two simple sentences that are related in their ideas and you don't use a coordinating conjunction, you can combine them with a **semicolon**.

two simple sentences:

S   V   S   V
I cooked the turkey. **She made** the stuffing.

two simple sentences combined with a semicolon:

S   V   ; S   V
I cooked the turkey; **she made** the stuffing.

Here's another example of this option in use:

S   V   V   ; S   V
Rain can be dangerous; **it makes** the roads slippery.

Notice that when you join two simple sentences with a semicolon, the second sentence begins with a lowercase letter, not a capital letter.

Remember these rules for punctuating combined simple sentences:

■ If a coordinating conjunction joins the combined sentences (remember option 1), put a comma in front of the coordinating conjunction.

S   V   ,   S   V
Tom had a barbecue in his backyard, and the **food was** delicious.

■ If there is no coordinating conjunction, put a semicolon in front of the second independent clause (option 2).

S   V   ;   S   V
Tom had a barbecue in his backyard; the **food was** delicious.

OPTION 3: USING A SEMICOLON AND A CONJUNCTIVE ADVERB

Sometimes, you want to join two simple sentences (independent clauses) with a connecting word called a **conjunctive adverb**. This word points out or clarifies a relationship between sentences. The Infobox provides a list of some conjunctive adverbs.

INFOBOX	SOME COMMON CONJUNCTIVE ADVERBS		
also	furthermore	likewise	otherwise
anyway	however	meanwhile	similarly
as a result	in addition	moreover	still
besides	incidentally	nevertheless	then
certainly	indeed	next	therefore
consequently	in fact	now	thus
finally	instead	on the other hand	undoubtedly

You can use a conjunctive adverb (*CA*) to join simple sentences, but when you do, you still need a semicolon in front of the adverb.

two simple sentences:

    S   V   S V

My **parents checked** my homework every night. **I did** well in math.

two simple sentences joined by a conjunctive adverb and a semicolon:

    S   V   ; CA S V

My **parents checked** my homework every night; **thus I did** well in math.

  S V   ; CA   S   V

She **gave** me good advice; **moreover**, **she helped** me follow it.

Punctuating after a Conjunctive Adverb

Notice the comma *after* the conjunctive adverb in the preceding sentence. Here's the generally accepted rule:

Put a comma after the conjunctive adverb if the conjunctive adverb is more than one syllable long.

For example, if the conjunctive adverb is a word like *consequently*, *furthermore*, or *moreover*, you use a comma. If the conjunctive adverb is one syllable, you don't have to put a comma after the conjunctive adverb. One-syllable conjunctive adverbs are words like *then* and *thus*.

We worked on the project all weekend; **consequently**, we finished a week ahead of the deadline.

I saw her cruel behaviour to her staff; **then** I lost respect for her.

EXERCISE 3

COMBINING SIMPLE SENTENCES THREE WAYS

Add a comma, or a semicolon, or a semicolon and a comma to the following sentences. Don't add, change, or delete any words; just add the correct punctuation.

1. For many years, scientists have been warning the public about the effects of climate change yet some people feel these claims are being exaggerated.

2. Geographically, Canada covers many cold-weather climates thus some scientists predict that Canada will be more affected by climate change.
3. Temperature increases could drastically affect Canada's fresh water supply consequently the prairies could suffer significant droughts.
4. Canada signed the Kyoto Accord, but has been criticized for not being committed to this international environmental agreement.
5. The Canadian government said it would create an environmental plan to replace Canada's Kyoto commitment critics claim this plan is deficient.
6. The government imposed regulations on emissions yet it was believed that heavy polluters were not sufficiently penalized.
7. Environmentalists believed that these new regulations could not compare to the Kyoto Accord and they voiced their concerns.
8. Polar bears have found their natural habitat shrinking due to global warming as a result many activists have used the polar bear as a symbol in the fight against global warming.
9. Studies show that most Canadians believe the science behind climate change and that they would like to see the government take more action.
10. More Canadians than Americans are willing to pay some sort of tax on the fuel they use they feel the environment is an important part of Canada's identity.

EXERCISE 4 | MORE ON COMBINING SIMPLE SENTENCES THREE WAYS

Add a comma, or a semicolon, or a semicolon and a comma to the following sentences. Don't add, change, or delete any words; just add the correct punctuation.

1. Margaret Atwood is one of Canada's most popular writers but she is known for her novels more than her poetry.
2. Atwood grew up in northern Ontario her father studied insects that plagued Ontario's spruce trees.
3. She attended the University of Toronto and later she did graduate studies at Harvard University.
4. Much of her poetry revolves around the imagery of mirrors and cameras these symbols were important in the search for identity.
5. Her book *Survival*, published in 1972, theorized that Canadian literature at that time was searching for an identity this identity was of survival.
6. Atwood's novel *The Handmaid's Tale* was made into a movie and there is talk of *Oryx and Crake* also being made into a movie.
7. Atwood and her partner, Graeme Gibson, are members of Canada's Green Party and Atwood has been president of PEN Canada, an organization supporting oppressed writers around the world.
8. Few people are aware that Atwood has written children's books one is called *Princess Prunella and the Purple Peanut*.
9. Several of her later novels are considered science fiction they often envision a bleak future.
10. Atwood has won numerous awards for her work Canadians are proud of her international acclaim.

EXERCISE 5

COMBINING SIMPLE SENTENCES

Below are pairs of simple sentences. Working with a partner or partners, combine each pair into one sentence. Use any of the three combining options discussed in this section: (1) a comma and a coordinating conjunction, (2) a semicolon, (3) a semicolon and a conjunctive adverb (with a comma, if it's needed). Then use a different option to create a second combination. The first one has been done for you.

Pick the options that make the most sense for each sentence.

1. Jim missed the beginning of the movie.

    I had to explain the story to him.

    combinations:

    a. Jim missed the beginning of the movie, so I had to explain the story to him.

    b. Jim missed the beginning of the movie; therefore, I had to explain the story to him.

2. Canada signed the Kyoto Accord in 2002.

    Canada withdrew from the Kyoto Accord in 2011.

    combinations:

    a. _____

    _____

    b. _____

    _____

3. Tommy Douglas was the NDP's first leader in Canada.

    He is considered "the father of medicare."

    combinations:

    a. _____

    _____

    b. _____

    _____

4. Margaret Atwood is one of Canada's most popular writers.

    She writes poetry, children's books, short stories, and novels.

    combinations:

    a. _____

    _____

    b. _____

    _____

5. Terry Fox had raised $1.7 million by the time he had to halt his Marathon of Hope.

   More than $500 million have been raised in his name for cancer research since his death.

   combinations:

   a. _____

   _____

   b. _____

   _____

EXERCISE

6

EDITING A PARAGRAPH FOR ERRORS IN COORDINATION

Edit the following paragraph for errors in coordination. Don't add or change words; just add, delete, or change punctuation. There are five errors in the paragraph.

A bad cold is a minor illness but it can be one of the most miserable ailments in the world. Most people soon forget their own colds, and don't sympathize with someone else's bad cold. A cold is supposed to be a silly, sniffling disturbance in the head however, the person with a cold feels very sick. He or she is sneezing, wheezing, and grabbing at tissues. Fever, headache, and stuffiness suddenly attack the sufferer and no remedy seems to work. Cold pills cannot make a person feel less congested nor can chicken soup clear up a headache. The victim of a cold can only wait for the misery to pass then the cold bug brings its nasty symptoms to a new victim.

CHAPTER 15
The Complex Sentence:
Subordination

MORE OPTIONS FOR COMBINING SIMPLE SENTENCES

Before you go any further, look back. Review the following:

- A clause has a subject and a complete predicate (the verb, plus the objects and phrases modifying the verb).
- An independent clause is a simple sentence; it is a group of words, with a subject and verb, that makes sense on its own.
- Independent clauses can be combined in various ways to make compound sentences.

There is another kind of clause, called a **dependent clause**. It has a subject and a verb, but it doesn't make sense by itself. It can't stand alone. It isn't complete by itself. That is, it *depends* on the rest of the sentence to give it meaning. You can use a dependent clause in combining simple sentences.

Using a Subordinating Conjunction

Changing an independent clause to a dependent one is called subordinating. How do you do it? You add a certain word, called a **subordinating conjunction**, to an independent clause, which makes it dependent, less important, or subordinate in the new sentence.

Keep in mind that the subordinate clause is still a clause; it has a subject and a complete predicate, but it doesn't make sense on its own. For example, here's an independent clause:

       S   V

Caroline studies.

Somebody (*Caroline*) does something (*studies*). The statement makes sense by itself. But if you add a subordinating conjunction to the independent clause, the clause becomes dependent, incomplete, and unfinished, like this:

When Caroline studies. (When she studies, what happens?)

Unless Caroline studies. (Unless she studies, what will happen?)

If Caroline studies. (If Caroline studies, what will happen?)

Now, each dependent clause needs an independent clause to finish the idea:

dependent clause   independent clause

When Caroline studies, she gets good grades.

dependent clause   independent clause

Unless Caroline studies, she forgets key ideas.

dependent clause independent clause

If Caroline studies, she will pass the course.

There are many subordinating conjunctions. When you put any of these words in front of an independent clause, you make that clause dependent. The Infobox provides a list of some common subordinating conjunctions.

INFOBOX	SOME COMMON SUBORDINATING CONJUNCTIONS		
after	because	in order that	whatever
although	before	since	when
as	even if	though	whenever
as if	even though	unless	whereas
as soon as	if	until	while

You can use these subordinating conjunctions to create dependent clauses in two more options for combining simple sentences.

OPTION 4: USING A DEPENDENT CLAUSE TO BEGIN A SENTENCE

Often, you can combine simple sentences by changing the independent clause from one sentence into a dependent clause and placing it at the beginning of a new sentence.

two simple sentences:

S V   S V

I was late for work. My car had a flat tire.

changing one simple sentence into a beginning dependent clause:

S V   S V

Because my car had a flat tire, I was late for work.

Note that you can begin a sentence with a subordinating conjunction such as *because* as long as you follow it with an independent clause to make a complete sentence.

OPTION 5: USING A DEPENDENT CLAUSE TO END A SENTENCE

You can also combine simple sentences by changing an independent clause into a dependent clause and placing it at the end of a new sentence:

the same two simple sentences as above:

S V   S V

I was late for work. My car had a flat tire.

changing one simple sentence into a dependent clause at the end:

S   V   S   V

I was late for work because my **car had** a flat tire.

Choosing a Subordinating Conjunction

If you pick the right subordinating conjunction, you can effectively combine simple sentences (independent clauses) into a more sophisticated sentence pattern. Such combining helps you add sentence variety to your writing and helps to explain relationships between ideas.

simple sentences:

S   V   V   S   V

Leo could not **read** music. His **performance was** exciting.

new combination:

dependent clause   independent clause

Although Leo could not read music, his performance was exciting.

simple sentences:

S   V   S   V

I caught a bad cold last night. **I forgot** to bring a sweater to the baseball game.

new combination:

independent clause   dependent clause

I caught a bad cold last night because I forgot to bring a sweater to the baseball game.

Punctuating Complex Sentences

A sentence that has one independent clause and one or more dependent clauses is called a **complex sentence**. Complex sentences are easy to punctuate. See if you can figure out by yourself the usual rule for punctuating. Look at the following examples. All are punctuated correctly.

example 1:

dependent clause   independent clause

Whenever the baby smiles, his mother is delighted.

independent clause   dependent clause

His mother is delighted **whenever the baby smiles**.

example 2:

dependent clause   independent clause

While you were away, I saved your mail for you.

independent clause   dependent clause

I saved your mail for you **while you were away**.

In the previous two examples, look at the sentences that have a comma. Now look at the ones that don't have a comma. Both kinds of sentences are punctuated correctly. Do you see the rule?

Rule: When a dependent clause comes at the beginning of a sentence, the clause is followed by a comma. When a dependent clause comes at the end of a sentence, the clause usually doesn't need a comma.

Using a Relative Pronoun

Another type of dependent clause can be created by adding a **relative pronoun** such as *that, who, whoever, whom, what, which,* and *whose.*

This **relative clause** can be used as an adjective or a noun:

used as a noun (subject):

Whoever eats with us will enjoy a terrific meal. (Note that the clause actually forms the subject of the sentence—the subject of the independent clause.)

used as a noun (object of the verb):

She wanted to know **whom he would be visiting.** (answers the question "to know what?")

used as an adjective:

John recorded the game **that was played last night.** (describes what game)

The preceding examples of complex sentences have one independent clause and one dependent clause. A complex sentence can have one independent clause and *one or more* dependent clauses. Note the following example of a complex sentence with one independent clause and *two* dependent clauses:

independent clause	dependent clause	dependent clause

He tried to call her at home before she left with the man whose background was a mystery.

EXERCISE 1

PUNCTUATING COMPLEX SENTENCES

All the following sentences are complex sentences; that is, they have one independent clause and one or more dependent clauses. Add a comma to the sentences that need one.

1. Until I became a parent I never realized that parenting could be so difficult.
2. Because they wanted me to have the best education my parents each worked two jobs.
3. My mother worked full-time as a teacher while she cleaned offices at night.
4. I knew how stressed my parents were even though they thought they were hiding their worries from me.

5. When I'm dealing with my own concerns I try to shelter my son from them.

6. I want my son to enjoy his childhood until he's old enough to have his own responsibilities.

7. My husband and I try to take our son on family outings whenever we can.

8. Although I would like to give my son everything he wants I know that would spoil him.

9. I want to raise a healthy, well-adjusted child as my parents did.

10. Whereas I didn't have many luxuries growing up my son will have an easier life.

EXERCISE 2 — MORE ON PUNCTUATING COMPLEX SENTENCES

All the sentences below are complex sentences; that is, they have one independent clause and one or more dependent clauses. Add a comma to each sentence that needs one.

1. It amazes me that my wife and I get along so well because we are two entirely different people.

2. Whereas my dream vacation involves a five-star hotel my wife's dream vacation means hiking and camping.

3. Even though she'd like to visit Gros Morne National Park before the end of the summer I have other plans.

4. I would prefer to spend a week on a beach somewhere though my wife insists it would be a nice change to go camping.

5. Why would I want to sleep on the rocky ground while I'm being bitten by mosquitoes?

6. My wife would like to take our daughter camping before she goes back to school.

7. While we do have our differences I love my wife.

8. We'll go camping this summer as long as we can go to the beach next year.

9. If I remember to bring mosquito repellent I might just have a good time.

10. As I write this my wife is already packing the tent.

COMBINING SENTENCES: A REVIEW OF YOUR OPTIONS

You've seen several ways to combine simple sentences. The following chart will help you to see them all at a glance:

INFOBOX	OPTIONS FOR COMBINING SENTENCES

Coordination

Option 1:

Independent clause + comma + coordinating conjunction + independent clause.

> , for
> , and
> , nor
> , but
> , or
> , yet
> , so

Option 2:

Independent clause + semicolon + independent clause.

Option 3:

Independent clause + semicolon + conjunctive adverb + independent clause.

> ; also,
> ; anyway,
> ; as a result,
> ; besides,
> ; certainly,
> ; consequently,
> ; finally,
> ; furthermore,
> ; however,
> ; incidentally,
> ; in addition,
> ; in fact,
> ; indeed,
> ; instead,
> ; likewise,
> ; meanwhile,
> ; moreover,
> ; nevertheless,
> ; next
> ; now
> ; on the other hand,
> ; otherwise,
> ; similarly,
> ; still
> ; then
> ; therefore,
> ; thus
> ; undoubtedly,

(continued)

Subordination

Option 4:

Subordinating conjunction + dependent clause + comma + independent clause.

After	
Although	
As	
As if	
As soon as	
Because	
Before	
Even if	
Even though	
If	(Put a comma at
In order that	the end of the
Since	dependent clause.)
So that	
Though	
Unless	
Until	
Whatever	
When	
Whenever	
Whereas	
Whether	
While	

Option 5:

Independent clause + subordinating conjunction + dependent clause.

after
although
as
as if
as soon as
because
before
even if
even though
if
in order that
since
so that
though
unless
until
whatever
when
whenever
whereas
whether
while

Note: In Option 4, words are capitalized because the dependent clause will begin your complete sentence.

Creating Compound-Complex Sentences

Another type of sentence is the **compound-complex sentence**. This type of sentence has *two or more* independent clauses and *one or more* dependent clauses. You can join simple sentences to create the compound-complex sentence by using the same punctuation and conjunctions you've already learned.

> dependent clause　　independent clause　　dependent clause　　CA
> When we left for school, we knew that we were already late; however,
>
> independent clause
> the instructor was late, too.

> independent clause　　　dependent clause　　　CA　　　independent clause
> Stefan tried to tell her that she shouldn't go; however, she wanted to make
>
> 　　　　　　　independent clause　　dependent clause
> her own decision, so she left before anyone else awoke.

EXERCISE 3

USING THE FIVE OPTIONS FOR COMBINING SENTENCES

Add the missing commas and/or semicolons to the following compound, complex, or compound-complex sentences. Some sentences are correct as written.

1. People can be more environmentally friendly if they make just a few simple changes.
2. My family has long been environmentally aware so I've always conserved energy.
3. Don't use incandescent light bulbs instead replace them with compact fluorescent ones.
4. My parents always turn off the lights when they leave a room.
5. We don't run the dishwasher unless it's completely full.
6. We hang our clothes up to dry even if it's raining we just hang them up in the basement.
7. We bought a programmable thermostat so that the furnace will turn itself off when we aren't home.
8. Before the cold weather set in we added insulation to our house.
9. Even though we live in the suburbs we have only one car and it's fuel-efficient.
10. We buy our groceries in bulk and don't use plastic bags.
11. My son and I plant vegetables in our garden when the threat of frost has passed.
12. We use our composter regularly so that we have very little trash to put out every two weeks.
13. We put out one bag of trash however we usually put out three recycling bins.

14. Even though we live in the suburbs I take the bus whenever I can.

15. There's a rain barrel in our backyard we use the water in the garden.

16. Because native plants require less watering I've replaced the non-native plants in our garden with native ones.

17. When the leaves appear on the large tree in our garden the tree shades our house in the summer.

18. Often we don't have to turn on the air conditioner in the summer because the house is shaded by the tree.

19. We water the garden first thing in the morning and for just twenty minutes at a time.

20. I like to think that I'm helping the environment and teaching my son about environmental responsibility.

EXERCISE 4

COMBINING SENTENCES

Do this exercise with a partner or with a group. Combine each pair of sentences below into one clear, smooth sentence in two different ways. You can add words as well as punctuation. The first pair of sentences is done for you.

1. Many cafés have become workplaces and social hubs.
   Customers can spend hours using free WiFi or playing cards.

   combination 1: Many cafés have become workplaces and social hubs, as
   customers can spend hours using free WiFi or playing cards.

   combination 2: Many cafés have become workplaces and social hubs;
   customers can spend hours using free WiFi or playing cards.

2. Many cafés have patio seating.
   Sitting on the patio allows customers to take advantage of beautiful weather.

   combination 1: _____

   _____

   combination 2: _____

   _____

3. Canadian summers can be short.
   Canadians like to be outdoors as much as possible.

   combination 1: _____

   _____

   combination 2: _____

   _____

4. Doctors have been informing the public about the dangers of sun exposure.

   People need vitamin D from sun exposure to stay healthy.

   combination 1: _____

   _____

   combination 2: _____

   _____

5. Vitamin D is essential for the proper function of the heart, muscles, and brain.

   Studies have shown that most people don't get enough vitamin D.

   combination 1: _____

   _____

   combination 2: _____

   _____

6. Vitamin D supplements are available.

   The sun remains the best source for vitamin D.

   combination 1: _____

   _____

   combination 2: _____

   _____

7. A lack of vitamin D can lead to higher risk of certain cancers and high blood pressure.

   Some doctors recommend at least some sun exposure.

   combination 1: _____

   _____

   combination 2: _____

   _____

8. Vitamin D can be found in foods such as egg yolks, fish, and cheese.

   Foods alone don't contain enough vitamin D for a person to stay healthy.

   combination 1: _____

   _____

   combination 2: _____

   _____

EXERCISE 5

CREATE YOUR OWN TEXT ON COMBINING SENTENCES

Below is a list of rules for coordinating and subordinating sentences. Working with a group, create two examples of each rule.

Option 1: You can join two simple sentences (two independent clauses) into a compound sentence with a coordinating conjunction and a comma in front of it.

The coordinating conjunctions are *for, and, nor, but, or, yet,* and *so.*

example 1: _____

_____

example 2: _____

_____

Option 2: You can combine two simple sentences (two independent clauses) into a compound sentence with a semicolon between independent clauses.

example 1: _____

_____

example 2: _____

_____

Option 3: You can join two simple sentences (two independent clauses) into a compound sentence with a semicolon and a conjunctive adverb between independent clauses.

Some conjunctive adverbs are *also, anyway, as a result, besides, certainly, consequently, finally, furthermore, however, incidentally, in addition, in fact, indeed, instead, likewise, meanwhile, moreover, nevertheless, next, now, on the other hand, otherwise, similarly, still, then, therefore, thus, undoubtedly.*

example 1: _____

_____

example 2: _____

_____

Option 4: You can combine two simple sentences (two independent clauses) into a complex sentence by making one clause dependent. The dependent clause starts with a subordinating conjunction. Then, if the dependent clause begins the sentence, the clause ends with a comma.

Some common subordinating conjunctions are *after, although, as, as if, as soon as, because, before, even if, even though, if, in order that, since, though, unless, until, whatever, when, whenever, whereas, whether, while.*

example 1: _____

_____

example 2: _____

_____

Option 5: You can combine two simple sentences (two independent clauses) into a compound sentence by making one clause dependent. Then, if the dependent clause comes after the independent clause, usually no comma is needed.

example 1: _____

_____

example 2: _____

_____

EXERCISE 6

EDITING A PARAGRAPH FOR ERRORS IN COORDINATION AND SUBORDINATION

Edit the following paragraph for errors in coordination and subordination. Do not add words to the paragraph; just add, delete, or change punctuation. There are ten errors.

I am beginning to realize the importance of punctuality. This lesson came to me the hard way when I almost lost my job at a small, friendly insurance office certainly, I felt at ease with its casual and open atmosphere. I think I confused friendliness with slackness and soon found trouble. Since my boss and the other agents are often busy they rely on me to open up in the morning. I usually arrive on time at least I try to get there on time. I figured it didn't matter if I was ten or fifteen minutes late. When I arrived late last Friday it did matter. My boss came in thirty minutes after I did so I figured everything was fine. As soon as she took one call she came up to my desk and started shouting. The call was a customer with an emergency. That customer had called the office six times early in the morning no one had answered. Of course, I hadn't yet opened the office. My boss explained the seriousness of the problem finally, she gave me one more chance. I'll be on time from now on for I won't risk losing that chance.

CHAPTER 16
Avoiding Run-on Sentences and Comma Splices

RUN-ON SENTENCES

Run-on sentences are independent clauses that haven't been joined correctly. This error, also called a **fused sentence,** is a major grammatical error.

run-on sentence error:

People have long thought that students who sit in the front row of class get better grades studies show that these students have 20 percent higher GPAs than students who sit in the back row.

run-on sentence error corrected:

People have long thought that students who sit in the front row of class get better grades, and studies show that these students have 20 percent higher GPAs than students who sit in the back row.

run-on sentence error:

Technology has changed today's lifestyles social networking sites have replaced face-to-face socializing.

run-on sentence error corrected:

Technology has changed today's lifestyles; social networking sites have replaced face-to-face socializing.

run-on sentence error:

The causes of many illnesses have been found scientists have done much research.

run-on sentence error corrected:

The causes of many illnesses have been found because scientists have done much research.

Note: Two independent clauses could also be punctuated correctly as two separate sentences.

People have long thought that students who sit in the front row of class get better grades. Studies show that these students have 20 percent higher GPAs than students who sit in the back row.

CORRECTING RUN-ON SENTENCES

When you edit your writing, you can correct run-on sentences by following the steps shown in the Infobox.

INFOBOX	**TWO STEPS IN CORRECTING RUN-ON SENTENCES**

Step 1: Check for two independent clauses.
Step 2: Check that the clauses are separated by a comma and coordinating conjunction, by a semicolon, or by a subordinating conjunction.

Follow the steps in checking this sentence:

The meeting was a waste of time the councillors argued about silly issues.

Step 1: Check for two independent clauses. You can do this by checking for the subject–verb, subject–verb pattern that indicates two independent clauses:

    S   V   S   V

The **meeting was** a waste of time the **councillors argued** about silly issues.

The pattern indicates that you have two independent clauses.

Step 2: Check that the clauses are separated either by a comma and coordinating conjunction (*for, and, nor, but, or, yet,* and *so*), by a semicolon, or by a subordinating conjunction.

The independent clauses aren't separated by any of those options, so you have a run-on sentence. You can correct the run-on sentence in three ways:

run-on sentence corrected with a comma and a coordinating conjunction:

The meeting was a waste of time, **for** the councillors argued about silly issues.

run-on sentence corrected with a semicolon:

The meeting was a waste of time; the councillors argued about silly issues.

run-on sentence corrected with a subordinating conjunction:

The meeting was a waste of time **since** the councillors argued about silly issues.

or

Since the councillors argued about silly issues, the meeting was a waste of time.

Follow the steps once more as you check this sentence:

I had the flu I missed class last week.

Step 1: Check for two independent clauses. Do this by checking the subject–verb, subject–verb pattern:

S V   S V

I had the flu **I missed** class last week.

Step 2: Check that the clauses are separated either by a comma and coordinating conjunction (*for, and, nor, but, or, yet, so*), by a semicolon, or by a subordinating conjunction.

The independent clauses aren't separated by any of those options, so you have a run-on sentence. You can correct the run-on sentence three ways:

run-on sentence corrected with a comma and coordinating conjunction:

I had the flu, **so** I missed class last week.

run-on sentence corrected with a semicolon:

I had the flu; I missed class last week.

run-on sentence corrected with a subordinating conjunction:

Because I had the flu, I missed class last week.

Using the steps to check for run-on sentences can also help you avoid unnecessary punctuation. Consider this sentence:

The manager gave me my schedule for next week, and told me about a special sales promotion.

Step 1: Check for two independent clauses. Do this by checking the subject–verb, subject–verb pattern:

    S   V   V

The **manager gave** me my schedule for next week, and **told** me about a special sales promotion.

The pattern is *SVV*, not *SV, SV*. The sentence is not made up of two independent clauses, so it doesn't need a comma before the coordinating conjunction. The sentence should read as follows:

The **manager gave** me my schedule for next week and **told** me about a special sales promotion.

Following these steps in correcting run-on sentences can help you combine sentences effectively.

| EXERCISE 1 | CORRECTING RUN-ON (FUSED) SENTENCES |

Some of the sentences below are correctly punctuated. Some are run-on (fused) sentences; that is, they are two simple sentences run together without any punctuation. If a sentence is correctly punctuated, write *OK* in the space provided. If it's a run-on sentence, put an *X* in the space provided and correct the sentence above the lines.

1. _____ With the help of computers and wireless technology, many people can work from home so employers are granting many more flex hours.

2. _____ Some companies maintain remote offices for employees to have the occasional meeting or to print documents otherwise these employees work from home.

3. _____ Job sharing has been an innovative way to save jobs in difficult economic times instead of eliminating jobs, two people may share a job.

4. _____ Workers can conduct meetings through webcams and conference calls without leaving home.

5. _____ Virtual private networks allow workers access to their documents and company network at home thus it's almost like being at work.

6. _____ The portability of laptops and the widespread availability of wireless internet allow people to work from anywhere, from their backyards to the local coffee shop.

7. _____ The ready availability of work documents and the internet can mean that people may work at any time so many employees are constantly checking email.

8. _____ Studies have shown that more than 50 percent of workers check their email on vacation they say they're afraid of falling behind when they get back to work.

9. _____ Some people keep their smartphones or BlackBerrys on and beside them when they sleep at night.

10. _____ This blurring of the lines between work and personal time is called *work creep*.

EXERCISE 2	**MORE ABOUT CORRECTING RUN-ON (FUSED) SENTENCES**

Some of the sentences below are correctly punctuated. Some are run-on (fused) sentences; that is, they are two simple sentences run together without any punctuation. If a sentence is correctly punctuated, write *OK* in the space provided. If it's a run-on sentence, put an *X* in the space provided and correct the sentence above the lines. You may add words if necessary.

1. _____ Many people work downtown but they live in the suburbs.

2. _____ Families can afford a detached house in the suburbs they can afford only a small condominium in the city.

3. _____ Suburban properties usually include some kind of outdoor space however condominiums may have just a balcony.

4. _____ Many people, especially young couples, prefer to live downtown they can walk to work and shops.

5. _____ City dwellers escape rush hour traffic and stressful commutes.

6. _____ They save money by walking or taking public transit so they may not even own a car.

7. _____ Many people prefer being maintenance-free condominium residents don't have to shovel snow or mow a lawn.

8. _____ Condominiums offer amenities such as swimming pools, workout rooms, and party rooms.

9. _____ It can be noisy living downtown for late-night partygoers can disrupt the quiet of the night.

10. _____ Maintenance people can come into your unit when you're not home to inspect and maintain the property.

COMMA SPLICES

A **comma splice** is an error that occurs when you punctuate with a comma when you should instead be using either a comma plus a coordinating conjunction (*for, and, nor, but, or, yet, so*) or a semicolon. A comma alone is not enough.

comma-splice error:

The crowd pushed forward, people began to panic.

comma-splice error corrected:

The crowd pushed forward, and people began to panic.

or

The crowd pushed forward; people began to panic.

comma-splice error:

I forgot my glasses, I couldn't read the small print in the contract.

comma-splice error corrected:

I forgot my glasses, so I couldn't read the small print in the contract.

or

I forgot my glasses; I couldn't read the small print in the contract.

CORRECTING COMMA SPLICES

When you edit your writing, you can correct splices by following these steps:

INFOBOX	TWO STEPS IN CORRECTING COMMA SPLICES

Step 1: Check for two independent clauses.
Step 2: Check that the clauses are separated by a coordinating conjunction (FANBOYS: *for, and, nor, but, or, yet, so*) after the comma. If they are, then a comma is sufficient. If they're not separated by a coordinating conjunction, you have a comma splice. Correct the comma splice by adding a coordinating conjunction after the comma or by changing the comma to a semicolon.

Follow the steps to check for a comma splice in this sentence:

I dropped the glass, it shattered on the tile floor.

Step 1: Check for two independent clauses. You can do this by checking for the subject–verb, subject–verb pattern that indicates two independent clauses.

S   V   S   V

I dropped the glass, **it shattered** on the tile floor.

The pattern indicates that you have two independent clauses.

Step 2:   Check that the clauses are separated by a coordinating conjunction after the comma.

There is no coordinating conjunction. To correct the comma-splice error, you must add a coordinating conjunction or use a semicolon instead of a comma.

comma-splice error corrected:

I dropped the glass, and it shattered on the tile floor.

or

I dropped the glass; it shattered on the tile floor.

Be careful not to mistake a short word like *then* or *thus* for a coordinating conjunction. Only the seven coordinating conjunctions (*for, and, nor, but, or, yet, so*) can join independent clauses with a comma. *Then* is not a coordinating conjunction; it's a conjunctive adverb. When it joins two independent clauses, it needs a semicolon in front of it.

comma-splice error:

Susie prepared her résumé, then she applied for the job.

comma-splice error corrected:

Susie prepared her résumé; then she applied for the job.

Also remember that conjunctive adverbs that are two or more syllables long (like *consequently*, *however*, and *therefore*) need a comma after them as well as a semicolon in front of them when they join independent clauses:

Harry has been researching plane fares to Vancouver; consequently, he knows how to spot a cheap flight.

(For a list of some common conjunctive adverbs, see page 352 in Chapter 14.)

Sometimes, writers see commas before and after a conjunctive adverb and think the commas are sufficient. Check this sentence for a comma splice by following the steps:

Jonathan loves his job, however, it pays very little.

Step 1:   Check for two independent clauses by checking for the subject–verb, subject–verb pattern.

S   V   S   V

Jonathan loves his job, however, **it pays** very little.

The pattern indicates that you have two independent clauses.

Step 2:   Check for a coordinating conjunction.

There is no coordinating conjunction. *However* is a conjunctive adverb, not a coordinating conjunction. Because there is no coordinating conjunction, you need a semicolon between the two independent clauses.

comma-splice error corrected:

Jonathan loves his job; however, it pays very little.

EXERCISE 3	CORRECTING COMMA SPLICES

Some of the sentences below are correctly punctuated. Some contain comma splices. If the sentence is correctly punctuated, write *OK* in the space provided. If it contains a comma splice, put an *X* in the space provided and correct the sentence above the lines. To correct a sentence, add the necessary punctuation. Do not add any words.

1. _____ Many traditional exchanges of money are now being done online, therefore it's wise to be aware of high-tech scams.

2. _____ It's important to protect your personal information, never respond to emails asking for your bank account information or credit card number.

3. _____ You should also be careful at the ATM, thieves have been known to hide cameras there.

4. _____ The cameras record you as you enter your PIN, then the thieves use that number to access your bank account and drain your funds.

5. _____ Try to cover the keypad with your hand as you enter your PIN, in addition never write your PIN down.

6. _____ Many credit cards are now chip-enabled, this means they have microchips embedded in them to prevent fraud.

7. _____ Owners must enter a PIN to make a purchase with a credit card, in the past just a signature was required.

8. _____ Because some salespeople didn't verify the shopper's signature, thieves could use a stolen credit card; this caused difficulties for both the credit card owner and the issuer of the credit card.

9. _____ Credit card fraud costs the industry millions of dollars, and this cost is passed on to consumers.

10. _____ Experts recommend that consumers check their credit statements regularly and report any suspicious activity.

EXERCISE 4	MORE ABOUT CORRECTING COMMA SPLICES

Some of the sentences below are correctly punctuated. Some contain comma splices. If the sentence is correctly punctuated, write *OK* in the space provided. If it contains a comma splice, put an *X* in the space provided and correct the sentence above the lines. To correct a sentence, add the necessary punctuation. Do not add any words.

1. _____ The carpenter used nails instead of screws to lay the floor, as a result, the floor creaked.

2. _____ Malakeh loves children, so she got her early childhood education diploma.

3. _____ The government was trying to encourage the public to save electricity, it offered rebates on compact fluorescent light bulbs.

4. _____ Manufacturers claim that these bulbs will last up to seven years, but in my experience, they last an average of three months.

5. _____ Compact fluorescent bulbs contain small amounts of mercury, a toxic substance.

6. _____ If a compact fluorescent bulb breaks in your home, experts recommend that you open all the windows in the room, they also recommend that everyone evacuate the room.

7. _____ You must pick up the larger broken pieces and use tape to pick up the smaller pieces, you must not use a vacuum cleaner.

8. _____ To prevent spreading mercury throughout your house, experts also recommend turning off your heating and cooling system.

9. _____ The newest innovation in lighting is the LED light, *LED* stands for "light-emitting diode."

10. _____ LEDs are more energy efficient than incandescent light bulbs for they produce more light per unit of energy.

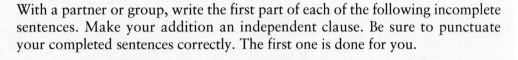

EXERCISE 5

COMPLETING SENTENCES

With a partner or group, write the first part of each of the following incomplete sentences. Make your addition an independent clause. Be sure to punctuate your completed sentences correctly. The first one is done for you.

1. <u>The driver ignored the railroad warning signals,</u> and his car was hit by the train.

2. _____ then students can register for class.

3. _____ furthermore, strong communication skills are required.

4. _____ or traffic will continue to worsen.

5. _____ now candidates may apply online.

6. _____ professional attire is recommended.

7. _____ however, there is an additional fee.

8. _____ but it's a good experience for international students.

9. _____ the hiring manager is on leave.

10. _____ otherwise, a laptop would be a better choice.

EXERCISE 6

EDITING A PARAGRAPH FOR RUN-ON SENTENCES AND COMMA SPLICES

Edit the following paragraph for run-on sentences and comma splices. There are seven errors.

Choosing a career is difficult I'm torn between two fields. My best grades have been in my math classes and my father wants me to be an accountant. Accountants make a good salary in addition, they're always in demand. My uncle is an accountant and has found good jobs in four exciting cities. I would like the security and opportunity of such employment on the other hand, I dream of a different career. I've been working at a restaurant for four years as a result, I have learned about the inner workings of the restaurant business. The job is tough nevertheless, I would love to have my own restaurant. Everyone warns me about the huge financial risks and long hours yet these challenges can be exciting. Someday I'll have to choose between a risky venture in the restaurant business and a safe, well-paying career in accounting.

CHAPTER 17
Avoiding Sentence Fragments

A **sentence fragment** is a group of words that looks like a sentence and is punctuated like a sentence but isn't a sentence. Writing a sentence fragment is a major error in grammar because it reveals that the writer isn't sure what a sentence is.

The following groups of words are all fragments:

Because customer service is an often neglected, yet crucial, aspect to any business.

My job being very stressful and fast-paced.

For example, the trend of serving tapas, or appetizer-sized portions.

Two simple steps that can help you check your writing for sentence fragments are provided in the Infobox.

INFOBOX	TWO STEPS IN RECOGNIZING SENTENCE FRAGMENTS

Step 1: Check each group of words punctuated like a sentence; look for a subject and a complete predicate.

Step 2: If you find a subject and a complete predicate, check that the group of words makes a complete statement.

RECOGNIZING FRAGMENTS: STEP 1

Check for a subject and a complete predicate (verb plus object and modifiers). Some groups of words that look like sentences may actually have a subject, but no complete predicate; or they may have a complete predicate, but no subject; or they may have neither a subject *nor* a complete predicate.

The customer by the cashmere sweaters. (***Customer*** could be the subject of a sentence, but there's no complete predicate.)

Doesn't matter to me one way or the other. (There is a complete predicate, ***doesn't matter***, but there is no subject.)

In the back of my mind. (There are two prepositional phrases, ***In the back*** and ***of my mind***, but there is no subject or complete predicate.)

Remember that the *-ing* form of a verb by itself cannot be the main verb in a sentence (see Chapter 13). Therefore, groups of words like the ones below may look like sentences, but they're missing a complete predicate and are really fragments:

> Your sister having all the skills required of a good salesperson.
>
> The two top tennis players struggling with exhaustion and the stress
>
> of a highly competitive tournament.
>
> Jack being the only one in the room with a piece of paper.

An infinitive (*to* plus a verb) can't be a main verb in a sentence either. The following groups of words are also fragments:

> The manager of the store to attend the meeting of regional managers next
>
> month in Brampton.
>
> The purpose to explain the fine points of the game to new players.

Groups of words beginning with words like *also*, *especially*, *except*, *for example*, *in addition*, and *such as* need subjects and complete predicates, too. Without subjects and complete predicates, these groups can be fragments, like the ones below:

> Also a good place to grow up.
>
> Especially the youngest member of the family.
>
> For example, a person without a high school diploma.

Note that there is one type of sentence that may look as if it has no subject but in fact is complete. With a verb that gives a direct command or instruction, the subject *you* is understood. Thus, the following are complete sentences:

> Hang up your coat.
>
> Don't plagiarize.
>
> Please sit down.

EXERCISE 1 — CHECKING GROUPS OF WORDS FOR SUBJECTS AND COMPLETE PREDICATES

Check the following groups of words for subjects and complete predicates. Some have subjects and complete predicates and are sentences. Some are missing subjects, complete predicates, or both: they are fragments. Put an *S* beside the ones that are sentences; put an *F* beside the ones that are fragments.

1. _____ For example, the Alberta oil sands represent the world's second largest reserve of crude oil.

2. _____ Under these oil sands lie hundreds of billions of barrels of crude oil.

3. _____ Big, 400-ton trucks transporting crude to the refinery, impacting the environment.

4. _____ Can't possibly be sustainable.

5. _____ Especially the challenges of transporting over large distances.

6. _____ Transporting oil by pipeline and by rail are both politically contentious.

7. _____ Tree-planting initiatives in an attempt to offset the environmental impact.

8. _____　The energy used to develop the oil sands causes spikes in greenhouse gas emissions.

9. _____　Alberta's rivers and streams shown to be affected.

10. _____　No easy answers, without a doubt.

EXERCISE 2

MORE ABOUT CHECKING GROUPS OF WORDS FOR SUBJECTS AND COMPLETE PREDICATES

Some of the following groups of words have subjects and complete predicates; these are sentences. Some are missing subjects, complete predicates, or both; these are fragments. Put an *S* beside each sentence; put an *F* beside each fragment.

1. _____　Mona Parsons, one of Canada's great unsung heroes.

2. _____　Born and raised in Nova Scotia, but moved to Amsterdam with her husband.

3. _____　She and her husband, joining the Resistance at the beginning of the war, hiding Allied airmen.

4. _____　They hid these airmen for almost a year and a half before they were discovered by the Nazis.

5. _____　Parsons was tried and sentenced to death.

6. _____　Her sentence commuted to life, moved from prison camp to prison camp.

7. _____　Escaping with a fellow prisoner.

8. _____　Then hid with a German farm family.

9. _____　Parsons made her way back to Holland near the end of the war.

10. _____　Returned to Canada, where few people were aware of her story.

RECOGNIZING FRAGMENTS: STEP 2

If you find a subject and a complete predicate, check that the group of words makes a complete statement. Many groups of words have both a subject and a verb, but they don't make sense by themselves. They are **dependent clauses.**

How can you tell if a clause is dependent? After you've checked each group of words for a subject and complete predicate, check to see whether it begins with one of the **subordinating conjunctions** that start dependent clauses. (Here again are some common subordinating conjunctions: *after, although, as, because, before, even if, even though, if, in order that, since, though, unless, until, when, whereas, while.*)

A clause that begins with a subordinating conjunction is a dependent clause. When you punctuate a dependent clause as if it were a sentence, you have a kind of fragment called a **dependent clause fragment:**

> After I woke up this morning.
>
> Because he liked cricket better than soccer.
>
> Unless it stops raining by lunchtime.

It's important to remember both steps in checking for fragments:

Step 1: Check for a subject and a complete predicate.

Step 2: If you find a subject and a complete predicate, check that the group of words makes a complete statement.

EXERCISE **3**	**CHECKING FOR DEPENDENT CLAUSE FRAGMENTS**

Some of the following groups of words are sentences. Some are dependent clauses punctuated like sentences; these are sentence fragments. Put an *S* beside the sentences and an *F* beside the fragments.

1. _____ As he carefully washed the outside of the car and polished the chrome trim with a special cloth.

2. _____ Commuters rushed past the ticket windows and jumped onto the train at the last possible minute.

3. _____ Because no one in the class had been able to buy a copy of the required text in the campus bookstore.

4. _____ Even though many people expect to own a home and to be able to meet the mortgage payments.

5. _____ Most of the movies were sequels to the popular movies of last summer.

6. _____ While I wanted to go to a place in the desert with dry air and bright sunshine.

7. _____ Although defendants in some countries are considered guilty until they prove their innocence.

8. _____ If people in our community were more serious about conserving water.

9. _____ Ever since Ron began taking martial arts classes.

10. _____ When prospective students don't have the finances to pay for school.

EXERCISE **4**	**MORE ABOUT CHECKING FOR DEPENDENT CLAUSE FRAGMENTS**

Some of the following groups of words are sentences. Some are dependent clauses punctuated like sentences; these are sentence fragments. Put an *S* beside each sentence and an *F* beside each fragment.

1. _____ After I finish my shift at work.

2. _____ Down the ladder came a firefighter with a child in his arms.

3. _____ Since we met at the student centre for a cup of coffee.

4. _____ Near the hospital is a huge medical building.

5. _____ Before I had a chance to put the key in the door.

6. _____ Because anyone could have broken into the gym.

7. _____ While Sergei painted the green trim on the outside of the house.

8. _____ Suddenly my car alarm sounded.

9. _____ Unless you can give me a better deal on this smartphone.

10. _____ Whenever Tanya borrows my USB drive.

| EXERCISE 5 | USING TWO STEPS TO RECOGNIZE SENTENCE FRAGMENTS |

Some of the following are complete sentences; some are fragments. To recognize the fragments, check each group of words by using the two-step process:

Step 1: Check for a subject and a complete predicate.
Step 2: If you find a subject and a complete predicate, check that the group of words makes a complete statement.

After you've completed both steps, put an *S* beside the groups of words that are sentences and an *F* beside the ones that are fragments.

1. _____ The reason being a concern about an oil spill's environmental impact.

2. _____ As the prime minister approached the podium to give his speech.

3. _____ Protesters claim that any breach to an oil-carrying pipeline could devastate the surrounding environment.

4. _____ Alberta's oil sands, contributing billions of dollars to Canada's economy every year.

5. _____ Also providing many jobs.

6. _____ Some argue that a pipeline is a safer method of transport than rail.

7. _____ In Canada's oil sands, some Americans believe they have secured an oil source unaffected by political turmoil.

8. _____ Biggest trucks in the world used to transport the oil.

9. _____ Women preferred to drive them.

10. _____ The reason being that women are easier on the trucks.

11. _____ However, at the oil sands, many more men than women.

12. _____ Canadians moving west to find lucrative salaries.

13. _____ Need to create steam to extract the oil-sand mixture.

14. _____ Its creation also contributing to the greenhouse effect.

15. _____ For example, local flora and fauna to be affected.

16. _____ The oil spill at Lac-Mégantic.

17. _____ From coast to coast, this rail disaster has prompted inquiries into rail transport of oil and other hazardous materials.

18. _____ Tragically killed forty-seven people.

19. _____ In less than a decade, oil transports by rail have increased significantly.

20. _____ Safest tracks often running through residential areas, which have been built around the tracks.

CORRECTING FRAGMENTS

You can correct fragments easily if you follow the two steps for identifying them.

Step 1: Check for a subject and a complete predicate. Then, if a group of words is a fragment because it lacks a subject or a complete predicate, or both, *add what's missing*.

fragment: My father being a very strong person.

(This fragment lacks a main verb, since an *-ing* form by itself is not a main verb.)

corrected: My father is a very strong person.

(The verb *is* replaces the *-ing* form **being**.)

fragment: Doesn't care about the party. (This fragment lacks a subject.)

corrected: Alicia doesn't care about the party. (A subject, **Alicia**, is added.)

fragment: Especially on dark winter days. (This fragment has neither a subject nor a verb.)

corrected: I love hot chocolate, especially on dark winter days. (A subject, **I**, and a verb, **love**, are added.)

Step 2: If you find a subject and a verb, check that the group of words makes a complete statement. Then, to correct the fragment, (a) you can turn a dependent clause into an independent one by removing the subordinating conjunction, *or* (b) you can add an independent clause to the dependent one to create a statement that makes sense by itself.

fragment: When the rain beat against the windows. (The statement does not make sense by itself. The subordinating conjunction **when** leads the reader to ask, "What happened when the rain beat against the windows?" The subordinating conjunction makes this a dependent clause, not a sentence.)

corrected using (a): The rain beat against the windows. (Removing the subordinating conjunction makes this an independent clause, a sentence.)

corrected using (b): When the rain beat against the windows, I reconsidered my plans for the picnic. (Adding an independent clause turns this into something that makes sense.)

Note: Sometimes you can correct a fragment by linking it to the sentence before it or after it.

fragment (underlined):

I have always enjoyed outdoor concerts. <u>Like the ones at Pioneer Park.</u>

corrected:

I have always enjoyed outdoor concerts like the ones at Pioneer Park.

fragment (underlined): <u>Even if she apologizes for that nasty remark.</u> I will never trust her again.

corrected: Even if she apologizes for that nasty remark, I will never trust her again.

You have several options for correcting fragments: you can add words, phrases, or clauses; you can take words out; or you can combine independent and dependent clauses. You can transform fragments into simple sentences or create compound (see Chapter 14) or complex sentences (see Chapter 15). To punctuate your new sentences, remember the options for combining sentences (see the Infobox in Chapter 15, pages 361–362).

EXERCISE 6

CORRECTING FRAGMENTS

Correct each sentence fragment below in the most appropriate way.

1. It can be difficult to learn the finer points of grammar. Such as identifying comma splices, run-on sentences, and sentence fragments.

   corrected: _____

   _____

2. If you pay attention in class and do all the practice exercises. You will probably find it easier to identify grammatical errors.

   corrected: _____

   _____

3. Writing my draft at the last minute. I had the feeling I missed some details in my paragraph.

   corrected: _____

   _____

4. I find some of the elements of the essay difficult to write. Especially the conclusion.

   corrected: _____

   _____

5. Because the topic sentence is so important. Sometimes I get writer's block.

   corrected: _____

   _____

6. Brainstorming being the best way to overcome writer's block.

   corrected: _____

   _____

7. I have lots of ideas. Once I get started.

   corrected: _____

   _____

8. After taking four weeks of this course. I feel more confident organizing my ideas.

    corrected: _____

    _____

9. Students editing their writing. Write more effective paragraphs.

    corrected: _____

    _____

10. Effective writing important for success in college.

    corrected: _____

    _____

EXERCISE 7

MORE ABOUT CORRECTING FRAGMENTS

With a partner or a group, correct each fragment below in two ways. The first one is done for you.

1. Whenever I'm waiting for an important phone call.

    corrected: <u>I'm waiting for an important phone call.</u>

    corrected: <u>Whenever I'm waiting for an important phone call, I feel extremely impatient and anxious.</u>

2. Children have two months' summer vacation. While their parents still have to work.

    corrected: _____

    _____

    corrected: _____

    _____

3. When parents can't stay at home with the children. Parents often enrol the children in camps.

    corrected: _____

    _____

    corrected: _____

    _____

4. Camps being very expensive.

    corrected: _____

    _____

    corrected: _____

    _____

5. Although some experts are recommending year-round schooling. Others say that long summer vacations are the basis for fond childhood memories.

   corrected: _____

   _____

   corrected: _____

   _____

6. Many children forgetting most of what they learned at school.

   corrected: _____

   corrected: _____

   _____

7. In North America, where there are fewer and fewer full-time summer jobs.

   corrected: _____

   _____

   corrected: _____

   _____

8. Because students get bored over a long summer break.

   corrected: _____

   _____

   corrected: _____

   _____

9. Critics don't like the idea of school during the summer. As most schools are not air-conditioned.

   corrected: _____

   _____

   corrected: _____

   _____

10. While students do better with shorter and more frequent breaks. Teachers fare better, too.

   corrected: _____

   _____

   corrected: _____

   _____

EXERCISE **8**	EDITING A PARAGRAPH FOR SENTENCE FRAGMENTS

Correct the sentence fragments in the following paragraph. There are six fragments.

Nick would love to meet a celebrity. Like a famous athlete. He sees these celebrities on television. Where they drive expensive cars and wear wild clothes. They seem to have it all. Talent, looks, money, and fame. These things all appear to come easily to celebrities. They can live anywhere they want and buy anything they desire. These famous people filling Nick's dreams. To talk to one basketball or music star and get the person's autograph. Being close to a celebrity would make Nick feel important. Since Nick is only six years old. He has plenty of time to find other dreams.

CHAPTER 18
Using Parallelism in Sentences

Parallelism means balance in a sentence. To create sentences with parallelism, remember this rule:

Similar points should be written with a similar structure.

In your writing, you'll likely often include two or three (or more) related ideas, examples, or details in one sentence. If you express these ideas in a parallel structure, they will be clearer, smoother, and more convincing. Speechwriters, for instance, frequently use parallel structure for a more powerful and memorable impact. Here are three well-known examples of parallel structure:

- "Veni, vidi, vici." ("I came, I saw, I conquered.") ~ *Julius Caesar*
- "If some countries have too much history, we have too much geography." ~ *William Lyon Mackenzie King*
- "It was the best of times, it was the worst of times." ~ *Charles Dickens*

Here are some pairs of sentences with and without parallelism:

> **not parallel:** Of all the sports I've played, I prefer tennis, handball, and playing golf.
>
> **parallel:** Of all the sports I've played, I prefer **tennis, handball, and golf**. (Three words are parallel.)
>
> **not parallel:** If you're searching for the car keys, you should look under the table, the kitchen counter, and they might be behind the refrigerator.
>
> **parallel:** If you're searching for the car keys, you should look **under the table, on the kitchen counter, and behind the refrigerator**. (Three prepositional phrases are parallel.)
>
> **not parallel:** He's a good choice for manager because he works hard, he keeps calm, and well-liked.
>
> **parallel:** He's a good choice for manager because **he works hard, he keeps calm, and he's well-liked**. (Three clauses are parallel.)

From these examples you can see that parallelism involves matching the structures of parts of your sentence.

ACHIEVING PARALLELISM

There are two steps that can help you check your writing for parallelism, as shown in the following Infobox.

INFOBOX	TWO STEPS IN CHECKING A SENTENCE FOR PARALLEL STRUCTURE

Step 1: Look for the list in the sentence.
Step 2: Put the parts of the list into a similar structure.

(You may have to change or add something to get a parallel structure.)

Let's correct the faulty parallelism of the following sentence:

> **sample sentence:** The committee for neighbourhood safety met to set up a schedule for patrols, coordinating teams of volunteers, and also for the purpose of creating new rules.

To correct this sentence, we'll follow the steps.

Step 1:   Look for the list. The committee met to do three things:

1. to set up a schedule for patrols
2. coordinating teams of volunteers
3. for the purpose of creating new rules

Step 2:   Put the parts of the list into a similar structure:

1. *to set up* **a schedule for patrols**
2. *to coordinate* **teams of volunteers**
3. *to create* **new rules**

Now revise to get a parallel sentence.

> **parallel:** The committee for neighbourhood safety met **to set up** a schedule for patrols, **to coordinate** teams of volunteers, and **to create** new rules.

When writing a parallel list with an infinitive (*to* plus the verb), either use *to* with every item in the list (*to* set up . . . *to* coordinate . . . and *to* create) or use it just once at the beginning of the list (*to* set up . . . coordinate . . . and create). Don't write an unbalanced list (*to* set up . . . coordinate . . . and *to* create).

Caution: Sometimes making ideas parallel means adding something to a sentence because all the parts of the list can't match exactly.

> **sample sentence:** In his pocket the little boy had a ruler, rubber band, baseball card, and apple.

Step 1: Look for the list.

In his pocket the little boy had a

1. ruler
2. rubber band
3. baseball card
4. apple

As the sentence is written, the *a* goes with *a ruler, a rubber band, a baseball card*, and *a apple*. But *a* isn't the right word to put in front of *apple*. Words beginning with vowels (a, e, i, o, u) need *an* in front of them: *an apple*. So to make the sentence parallel, you have to change something in the sentence.

Step 2: Put the parts of the list into a parallel structure.

parallel: In his pocket the little boy had **a ruler, a rubber band, a baseball card**, and **an apple**.

Here's another example:

sample sentence: She was amused and interested in the silly plot of the movie.

Step 1: Look for the list.

She was

1. amused
2. interested in

the silly plot of the movie.

Check the sense of this sentence by looking at each part of the list and determining how it's working in the sentence: "She was *interested in* the silly plot of the movie." That part of the list seems clear. But "She was *amused* the silly plot of the movie"? Or "She was *amused in* the silly plot of the movie"? Neither sentence is right. People are not *amused in*.

Step 2: Put the parts of the list into a parallel structure. In this case, the sentence needs a word added to make the structure parallel.

parallel: She was **amused by** and **interested in** the silly plot of the movie.

Sometimes, the clauses in a compound or complex sentence are not written in a parallel structure. You may need to change the subject of one of the clauses or reorder the words in the sentence so that the clauses are parallel:

sample sentence: Adarsh carried three books in his knapsack; **Lael's knapsack held** five.

parallel: Adarsh carried three books in his knapsack; **Lael carried** five in hers.

sample sentence: Before **you write** an essay, **research needs** to be done.

parallel: Before **you write** an essay, **you need** to do research.

When you follow the two steps to check for parallelism, you can write clear sentences and improve your style.

EXERCISE

1

REVISING SENTENCES FOR PARALLELISM

Some of the following sentences need to be revised so that they have parallel structures. Revise the ones that need parallelism. Write C for the sentences that are already correct.

1. The workday begins at 9:00 a.m.; at 5:00 p.m. is when it ends.

   revised: _____

   _____

2. The restaurant is very popular, noisy, and has crowds.

   revised: _____

   _____

3. My workday is so busy with activities that I have to shop for groceries, washing and ironing my clothes, and clean my room at night.

   revised: _____

   _____

4. You can get to the carnival by chartered bus or by special train.

   revised: _____

   _____

5. He's a player with great energy and who is ambitious.

   revised: _____

   _____

6. When we meet tomorrow, I'd like to discuss your job description, explaining your health benefits, and a description of the package of retirement options you will have.

   revised: _____

   _____

7. The location of the house, its size, and how much it cost made it the best choice for the family.

   revised: _____

   _____

8. Going to college isn't the same as when you go to high school.

   revised: _____

   _____

9. Job interviews are stressful because you have to dress professionally, answering questions, and you must show you're the best person for the job.

   revised: _____

   _____

10. Ramona would rather sew her own wedding gown than paying a fortune to buy one.

    revised: _____

    _____

EXERCISE 2

WRITING SENTENCES WITH PARALLELISM

With a partner or with a group, complete each sentence. Begin by brainstorming a draft list; then revise the list for parallelism. Finally, complete the sentence in parallel structure. (Note: A colon isn't necessary before the list of items in the sentences in this exercise; see Chapter 25 on the correct use of a colon.) You may want to assign one task (brainstorming a draft list, revising it, etc.) to each group member, then switch tasks on the next sentence. The first one is done for you:

1. Three habits I'd like to break are

   draft list: **revised list:**

   a. worry too much   a. worrying too much
   b. talking on the phone for hours   b. talking on the phone for hours
   c. lose my temper   c. losing my temper

   sentence: Three habits I'd like to break are worrying too much, talking on the phone for hours, and losing my temper.

2. Three ways to look for a job are

   draft list: **revised list:**

   a. _____   a. _____
   b. _____   b. _____
   c. _____   c. _____

   sentence: _____

3. Three reasons to volunteer are

   draft list: **revised list:**

   a. _____   a. _____
   b. _____   b. _____
   c. _____   c. _____

   sentence: _____

4. Three irritations in my daily life are

   draft list: **revised list:**

   a. _____   a. _____
   b. _____   b. _____
   c. _____   c. _____

   sentence: _____

5. Exercise is good for you because [add three reasons]

   draft list: **revised list:**

   a. _____   a. _____
   b. _____   b. _____
   c. _____   c. _____

sentence: _____

_____

6. Getting enough sleep is important because [add three reasons]

draft list: revised list:

a. _____   a. _____

b. _____   b. _____

c. _____   c. _____

sentence: _____

_____

7. Five years from now, I want to [add two goals]

draft list: revised list:

a. _____   a. _____

b. _____   b. _____

sentence: _____

_____

8. Travelling can be stressful because [add three reasons]

draft list: revised list:

a. _____   a. _____

b. _____   b. _____

c. _____   c. _____

sentence: _____

_____

9. I am most carefree when [add two times or occasions]

draft list: revised list:

a. _____   a. _____

b. _____   b. _____

sentence: _____

_____

10. Three characteristics of a good parent are

draft list: revised list:

a. _____   a. _____

b. _____   b. _____

c. _____   c. _____

sentence: _____

_____

11. Three experiences most people dread are

draft list:	revised list:
a. _____	a. _____
b. _____	b. _____
c. _____	c. _____

sentence: _____

_____

EXERCISE 3

COMBINING SENTENCES AND CREATING A PARALLEL STRUCTURE

Combine each of the following clusters of sentences into one clear, smooth sentence. The first one is done for you:

1. Before you buy a used car, you should research what similar models are selling for.

   It would be a good idea to have a mechanic examine the car.

   Also, how much mileage it has racked up is a consideration.

   combination: _Before you buy a used car, you should compare prices of similar models, get a mechanic to examine the car, and think carefully about the mileage._

2. The service at Cyber Barn was excellent.

   The sales representative was patient and friendly.

   The fact that there was a full three-year warranty on my tablet was a bonus, too.

   combination: _____

   _____

3. If you want to lose weight, you should limit the amount of fat in your diet.

   Cutting back on junk food is also a good idea.

   Regular exercise is important, too.

   combination: _____

   _____

4. Business people advertise by computer.

   Children use computers to play video games.

   Computers are used by teachers to communicate outside of class time.

   combination: _____

   _____

5. She was a dynamic professor.

 She had energy.

 She had enthusiasm.

 combination: _____

 _____

6. As a friend, he was extremely loyal.

 As a friend, he also told the truth.

 He was also a compassionate friend.

 combination: _____

 _____

7. Richard joined the conversation club.

 Richard spoke with other members three times a week.

 Richard's pronunciation improved significantly.

 combination: _____

 _____

8. The demonstrators came from small towns.

 The demonstrators came from major cities.

 The demonstrators came from farms.

 The demonstrators came from factories.

 The demonstrators came to express their concern about the environment.

 combination: _____

 _____

9. People crowded the entrances to the electronics store.

 They hoped to be the first inside the store.

 Their goal was to find a bargain at the sale.

 combination: _____

 _____

10. The city was well-planned.

 It had wide sidewalks.

 It had many mixed-use areas.

 It had lots of community centres.

 The city was a welcoming place to live.

 combination: _____

 _____

11. People don't interact face to face anymore.
    They prefer to communicate through social media.

    Texting is another method people like.

    Email is still common.

    combination: _____

    _____

12. The federal government should provide more funding to the arts.
    An appreciation of the arts can build a sense of community.

    Exposure to the arts encourages children to become more flexible thinkers.

    More independent local artists are supported.

    combination: _____

    _____

EXERCISE 4	EDITING A PARAGRAPH FOR ERRORS IN PARALLELISM

Correct any errors in parallelism in the following paragraph. There are six errors.

I can't understand why my brother is a big baseball fan; I think the game is slow, causes me to get bored, and it's outdated. My brother always drags me to baseball games where he pays close attention to every minute of the game. Meanwhile, I'm waiting for the action to begin. I can see only players standing around the field, talking to each other, chew gum, or they spit tobacco juice. I don't see why this behaviour is exciting. In addition, there are the boring moments when the game seems to stop completely. Then the coaches or the umpire or the players seem to be having a conference on the field. These little talks seem endless. My last complaint is about the atmosphere of a ball game. Even the big, nationally televised games seem old-fashioned. The games feature the same kinds of uniforms, music playing, and fans as a baseball game in a fifty-year-old movie. While my brother enjoys this slow, traditional game, I want the action, excitement, and sense of aggression of modern hockey or basketball.

CHAPTER 19
Correcting Problems with Modifiers

Modifiers are words, phrases, or clauses that describe or *modify* something in a sentence. The following words, phrases, and clauses that appear in bold are modifiers.

the **blue** van (word)

the van **in the garage** (phrase)

the van **that she bought** (clause)

foreign tourists (word)

tourists **coming to Charlottetown** (phrase)

Coming to Charlottetown, tourists . . . (phrase)

To meet friends, she . . . (phrase)

tourists **who visit the province** (clause)

Modifiers limit another word (or words) and make it more specific.

the girl **in the corner** (tells exactly which girl)

fifty metres (tells exactly how many metres)

the movie **that I liked best** (tells which movie)

He **never** calls. (tells how often)

EXERCISE	RECOGNIZING MODIFIERS
1	

In each of the following sentences, underline the modifiers (words, phrases, or clauses) that describe the italicized word or phrase.

1. *The movie* about global warming won an Academy Award.
2. *The community* fighting the building of the garbage-burning plant won a reprieve.
3. *The companies* that responded to market conditions survived the recession.
4. *The final exam*, which was worth 30 percent of the overall mark, was very challenging.
5. Julie and Sabina always complete their weekly *labs*.
6. To learn a new trade, *my father* enrolled in college.
7. Hoping to attract more international students, *the community college* set up an information booth.
8. The multinational corporation drew criticism for its *treatment* of its employees.
9. Staying up late at night, *the* exhausted *student* finally finished his assignment.
10. The tired, outdated *campus*, with its peeling paint and water-stained walls, was finally renovated.

CORRECTING MODIFIER PROBLEMS

Modifiers can make your writing more specific and more concrete. Used effectively, modifiers give the reader a clear, exact picture of what you want to say. But modifiers have to be used correctly. You can check for errors with modifiers as you revise your sentences.

INFOBOX	THREE STEPS IN CHECKING FOR SENTENCE ERRORS WITH MODIFIERS

Step 1: Find the modifier.
Step 2: Ask, "Does the modifier have something to modify?"
Step 3: Ask, "Is the modifier in the right place, as close as possible to the word, phrase, or clause it modifies?"

If you answer *No* to either Step 2 or Step 3, you need to revise your sentence.

Correcting Misplaced Modifiers

Let's use the steps in the following example.

sample sentence: I saw a woman driving a Porsche texting on a cellphone.

Step 1: Find the modifier. The modifiers are *driving a Porsche* and *texting on a cellphone*.

Step 2: Ask, "Does the modifier have something to modify?" The answer is *yes*. A woman is driving a Porsche. A woman is texting on a cellphone. Both modifiers go with *a woman*.

Step 3: Ask, "Is the modifier in the right place?" The answer is *yes* and *no*. One modifier is in the right place:

I saw **a woman driving a Porsche**

The other modifier is not in the right place:

a Porsche texting on a cellphone

The Porsche is not texting on a cellphone.

revised: I saw a woman texting on a cellphone while driving a Porsche.

Let's work through the steps once more:

sample sentence: Hurriedly taking orders, the diners motioned to the harried server.

Step 1: Find the modifier. The modifiers are *hurriedly taking orders* and *harried*.

Step 2: Ask, "Does the modifier have something to modify?" The answer is *yes*. There is the *harried server*. The *harried server* is *hurriedly taking orders*. Both modifiers go with *server*.

Step 3: Ask, "Is the modifier in the right place?" The answer is *yes* and *no*. The word *harried* is in the right place:

harried server

But *Hurriedly taking orders* is in the wrong place:

Hurriedly taking orders, the diners

The diners are not hurriedly taking orders. The server is.

revised: The diners motioned to the harried server **hurriedly taking orders.**

Caution: Make sure to put words like *almost, even, exactly, hardly, just, merely, nearly, only, scarcely,* and *simply* as close as possible to what they modify. If you put them in the wrong place, you may write a confusing sentence.

sample sentence: Etienne **only wants** to grow carrots and zucchini.

The modifier that creates confusion here is *only.* Does Etienne have only one goal in life—to grow carrots and zucchini? Or are these the *only* vegetables that he wants to grow? To create a clearer sentence, move the modifier.

possible revision: Etienne wants **only to grow** carrots and zucchini.

This could still be confusing. Does Etienne want only *to grow* the carrots and zucchini but not to harvest them, market them, etc.?

further revision (and probably most accurate): Etienne wants to grow **only carrots and zucchini.**

The examples you've just worked through show one common error in using modifiers. This error involves **misplaced modifiers**, words that describe something but are not where they should be in the sentence. Here's the rule to remember:

Put the modifier as close as possible to the word, phrase, or clause it modifies.

EXERCISE **2**	**CORRECTING SENTENCES WITH MISPLACED MODIFIERS**

Some of the following sentences contain misplaced modifiers. Revise any sentence that has a misplaced modifier by putting the modifier as close as possible to whatever it modifies. Write C beside any sentences that are already correct.

1. Falling from the top of my refrigerator, I saw my best glass dish.

   revised: _____

   _____

2. When the manager offered her the job, the candidate was ready to nearly jump for joy.

   revised: _____

   _____

3. When I prepare my résumé, I only want to include my most relevant work experience.

   revised: _____

   _____

4. Packed to capacity, we entered the college parking lot.

    revised: _____

    _____

5. The doctor gave the prescription for sedatives to the nervous patient.

    revised: _____

    _____

6. When he starts college next fall, he wants to take only business courses.

    revised: _____

    _____

7. Cracked in two places, she was sure the window would have to be replaced.

    revised: _____

    _____

8. Using negative radio advertisements, voters don't like the political party.

    revised: _____

    _____

9. Haunted by the looming deadline, the project was completed at the last minute.

    revised: _____

    _____

10. Flailing wildly, Jim avoided the downed electrical wire.

    revised: _____

    _____

Correcting Dangling Modifiers

The three steps for correcting modifier problems can help you recognize another kind of error. For example, let's use the steps to check the following sentence.

> **sample sentence:** Strolling through the tropical paradise, many colourful birds could be seen.

> **Step 1:** Find the modifier. The modifiers are *Strolling through the tropical paradise* and *many colourful.*

> **Step 2:** Ask, "Does the modifier have something to modify?" The answer is *yes* and *no.* The words *many* and *colourful* modify *birds.* But who or what is *Strolling through the tropical paradise*? There is no person mentioned in this sentence. The birds aren't strolling.

This kind of error is called a **dangling modifier**. It means that the modifier doesn't have anything to modify; it just dangles in the sentence. To correct this kind of error, you can't just move the modifier:

> **still incorrect:** Many colourful birds could be seen strolling through the tropical paradise.

(There is still no person strolling.)

The way to correct this kind of error is to add something to the sentence. If you gave the modifier something to modify (let's use *the tourists*), you might come up with several different revised sentences:

> **Strolling through the tropical paradise, the tourists** could see many colourful birds.

(Keep the structure of the sentence the same as in the sample, but add the appropriate words *the tourists* to the sentence in the subject position.)

or

> **The tourists strolling through the tropical paradise** could see many colourful birds.

(Move the phrase *strolling through the tropical paradise* so that it's clearly modifying *tourists*.)

or

> **As the tourists were strolling through the tropical paradise,** many colourful birds could be seen.

(Change the phrase *strolling through the tropical paradise* to a dependent clause with its own subject; then the subject of the independent clause [*many colourful birds*] can remain the same.)

or (better)

> **As the tourists were strolling through the tropical paradise, they** could see many colourful birds.

(Avoid the wordier passive structure [see Chapter 21, pages 421–423] of *many colourful birds could be seen.*)

or

> Many colourful birds could be seen **as the tourists were strolling through the tropical paradise**.

(As in the previous revision, change the phrase *strolling through the tropical paradise* to a dependent clause; then place it at the end of the sentence.)

Be careful with this revision:

> The **tourists** could see many colourful birds **as they were strolling through the tropical paradise**.

(This one could create a pronoun reference problem because *they* in the second clause of the sentence could refer to either tourists or birds.)

Try the process for correcting dangling modifiers once more:

> **sample sentence:** Ascending in the glass elevator, her eyes needed to be closed because of her terrible fear of heights.

Step 1: Find the modifier. The modifiers are *Ascending in the glass elevator* and *terrible*.

Step 2: Ask, "Does the modifier have anything to modify?" The answer is *yes*—*terrible* modifies *fear*, and *no*—*Ascending in the glass elevator* doesn't modify anything. Who or what is ascending in the elevator? *Her eyes* are mentioned, but not the person herself. To revise this sentence, put somebody or something in the sentence for the modifier to describe.

revised sentences: **Ascending in the glass elevator, the guest needed** to close her eyes because of her terrible fear of heights.

or

As the guest ascended in the glass elevator, she needed to close her eyes because of her terrible fear of heights.

Remember that you can't correct a dangling modifier just by moving the modifier. You have to give the modifier something to modify; you have to add something to the sentence.

EXERCISE **3**	CORRECTING SENTENCES WITH DANGLING MODIFIERS

Some of the following sentences use modifiers correctly. Some sentences have dangling modifiers. Revise the sentences with dangling modifiers. To revise, you'll have to add and change words. Write *C* beside the sentences that are already correct.

1. Racing across the station, the train was reached before the doors closed.

   revised: _____

   _____

2. Breaking into the house at night, the homeowners lost their most valuable possessions.

   revised: _____

   _____

3. At the age of five, my family moved to Regina.

   revised: _____

   _____

4. Lost in the fog, the lighthouse could not be seen.

   revised: _____

   _____

5. Stumbling across the finish line, the runner gasped for breath.

   revised: _____

   _____

6. When taking the geometry exam, an argument between the teacher and a student began.

   revised: _____

   _____

7. While mowing the lawn, a wasp stung him.

   revised: _____

   _____

8. Tired and irritable, the workday seemed endless.

   revised: _____

   _____

9. Visiting Mexico for the first time, I thought the country was strange and exciting.

   revised: _____

   _____

10. To enter that contest, an entry fee of $50 is needed.

    revised: _____

    _____

REVIEWING THE STEPS AND THE SOLUTIONS

It's important to recognize problems with modifiers and to correct these problems. Modifier problems can result in confusing or even silly sentences. And when you confuse or unintentionally amuse your reader, you're not making your point.

Remember to check for modifier problems by using three steps, and to correct each kind of problem in the appropriate way.

INFOBOX	A SUMMARY OF MODIFIER PROBLEMS

Checking for Modifier Problems

Step 1: Find the modifier.
Step 2: Ask, "Does the modifier have something to modify?"
Step 3: Ask, "Is the modifier in the right place?"

Correcting Modifier Problems

* If a modifier is in the wrong place (a misplaced modifier), put it as close as possible to the word, phrase, or clause it modifies.
* If a modifier has nothing to modify (a dangling modifier), add or change words so that it has something to modify.

REVISING SENTENCES WITH MODIFIER PROBLEMS

Each of the following sentences has some kind of modifier problem. Write a new, correct sentence for each one. You can move words, add words, change words, or remove words. The first one is done for you.

1. Stopping suddenly, the box with the cake in it fell from the seat of the car.

   revised: When I had to stop suddenly, the box with the cake in it fell from the seat of the car.

2. Without a trace of bitterness, the argument between the neighbours was settled.

   revised: _____

   _____

3. Staring into space, the teacher scolded the student.

   revised: _____

   _____

4. After considering the alternatives, a compromise was reached by the two sides.

   revised: _____

   _____

5. After drag racing down the street until 3:00 a.m., the neighbours decided to complain to the teenagers' parents.

   revised: _____

   _____

6. Shivering from the cold, the winter took its toll on the homeless man.

   revised: _____

   _____

7. Susan nearly missed all the multiple-choice questions on the test.

   revised: _____

   _____

8. Taking every precaution, safety was a priority at the machining shop.

   revised: _____

   _____

9. To make friends at school, an outgoing personality is necessary.

   revised: _____

   _____

10. When packing a suitcase for a trip, a little ingenuity and planning go a long way.

revised: _____

_____

EXERCISE 5

EDITING A PARAGRAPH FOR MODIFIER PROBLEMS

Correct any errors in modifiers in the following paragraph. There are four errors. Write your corrections above the lines.

When entering a new school, it's difficult to make new friends. If the school is a college, the process can be especially hard. Colleges have students of all ages, and new students may think they can only see a few people of their own age. Everyone else may look much younger or older. College also seems to be a more serious place than high school, so students may feel shy about starting a conversation. Standing alone in the hall before class, nervousness paralyzes a newcomer. It may seem as if everyone else has a close friend to talk to. Then, when the newcomer starts to meet one or two people, another problem arises. A new student may hesitate before giving a phone number or email address to a classmate, fearing too much intimacy too soon. Fortunately, time passes, and new students become a part of school and of new friendships.

MyWritingLab

Go to MyWritingLab to access a diagnostic test that creates your own personalized learning path supported by rich multimedia resources and a variety of animated tutorials, all aimed at helping you improve your writing. MyWritingLab also includes a complete eText version of the book that is fully searchable and accessible through your web browser or most mobile devices.

CHAPTER 20
Using Verbs Correctly

USING STANDARD VERB FORMS

Many people use non-standard verb forms in everyday conversation. But everyone who wants to write and speak effectively should know the difference between the slang and dialect you might hear in everyday conversation and the **standard English** of college, business, and professional environments.

In everyday conversation, you might hear non-standard forms like

I goes	he don't	we was
you was	it don't	she smile
you be	I be	they walks

But these are not correct forms in standard English.

Verbs are words that show some kind of action or being. These verbs show action.

>   verb
> He **runs** to the park.

>   verb
> Ashraf **tastes** the pizza.

These verbs show being.

>   verb
> Melanie **is** my best friend.

>   verb
> The pizza **tastes** delicious.

(The verb *tastes* in this sentence shows "being" rather than action because the pizza isn't actually tasting something. Instead, the verb is used in this sentence to describe the pizza's condition.)

Verbs also describe when something takes place (time).

> He **will run** to the park. (The time is future.)

> Melanie **was** my best friend. (The time is past.)

> The pizza **tastes** delicious. (The time is present.)

The time of a verb is called its *tense*. You can say that a verb is in the *future tense*, the *past tense*, the *present tense*, or many other tenses.

Using verbs correctly involves knowing which form of the verb to use, choosing the right verb tense, and being consistent in verb tense.

THE PRESENT TENSE

Look at the standard verb forms for the **present tense** of *to listen*.

verb: to listen

I listen	we listen
you listen	you listen
he, she, it listens	they listen

Take a closer look at the standard verb forms. Only one form is different:

he, she, it *listens*

This is the only form that ends in *s* in the present tense.

INFOBOX	PRESENT TENSE ENDINGS

In the present tense, use an *s* or *es* ending on the verb only when the subject is *he*, *she*, or *it*, or the equivalent of *he*, *she*, or *it*.

Notice how the *s* is used at the end of the verb forms in each of the following examples because the subject is *he*, *she*, or *it* or the equivalent:

He calls his mother every day.

She watches television after she puts her children to bed.

It runs like a new car.

Lane calls his mother every day.

Jie watches television after she puts her children to bed.

The jalopy runs like a new car.

Take another look at the present tense. If the verb is a regular verb, it will follow this form in the present tense:

I attend every lecture.

You care about the truth.

He visits his grandfather regularly.

She drives a new car.

The new album sounds great.

We follow that team.

You work well when you both compromise.

They buy the store brand of cereal.

In the list above, the only forms that end in *s* are those used with *he*, *she*, and *the new album* (the equivalent of *it*).

EXERCISE	CHOOSING THE RIGHT VERB IN THE PRESENT TENSE
1	

Underline the subject and circle the correct verb form in parentheses in each of the following sentences.

1. Underemployment (seem/seems) to be a growing concern in Canada.

2. Many people (work/works) at part-time jobs or for minimum wage.

3. Almost three-quarters of new jobs (fall/falls) into this category.

4. The prospect of providing for a family on minimum wage rightly (frighten/frightens) many people.

5. Sometimes people (travel/travels) to other provinces in search of better wages.

6. Underemployment numbers for young people (show/shows) a percentage double that of the general population.

7. Over and above the challenges presented by underemployment (stand/ stands) the federal government's position on job creation.

8. With few job prospects, some recent graduates (choose/chooses) to go back to school.

9. High student debt and low income (contribute/contributes) to a delay.

10. It (seem/seems) like a good idea.

EXERCISE **2**	**MORE ABOUT CHOOSING THE RIGHT VERB IN THE PRESENT TENSE**

Underline the subject and circle the correct verb form in parentheses in each sentence below.

1. On warm days, our neighbour (relax/relaxes) on the patio.

2. You (talk/talks) about yourself too much.

3. The chief of detectives (drive/drives) an unmarked car.

4. A clean workspace (make/makes) a good impression.

5. Behind the factories (sit/sits) a small stone house.

6. Some of my friends (post/posts) every day on Facebook.

7. Every Saturday night, they (rent/rents) an old horror movie.

8. Humour (get/gets) people through tough situations.

9. A representative of the student government (attend/attends) the conference.

10. At that price, it (sound/sounds) like a bargain.

THE PAST TENSE

The **past tense** of most verbs is formed by adding *d* or *ed* to the verb.
verb: to listen

I listened	we listened
you listened	you listened
he, she, it listened	they listened

Add *ed* to *listen* to form the past tense. For some verbs that already end in *e*, you will add just *d*:

The sun **faded** from the sky.

He **quaked** with fear.

She **crumpled** the paper into a ball.

EXERCISE 3

WRITING THE CORRECT FORM OF THE PAST TENSE

Write *d* or *ed* in the blank to create the correct past-tense form of each verb in parentheses in the sentences below.

1. Last week, he and I (remove__) the stain from the counter.
2. The coach in high school (warn__) some players to pay attention to the game.
3. As a child, I (perform__) in an annual piano recital.
4. After doing some research into the company, I (reject__) its offer of a job.
5. Last night, we (compromise__) on the issue of whether to fix the furnace or the roof.
6. Yesterday, Christine (call__) me about driving to the party.
7. Reporters at the scene of last night's train accident (interview__) a witness.
8. Years ago, Arnold and Bruce (start__) a climb to success in Hollywood.
9. The girl at the desk (wave__) at me.
10. You (waste__) too much time on it yesterday.

THE FOUR MAIN VERB FORMS: PRESENT, PAST, PRESENT PARTICIPLE, AND PAST PARTICIPLE

When you're deciding what form of a verb to use, you'll probably rely on one of four forms: the present tense, the past tense, the present participle, or the past participle. Most of the time, you will use one of these forms or add a helping verb to it. As an example, look at the four main forms of the verb *to listen*.

Present	Past	Present Participle	Past Participle
listen	listened	listening	listened

When a verb is regular, like *fade* or *listen*, the past form is created by adding *d* or *ed* to the present form. The present participle is formed by adding *ing* to the present form, and the past participle is the same as the past form.

You use the four verb forms—present, past, present participle, past participle—alone or with helping verbs to express time (tense). They're very easy to remember when a verb is a **regular verb**, like *listen*. Use the present form for the present tense:

> We **listen** to the news on the radio.

The past form expresses past tense:

> I **listened** to language tapes for three hours yesterday.

The present participle, or *-ing* form, is used with helping verbs:

> I **am listening** to you.
>
> He **was listening** to me.
>
> You **should have been listening** more carefully.

Notice from the above examples that the *-ing* form plus helping verb(s) can be used to discuss events in the present, in the past, or in other situations.

The past participle of regular verbs is the *-d* or *-ed* form used with helping verbs:

I **have listened** for hours.

She **has listened** to the tape.

We **could have listened** to the tape before we bought it.

Of course, you can also add many helping verbs to the present tense:

present tense:

We **listen** to the news on the car radio.

add helping verbs:

We **will** listen to the news on the car radio.

We **should** listen to the news on the car radio.

We **can** listen to the news on the car radio.

INFOBOX	FREQUENTLY USED HELPING VERBS		
am	do	might	was
are	have	must	were
can	is	shall	will
could	may	should	would

IRREGULAR VERBS

The Present Tense of *Be, Have,* and *Do*

Irregular verbs don't follow the same rules for creating verb forms that regular verbs do. Three verbs that we use all the time—*be, have,* and *do*—are irregular verbs. You need to study them closely. Look at the present-tense forms for all three, and compare the standard present-tense forms to the non-standard ones you might hear in everyday conversation. *Remember always to use the standard forms when speaking or writing in college, business, and professional environments.*

verb: to be

Non-standard	Standard
I be or I is	I am
you be	you are
he, she, it be	he, she, it is
we be	we are
you be	you are
they be	they are

verb: to have

Non-standard	Standard
I has	I have
you has	you have
he, she, it have	he, she, it has
we has	we have
you has	you have
they has	they have

verb: to do

Non-standard	Standard
I does	I do
you does	you do
he, she, it do	he, she, it does
we does	we do
you does	you do
they does	they do

Caution: Be careful when you add *not* to *does*. If you're writing a contraction of *does not*, be sure you write *doesn't* instead of *don't*.

not this: The light don't work.

but this: The light doesn't work.

EXERCISE 4

CHOOSING THE CORRECT FORM OF *BE, HAVE,* OR *DO* IN THE PRESENT TENSE

Circle the correct form of the verb in parentheses in each sentence below.

1. Two of the salespeople (is/are/am) meeting at the branch office.
2. I'm sure the dancers (has/have) the ability to reach the top.
3. My mother (don't/doesn't) need another set of earrings for her birthday.
4. The winner of the contest (do/does) whatever he wants with the money.
5. Without an excuse, he (has/have) no choice but to apologize.
6. Every weekend, I (do/does) the laundry for the whole family.
7. The musicians (has/have) a huge bus equipped for travelling long distances.
8. I (is/am/are) very embarrassed.
9. They know he (do/does) his exercises early in the morning.
10. Amin and Lee (be/are/is) coming over in half an hour.

EXERCISE 5

MORE ABOUT CHOOSING THE CORRECT FORM OF *BE, HAVE,* OR *DO* IN THE PRESENT TENSE

Circle the correct form of the verb in parentheses in each sentence below.

1. Consequently, her son (do/does) nothing about the arguments.
2. Today, I (be/am/is) the youngest member of the cricket team.
3. Lamont (has/have) nothing but praise for his boss.
4. Regular exercise is important; it (do/does) affect your health.
5. Even though you pretend to be carefree, you (do/does) too much worrying.
6. Most of the time, a paperback book (don't/doesn't) cost as much as a hardcover book.
7. At New Year's, we (has/have) a traditional meal.
8. My shifts (be/are/is) too long; I never have enough time to see my friends.
9. The new gym (has/have) great air conditioning.
10. If you (has/have) a student ID, you can get a discount.

The Past Tense of *Be, Have,* and *Do*

The past-tense forms of these irregular verbs can be confusing. Again, compare the non-standard forms to the standard forms. *Remember to always use the standard forms when speaking or writing in college, business, and professional environments.*

verb: to be

Non-standard	Standard
I were	I was
you was	you were
he, she, it were	he, she, it was
we was	we were
you was	you were
they was	they were

verb: to have

Non-standard	Standard
I has	I had
you has	you had
he, she, it have	he, she, it had
we has	we had
you has	you had
they has	they had

verb: to do

Non-standard	Standard
I done	I did
you done	you did
he, she, it done	he, she, it did
we done	we did
you done	you did
they done	they did

In college and professional writing, you sometimes need to express doubtful ideas or unproven facts. For example,

> Manpreet eats very little. (expresses a fact)
>
> **If she were** fat, she could easily lose weight. (expresses an idea that is not necessarily true)
>
> I am already two hours late for the class. (expresses a fact)
>
> **If I were** two minutes earlier, I could catch the 7:42 train to Union Station.

(expresses an idea that is possible but not probable)

Note that the verb tenses *she were* and *I were* appear to be non-standard English. However, the choices are correct *if you wish to show a doubtful condition.*

EXERCISE 6

CHOOSING THE CORRECT FORM OF *BE, HAVE,* OR *DO* IN THE PAST TENSE

Circle the correct verb form in parentheses in each sentence.

1. The people next door (was/were) mysterious in their habits.

2. Last night, Alonzo (done/did) the decorating for the Grey Cup party.
3. In spite of the rain, the club (had/have) a large turnout for the picnic.
4. Three hours after the deadline, we (was/were) still busy.
5. Yesterday, at that intersection, I (had/have) a minor car accident.
6. As a little girl, Shireen (was/were) quiet and shy around strangers.
7. Believing in helping others, the volunteers (done/did) a good deed for two lost people.
8. I (was/were) unhappy with the grade on my math test.
9. Two years ago, you (was/were) the most valuable player on the team.
10. Her class in music appreciation (done/did) the most to interest her in music.

EXERCISE 7

MORE ABOUT CHOOSING THE CORRECT FORM OF *BE*, *HAVE*, OR *DO* IN THE PAST TENSE

Circle the correct verb form in parentheses in each sentence below.

1. Lorenzo and I (was/were) once clerks at the same bank.
2. Last winter, my sister (had/have) an encounter with a black bear.
3. I learned Portuguese when I (was/were) a student in Brazil.
4. Brendan (done/did) what he could to help his parents find a place to live.
5. We (was/were) minding our own business when the robbery occurred.
6. Last month, my cousin Raj (had/have) a job interview with the parks department.
7. Yesterday, you and I (was/were) calm and confident.
8. After the car accident, Monica (had/have) to fill out a statement for the police.
9. I have the evening free because I (done/did) the laundry and the ironing yesterday.
10. The student lounge at the college (had/have) comfortable chairs.

More Irregular Verb Forms

Be, *have*, and *do* aren't the only verbs with irregular forms. There are many such verbs, and everyone who writes uses some form of an irregular verb. When you're not certain if you're using the correct form of a verb, check the following list of irregular verbs.

For each irregular verb listed, the *present*, the *past*, and the *past participle* forms are given. The present participle isn't included because it's always formed by adding *ing* to the present form.

Irregular Verb Forms

Present	Past	Past Participle
(Today I *arise*.)	(Yesterday I *arose*.)	(I have/had *arisen*.)
arise	arose	arisen
awake	awoke, awaked	awoken, awaked
bear	bore	borne, born

beat	beat	beaten
become	became	become
begin	began	begun
bend	bent	bent
bite	bit	bitten
bleed	bled	bled
blow	blew	blown
break	broke	broken
bring	brought	brought
build	built	built
burst	burst	burst
buy	bought	bought
catch	caught	caught
choose	chose	chosen
cling	clung	clung
come	came	come
cost	cost	cost
creep	crept	crept
cut	cut	cut
deal	dealt	dealt
draw	drew	drawn
dream	dreamt, dreamed	dreamt, dreamed
drink	drank	drunk
drive	drove	driven
eat	ate	eaten
fall	fell	fallen
feed	fed	fed
feel	felt	felt
fight	fought	fought
find	found	found
fling	flung	flung
fly	flew	flown
freeze	froze	frozen
get	got	got, gotten
give	gave	given
go	went	gone
grow	grew	grown
hear	heard	heard
hide	hid	hidden
hit	hit	hit
hold	held	held
hurt	hurt	hurt
keep	kept	kept
know	knew	known
lay (means to put)	laid	laid
lead	led	led
leave	left	left
lend	lent	lent
let	let	let
lie (means to recline)	lay	lain
light	lit, lighted	lit, lighted
lose	lost	lost
make	made	made

mean	meant	meant
meet	met	met
pay	paid	paid
ride	rode	ridden
ring	rang	rung
rise	rose	risen
run	ran	run
say	said	said
see	saw	seen
sell	sold	sold
send	sent	sent
sew	sewed	sewn, sewed
shake	shook	shaken
shine	shone, shined	shone, shined
shrink	shrank	shrunk
shut	shut	shut
sing	sang	sung
sit	sat	sat
sleep	slept	slept
slide	slid	slid
sling	slung	slung
speak	spoke	spoken
spend	spent	spent
stand	stood	stood
steal	stole	stolen
stick	stuck	stuck
sting	stung	stung
stink	stank, stunk	stunk
string	strung	strung
swear	swore	sworn
swim	swam	swum
teach	taught	taught
tear	tore	torn
tell	told	told
think	thought	thought
throw	threw	thrown
wake	woke, waked	woken, waked
wear	wore	worn
win	won	won
write	wrote	written

EXERCISE 8

CHOOSING THE CORRECT FORM OF IRREGULAR VERBS

Write the correct form of the verb in parentheses in the following sentences. Make sure to check the list of irregular verbs.

1. I bought a huge bag of potato chips last night, and by midnight, I had _____ (eat) the whole thing.

2. Patty and Tom should have _____ (know) how to get to the store; they've been there before.

3. Last night, I _____ (lie) awake for three hours before I finally fell asleep.

4. I bought my five-year-old a new pair of blue jeans yesterday, but she has _____ (tear) them already.

5. I don't know what he _____ (mean) when he said, "I'm not interested."

6. Virginia asked Jack if he had ever _____ (lend) money to a friend.

7. Normally, my teacher begins the class with "Good morning," but yesterday she_____ (lay) her books on the table and said, "Today we're doing something different."

8. For years, that pawnbroker has _____ (deal) in stolen merchandise, but now he's being investigated.

9. The children have _____ (drink) all the milk in the refrigerator.

10. The child was hoping to get toys for his birthday, but instead his uncle _____ (bring) a sweater.

EXERCISE

9

WRITING SENTENCES WITH CORRECT VERB FORMS

With a partner or with a group, write two sentences that correctly use each of the following verb forms. In writing these sentences, you may add helping verbs to the verb forms, but you may *not* change the verb form itself. The first one is done for you.

1. sent

   a. He sent her a dozen roses on Valentine's Day. _____

   b. I have sent him all the information he needs. _____

2. seen

   a. _____

   b. _____

3. cost

   a. _____

   b. _____

4. drew

   a. _____

   b. _____

5. lain

   a. _____

   b. _____

6. felt

   a. _____

   b. _____

7. hurt

   a. _____

   b. _____

8. laid

   a. _____

   b. _____

9. got

   a. _____

   b. _____

10. eaten

   a. _____

   b. _____

EXERCISE
10

EDITING A PARAGRAPH FOR CORRECT VERB FORMS

Correct the errors in verb forms in the following paragraph. There are seven errors.

My responsibilities at home often interferes with my responsibilities at school. I'm not a parent, but I live with my parents and my two younger brothers. Because my mother and father work full time, they turn to me when they has a family emergency. Last week, my five-year-old brother was sick and feverish. My mother thought he had catched a cold and wanted to keep him out of school. That meant I had to stay out of school, too. I missed a quiz in my English class because I was stuck in the house with my sick brother. Something similar happened yesterday. My father's car breaked down on the highway, so he called me at school on my cellphone. He needed help, so I leaved my math class and picked him up on the road. Some students skip class because they have sleeped through the alarm or spent all night at a party, but I miss class because I be busy with my family.

CHAPTER 21
More about Verbs:
Consistency and Voice

Remember that your choice of verb form indicates the time (tense) of your statements. Be careful not to shift from one tense to another unless you have a reason to change the time.

CONSISTENT VERB TENSES

Staying in one tense (unless you have a reason to change tenses) is called **consistency of verb tense.**

incorrect shifts in tense:

The waitress **ran** to the kitchen with the order in her hand, **raced** back to her customers with glasses of water, and **smiles** calmly.

He **grins** at me from the ticket booth and **closed** the ticket window.

You can correct these errors by putting all the verbs in the same tense.

consistent present tense:

The waitress **runs** to the kitchen with the order in her hand, **races** back to her customers with glasses of water, and **smiles** calmly.

or

consistent past tense:

The waitress **ran** to the kitchen with the order in her hand, **raced** back to her customers with glasses of water, and **smiled** calmly.

consistent present tense:

He **grins** at me from the ticket booth and **closes** the ticket window.

or

consistent past tense:

He **grinned** at me from the ticket booth and **closed** the ticket window.

Whether you correct by changing all the verbs to the present tense or to the past tense, you're making the tenses consistent. Consistency of tense is important in the events you're describing because it helps the reader understand what happened and when it happened.

| **EXERCISE 1** | **CORRECTING SENTENCES THAT ARE INCONSISTENT IN TENSE** |

In each sentence below, one verb is inconsistent in tense. Cross it out and write the correct tense above.

1. Every month I stack all the household bills in a pile and drive to the ATM; then I paid all the bills at one time.
2. On the news, the reporter described the scene of the accident and interviewed a witness, but the reporter never explains how the accident happened.
3. When my father comes home from work, he sits in his recliner and turns on the television because he was too tired to talk.
4. Hundreds of pieces of junk mail come to our house every year and offered us magazine subscriptions, gifts, clothes, and fabulous prizes, but I throw all that junk mail into the recycling bin.
5. They were the top athletes in their class because they trained rigorously and follow a strict exercise routine.
6. In the kitchen, Adam struggled with the pipes under the sink and swore loudly; meanwhile, his wife calls a plumber.
7. Whenever she's depressed, she buys something chocolate and devoured it.
8. Because the parking lot at the supermarket is always crowded, people parked next door and walk the extra distance.
9. Working nights is hard for me because I had to get up early for classes and I have to find time for my family.
10. Although my friend says he's not afraid of heights, he shrank back whenever he's at the edge of a balcony or apartment railing.

| **EXERCISE 2** | **EDITING PARAGRAPHS FOR CONSISTENCY OF TENSE** |

Read the following paragraphs. Then cross out any verbs that are inconsistent in tense and write the correction above. There are four errors in the first paragraph and five errors in the second paragraph.

1. The rain came suddenly and pelts the holiday crowd with hail-sized nuggets. The storm transformed the scene. People grabbed their blankets and picnic baskets and run for cover. Several people congregated under nearby trees, but the lightning flashed nearby and worried them. Others sit under a picnic table while some raced to their cars. Everyone was soaking wet, and the picnic area becomes a scene of sopping paper plates and waterlogged barbecue grills.

2. The alarm clock blasted into my ear. I cringed, crawl out from under the covers, and reached my arm across the nightstand. I fling the stupid clock across the room and burrowed back under the covers. The bed feels warm and cozy. I tried to fall back into my dream. But soon my dog leaped into the room, jumped onto the bed, and plants kisses all over my face. In spite of all my attempts to go back to sleep, all the signs told me that it is time to get up.

EXERCISE 3	WRITING A PARAGRAPH WITH CONSISTENT VERB TENSES

The following paragraph has many inconsistencies in verb tense; it shifts between past and present tenses. Working with a group, write two versions of the paragraph: one in the present tense and one in the past tense. Half the group can record the present tense version; then the other half can record the past tense version. After both rewrites are complete, read the new paragraph aloud to the whole group.

The day starts off well, but it doesn't end that way. At first, I'm confident about taking my driving test and getting my driver's licence. Then I got into the car with the examiner and wait for him to tell me to start. When he does, I turned the key in the ignition and slowly pull out of the parking lot. For some reason, I'm sweating with fear, but I tried not to show it. I managed to drive without hitting another car. I remember to stop at a stop sign. But when it came to parallel parking, I knocked down all those orange markers! My driving examiner never cracks a smile or even talked to me. He just gives instructions. But I knew what he was thinking, and I know I won't get a licence. I feel like the worst driver in the world.

Paragraph Revised for Consistent Tenses:

_____
_____
_____
_____
_____
_____
_____
_____
_____
_____
_____
_____
_____
_____
_____
_____
_____
_____
_____

THE PERFECT TENSES

When you're choosing the right verb tense, you need to know about two verb tenses that can make your meaning clear: the present perfect and the past perfect.

The Present Perfect Tense

The **present perfect tense** is made up of the past participle form of the verb plus *have* or *has* as a helping verb. It's used to show an action that started in the past but is still going on in the present.

past tense: My father **drove** a truck for five months. (He doesn't drive a truck anymore, but he did drive one in the past.)

present perfect tense: My father **has driven** a truck for five months. (He started driving a truck five months ago; he is still driving a truck.)

past tense: For years, I **studied** ballet. (I don't study ballet now; I used to.)

present perfect tense: For years, I **have studied** ballet. (I still study ballet.)

Remember, use the present perfect tense to show that an action started in the past and is still going on.

EXERCISE 4	DISTINGUISHING BETWEEN THE PAST TENSE AND THE PRESENT PERFECT TENSE

Circle the correct verb tense in parentheses in each of the following sentences. Make sure to look carefully at the meaning of the sentence.

1. Parvi (has borrowed/borrowed) my marketing textbook last night.
2. William (sang/has sung) in the choir for many years now.
3. The old car (was/has been) having mechanical problems, but no one wants to get rid of it.
4. I called the office and (have asked/asked) for the supervisor.
5. The comedians (performed/have performed) together for two years and are now appearing at our campus theatre.
6. Two of my best friends (were/have been) musicians but gave music up for business careers.
7. Music videos (were/have been) influencing teenagers for years now.
8. While he was in basic training, he (has written/wrote) many letters home.
9. He (sent/has sent) his résumé to fifty companies and accepted a job from the first company that responded.
10. Melissa (lost/has lost) that bracelet three weeks ago.

The Past Perfect Tense

The **past perfect tense** is made up of the past participle form of the verb plus *had* as a helping verb. You can use the past perfect tense to show more than one event occurring in the past; that is, when more than one thing happened in the past but at different times.

past tense: He **washed** the dishes.

past perfect tense: He **had washed** the dishes by the time I came home. (He washed the dishes before I came home. Both actions happened in the past, but one happened earlier than the other.)

past tense: Susan **waited** for an hour.

past perfect tense: Susan **had waited** for an hour when she gave up on him. (Waiting came first; giving up came second. Both actions are in the past.)

The past perfect tense is especially useful because you write most of your essays in the past tense, and you often need to get further back into the past. Just remember to use *had* with the past participle of the verb, and you'll have the past perfect tense.

EXERCISE **5**	DISTINGUISHING BETWEEN THE PAST TENSE AND THE PAST PERFECT TENSE

Circle the correct verb tense in parentheses in the following sentences. Make sure to look carefully at the meaning of the sentence.

1. The child (had hidden/hid) the shattered vase just minutes before his aunt entered the living room.
2. My father drove a rental car last week because he (had wrecked/wrecked) his own car last month.
3. Bernie bought a new laptop yesterday; he (had saved/saved) for it for months.
4. Every week, I (had revised/revised) my résumé and searched for new job postings.
5. The customer service agent asked whether we (had received/received) the merchandise yet.
6. As I (had cut/cut) the pattern for another dress, I thought about becoming a dress designer.
7. They (had left/left) for the party by the time we came to pick them up.
8. She (threw/had thrown) the candy wrapper on the grass and ignored a nearby trash bin.
9. I wasn't sure whether he (had returned/returned) my tools earlier in the day.
10. When the little boy screamed, the mother (had jumped/jumped) up with a worried look on her face.

PASSIVE AND ACTIVE VOICE

Not only do verbs have tenses, but they also have voices. When the subject in the sentence is doing something, the verb is in the **active voice**. When something is done to the subject—when it receives the action of the verb—the verb is in the **passive voice**.

active voice: I painted the house. (**I**, the subject, did it.)

The people on the corner made a donation to the emergency fund.

(The **people**, the subject, did it.)

passive voice: The house was painted by me. (The **house**, the subject, didn't do anything. It received the action—it was painted.)

A donation to the emergency fund was made by the people on the corner.

(The **donation**, the subject, didn't do anything. It received the action—it was given.)

Notice what happens when you use the passive voice instead of the active:

active voice: I painted the house.

passive voice: The house was painted by me.

The sentence in the passive voice is two words longer than the one in the active voice. Yet the sentence using the passive voice doesn't say anything different, and it doesn't say it more clearly than the one using the active voice does.

Using the passive voice can make your sentences wordy, it can slow them down, and it can make them boring. The passive voice can also confuse readers. When the subject of the sentence isn't doing anything, readers may have to look carefully to see who or what *is* doing something. Look at this sentence, for example:

> *A decision to fire you was reached.*

Who decided to fire you? In this sentence, it's hard to find the answer to that question.

Of course, there will be times when you have to use the passive voice. For example, you may have to use it when you don't know who did something:

> *Our house was broken into last night.*

> *A leather jacket was left behind in the classroom.*

But in general, you should avoid using the passive voice and rewrite sentences so that they're in the active voice.

EXERCISE 6 | **REWRITING SENTENCES, CHANGING THE PASSIVE VOICE TO THE ACTIVE VOICE**

In the following sentences, change the passive voice to the active voice. If the original sentence doesn't tell you who or what performed the action, add words that tell who or what did it. An example is done for you.

example: He was appointed chief negotiator last night.

rewritten: *The union leaders appointed him chief negotiator last night.*

1. The scholarship was won by the student with the highest GPA.

    rewritten: _____

    _____

2. A compromise has been reached by the lawyers on both sides.

    rewritten: _____

    _____

3. The wrong number was called several times.

    rewritten: _____

    _____

4. Finally, a candidate was selected by the hiring committee.

    rewritten: _____

    _____

5. Great care was taken to protect the fragile package.

    rewritten: _____

    _____

6. Honorary degrees are conferred every year by universities across the country.

    rewritten: _____

    _____

7. Every day, the park is patrolled by a security guard.

    rewritten: _____

    _____

8. Last week, I was called by an insurance agent.

    rewritten: _____

    _____

9. The real reason for his tardiness was not known by his teacher.

    rewritten: _____

    _____

10. The murder is being investigated by the police.

    rewritten: _____

    _____

Avoiding Unnecessary Shifts in Voice

Just as you should be consistent in the tense of verbs, you should be consistent in the voice of verbs. Don't shift from active voice to passive voice, or vice versa, without a good reason to do so.

                        active   *passive*
shift: I **designed** the decorations for the dance; **they were hung** by Chuck.

                        active   *active*
rewritten: I **designed** the decorations for the dance; **Chuck hung them.**

                        passive   *active*
shift: Many **problems were discussed** by the council members, but **they found** no easy answers.

                            active   *active*
rewritten: The council **members discussed** many problems, but **they found** no easy answers.

Being consistent in voice can help you write clearly and smoothly.

| EXERCISE
7 | **REWRITING SENTENCES TO CORRECT
SHIFTS IN VOICE** |

Rewrite the following sentences so that all the verbs are in the active voice. You may change the wording to make the sentences clear, smooth, and consistent in voice.

1. Christine called Jack yesterday, but I was called by Tom today.

   rewritten: _____

   _____

2. A revised set of rules is being written by the disciplinary committee; the committee is also writing a list of penalties.

   rewritten: _____

   _____

3. That girl can be helped by your advice because you know her problems.

   rewritten: _____

   _____

4. The windows were opened by the office workers as the temperature soared above 30 degrees.

   rewritten: _____

   _____

5. It was decided by a team of experts that the water contains harmful bacteria.

   rewritten: _____

   _____

6. Some people worship celebrities; musicians, actors, and athletes are regarded as superhuman.

   rewritten: _____

   _____

7. Parvinder showed his dismay when his brother Sikander was rejected by the admissions committee.

   rewritten: _____

   _____

8. If a deal was made by the officers, I never knew about it.

   rewritten: _____

   _____

9. When the crime was committed by my brothers, they didn't tell me about it.

rewritten: _____

_____

10. Denise expressed her happiness when her father was praised in the newspaper.

rewritten: _____

_____

Small Reminders about Verbs

There are a few errors that people tend to make with verbs. If you're aware of these errors, you'll be on the lookout for them as you edit your writing.

Used To Be careful when you write that someone *used to* do, say, or feel something. It is incorrect to write *use to*.

> **not this:** Janine ~~use to~~ visit her mother every week. They ~~use to~~ like Thai food.

> **but this:** Janine **used to** visit her mother every week. They **used to** like Thai food.

Could Have, Should Have, Would Have Using *of* instead of *have* with *could*, *should*, and *would* is another common error with verbs.

> **not this:** I ~~could of~~ done better on the test.

> **but this:** I **could have** done better on the test.

> **not this:** He ~~should of~~ been paying attention.

> **but this:** He **should have** been paying attention.

> **not this:** The girls ~~would of~~ liked to visit Ottawa.

> **but this:** The girls **would have** liked to visit Ottawa.

Would Have/Had If you're writing about something that might have been possible but that didn't happen, use *had* as the helping verb.

> **not this:** If I ~~would have~~ taken a foreign language in high school, I wouldn't have to take one now.

> **but this:** If I **had** taken a foreign language in high school, I wouldn't have to take one now.

> **not this:** I wish they ~~would have~~ won the game.

> **but this:** I wish they **had** won the game.

> **not this:** If she ~~would have~~ been smart, she would have called a plumber.

> **but this:** If she **had** been smart, she would have called a plumber.

EXERCISE 8	WRITING SENTENCES WITH THE CORRECT VERB FORMS

Complete this exercise with a partner or with a group. Follow directions to write or complete each of the following sentences.

1. Complete this sentence and add a verb in the correct tense: I had cleaned the whole house by the time

   _____

   _____

   _____

2. Write a sentence that is more than six words long and that uses the words *has studied karate* in the middle of the sentence.

   _____

   _____

   _____

3. Write a sentence that uses the past-tense form of both these words: *run, stumble.*

   _____

   _____

   _____

4. Write a sentence in the passive voice.

   _____

   _____

   _____

5. Write a sentence in the active voice.

   _____

   _____

   _____

6. Write a sentence that uses *would have* and *had.*

   _____

   _____

   _____

7. Write a sentence that is more than six words long and that uses the words *had prepared* and *before.*

   _____

   _____

   _____

8. Write a sentence of more than six words that uses the words *used to*.

_____

_____

_____

9. Write a sentence that contains two verbs in the same tense.

_____

_____

_____

10. Write a sentence that uses the words *should have*.

_____

_____

_____

EXERCISE 9

EDITING A PARAGRAPH FOR ERRORS IN VERBS: CONSISTENCY, CORRECT TENSES, AND VOICE

Edit the following paragraph for errors in verb consistency, tense, or voice. There are eight errors.

Last week, a tragedy struck our town, and it was particularly terrible because it was so senseless. Two cars sped down a dark country road, one driver loses control, and four high-school students died. The dangers of that road were known by everyone at the high school; two accidents already occurred there earlier in the year. It was a notoriously unsafe road for years, yet nothing was done by the local police. More and better enforcement could of saved lives. Even speed bumps could have helped. Of course, the two drivers who drove down that stretch of concrete at more than 140 kilometres per hour do not use their heads. They choose to risk their lives long before they crashed. If they were more rational and less in love with street racing, four people would be alive today.

MyWritingLab

CHAPTER 22
Making Subjects and Verbs Agree

Subjects and verbs must *agree in number*. **Subject–verb agreement** means that a singular subject must be matched with a singular verb form; a plural subject must be matched with a plural verb form.

singular subject   singular verb

My **sister walks** to work every morning.

plural subject   plural verb

Nadeer, Myoungok, and Joel study hard.

singular subject   singular verb

That **movie is** too violent for me.

plural subject   plural verb

Bulky **packages are** difficult to carry.

Caution: Remember that a *regular verb* has an *s* ending in one singular form in the present tense—the form that goes with *he*, *she*, *it*, or their equivalent.

He **makes** me feel confident.

She **appreciates** intelligent conversation.

It **seems** like a good buy.

Raheel **runs** every day.

That girl **swims** well.

The machine **breaks** down too often.

EXERCISE 1	SUBJECT–VERB AGREEMENT: SELECTING THE CORRECT VERB FORM

Select the correct form of the verb in parentheses in each sentence below.

1. Since the advent of email, employees (spend/spends) much of their day reading and responding to incoming messages.
2. Some (like/likes) to stay abreast of their communication, so they answer email even on weekends.
3. Stress (keep/keeps) employees from enjoying their vacations.
4. They (start/starts) taking their laptops and tablets with them wherever they go.
5. Employees (feel/feels) overwhelmed with work when they return.

6. However, we all (need/needs) a break from work.
7. For most people, the weekend (make/makes) for a long enough break.
8. Stress (place/places) a strain on interpersonal relationships.
9. Stress (cost/costs) companies more in terms of lost productivity.
10. It (is/are) important to unplug from time to time.

EXERCISE 2

CORRECTING ERRORS IN SUBJECT–VERB AGREEMENT IN A PARAGRAPH

There are errors in subject–verb agreement in the following paragraph. If a verb doesn't agree with its subject, change the verb form. Cross out the incorrect verb form and write the correct one above. There are four errors in agreement in the paragraph.

Every night, my sister follows the same routine. She pours a big glass of diet cola, sit down in an old easy chair, and settles down for a night on the telephone. My sister always call the same person, her best friend Irene. She and Irene talks for hours about the most trivial subjects. The two girls gossip about their friends, about their enemies, about what happened that day, and about what will happen the next day. My brother says guys never spend as much time on the phone. But he always say that while he's trying to get the phone from my sister so he can make his evening calls!

PRONOUNS AS SUBJECTS

Pronouns can be used as subjects. Pronouns are words that take the place of nouns. When pronouns are used as subjects, pronouns and verbs must *agree in number*.

The Infobox provides a list of personal pronouns (those referring specifically to a person or thing) and the regular verb forms that agree with them in the present tense.

INFOBOX

SUBJECTIVE PRONOUNS AND A PRESENT-TENSE REGULAR VERB

pronoun	verb	
I	listen	
you	listen	all singular forms
he, she, it	listens	
we	listen	
you	listen	all plural forms
they	listen	

In the following sentences, the pronoun used as the subject of the sentence agrees in number with the verb.

singular pronoun singular verb
I make the best lassi in town.

singular pronoun singular verb
You dance very well.

singular pronoun singular verb
She performs like a trained athlete.

plural pronoun plural verb
We need a new refrigerator.

plural pronoun plural verb
They understand the situation.

SPECIAL PROBLEMS WITH AGREEMENT

Agreement seems fairly simple: If a subject is singular, use a singular verb form. If a subject is plural, use a plural verb form. However, there are special problems with agreement that will come up in your writing. Sometimes, it's hard to find the subject of a sentence; at other times, it's hard to determine whether a subject is singular or plural.

Finding the Subject

When you're checking for subject–verb agreement, you can find the real subject of the sentence by first eliminating the prepositional phrases. To find the real subject, put parentheses around the prepositional phrases. Then it's easy to find the subject, because nothing in a prepositional phrase can ever be the subject of a sentence (see Chapter 13). In the sentences below, the prepositional phrases have been placed in parentheses to reveal the subject and verb.

S   V
One (of my oldest friends) **became** a social worker.

S   V
A **student** (from one) (of the nearby school districts) **has won** the championship.

S   V
The **stores** (across the street) (from my house) **open** early in the morning.

S   V
You, (with all your silly jokes), **are** a nice person.

EXERCISE 3	FINDING THE REAL SUBJECT BY RECOGNIZING PREPOSITIONAL PHRASES

Put parentheses around all the prepositional phrases in the following sentences. Put an *S* above each subject and a *V* above each verb.

1. Two of my favourite television shows are crime dramas with lots of action scenes.

2. The smartphone with an unlimited data plan is the best choice.

3. One of the three people on the decorations committee works as a professional artist.

4. The clerk in the "Geek Squad" T-shirt became a valued employee.

5. A representative of the company from the proposed site has presented a convincing plan.

6. The tree behind the house is a hundred years old.

7. The elementary school with the modern architecture was built down the road from my house.

8. With a great deal of poise, she took the termination notice from her employer's hand.

9. The coat in the downstairs closet has my keys in its pocket.

10. The house with the solar panels contributes to the city's power source.

EXERCISE 4	SELECTING THE CORRECT VERB FORM BY IDENTIFYING PREPOSITIONAL PHRASES

In the following sentences, put parentheses around all the prepositional phrases; then circle the correct verb form in parentheses in each sentence.

1. A speaker from the Council of Cities (is/are) lecturing in our anthropology class today.

2. Several of the biggest bargains in the shop (lie/lies) stashed in the back room.

3. One of the contestants from the semifinal rounds (face/faces) the winner of this round.

4. The consequences of her argument with her father (seem/seems) severe.

5. A salesperson with a background in communications (has/have) a competitive advantage.

6. With a brand-new backpack and new shoes, the little girl on the bus (look/looks) excited on the first day of school.

7. A friend of mine from the Queen Charlotte Islands (love/loves) the West Edmonton Mall.

8. A change of plans (is/are) no reason for a change in your attitude.

9. An honest statement of the facts (is/are) behind the mayor's popularity in this city.

10. A person with energy, intelligence, and drive (meet/meets) the requirements for this job.

Changed Word Order

You're probably used to looking for the subject of a sentence in front of the verb, but not all sentences follow this pattern. Questions, sentences beginning with words like *here* or *there*, and other sentence patterns change the word order. So you have to look carefully to check for subject–verb agreement.

$$\overset{V}{} \qquad \overset{S}{}$$

Where **are** my **homework assignments?**

$$\overset{V}{}\overset{S}{}\overset{V}{}$$

When **is he going** to work?

$$\overset{V}{} \qquad \overset{S}{}$$

Behind the courthouse **stands** a huge **statue.**

$$\overset{V}{} \qquad \overset{S}{}$$

There **are potholes** in the road.

$$\overset{V}{} \qquad \overset{S}{}$$

Here **is** the **reason** for his impatience.

EXERCISE 5

MAKING SUBJECTS AND VERBS AGREE IN SENTENCES WITH CHANGED WORD ORDER

In each of the following sentences, underline the subject; then circle the correct verb form in parentheses.

1. Included in the package of coupons (was/were) a coupon for a free breakfast.

2. Among my happiest memories (is/are) the memory of a day at the beach.

3. Along the side of the road (sit/sits) a fruit stand and a gas station.

4. There (was/were) several explanations for his tantrum.

5. Here (is/are) my brother and sister, in the midst of an argument about my birthday party.

6. Behind the fence (wait/waits) a fierce and vicious dog.

7. There (was/were) a sudden increase in the price of groceries.

8. Under the porch (hide/hides) a mound of termites.

9. Where (was/were) the photographs of your trip to Mexico?

10. Here (is/are) the insurance policy for the car.

EXERCISE 6	MORE ON SELECTING THE CORRECT VERB FORM BY IDENTIFYING PREPOSITIONAL PHRASES

Put parentheses around all the prepositional phrases in the sentences below. Then circle the correct verb form in parentheses in each sentence.

1. A volunteer from Citizens for a Green Earth (speak/speaks) at the city council meeting on Wednesdays.

2. Several of the winners of the provincial semifinals (is/are) at the opening ceremonies.

3. One of the photographs from Mr. Khouri's portfolio (hang/hangs) on exhibit at the Photography Centre.

4. The protesters at the G8 trade conference (comes/come) from all parts of the world.

5. A person with weak managerial skills (has/have) little chance of success in business.

6. With his experience and hours of training, the Canadian swimmer (ranks/rank) far above the other swimmers at the meet.

7. One of the bushes at the edge of the fields (is/are) a rare type of wildflower from England.

8. Spending beyond your means (leads/lead) to money problems.

9. Her impressive background in medicine (makes/make) Dr. Baimel the most respected doctor at the clinic.

10. A college with a diverse student body, good teachers, and small classes (is/are) located within ten kilometres of your house.

COMPOUND SUBJECTS

A **compound subject** is two or more subjects joined by *and*, *or*, or *nor*. When subjects are joined by *and*, they are usually plural.

       S   S V

Jermaine and **Lisa are** bargain hunters.

       S   S V

The **house** and the **garden need** attention.

       S   S V

A **wireless card** and a **fingerprint reader are** in the box with the laptop.

Caution: Be careful to check for a compound subject when the word order changes.

>   V   S   S
>
> In the box with the laptop **are** a **wireless card** and a **fingerprint reader**.
>
> (Two things, a *wireless card* and a *fingerprint reader*, are in the box with the laptop.)

>   V   S   S
>
> Here **are** a **picture** of your father and a **copy** of his birth certificate.
>
> (Two things, a *picture* and a *copy*, are here.)

When subjects are joined by *or*, *either/or*, *neither/nor*, or *not only/but also*, the verb form agrees with the subject closer to the verb.

>   singular S   plural S plural V
>
> Not only the restaurant **manager** but also the **waiters were** pleased with the new policy.
>
>   plural S   singular S singular V
>
> Not only the **waiters** but also the restaurant **manager was** pleased with the new policy.

>   plural S singular S singular V
>
> Either the **parents** or the **boy walks** the dog every morning.

>   singular S   plural S   plural V
>
> Either the **boy** or the **parents walk** the dog every morning.

Caution: Sometimes, a connecting word or phrase will come between the subject and the verb. Connectors such as *as well as*, *along with*, *in addition to*, *including*, *together with*, *plus*, and *with* are prepositions rather than coordinating conjunctions, so they don't form compound subjects.

>   S   V
>
> Her **sister** as well as her brothers **comes** home every weekend. (The subject is *sister*, so it takes a singular verb form.)

>   S   V
>
> My favourite **movies** as well as my novel **were taken** from me until my assignment was finished. (The subject is *movies*, so it takes a plural verb form.)

EXERCISE **7**	**MAKING SUBJECTS AND VERBS AGREE: COMPOUND SUBJECTS**

Circle the correct form of the verb in parentheses in each of the following sentences.

1. Neither my sisters nor my cousin (excels/excel) at sports.
2. When they came to this country, Aziz and Omid (was/were) eager to find employment.

3. Here (sits/sit) the guest of honour and her husband.

4. Either Kevin or his sisters (takes/take) out the garbage on Saturdays.

5. Either his sisters or Kevin (takes/take) out the garbage on Saturdays.

6. A coffee cake as well as doughnuts (was/were) in the bag.

7. Under the sofa there (is/are) an old ragged slipper and a shrivelled apple.

8. Her impressive background in medicine, together with her calm and soothing bedside manner, (makes/make) Dr. Baimel the most respected doctor at the clinic.

9. Not only the teacher but also the students (like/likes) the new classroom.

10. Hanging out with my friends and complaining about my parents (was/were) my principal activities in high school.

EXERCISE 8

MORE ABOUT MAKING SUBJECTS AND VERBS AGREE: COMPOUND SUBJECTS

Circle the correct form of the verb in parentheses in each of the following sentences.

1. Not only the sausages but also the garlic bread (was/were) dripping with olive oil.

2. Neither the tire nor the shock absorbers (is/are) in good shape.

3. There (stands/stand) a small boy and his parents waiting at the end of the line.

4. Certainly, either Mr. Lopez or Mr. Woo (qualifies/qualify) for the position.

5. Here (was/were) my parents, tired after the long trip.

6. Kindness and generosity (make/makes) a person welcome in any group.

7. Here (is/are) a video of the crime and eyewitness testimony from a neighbour.

8. Whenever I come home for a visit, either my father or my brother (says/say) I look tired.

9. Within weeks of Mela's graduation, there (was/were) a family crisis as well as an accident facing her.

10. On Fridays, neither crazy drivers nor my nasty boss (spoils/spoil) my good mood.

INDEFINITE PRONOUNS

Indefinite pronouns, unlike personal pronouns, do not refer to a specific person or thing. Some indefinite pronouns always take a singular verb.

INFOBOX	INDEFINITE PRONOUNS THAT TAKE SINGULAR VERBS		
anybody	either	neither	somebody
anyone	everybody	nobody	someone
anything	everyone	nothing	something
each	everything	one	

If you want to write clearly and correctly, you must memorize these words and remember that they always take a singular verb. Using your common sense isn't enough because some of these words seem plural: for example, *everybody* seems to mean more than one person, but in grammatically correct English it takes a singular verb. Here are some examples of the pronouns used with singular verbs:

singular S   singular V

Everyone in town **is talking** about the scandal.

singular S   singular V

Each of the boys **is** talented.

singular S   singular V

One of their biggest concerns **is** crime in the streets.

singular S   singular V

Neither of the cats **is** mine.

Hint: You can memorize the indefinite pronouns as the *-one, -thing,* and *-body* words—every*one,* every*thing,* every*body,* and so forth—plus *each, either,* and *neither.*

Other indefinite pronouns such as *some, most,* and *all* can take either singular or plural verbs, depending on the sentence. If the sentence is talking about something you can count, then the verb must be plural; if the sentence is talking about something you cannot count, then the verb must be singular.

All the students *are going* to graduation. (You can count the number of students.)

All of my flour *is* whole wheat. (You can't count flour.)

EXERCISE **9**	MAKING SUBJECTS AND VERBS AGREE: USING INDEFINITE PRONOUNS

Circle the correct verb form in parentheses in the following sentences.

1. Everyone in the suburbs (knows/know) the way to that highway exit.

2. Nothing in the sales racks (is/are) sufficiently marked down.

3. Somebody (has/have) painted graffiti all over the walls.

4. All of the jewellery from that store (was/were) stolen.

5. (Has/Have) some of the toddlers had lunch?

6. Everybody in both schools (listens/listen) to the same radio station.

7. Nobody from either campus (volunteers/volunteer) for this project.

8. (Is/Are) some of these houses more environmentally friendly than others?

9. One of my most foolish decisions (was/were) to call in sick last week.

10. Here (is/are) someone who has come to see you.

EXERCISE 10

MORE ABOUT MAKING SUBJECTS AND VERBS AGREE: USING INDEFINITE PRONOUNS

Circle the correct verb form in parentheses in the following sentences.

1. After the graduation ceremony, most of the guests (is/are) invited to a reception in the lobby.

2. Either of the applicants for the job (satisfies/satisfy) the criteria for hiring.

3. Someone (deliver/delivers) the paper very early in the morning.

4. Each of Michael's business trips (costs/cost) the office thousands of dollars.

5. Neither of my parents (like/likes) the same hockey team as I.

6. On Canada Day, everyone in the neighbourhood (goes/go) to see the fireworks at the marina.

7. Something in the stranger's explanation (hint/hints) at a mystery.

8. Beneath the stack of documents, there (was/were) nothing except an old coffee stain.

9. At the end of the movie, (was/were) anyone crying?

10. Everything about cricket (confuse/confuses) me.

COLLECTIVE NOUNS

Collective nouns refer to more than one person or thing.

INFOBOX	SOME COLLECTIVE NOUNS	
audience	corporation	government
board	council	group
class	couple	jury
committee	crowd	staff
company	family	team

Collective nouns usually take a singular verb.

singular S   singular V

The **committee is sponsoring** a fundraiser.

singular S   singular V

The **audience was** impatient.

singular S   singular V

The **jury has reached** a verdict.

The singular verb is used because the group is sponsoring, or getting impatient, or reaching a verdict *as one unit*. Collective nouns take a plural verb only when the members of the group are acting individually, not as a unit.

The senior **class are fighting** among themselves. (The phrase *among themselves* shows that the class isn't acting as one unit.)

EXERCISE 11	MAKING SUBJECTS AND VERBS AGREE: USING COLLECTIVE NOUNS

Circle the correct verb form in parentheses in each of the following sentences.

1. My family (is/are) moving to another province next month.

2. The company with the safest work environment (receives/receive) an award tomorrow.

3. Our class (has/have) less school spirit than other classes.

4. The student council (meet/meets) every Tuesday afternoon.

5. My group of friends (is/are) attending two different colleges.

6. A team from the Philippines (was/were) competing in the international contest.

7. After Labour Day, the crowd at the beach (isn't/aren't) so large.

8. A truly enthusiastic audience (help/helps) the performers.

9. The governing board (vote/votes) on the annual budget tomorrow night.

10. The environmental group (has/have) never endorsed candidates for political office.

MAKING SUBJECTS AND VERBS AGREE: THE BOTTOM LINE

As you've probably realized, making subjects and verbs agree isn't as simple as it first appears. But if you can remember the basic ideas in this section, you'll be able to apply them automatically as you edit your own writing. The following Infobox provides a quick summary of subject–verb agreement.

| **INFOBOX** | **MAKING SUBJECTS AND VERBS AGREE: A SUMMARY** |

1. Subjects and verbs should agree in number: singular subjects take singular verb forms; plural subjects take plural verb forms.
2. When pronouns are used as subjects, they must agree in number with verbs.
3. Nothing in a prepositional phrase can be the subject of the sentence.
4. Word order can change in questions, in sentences beginning with *here* or *there*, and in other sentences, so look carefully for the subject.
5. When subjects are joined by *and*, they are usually plural.
6. When subjects are joined by *or*, *either/or*, *neither/nor*, or *not only/but also*, the verb form agrees with the subject closer to the verb.
7. Many indefinite pronouns take singular verbs.
8. Collective nouns usually take singular verbs unless the members of the group are acting individually.

EXERCISE 12

A COMPREHENSIVE EXERCISE ON SUBJECT–VERB AGREEMENT

Circle the correct verb form in parentheses in the following sentences.

1. Some of the cooks at the restaurant (was/were) in my math class last year.
2. Anybody from Saskatchewan (know/knows) how to stay cool in the summer.
3. When (was/were) the packages delivered?
4. Each of the cars on the showroom floor (was/were) polished to a dazzling brightness.
5. Within the circle of diamonds (sit/sits) a deep red stone.
6. Neither my cousin nor his parents ever (think/thinks) about home security.
7. Every day, apathy and pessimism (grow/grows) stronger in the city.
8. Nothing in ten years (has/have) pleased her more than that party.
9. The candidate with a strong background in liberal arts and good leadership skills (remain/remains) my first choice for the position.
10. Behind the refrigerator (sit/sits) a giant cockroach.
11. Everything in the botanical gardens (seem/seems) rare and exotic.
12. Down the street from the bank there (is/are) a Chinese restaurant and an Italian deli.
13. Because of the lateness of the hour, the jury (is/are) adjourning until tomorrow.
14. The company (was/were) not eager to recruit college graduates.
15. Clearly defined steps and a realistic schedule (help/helps) you complete a difficult project.
16. If the city doesn't fix that road soon, someone (is/are) going to have an accident.

17. Last year, there (was/were) a shooting and two muggings in the parking lot by the club.

18. Neither of my parents (is/are) anxious about my decision.

19. In spite of the rejection letters, Julie still (try/tries) to get her books published.

20. Here (is/are) your final marks.

EXERCISE
13

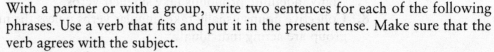

WRITING SENTENCES WITH SUBJECT–VERB AGREEMENT

With a partner or with a group, write two sentences for each of the following phrases. Use a verb that fits and put it in the present tense. Make sure that the verb agrees with the subject.

1. A crate of oranges _____

   A crate of oranges _____

2. Either Superman or Batman _____

   Either Superman or Batman _____

3. The committee _____

   The committee _____

4. Thelma and Jody _____

   Thelma and Jody _____

5. Everything in my closet _____

   Everything in my closet _____

6. Someone from the suburbs _____

   Someone from the suburbs _____

7. Not only the child but also his parents _____

   _____

   Not only the child but also his parents _____

   _____

8. Anybody in town _____

   _____

   Anybody in town _____

   _____

9. One of my greatest fears _____

   _____

   One of my greatest fears _____

   _____

10. Everyone in the office _____

    _____

    Everyone in the office _____

    _____

EXERCISE

14

👤+👤

CREATE YOUR OWN TEXT ON SUBJECT–VERB AGREEMENT

Working with a partner or with a group, create your own grammar handbook. Below is a list of rules on subject–verb agreement. Write one sentence that is an example of each rule. The first one is done for you.

Rule 1: Subjects and verbs should agree in number: singular subjects take singular verb forms; plural subjects take plural verb forms.

example: <u>A battered old car stands in the front yard.</u>

Rule 2: When pronouns are used as subjects, they must agree in number with verbs.

example: _____

_____

Rule 3: Nothing in a prepositional phrase can be the subject of the sentence.

example: _____

_____

Rule 4: Word order can change in questions, in sentences beginning with *here* or *there*, and in other sentences, so look carefully for the subject.

example: _____

_____

Rule 5: When subjects are joined by *and*, they are usually plural.

example: _____

_____

Rule 6: When subjects are joined by *or, either/or, neither/nor,* or *not only/ but also,* the verb form agrees with the subject closer to the verb.

example: _____

_____

Rule 7: Many indefinite pronouns take singular verbs.

example: _____

_____

Rule 8: Collective nouns usually take singular verbs unless the members of the group are acting individually.

example: _____

_____

EXERCISE 15

EDITING A PARAGRAPH FOR ERRORS IN SUBJECT–VERB AGREEMENT

Edit the following paragraph by correcting any verbs that don't agree with their subjects. Write your corrections above the lines. There are five errors.

There is two simple lessons adults could learn from very young children. First of all, have anybody ever seen a toddler hesitate to have fun? Small children do not hold back; they run directly toward the joy of a bright flower or a pet or a parent's embrace. Yet everybody over the age of fifteen seem to worry about enjoying a moment of happiness. People debate whether they have time to enjoy the flower or play with the dog. They think hugging a child can be done later, after they have gone to work and made money to support the child. Toddlers, in contrast, lives fully in the moment, and that is the second lesson we can learn from them. When small children are building a house with their plastic blocks, they are fully focused on that project. Adults may be building a patio out of real bricks, but at the same time they are also talking on their cellphones and obsessing about tomorrow's workload. The adults have lost their ability to enjoy and to focus on a single, present moment. A group of children are often wiser than stressed and anxious adults.

CHAPTER 23
Using Pronouns Correctly: Agreement and Reference

NOUNS AND PERSONAL PRONOUNS

Nouns are the names of persons, places, or things:

Jack is a good friend. (*Jack* is the name of a person.)

The band is from **Winnipeg**. (*Winnipeg* is the name of a place.)

I hate the **movie**. (*Movie* is the name of a thing.)

Pronouns are words that substitute for nouns. A pronoun's **antecedent** is the word or words the pronoun replaces. Personal pronouns refer to specific persons (or animals or objects); they can act as subjects or objects, or can show possession (see Chapter 24).

antecedent   pronoun

Jack is a good friend; **he** is very trustworthy.

antecedent   pronoun

I wasn't interested in **the movies** but my friend made me watch **them**.

antecedent   pronoun

Playing hockey was fun, but **it** started to take up too much of my time.

antecedent   pronoun

Mike and Michelle are sure that the money is **theirs** to enjoy.

antecedent   pronoun

Anya and I gave away **our** old clothes.

antecedent   pronoun

The car almost lost **its** muffler; it was dragging on the ground.

EXERCISE 1 — IDENTIFYING THE ANTECEDENTS OF PRONOUNS

In each of the following sentences, a pronoun is underlined. Underline the word or words that are the antecedents of the underlined pronoun. Note that the sentences may contain other pronouns that are not underlined.

1. Kim and I are quitting tomorrow because <u>we</u> can't make enough money at the job.

2. Targeting your résumé for each job position is recommended because <u>it</u> shows that you're serious about the job.

3. The leaders at the G8 summit said <u>they</u> were committed to emissions reduction.

4. The social media site claimed that <u>its</u> data was secure.

5. Deirdre, <u>you</u> are the best candidate for the job.

6. Daniel was named employee of the month; <u>his</u> work ethic is impeccable.

7. Although <u>it</u> can be challenging, preparing an effective résumé is worth the time and effort.

8. Though I called the recruiter several times, <u>he</u> did not return my calls.

9. All employees must submit <u>their</u> monthly reports by next week.

10. Constant criticism is dangerous; in fact, <u>it</u> can destroy a person's confidence.

AGREEMENT OF A PRONOUN AND ITS ANTECEDENT

A pronoun must agree in number with its antecedent. If the antecedent is singular, the pronoun must be singular. If the antecedent is plural, then the pronoun must be plural.

> singular antecedent   singular pronoun
> **Susan** tried to arrive on time, but **she** got caught in traffic.
>
> plural antecedent   plural pronoun
> **Susan and Ray** tried to arrive on time, but **they** got caught in traffic.
>
> plural antecedent   plural pronoun
> **The visitors** tried to arrive on time, but **they** got caught in traffic.

Agreement of pronoun and antecedent seems fairly simple. If an antecedent is singular, use a singular pronoun. If an antecedent is plural, use a plural pronoun. There are, however, some special problems with agreement of pronouns, and these problems will come up in your writing. If you become familiar with the explanations, examples, and exercises that follow, you'll be ready to handle the special problems.

INDEFINITE PRONOUNS

As we discussed in Chapter 22, certain words, called **indefinite pronouns**, are always singular. Therefore, if an indefinite pronoun is the antecedent, the pronoun that replaces it must be singular. Examples of indefinite pronouns are listed in the Infobox in Chapter 22, page 436.

You may think that *everybody* is plural, but in grammatically correct English it is a singular word. Therefore, if you want to write clearly and correctly, memorize these words as the *-one*, *-thing*, and *-body* words—every*one*, every*thing*, every*body*, and so forth—plus *each*, *either*, *neither*. If any of these words is an antecedent, the pronoun that refers to it must be singular.

singular antecedent   singular pronoun

Each of the Boy Scouts received **his** merit badge.

singular antecedent   singular pronoun

Everyone on the girls' volleyball team donated **her** time to the project.

Using Gender-Neutral Language

Consider this sentence:

Everybody in the math class brought _____ own calculator.

How do you choose the correct pronoun to fill in the blank? If everybody in the class is male, you can write

Everybody in the math class brought **his** own calculator.

Or, if everybody in the class is female, you can write

Everybody in the math class brought **her** own calculator.

Or, if the class has students of both sexes, you can write

Everybody in the math class brought **his or her** own calculator.

In the past, most writers used the pronoun *his* to refer to both men and women. Today, many writers try to use *his or her* to avoid sexual bias. If you find that using *his or her* is getting awkward or repetitive, you can rewrite the sentence and *make the antecedent plural*:

correct: **The students** in the math class brought **their** own calculators.

But you can't shift from singular to plural. You can't write

incorrect: **Everybody** in the math class brought **their** own calculators.

EXERCISE **2**	**MAKING PRONOUNS AND ANTECEDENTS AGREE**

Write the appropriate pronoun in the blank space in each of the following sentences. Look carefully for the antecedent before you choose the pronoun.

1. My essay is disorganized and confusing; I really should edit _____.

2. Years ago, most people were careful with their cash; _____ were taught to save money, not to spend it.

3. I noticed that a woman was advertising a reward for the return of _____ BlackBerry.

4. The restaurant was very luxurious; all of _____ glassware was made of crystal.

5. When the little girl had a birthday party, _____ wanted to invite the whole neighbourhood.

6. Children with nothing to do all summer may wind up getting into trouble with _____ friends because of boredom.

7. Neither of the men chosen to lead the campaign wanted to devote _____ time to fundraising.

8. Everyone named an Outstanding Father of the Year had _____ own opinion about the ceremony.

9. Each of the sisters has won an athletic scholarship to the college of _____ choice.

10. I am beginning to enjoy my exercise class; _____ helps me relax.

EXERCISE 3 — MORE ABOUT MAKING PRONOUNS AND ANTECEDENTS AGREE

Write the appropriate pronoun in the blank in each of the following sentences. Look carefully for the antecedent before you choose the pronoun.

1. Bring home anything from Perfect Pizzas; _____ will taste good to me.

2. At the women's basketball tournament, one of the players hurt _____ back.

3. Every Saturday, Lennie and Geraldo take _____ cars to the car wash.

4. One of my antique cups is cracked so badly that _____ cannot be repaired.

5. All of my aunts gave me _____ version of the family feud that has been going on for years.

6. Everyone in the management program wore _____ best dress to the graduation dinner dance.

7. Ray cleaned his house thoroughly because he wanted everything to look _____ best for the visitors.

8. I think somebody from the men's soccer team left _____ cleats behind.

9. Nothing at the movies looked as if _____ would appeal to a teenage audience.

10. Either of the men could have given _____ seat to the elderly woman.

COLLECTIVE NOUNS AND THEIR PRONOUNS

Collective nouns refer to more than one person or thing. See the examples in the Infobox in Chapter 22, page 437.

Most of the time, collective nouns take a singular pronoun.

collective noun   singular pronoun

The **team** that was ahead in the playoffs lost **its** home game.

collective noun   singular pronoun

The **corporation** changed **its** policy on parental leave.

Collective nouns are usually singular because the group is losing a game or changing a policy *as one*, as a unit. Collective nouns take a plural pronoun only when the members of the group are acting individually, not as a unit.

The **class** picked up **their** class rings this morning. (The members of the class picked up their own rings, individually.)

EXERCISE 4	**MAKING PRONOUNS AND ANTECEDENTS AGREE: COLLECTIVE NOUNS**

Circle the correct pronoun in parentheses in each of the following sentences.

1. The computer company has a reputation for being extremely generous to (their/its) employees.

2. Skyward Airlines was involved in a campaign to change (their/its) image.

3. The flock of sheep enters the barn to have (their/its) coats shorn.

4. After the singer left the stage, the audience expressed (their/its) disappointment with boos and shouts.

5. Two of the teams were selling candy to raise money for (their/its) equipment.

6. The family lost (their/its) home in a fire last week.

7. I loved working at Castle Company because (it/they) gave me such a generous package of benefits.

8. The club made a list of (its/their) responsibilities.

9. The general was worried that the army wouldn't be able to hold (their/its) position.

10. The gang began to fall apart when the members started finding other things to do with (its/their) time.

EXERCISE 5	**EDITING A PARAGRAPH FOR ERRORS OF PRONOUN–ANTECEDENT AGREEMENT**

Read the following paragraph carefully, looking for errors in agreement of pronouns and their antecedents. Cross out any pronoun that does not agree with its antecedent and write the correct pronoun above. There are five pronouns that need to be corrected.

The Paper Company is a great place to work. The managers are firm but friendly in their relations with the employees, and working conditions are pleasant. The company has designed their policies to motivate employees, not to intimidate them. Everybody in the workplace knows they will be treated fairly. The Paper Company is not only considerate of workers, but it is also concerned for the environment. All the products are made of recycled paper. Thus, each of the items made for sale contributes their part to conservation. Workers and managers can feel good, knowing that he or she can help the planet. I wish everyone in this country would do their part, just as the Paper Company does.

EXERCISE **6** 	**WRITING SENTENCES WITH PRONOUN–ANTECEDENT AGREEMENT** With a partner or with a group, write a sentence for each of the following pairs of words, using each pair as a pronoun and its antecedent. The first pair is done for you.

1. students . . . their

   sentence: College students who have children need to plan their time
   carefully.

2. council . . . its

   sentence: _____
   _____

3. anyone . . . his or her

   sentence: _____
   _____

4. celebrities . . . they

   sentence: _____
   _____

5. complaining . . . it

   sentence: _____
   _____

6. neither . . . her

   sentence: _____
   _____

    7. each . . . his or her

      sentence: _____

      _____

    8. Canada . . . it

      sentence: _____

      _____

    9. movies and popular music . . . they

      sentence: _____

      _____

    10. credit card debt . . . it

      sentence: _____

      _____

      _____

PRONOUNS AND THEIR ANTECEDENTS: BEING CLEAR

Remember that pronouns are words that replace or refer to other words, and that those other words that are replaced or referred to are called antecedents.

Make sure that a pronoun has one clear antecedent. Your writing will be vague and confusing if a pronoun appears to refer to more than one antecedent or if it doesn't have any specific antecedent to refer to. In grammar, such confusing language is called a problem with **pronoun reference**.

Two or More Antecedents

When the pronoun could refer to more than one thing, the sentence can become confusing or silly. The following are examples of unclear reference.

> *Jim told his father that his bike had been stolen.* (Whose bike was stolen? Jim's? His father's?)
>
> *She put the cake on the table, took off her apron, pulled up a chair, and began to eat it.* (What did she eat? The cake? The table? Her apron? The chair?)

If there is no single clear antecedent, you must rewrite the sentence to make the reference clear. Sometimes, the rewritten sentence may seem repetitive, but a little repetition is better than a lot of confusion.

> **unclear:** *Jim told his father that his bike had been stolen.*
>
> **clear:** *Jim told his father that Jim's bike had been stolen.*
>
> **clear:** *Jim told his father that his father's bike had been stolen.*
>
> **clear:** *Jim told his father, "My bike has been stolen."*

unclear: She put the cake on the table, took off her apron, pulled up a chair, and began to eat it.

clear: She put the cake on the table, took off her apron, pulled up a chair, and began to eat the cake.

No Clear Antecedent

Sometimes, the problem is a little trickier. Can you spot what's wrong with this sentence?

unclear: Bill decided to take a part-time job, which worried his parents. (What worried Bill's parents? His decision to work part-time? Or the job itself?)

Be very careful with the pronoun *which.* If there is any chance that using *which* will confuse the reader, rewrite the sentence and get rid of *which.*

clear: Bill's parents were worried about the kind of part-time job he chose.

clear: Bill's decision to work part-time worried his parents.

Sometimes, a pronoun has nothing to refer to; it has no antecedent.

When Bill got to the train station, they said the train was going to be late. (Who said the train was going to be late? The ticket agents? Strangers whom Bill met on the platform?)

Maria has always loved medicine and has decided that's what she wants to be. (What does "that" refer to? The only word it could refer to is "medicine," but Maria certainly doesn't want to be "a medicine.")

If a pronoun lacks an antecedent, add an antecedent or get rid of the pronoun.

add an antecedent:
When Bill got to the train station and asked the ticket agents about the schedule, they said the train was going to be late.

get rid of the pronoun:
Maria has always loved medicine and has decided she wants to be a physician.

Note: To check for clear reference of pronouns, underline any pronoun that may not be clear. Then try to draw a line from that pronoun to its antecedent. Are there two or more possible antecedents? Is there no antecedent? In either case, you need to rewrite.

EXERCISE 7

REWRITING SENTENCES FOR CLEAR PRONOUN REFERENCE

Rewrite the following sentences so that the pronouns have clear references. You may add, take out, or change words.

1. Oscar told Victor that he had a bad temper.

2. The service at Island Rooster Restaurant was terrible; he was slow to bring our menus and forgot to take our orders.

3. I was offered a position at Express Service, which pleased me.

4. I loved my visit to Halifax; they are so friendly and warm.

5. My father is a computer systems analyst, but I'm not interested in it.

6. Parents often fight with adolescent children because they are stubborn and inflexible.

7. The supervisor told the assistant that his office would be moved to a new location.

8. The car crossed the median and hit a truck, but it wasn't badly damaged.

9. They never told me about the fine print when I signed a lease for my apartment.

10. Don finally made a sale, which encouraged him.

EXERCISE **8**	**EDITING A PARAGRAPH FOR ERRORS IN PRONOUN AGREEMENT AND REFERENCE**

Correct any errors in pronoun agreement or reference in the following paragraph. Write your corrections above the lines. There are six errors.

The food at Casa Taco is good, but the real attraction is the atmosphere. They are so friendly that a visit to the restaurant can seem like a family reunion. From the cashier to the counter staff, everybody does their best to make the customers feel special. For example, the people behind the counter know my order before I tell them, and they often tease me about being adventurous and trying new items. In addition, the lady at the cash register always has a smile and a joke for me. The good feeling spreads to all the customers. Nobody loses their temper or raises their voice over an incorrect order or a long wait. Even if the restaurant is crowded, the crowd never loses their patience. Casa Taco treats each customer like a special person and invites them into a special place.

CHAPTER 24
Using Pronouns Correctly: Consistency and Case

MAKING PRONOUNS CONSISTENT

When you write, you do it from a point of view, and each point of view requires certain pronouns. If you write from the first-person point of view, you use the pronoun *I* (singular) or *we* (plural). If you write from the second-person point of view, you use the pronoun *you*, whether your subject is singular or plural. (Keep in mind that there is no such word as "youse," often used in error as the second-person plural.) If you write from the third-person point of view, you use the pronouns *he*, *she*, or *it* (singular) or *they* (plural).

Different kinds of writing may require different points of view. When you're writing a set of directions, for example, you might use the second-person (*you*) point of view. For an essay about your childhood, you might use the first-person (*I*) point of view.

Whatever point of view you select, use **consistency** in choosing pronouns. That is, you shouldn't shift person without a good reason.

> **not consistent:** Every time I go shopping on Boxing Day, parking lots are so crowded that **you** have to drive around for hours looking for a parking space.

> **consistent:** Every time I go shopping on Boxing Day, parking lots are so crowded that I have to drive around for hours looking for a parking space.

| EXERCISE **1** | **CONSISTENCY IN PRONOUNS** |

Correct any inconsistency in point of view in the following sentences. Cross out the incorrect pronoun and write the correct one above it.

1. Breakfast is a meal on the run because I am always late for work and you never have time to cook a big breakfast.

2. After the students are seated in the classroom, the professor circulates an attendance sheet for you to sign.

3. Motorists should use caution when merging on the highway; if they don't check blind spots, you can be hit by another driver.

4. At my doctor's office, patients can wait for an hour before the doctor is ready to see you.

5. The law students filed into the auditorium, nervously waiting for the proctors to enter and give you the three-hour exam.

6. They were irritated by his conversation because you couldn't get a word into his endless chatter.

7. When we drove into Manitoba, the snow was coming down so heavily that you could barely see the road.

8. In the college cafeteria, students sit at long tables, socialize with their friends, or do your homework.

9. Every time I visit my sister's house, you know she's been cleaning and polishing all day.

10. When I contacted my cellphone service provider, I thought the staff was so rude that you swore you'd switch to another provider the next day.

EXERCISE 2	**CORRECTING SENTENCES WITH CONSISTENCY PROBLEMS**

Rewrite the following sentences, correcting any errors in consistency of pronouns. To make the corrections, you may have to change, add, or take out words.

1. You could tell the atmosphere was tense when we walked in and saw our friends sitting in silence.

   rewritten: _____

   _____

2. My grandmother's house was a favourite with all the grandchildren; you knew you would always have fun there.

   rewritten: _____

   _____

3. A supervisor can gain respect if you treat all the workers fairly and communicate openly.

   rewritten: _____

   _____

4. Students who are just starting college can be overwhelmed by the reading assignments; you are not used to reading so much so quickly.

   rewritten: _____

   _____

5. The best part about my public speaking class is that you can relax when someone else is giving a speech.

   rewritten: _____

   _____

6. I can't ask Miguel to help me because he'll talk your ear off about self-reliance.

   rewritten: _____

   _____

7. It doesn't matter how politely I try to explain my situation; she'll get angry with you every time.

   rewritten: _____

   _____

8. Students who miss the test can take a make-up test only after the instructor decides you have a valid excuse.

   rewritten: _____

   _____

9. The worst thing about my job at the restaurant is that you have to spend hours on your feet.

   rewritten: _____

   _____

10. If an employee genuinely cares about a pleasant work environment, you shouldn't gossip with co-workers.

    rewritten: _____

    _____

CHOOSING THE CASE OF PRONOUNS

Pronouns have forms that show number and person, and they also have forms that show **case**. Here's a list of three cases of pronouns:

singular pronouns

	subjective case	objective case	possessive case
1st person	I	me	my
2nd person	you	you	your
3rd person	he, she, it	him, her, it	his, her, its

plural pronouns

1st person	we	us	our
2nd person	you	you	your
3rd person	they	them	their

The rules for choosing the case of pronouns are simple:

1. When a pronoun is used as a subject, use the subjective case.
2. When a pronoun is used as the object of a verb or the object of a preposition, use the objective case.

3. When a pronoun is used to show ownership, use the possessive case.

pronouns used as subjects:

> **She** calls the office once a week.
>
> Sylvia wrote the letter, and **we** revised it.

pronouns used as objects:

> Ernestine called **him** yesterday.
>
> He gave all his money to **me**.

pronouns used to show possession:

> I'm worried about **my** grade in French.
>
> The nightclub has lost **its** popularity.

Problems Choosing Pronoun Case

One time when you need to be careful in choosing case is when the pronoun is part of a related group of words. If the pronoun is part of a related group of words, isolate the pronoun. Next, try out the pronoun choices. Then decide which pronoun is correct and write the correct sentence. For example, which of these sentences is correct?

> Aunt Sophie planned a big dinner for Tom and **I**.

or

> Aunt Sophie planned a big dinner for Tom and **me**.

Step 1: Isolate the pronoun. Eliminate the related words *Tom and*.

Step 2: Try each case:

> Aunt Sophie planned a big dinner for **I**.

or

> Aunt Sophie planned a big dinner for **me**.

Step 3: The correct sentence is

> Aunt Sophie planned a big dinner for Tom and **me**.

The pronoun acts as an object, so it takes the objective case.

To make sure you understand this principle, try working through the steps once more in order. Which of the following sentences is correct?

> Last week, **me** and my friend took a ride on the new commuter train.

or

> Last week, **I** and my friend took a ride on the new commuter train.

Step 1: Isolate the pronoun. Eliminate the related words *and my friend*.

Step 2: Try each case:

> Last week, **me** took a ride on the new commuter train.

or

> Last week, I took a ride on the new commuter train.

Step 3:   The correct sentence is

> Last week, I and my friend took a ride on the new commuter train.

The pronoun acts as a subject, so it takes the subjective case.
   Note: It is more correct to write it this way:

> Last week, my friend and I took a ride on the new commuter train.

Common Errors with Pronoun Case

Be careful to avoid these common errors:

1. *Between* **is a preposition.** The pronouns that follow it are objects of the preposition: between *us*, between *them*, between *you and me*. It is *never correct* to write *between you and I*.

   not this: The plans for the surprise party must be kept secret between you and I.

   but this: The plans for the surprise party must be kept secret between you and me.

2. **Never use** *myself* **as a replacement for** *I* **or** *me*.

   not this: My father and myself want to thank you for this honour.

   but this: My father and I want to thank you for this honour.

   not this: She thought the prize should be awarded to Arthur and myself.

   but this: She thought the prize should be awarded to Arthur and me.

   The correct use of pronouns ending in *-self* or *-selves* is for emphasis (*I myself loved the movie*) or as reflexive verbs (*They congratulated themselves*).

3. **The possessive pronoun** *its* **has no apostrophe.** Remember that the equivalent possessive pronouns are *my*, *your*, *her*, and *their*, and none of those has an apostrophe. *It's* is used only as the contraction of *it is*.

   not this: The car held it's value.

   but this: The car held its value.

4. **Pronouns that complete comparisons can be in the subjective, objective, or possessive case.**

   subjective: Christa speaks better than I.

   objective: The comment hurt Manny more than **her**.

   possessive: My car is as fast as **his**.

   To decide on the correct pronoun, add the words that complete the comparison and say them aloud:

Christa speaks better than I (speak).

The comment hurt Manny more than (the comment hurt) **her**.

My car is as fast as **his** (car is).

Note that the pronoun you choose can change the meaning.

The comment hurt Manny more than (the comment hurt) **her**.

versus

The comment hurt Manny more than **she** (hurt Manny).

EXERCISE **3**	**CHOOSING THE RIGHT PRONOUN CASE**

Circle the correct pronoun in parentheses in each of the following sentences.

1. The newspaper updates (its/it's) website every hour.
2. Though my brother is my family's favourite, I am smarter than (he/him).
3. When the neighbour couldn't get an answer, he kept calling Carla and (they/them) all night.
4. Without a guidebook, Mr. Martinez and (she/her) were lost in the big city.
5. I promise not to mention what we discussed; our conversation will be strictly between you and (I/me).
6. The nominating committee selected two applicants from out of town and (me/myself) as finalists for the position.
7. My pickup truck is twelve years old; it's on (it's/its) last legs.
8. His comments about the proposal were unfairly critical of my staff and (myself/me).
9. The security officer and (we/us) looked all over for the missing car.
10. The job was a wonderful opportunity; it was a new beginning for (me/I) and him.

EXERCISE **4**	**MORE ABOUT CHOOSING THE RIGHT PRONOUN CASE**

Circle the correct pronoun in parentheses in each of the following sentences.

1. After I met Frank at my sister's house, life began to change for (me/I) and him.
2. Before breakfast, Sylvia and (she/her) went out for an early morning run.

3. Dr. Leah Gupta is a dedicated researcher, but Dr. Andrew McKenna is just as committed as (she/her).

4. Marty is a much better listener than (he/him).

5. My husband planned a big surprise for the children and (I/me).

6. Even though you both speak French, your accent is different from (him/his).

7. James and I visited the old hockey arena, but it didn't have any of (its/it's) former magic.

8. I spent the whole afternoon looking for Tim and (she/her), but they must have gone out of town.

9. My grandfather's will left a small sum of money to be divided between my sister and (me/myself).

10. Officer Lee and (he/him) are looking into suspicious activity at the waterfront.

| EXERCISE **5** | **WRITING YOUR OWN TEXT ON PRONOUN CASE** |

With a partner or with a group, write two sentences that could be used as examples for each of the following rules. The first is done for you.

Rule 1: When a pronoun is used as a subject, use the subjective case.

examples: *He complained about the noise in the street.*

Tired and hungry, they stopped for lunch.

Rule 2: When a pronoun is used as the object of a verb or the object of a preposition, use the objective case.

examples: _____

_____

Rule 3: When a pronoun is used to show ownership, use the possessive case.

examples: _____

_____

Rule 4: When a pronoun is part of a related group of words, isolate the pronoun to choose the case. (For examples, write two sentences in which the pronoun is part of a related group of words.)

examples: _____

_____

EXERCISE 6

EDITING A PARAGRAPH FOR ERRORS IN PRONOUN CONSISTENCY AND CASE

Correct any errors in pronoun consistency or case in the following paragraph. Write your corrections above the lines. There are seven errors.

I love to go to the Downtown Flea Market because there are so many things you can do and buy there. My brother and me often spend a whole Saturday afternoon at the market, snacking on the many varieties of ethnic food, listening to the music, and watching the performers. My favourite place for shopping is the used furniture area; I am always looking for an old lamp or a framed poster for my room. My brother loves the Greek market; he says it's pastry is the best in the city. We both like to sit and listen to the music. Each weekend, a different group plays, and some of the music is excellent. My friend Dave takes his girlfriend to hear the groups every Friday night. Dave and her like to catch all the new talent. Even my best friend Carlos, who plays a guitar in a local band, says some of the performers are as good as him. In addition, the market has street entertainers. Little children can visit a friendly clown and get your faces painted, and street dancers crowd the sidewalks, making dramatic moves to the sounds of a portable DVD player. I think anyone can spend a pleasant afternoon at the flea market. It's been the highlight of many days for myself.

CHAPTER 25
Punctuation

You probably know a good deal about punctuation. In fact, you probably know most of the rules so well that you punctuate your writing automatically, without having to think about the rules. Nevertheless, there are times when every writer has to stop and think, "Do I put a comma here?" or "Should I capitalize this word?" The following review of the basic rules of punctuation can help you answer such questions.

THE PERIOD

Periods are used in two ways.

1. Use a period to mark the end of a sentence that makes a statement.

> We invited him to dinner at our house.
>
> When Richard spoke, no one paid attention.

2. Use a period after abbreviations.

> Mr. Ryan
>
> James Wing, Sr.
>
> 10:00 P.M.

Note: If a sentence ends with a period marking an abbreviation, do not add a second period.

THE QUESTION MARK

Use a **question mark** after a direct question.

> Aren't polar bears adorable?
>
> Do you have car insurance?

If a question is not a direct question, it does not get a question mark.

> They asked if I thought polar bears were adorable.
>
> She questioned whether I had car insurance.

EXERCISE 1	PUNCTUATING WITH PERIODS AND QUESTION MARKS

Add any missing periods and question marks to each of the following sentences.

1. My grandmother offered me some cookies and iced tea, and she tried to get me to eat a sandwich, too
2. When did Nadia start working at the credit card company

3. Felicia thinks Mr. Johannsen is a great math teacher
4. Manny is not sure whether his father has auto insurance
5. Is Drew bringing his guitar
6. Lorene will try to get there at 3:30 PM, but she may be a little late
7. Gurpreet wanted to know when the movie started
8. My girlfriend asked me if I was taking a break from studying
9. I wonder why he is always twenty minutes late for class
10. How much more orange juice is in the refrigerator

THE COMMA

There are four main ways to use a **comma**, as well as other, less important ways. *Memorize the four main ways.* If you can learn and understand these four rules, you'll be more confident and correct in your punctuation. That is, you'll use a comma only when you have a reason to do so; you won't be scattering commas in your sentences simply because you think a comma might fit, as many writers do.

The four main ways to use a comma are as a lister, a linker, an introducer, or an inserter (use two commas).

1. **Lister.** Commas support items in a series. These items can be words, phrases, or clauses.

    comma between words in a list:

    The most popular colours for business suits are navy blue, charcoal grey, and black.

    comma between phrases in a list:

    I wanted a house on a quiet street, in a friendly neighbourhood, and near a school.

    comma between clauses in a list:

    Last week he graduated from college, he found the woman of his dreams, and he won the lottery.

    Note: In a list, the comma before *and* is optional, but most writers use it. We recommend using this comma because in some sentences it avoids ambiguity.

2. **Linker.** A comma and a coordinating conjunction link two independent clauses. Remember from Chapter 14 that the coordinating conjunctions are *for, and, nor, but, or, yet,* and *so* (use the acronym FANBOYS to remember). The comma goes in front of the coordinating conjunction.

I have to get to work on time, or I'll get into trouble with my boss.

The movie was long, but the audience loved the action.

3. **Introducer.** Put a comma after introductory words, phrases, or clauses in a sentence.

comma after an introductory word:

No, I can't afford that car.

Dad, give me some help with the dishes.

comma after an introductory phrase:

By the way, the meeting was changed from noon to one o'clock.

In the long run, you'll be better off without him.

Before the anniversary party, my father bought my mother a necklace.

comma after an introductory clause:

If you call home, your parents will be pleased.

When the phone rings, I'm always in the shower.

4. **Inserter.** When words or phrases that are *not* necessary are inserted into a sentence, put a comma on *both* sides of the inserted material.

The game, unfortunately, was rained out.

My test score, believe it or not, was the highest in the class.

Potato chips, my favourite snack food, taste better when they're fresh.

James, caught in the middle of the argument, tried to keep the peace.

Using commas as inserters requires that you decide what is essential to the meaning of the sentence and what is not essential.

If you don't need material in a sentence, put commas around that material. If you do need material in a sentence, don't put commas around that material.

For example, consider this sentence:

The girl who called me was selling magazine subscriptions.

Do you need the words "who called me" to understand the meaning of the sentence? To answer this question, write the sentence without these words:

The girl was selling magazine subscriptions.

Reading the shorter sentence, you might ask, "Which girl?" If so, the words *who called me* are essential to the sentence. Therefore, you *do not* put commas around them.

correct: The girl who called me was selling magazine subscriptions.

Remember that the proper name of a person, place, or thing is often sufficient to identify it. Therefore, any information that follows a proper name is usually inserted material; it gets commas on both sides.

Mixmaster Coffee, which has free wireless access, is my favourite place to pass the time.

Sam Harris, the man who won the marathon, lives on my block.

However, if there is more than one of the person, place, or thing, the information is essential.

The Mixmaster Coffee that is near my house has free wireless access.
(There is another Mixmaster Coffee that is not near your house and that may or may not have free wireless access.)

The Sam Harris who won the marathon lives on my block. (There might be another Sam Harris, so you want to identify which Sam Harris you are referring to.)

Note: Sometimes, the material that is needed in a sentence is called **essential** (or restrictive), and the material that is not needed is called **non-essential** (or non-restrictive).

Remember the four main ways to use a comma—as a *lister, linker, introducer,* or *inserter*—and you'll solve many of your problems using punctuation.

EXERCISE	**PUNCTUATING WITH COMMAS: THE FOUR MAIN WAYS**
2	Add commas only where they're needed in the following sentences. Do not add any other punctuation, and do not change any existing punctuation. Some of the sentences don't need commas.

1. Whether you like it or not you have to get up early tomorrow.

2. Skiing snowboarding and surfing all demand tremendous agility and fitness.

3. I was forced to call the emergency towing service and waited two hours for help.

4. The two-storey house by the lake is the most attractive one in the neighbourhood.

5. Chicken Delights the only restaurant in my neighbourhood is always crowded on a Saturday night.

6. No you can't get a bus to the city on Saturdays unless you're prepared to leave early.

7. Dripping wet and miserable I crouched under a huge tree until the rain stopped.

8. Nick got a job right after college for he'd spent his final year making contacts and sending applications.

9. I wanted to look professional for my job interview so I wore a conservative suit.

10. Cleaning the kitchen is a chore because I have to scrub the sink wipe the counters empty the garbage and wash the floor.

Other Ways to Use a Comma

There are other places to use a comma. Reviewing these uses will help you feel more confident as a writer.

1. **Use commas with quotations.** Use a comma to set off direct quotations from the rest of the sentence.

   My father told me, "Money doesn't grow on trees."

   "Let's split the bill," Raymond said.

   He wrote, "I'll never love again."

   Note that the comma that introduces the quotation goes before the quotation marks. But once the quotation has begun, commas or periods generally go inside the quotation marks.

2. **Use commas with dates and addresses.** Use commas between the items in dates and locations or addresses.

   August 5, 1986, is Guraj's date of birth.

   We lived in Fernie, British Columbia, before we moved to Manitoba.

   Notice the comma after the year in the date and the comma after the province in the address. These commas are needed when you write a date or address within a sentence.

3. **Use commas for numbers.** Use commas in numbers of one thousand or larger.

   The price of equipment was $ 1,293.

   In SI style, which is now more commonly used in Canada, numerals of four digits have no separator (1293), and a space rather than a comma is used in numerals of five digits or more (563 000). Ask your instructor which method is preferred in your course.

4. **Use commas for clarity.** Insert a comma when you need it to make something clear.

   Whatever you did, did the trick.

   I don't like to dress up, but in this job I have to, to get ahead.

EXERCISE **3**	**PUNCTUATION: OTHER WAYS TO USE A COMMA**

Use commas wherever they're needed in the following sentences. Do not add any other punctuation, and do not change any existing punctuation.

1. Mr. Chen used to say "Every cloud has a silver lining."

2. My best friend was born on January 29 1976 in Mississauga Ontario.

3. "I would never borrow your car without asking first" my little brother asserted.

4. She bit into the apple and mumbled "This is the best apple I've ever tasted."

5. I graduated from Deerfield High School on June 19 2004 and started my first real job on June 19 2005 in the same town.

6. The repairs on my truck cost me $2392.

7. The Reilly mansion across town is selling for $359000.

8. He ordered a sandwich, and she a drink.

9. On April 30 2014 my father warned me "Don't forget to file your income tax forms."

10. "Nothing exciting ever happens around here" my cousin complained.

EXERCISE

PUNCTUATING WITH COMMAS: A COMPREHENSIVE EXERCISE

Put commas wherever they are needed in the following sentences. Do not add any other punctuation, and do not change any existing punctuation. Some of the sentences do not need commas.

1. I wanted a fabric with grey white and navy in it but I had to settle for one with grey and white.

2. He was born on July 15 1970 in a small town in Quebec.

3. I'm sure Jeffrey that you aren't telling me the whole story.

4. The family wanted to spend a quiet weekend at home but wound up doing errands all over town.

5. My favourite novel *Surfacing* is set in northern Ontario.

6. She devoted an entire day to cleaning the kitchen cabinets reorganizing the pantry shelves and scrubbing the hall floor.

7. The man who wrote you is a friend of mine.

8. Whether David likes it or not he has to work overtime again.

9. "Get out your notebooks" the teacher said.

10. Honestly I can't say which is a better buy.

11. I tried to reason with her I tried to warn her and I even tried to frighten her but she was determined to proceed with her plans.

12. Pizza Pronto my favourite restaurant is going out of business.

13. We can call him tomorrow or stop by his house.

14. For the third time the child whispered "Mommy I want to go home now."

15. People who have never seen the ocean are not prepared for its beauty.

16. My sister is in two important ways the opposite of my mother.

17. In two important ways my sister is the opposite of my mother.

18. The visitors were friendly and polite yet they seemed a little shy.

19. If you lose lose with style and class.

20. The car in the garage doesn't belong to me nor do I have permission to borrow it.

THE APOSTROPHE

Use the **apostrophe** in two ways.

1. Use an apostrophe in contractions to show that letters have been omitted.

do not = don't

I will = I'll

is not = isn't

she would = she'd

will not = won't

Also use the apostrophe to show that numbers have been omitted:

the summer of 2003 = the summer of '03

2. Use an apostrophe to show possession. Show ownership by adding an apostrophe and *s*.

the ring belonging to Jill = Jill's ring

the wallet belonging to somebody = somebody's wallet

the books that are owned by my father = my father's books

If two people jointly own something, put the '*s*** on the last person's name.**

Gillian and Mike own a house = Gillian and Mike's house

If two people each own something, put the '*s*** on each person's name**

Gillian and Mike each own a house = Gillian's and Mike's houses

Add only an apostrophe to plural words ending in *s*, but add an '*s*** to singular words ending in *s*.**

the dog owned by two boys = the boys' dog

the toys belonging to two cats = the cats' toys

the house belonging to Ms. Jones = Ms. Jones's house

Caution: Be careful with apostrophes. These words, the possessive pronouns, do not take apostrophes: *his, hers, theirs, ours, yours, its*.

not this: The pencils were their's.

but this: The pencils were theirs.

not this: The steak lost it's flavour.

but this: The steak lost its flavour.

| EXERCISE 5 | PUNCTUATING WITH APOSTROPHES |

Add apostrophes where they're needed in the following sentences. Some sentences don't need apostrophes.

1. I'm sure Johns intentions were good.
2. That movie sure doesnt live up to its reputation.
3. I love my cousins, but I disagree with their political views.
4. I was sure that the items recovered in the police raid would turn out to be ours.
5. I was delighted by Sioux Narrows natural beauty.
6. Professor Lyons is an expert in the field of childrens rights.
7. She had lost the womens hockey sweaters.
8. I know shes not interested in aerobics.
9. Theyll take the train to Jim and Davids house.
10. I can give the boys advice, but the problem is still theirs.

THE SEMICOLON

There are two ways to use **semicolons**.

1. Use a semicolon to join two independent clauses.

Michael loved his old Camaro; he worked on it every weekend.

The situation was hopeless; I couldn't do anything.

Note: If the independent clauses are joined by a conjunctive adverb, you still need a semicolon. You will also need a comma after the conjunctive adverb if the conjunctive adverb is more than one syllable long.

He was fluent in Spanish; consequently, he was the perfect companion for our trip to Venezuela.

I called the hotline for twenty minutes; then I called another number.

2. Use semicolons to separate items in a list that contains commas. Adding semicolons will make the list easier to read.

The contestants came from Kenora, Ontario; Brandon, Manitoba; and Estevan, Saskatchewan.

The new officers of the club will be Althea Bethell, president; François Rivière, vice-president; Ricardo Perez, secretary; and Lou Phillips, treasurer.

THE COLON

A **colon** is used at the end of a complete statement. It introduces a list or an explanation.

colon introduces a list: When I went grocery shopping, I picked up a few things: milk, eggs, and coffee.

colon introduces an explanation: The room was a mess: dirty clothes were piled on the chairs, wet towels were thrown on the floor, and an empty pizza box was tossed in the closet.

Remember that the colon comes after a complete statement. What comes after the colon explains or describes what came before the colon. Look once more at the two examples, and you'll see the point.

When I went grocery shopping, I picked up a few things: milk, eggs, and coffee. (The words after the colon, **milk, eggs, and coffee,** explain what few things I picked up.)

The room was a mess: dirty clothes were piled on the chairs, wet towels were thrown on the floor, and an empty pizza box was tossed in the closet. (In this sentence, all the words after the colon describe what the mess was like.)

Some people use a colon every time they put a list in a sentence, but this is not a good rule to follow. Instead, remember that a colon, even one that introduces a list, must come after a complete statement.

not this: When I go to the beach, I always bring: suntan lotion, a big towel, and a cooler with iced tea.

but this: When I go to the beach, I always bring my supplies: suntan lotion, a big towel, and a cooler with iced tea.

A colon may also introduce quotations (whether short and integrated into the sentence or long and set off from the text).

As early as 1961, historian W. L. Morton, in his book *The Canadian Identity*, observed the true nature of this country: "Not life, liberty, and the pursuit of happiness, but peace, order, and good government are what the national government of Canada guarantees."

EXERCISE 6

USING SEMICOLONS AND COLONS

Add semicolons and colons where they're needed to each sentence below. You might have to change a comma to a semicolon.

1. Eileen picked me up at the train station then she drove me to my sister's house.

2. Every Thanksgiving, we have the same meal roast turkey, stuffing, cranberry sauce, and pumpkin pie.

3. You should bring a jacket to the game otherwise, you're going to get cold.

4. When I started working at the restaurant, I had to be trained in three areas customer relations, menu selections, and financial procedures.

5. Last night the Athletic League voted for Greg Patel, president, Lisa Tobin, vice-president, Graham Pritchard, second vice-president, and Daisy Fiero, treasurer.

6. You can keep an eye on the baby, meanwhile, I'll call the doctor about the baby's fever.

7. If you're going to the bakery bring me my usual order some bagels, a loaf of whole grain bread, and some cinnamon buns.

8. Frank arrived at nine he's always prompt.

9. You can pick up a bath mat at The Bay, and don't forget your son's goodies a wooden puzzle and a small stuffed animal.

10. I would never eat Brussels sprouts the very thought of it makes me sick.

THE EXCLAMATION MARK

The **exclamation mark** is used at the end of sentences that express strong emotion.

appropriate: You've won the lottery!

inappropriate: We had a great time! ("*Great*" already implies excitement.)

Be careful not to overuse the exclamation mark. If your choice of words is descriptive and makes use of a good vocabulary, you should not have to rely on the exclamation point for emphasis.

THE DASH

Use a **dash** to interrupt a sentence; use a pair of dashes to set off words within a sentence. The dash is somewhat dramatic, so be careful not to overuse it. In word processing, show a dash clearly by using two or three hyphens, not just one.

This is my last chance to warn him—and he'd better listen to my warning.

That silly show—believe it or not—is number one in the ratings.

PARENTHESES

Use **parentheses** to enclose extra material and afterthoughts.

I was sure that Ridgefield (the town I'd just visited) was not the place for me.

If your sentence includes a comma, make sure you place it after the closing parenthesis:

not this: She was accepted at that college, (her first choice) but her parents wanted her to go to a school closer to home.

but this: She was accepted at that college (her first choice), but her parents wanted her to go to a school closer to home.

Note: Commas in pairs, dashes in pairs, and parentheses are all used as inserters. They set off material that interrupts the flow of the sentence. The least dramatic and smoothest way to insert material is to use commas.

THE HYPHEN

A **hyphen** joins two or more descriptive words that act as a single word.

> The old car had a souped-up engine.
>
> Bill was a smooth-talking charmer.

EXERCISE **7**	**PUNCTUATING WITH EXCLAMATION MARKS, DASHES, PARENTHESES, AND HYPHENS**

Add any exclamation marks, dashes, parentheses, and hyphens that are needed in the sentences below. A colon or comma would also be appropriate in some sentences; however, for this exercise, choose from the punctuation indicated.

1. His plan for making a million dollars was the most lame brained scheme I'd ever heard.

2. The Carlton Gallery of Fine Art the place where I had my first job is located east of the river.

3. My son can't go anywhere without his collection of amusements one hundred Pokémon cards, five Bakugan toys, Lego figurines, and a grimy stuffed lamb.

4. Rosa could tell that the speaker was nervous he fidgeted with his notes, stumbled over his words, and blushed beet red.

5. Godzilla is at the window

6. Bring a raincoat, sweaters, thermal underwear, and heavy socks it's going to be freezing cold out there.

7. Cocoa Forest the smallest town in Midland County is best known for its Victorian houses and restored town square.

8. Don't you ever speak to me like that again

9. There are two kinds of desserts desserts that are good for you and desserts that taste good.

10. Stop it

QUOTATION MARKS

Use **quotation marks** for direct quotes, for the titles of short works, and for other, special uses.

1. **Put quotation marks around direct quotes—a speaker or writer's exact words.**

> My mother told me, "There are plenty of fish in the sea."
>
> "I'm never going there again," said Irene.
>
> "I'd like to buy you dinner," Peter said, "but I'm out of cash."
>
> My best friend wrote, "Stay away from that guy. He will break your heart."

CHAPTER TWENTY-FIVE: *Punctuation*

Look carefully at the preceding examples. Notice that a comma is used to introduce a direct quote, and that, at the end of the quotation, the comma or period goes inside the quotation marks.

My mother told me, "There are plenty of fish in the sea."

Notice how direct quotes of more than one sentence are punctuated. If the quote is written in one unit, quotation marks go before the first quoted word and after the last quoted word.

My best friend warned me, "Stay away from that guy. He will break your heart."

But if the quote is not written as one unit, the punctuation changes.

"Stay away from that guy," my best friend wrote. "He will break your heart."

Caution: Do *not* put quotation marks around indirect quotations.

indirect quotation: He asked if he could come with us.
direct quotation: He asked, "Can I come with you?"

indirect quotation: She said that she wanted more time.
direct quotation: "I want more time," she said.

2. **Put quotation marks around the titles of short works.** If you're writing the title of a chapter, a short story, an essay, a newspaper or magazine article, an episode of a television series, a poem, or a song, use quotation marks.

In Grade 8, we read Robert Frost's poem "The Road Not Taken."
My little sister has learned to sing "Itsy Bitsy Spider."

However, if you're writing the title of a longer work, such as a book, movie, magazine, play, television show, or record album, put the title in italics.

Last night, I saw an old movie, *Stand by Me*.
I read an article called "Campus Crime" in *Maclean's* magazine.

If you're handwriting or don't have access to italics, underline the titles of long works.

3. **There are other uses of quotation marks.** You can use quotation marks around special words in a sentence.

When you said "never," did you mean it?
People from Nova Scotia pronounce "boy" differently than I do.

(Words used in this way may also be put in italics, as we do in this book.)

If you're using a quote within a quote, use single quotation marks.

My brother complained, "Every time we get in trouble, Mom has to say, 'I told you so.'"

Kyle said, "Linda has a way of saying, 'Excuse me' that is really very rude."

CAPITAL LETTERS

There are ten main situations in which you **capitalize.**

1. Capitalize the first word of every sentence.

Yesterday, we saw our first soccer game.

2. Capitalize the first word in a direct quotation if the word begins a sentence.

My aunt said, "This is a gift for your birthday."

"Have some birthday cake," my aunt said, "and have some more ice cream."

(Notice that the second section of this quote doesn't begin with a capital letter because it does not begin a sentence.)

3. Capitalize the names of people.

Nancy Perez and Frank Scarpitti came to see me at the store.

I asked Mom to feed my cat.

Do not capitalize words like *mother, father, uncle,* and *aunt* if you put a possessive in front of them.

I asked my mom to feed my cat.

4. Capitalize people's titles.

I was a patient of Dr. Woo.

He has to see Dean Singh.

Don't capitalize when the title isn't connected to a name.

I was a patient of that doctor.

He has to see the dean.

5. Always capitalize nationalities, religions, races, months, days of the week, documents, organizations, holidays, and historical events or periods.

In high school, we never studied the Korean War, just the Second World War.

The Polish-Canadian Club will hold a picnic on Labour Day.

Use lowercase letters for the seasons.

I love fall because I love to watch the leaves change colour.

6. Capitalize the names of particular places.

We used to hold our annual meetings at Northside Auditorium in Lachine, Quebec, but this year we're meeting at Riverview Theatre in London, Ontario.

Use lowercase letters if a particular place is not named.

We'e looking for an auditorium we can book for our meeting.

7. Use capital letters for geographic locations.

Jim was determined to find a good job in the West.

But use lowercase letters for geographic directions.

To get to my house, you have to drive west on the freeway.

8. **Capitalize the names of specific products.**

I always drink Diet Pepsi for lunch.

But use lowercase letters for a general type of product.

I always drink a diet cola for lunch.

9. **Capitalize the names of specific school courses.**

I have to take Child Psychology III next term.

But use lowercase letters for a general academic subject.

My adviser told me to take a child psychology course.

10. **Capitalize the first and last words in the titles of long or short works, and capitalize all other significant words in the titles.** Significant words include nouns, pronouns, verbs, adjectives, adverbs, and some conjunctions (but not the coordinating conjunctions), and usually don't include longer prepositions.

I've always wanted to read The Old Man and the Sea.

Whenever we go to see a musical, my uncle sings "Don't Cry for Me,

Argentina" in the car.

Remember that the titles of long works, like books, should be italicized (underlined in handwritten work); the titles of short ones, like songs, are quoted.

EXERCISE **8**	**PUNCTUATING WITH QUOTATION MARKS, ITALICS OR UNDERLINING, AND CAPITAL LETTERS**

Add any missing quotation marks, underlining (italics), and capital letters to the sentences below.

1. Don't ever call me again, the repair person said, unless it's an emergency.

2. No one expected Home Alone to be such a popular movie, but it broke all box office records at the Sunset mall theatre.

3. James, you should be careful what you wish for, my aunt said, because you may get it.

4. That old word jock is mistakenly applied to anyone who likes sports.

5. My sisters all attended Broward Community college, but I'm going to a community college in the maritimes.

6. When I was growing up, my favourite television show was Thundercats, but now I love to watch old movies like It's a wonderful life or citizen kane.

7. Yesterday I tried to buy tickets for the concert at the coral beach amphitheatre, but the man at the ticket office said, we're sold out.

8. You always say I'm sorry and you never mean it, my boyfriend complained.

9. I told uncle Phil to be on time, but my uncle is a procrastinator.

10. Next semester, I'm taking courses in public speaking, business, and economics; I've already taken the seminar course called preparing for a business career.

NUMBERS

1. Spell out numbers that are written as one or two words.

Alice mailed **two hundred** brochures.

I spent **ninety** dollars on car repairs.

2. Use the numbers themselves if it takes more than two words to spell them out.

We looked through **243** old photographs.

The sticker price was **$10,397.99**.

(Another accepted style, often used in scientific and business writing, is to write out the numbers one to nine and use numerals for numbers ten or larger.)

3. Also use numbers to write dates, times, and addresses.

We live at 24 Cambridge Street.

They were married on April 3, 1993.

ABBREVIATIONS

Although you should spell out most words rather than abbreviate them, you may use common **abbreviations** like *Mr., Ms., Mrs., Jr., Sr.,* and *Dr.* when they're used with a proper name. Abbreviations may also be used for references to time and for organizations widely known by initials.

The moderator asked Ms. Steinem to comment.

The bus left at 5:00 P.M., and the trip took two hours.

He works for CIBC.

Note: It has become more common for periods not to be used in abbreviations of three letters or more. You would write B.C., but *FAQ*.

You should spell out the names of places, months, days of the week, courses of study, and words referring to parts of a book.

not this: I missed the last class, so I never got the notes for Chap. Three.

but this: I missed the last class, so I never got the notes for Chapter Three.

not this: He lives on Chestnut Street in Winnipeg, MB.

but this: He lives on Chestnut Street in Winnipeg, Manitoba.

not this: Pete missed his trig. test.

but this: Pete missed his trigonometry test.

EXERCISE 9	USING NUMBERS AND ABBREVIATIONS

Correct any errors in the use of numbers or abbreviations in the following sentences. Some sentences may not need corrections.

1. We are looking for Thomas Pittman, Jr., the man who wrote the editorial in today's paper.

2. My mother was born in Prince Albert, Sask., the youngest of 4 children, all girls.

3. The rent for the one-room apartment on Orchard St. was $1,250 a month.

4. I graduated from high school on June twenty-sixth, 2007, and I started my new job the following Mon.

5. The new biology prof. takes 2 weeks to return our test papers.

6. The answer to the psych. question is in Chap. 2 of the child psychology textbook.

7. The alarm went off at 7:00 A.M., so I had plenty of time to get ready for the flight to Calgary, Alta.

8. Dr. Chen found seventeen new specimens of a rare tropical insect; she'll study them in her research facility at the Charter Chemical Co.

9. I sorted through three hundred and fifty photographs before I came across the one of our old house on Empire Ave. in Thunder Bay, Ont.

10. Mario missed his econ. class last Wed. because he fell and twisted his ankle about fifty m from the classroom building.

EXERCISE 10	A COMPREHENSIVE EXERCISE ON PUNCTUATION AND MECHANICS

Add any missing punctuation to the following sentences. Correct any errors in capitalization and in use of numbers or abbreviations.

1. My sister had a hard time meeting her three boys demands for attention but she did her best.

2. The people at the store were extremely helpful furthermore they were willing to handle special orders.

3. Making a roux which is a classic French technique is taught in cooking 101.

4. Every time I study with you she said I get good grades on my tests.

5. Parents should be willing to listen children should be willing to talk and both groups should be open to new ideas if families are going to live in harmony.

6. Repairing the damages caused by the fire cost three hundred and fifty-seven dollars.

7. My little sister walks around singing her favourite hannah montana song Lily do you want to know a secret all day in her squeaky little girl voice.

8. Dont forget to pick up the food we need for the picnic hamburgers hot dogs potato salad and corn.

9. No one told Jose about the job opening so he didn't apply for the position.

10. Leo was born in Fredericton NB on June 3 1968 and he grew up in a nearby town.

11. Christina Ruggiero who always sends me a birthday card is a considerate and thoughtful person.

12. We were sure that rain or shine he would be there.

13. I'm sorry dad that I was late for James farewell dinner.

14. Unless you replace those worn out tires you cant drive safely on rain slicked roads.

15. Philip asked Is there a shortcut to the warehouse

16. Philip asked if there was a shortcut to the warehouse

17. When he was in high school he took english courses but at Jackson college he is taking communication courses.

18. The girl running across the ice slipped and fell then she grabbed at a fence post and pulled herself up.

19. Bolton Furniture has kept its reputation for quality merchandise at a reasonable price thus its been able to survive in hard times.

20. I'm thinking of writing a book called how to manage your time but I never seem to have time to write it.

APPENDIX
Grammar for ESL Students

NOUNS AND ARTICLES

A **noun** names a person, place, or thing. There are count nouns and non-count nouns.

Count nouns refer to persons, places, or things that can be counted: three *doughnuts*, two *computers*, five *pencils*

Non-count nouns refer to things that can't be counted: *medicine, housework, mail*

Here are some more examples of count and non-count nouns:

count	non-count
rumour	gossip
violin	music
school	intelligence
suitcase	luggage

One way to remember the difference between count and non-count nouns is to put the word *much* in front of the noun. For example, if you can say *much luggage*, then *luggage* is a non-count noun.

EXERCISE 1	IDENTIFYING COUNT AND NON-COUNT NOUNS

Write *count* or *non-count* next to each word below.

1. _____ sailboat

2. _____ button

3. _____ time

4. _____ honesty

5. _____ valour

6. _____ health

7. _____ food

8. _____ milk

9. _____ gold

10. _____ tree

Using Articles with Nouns

Articles point out nouns. Articles are either **indefinite** (*a, an*) or **definite** (*the*). There are several rules for using these articles:

- Use *a* in front of consonant sounds and use *an* before vowel sounds:

a card	an orange
a radio	an answer
a button	an entrance
a house	an hour
a nightmare	an uncle
a BLT	an MBA

Notice that *hour* takes *an* because you pronounce it with a vowel sound as though it were *our*, but *house* takes *a* because you pronounce it with the consonant *h* sound. Also, notice that the indefinite article for an abbreviation is based on whether the first letter is pronounced as a consonant (the *bee* in BLT) or as a vowel (the *em* in MBA).

- Use *a* or *an* in front of singular count nouns whose specific identity is not known to the reader (*a* or *an* means "*any* one").

  I ate **an egg.**
  James planted **a tree.**

- Do not use *a* or *an* with most non-count nouns:

  not this: Selena filled the tank with ~~a gasoline.~~
  but this: Selena filled the tank with **gasoline.**

- Use *the* before both singular and plural count nouns whose specific identity is known to the reader:

  The dress with the beads on it is my party dress.
  Most of **the movies** I rent are science fiction films.

- Do not use *the* before plural count nouns if the specific identity is not known.

  Movies made in Canada are becoming more popular.
  He saw **horses** in the open pasture.

- Use *the* before non-count nouns only when they are specifically identified:

  not this: I need ~~the~~ help. (Whose help? What help? The non-count noun *help* is not specifically identified.)
  but this: I need **the help** of a good plumber. (Now *help* is specifically identified.)

  not this: Kindness of the people who took me in was remarkable. (The non-count noun *kindness* is being specifically identified, so you need *the*.)
  but this: The kindness of the people who took me in was remarkable.

EXERCISE **2**	**USING *A* OR *AN***

Put *a* or *an* in the spaces where it is needed. Some sentences are correct as they are.

1. Ms. Verinsky took us to _____ movie.

2. I need to buy _____ furniture for my new house.

3. My son was eating _____ orange.

4. My brother is studying _____ medicine and taking _____ course in anatomy.

5. Keith had _____ accident on Wednesday.

6. I can bring _____ coffee and _____ ice cream to Joe's birthday party.

7. Jimmy took me to _____ concert and _____ exhibition of famous racing cars.

8. All she wants is _____ respect.

9. Mark was carrying _____ umbrella with _____ hole in it.

10. Joanna has _____ confidence and _____ sense of humour.

EXERCISE 3

USING *THE*

Write *the* in the spaces where it is needed. Some sentences are correct as they are.

1. Tenzin missed _____ dinners his mother used to make.

2. Eventually, you will develop _____ patience to succeed in _____ child psychology.

3. I have always wanted to swim in _____ ocean.

4. I haven't had _____ luck that I need to win the lottery.

5. Stephanie goes to _____ supermarket near her house because that store has _____ best selection of _____ organic produce.

6. _____ newspapers in _____ garage need to be recycled.

7. Because of _____ hard work of _____ volunteers at our community garage sale, we made $500 for _____ community garden.

8. Getting a good job takes _____ determination and _____ hard work.

9. Some children watch _____ television after school instead of doing their homework.

10. Tom cleaned out _____ trash in _____ backyard but left _____ dead leaves under _____ porch for another day.

EXERCISE 4

CORRECTING A PARAGRAPH WITH ERRORS IN ARTICLES

Correct the errors with *a, an,* or *the* in the following paragraph. You may need to add, change, or eliminate articles. Write the corrections in the space above the errors. There are ten errors.

When I was twelve years old, I had a dog like no other dog in the world. This dog had the intelligence and the courage, and he also had a crazy streak in his personality. His name was Buzzy, and he was the border collie. On farms of England and Scotland, border collies are used to herd sheep, and these dogs love to chase anything that moves. They are full of the energy and have stamina of much larger dogs. Buzzy loved to run, and he could chase and herd almost any animal. I remember when he herded five ducks into a quacking group and pushed them into a pond. He was always looking for a opportunity to run and play. If he couldn't find anything to herd, he loved to play the fetch. He would retrieve a old tennis ball for a hour. He ran as fast as the bullet.

NOUNS OR PRONOUNS USED AS SUBJECTS

A noun or a **pronoun** (a word that takes the place of a noun) is the subject of each sentence or dependent clause. Be sure that all sentences or dependent clauses have a subject:

> **not this:** Drives to work every day.
> **but this: He** drives to work every day.

> **not this:** My sister is pleased when gets a compliment.
> **but this:** My sister is pleased when **she** gets a compliment.

Be careful not to *repeat* the subject:

> **not this:** The police officer ~~she~~ said I was speeding.
> **but this:** The police officer said I was speeding.

> **not this:** The car that I needed ~~it~~ was a sports car.
> **but this:** The car that I needed was a sports car.

| EXERCISE **5** | **CORRECTING ERRORS WITH SUBJECTS** |

Correct any errors with subjects in the sentences below. Write your corrections above the errors.

1. Anthony he never gets up when hears the alarm clock.

2. In the summer, my car it often gets overheated.

3. Action movies with a good soundtrack they are the best.

4. After a long day, is difficult to concentrate on homework.

5. Sweatshirts are warm in winter; are also very comfortable.

6. My friend Inez she likes to walk in all kinds of weather.

7. Yesterday, the right rear tire on my truck it was flat.

8. Always comes to visit on New Year's Day and brings a special gift.

9. Whenever sees a coupon in the newspaper, he cuts it out.

10. The scariest part of the amusement park it was a haunted house.

VERBS

Necessary Verbs

Be sure that a **main verb** isn't missing from your sentences or dependent clauses.

not this: My boyfriend very ambitious

but this: My boyfriend **is** very ambitious.

not this: Sylvia cried when the hero in the movie.

but this: Sylvia cried when the hero in the movie **died**.

-s Endings

Be sure to put the *-s* on present-tense verbs in the third-person singular:

not this: He ~~run~~ in the park every morning.

but this: He **runs** in the park every morning.

not this: The concert ~~start~~ at 9:00 p.m.

but this: The concert **starts** at 9:00 p.m.

-ed Endings

Be sure to put an *-ed* ending on the past-participle form of a verb when necessary. There are three main forms of a verb:

present: Today I **walk.**

past: Yesterday I **walked.**

past participle: I **have walked.** He **has walked.**

The past-participle form is used after *were, was, had, has,* and *have*:

not this: He **has** ~~call~~ me every day this week.

but this: He **has called** me every day this week.

not this: My neighbour **was** ~~surprise~~ by the sudden storm.

but this: My neighbour **was surprised** by the sudden storm.

Caution: Do not add *-ed* endings to infinitives. An infinitive is the verb form that uses *to* plus the present form of the verb:

infinitives: to consider   to obey

not this: Dean wanted me **to** ~~considered~~ the proposal.

but this: Dean wanted me **to consider** the proposal.

not this: I taught my dog **to** ~~obeyed~~ commands.

but this: I taught my dog **to obey** commands.

EXERCISE **6**	**CORRECTING ERRORS IN VERBS: NECESSARY VERBS, THIRD-PERSON PRESENT TENSE, PAST PARTICIPLES, AND INFINITIVES**

Correct any errors in verbs in the sentences below. Write your corrections above the lines. Some sentences do not need any corrections.

1. The letter was mail at the post office where my uncle work.

2. After I got divorced, I wanted to examining the good and bad points of moving to Alberta.

3. As a child, I was fascinating by dinosaurs and other prehistoric creatures.

4. Once a week, Flor calls her family in Manila and tells them all her news.

5. Your new haircut look good on you; it make you look very handsome.

6. Laura had wrap all the gifts before the children arrived.

7. Two of the most generous neighbours in my building, Chet and Semra, from the third floor.

8. Do not come to the dinner table unless you have wash your hands.

9. Good communication skills essential in any close relationship.

10. When Ms. Simone need to relaxed, she lie on the couch and read a mystery novel.

EXERCISE **7**	**CORRECTING A PARAGRAPH WITH ERRORS IN NECESSARY VERBS, THIRD-PERSON PRESENT TENSE, PAST PARTICIPLES, AND INFINITIVES**

Correct the verb errors in the following paragraph. Write your corrections above the lines. There are seven errors.

Whenever we have a sale at the store where I work, we have to prepared for it for days. If the sale start on a Wednesday, for example, we work for hours on Monday and Tuesday, sorting the sale items and marking the merchandise with special sales tags. All this sorting and marking must be done after the store close, so the work continue late into the night. Then, at about 5:00 a.m. on Wednesday morning, the really hard work begins. We rush to put up the "Sale" signs, to displayed the marked-down items, and to be ready when the customers come in at 9:00. Before a sale begins, I have often earn as much as fifteen hours of overtime. A sale is fun for customers, but for salespeople it a hard way to make extra money.

Two-Word Verbs

Two-word verbs contain a verb plus another word, either a preposition or an adverb. The meaning of each word by itself is different from the meaning the two words have when they are together. Look at this example:

Sometimes Hamida **runs across** her sister at the park.

You might check *run* in the dictionary and find that it means "to move quickly." *Across* means "from one side to the other." But *run across* means something different:

not this: Sometimes Hamida ~~moves quickly from one side to the other of~~ her sister at the park.

but this: Sometimes Hamida **encounters** her sister at the park.

Sometimes, a word or words come between the words of a two-word verb:

On Friday night, I **put** the garbage **out**; the sanitation department collects it early Saturday morning.

Here are some common two-word verbs:

ask out	Jamal wants to *ask* Teresa *out* for dinner.
break down	I hope my car doesn't *break down*.
call off	You can *call off* the party.
call on	I need to *call on* you for help.
come across	I often *come across* bargains at thrift shops.
drop in	I will *drop in* tomorrow to check on your progress.
drop off	My father will *drop* the package *off*.
fill in	You can *fill in* your name.
fill out	Danny has to *fill out* a complaint form.
hand in	We have to *hand in* our assignments.
hand out	I hope the theatre *hands out* free passes.
keep on	You must *keep on* practising your speech.
look into	Jonelle will *look into* the situation.
look over	Jake needs to *look* the plans *over*.
look up	I had to *look up* the street in the directory.
pick up	Tomorrow, I *pick up* my first paycheque.
quiet down	The teacher told the class to *quiet down*.
run into	Nancy will *run into* Alan at the gym.
run out	The family has *run out* of money.
try on	Before you buy the shirt, *try* it *on*.
try out	She wants to *try* the lawnmower *out*.
turn on	*Turn* the television *on*.
turn down	Sal thinks Wayne should *turn* the job *down*.
turn up	Nick is sure to *turn up* uninvited.

EXERCISE 8

WRITING SENTENCES WITH TWO-WORD VERBS

Write a sentence for each of the following two-word verbs. Use the examples above as a guide, but consult a dictionary if you are not sure what the verbs mean.

1. call off _____

2. look up _____

3. keep on _____

4. fill out _____

5. run across _____

6. turn up _____

7. drop off _____

8. pick up _____

9. try out _____

10. ask out _____

Contractions and Verbs

Affirmative Contractions   **Negative Contractions**

am = 'm (I'm)   am not = 'm not (I'm not)

is = 's (he's)   is not = isn't or 's not (he isn't or he's not)

are = 're (you're)   are not = aren't or 're not (you aren't or you're not)

have = 've (I've)   have not = haven't or 've not (I haven't or I've not)

has = 's (he's)   has not = hasn't or 's not (he hasn't or he's not)

had = 'd (he'd)   had not = hadn't (he hadn't)

will = 'll (they'll)   will not = won't (they won't)

would = 'd (I'd)   would not = wouldn't (I wouldn't)

The following verbs don't have contractions in the affirmative, but do in the negative:

cannot = can't	could not = couldn't	did not = didn't
do not = don't	does not = doesn't	might not = mightn't
should not = shouldn't	was not = wasn't	were not = weren't

EXERCISE **9**	**CONTRACTIONS AND VERBS**

In the space above each italicized contraction, write its long form. The first one is done for you.

She would

1. *She'd* let me know if she needed help.

2. *Alberto's* building a new house.

3. *Alberto's* built a new house.

4. *You'll* be sorry you missed the game.

5. The *car's* in the body shop for repairs.

6. On a rainy day, *I'm* likely to stay home and sleep.

7. *They'll* never sell their boat.

8. Do you think *you'd* like to visit Hong Kong?

9. *We've* proposed a good idea.

10. The neighbours *won't* turn down their television.

PREPOSITIONS

Prepositions are little words such as *with, for, of, around,* or *near.* (For more examples, see the Infobox in Chapter 13 on page 335.) Some prepositions can be confusing; these are the ones that show time and place.

Prepositions That Show Time

Use *at* to show a specific or precise time:

> I will call you **at** 7:30 P.M.
>
> The movie starts **at** midnight.

Use *on* with a specific day or date:

> The meeting is **on** Friday.
>
> Frances begins basic training **on** June 23.

Use *by* when you mean "no later than that time":

> Jean has to be at work **by** 8:00 A.M.
>
> We should be finished with the cleaning **by** 5:00 P.M.

Use *until* when you mean "continuing up to a time":

> Yesterday I slept **until** 10:00 A.M.
>
> The dentist cannot see me **until** tomorrow.

Use *in* when you refer to a specific time period (minutes, hours, days, weeks, months, years):

> I'll be with you **in** a minute.
>
> Nikela works **in** the morning. (You can also say *in* the afternoon, or *in* the evening, but *at* night.)

Use *during* when you refer to a continuing time period or within the time period:

> I fell asleep **during** his speech.
>
> My sister will study management **during** the summer.

Use *for* to tell the length of a period of time:

> We have been married **for** two years.
> Wanda and Max cleaned the attic **for** three hours.

Use *since* to tell the starting time of an action:

> He has been calling **since** 9:00 A.M.
> We have been best friends **since** Grade 3.

Prepositions That Show Place

Use *in* to refer to a country, region, province, city, or neighbourhood:

> He studied **in** Ecuador.
> Mr. Etienne lives **in** St. Boniface.

Use *in* to refer to an enclosed space:

> He put the money **in** his wallet.
> Delia waited for me **in** the dining room.

Use *at* to refer to a specific address:

> The repair shop is **at** 7330 Glades Road.
> I live **at** 7520 Maple Lane.

Use *at* to refer to a corner or intersection:

> We went to a garage sale **at** the corner of Spring Street and High Park Avenue.
> The accident occurred **at** the intersection of Lakeshore Boulevard and Temple Road.

Use *on* to refer to a street or a block:

> Dr. Lopez lives **on** Hawthorne Street.
> Malcolm bought the biggest house **on** the block.

Use *on* to refer to a surface:

> Put the sandwiches **on** the table.
> There was a bright rug **on** the floor.

Use *off* to refer to a surface:

> Take the sandwiches **off** the table.
> She wiped the mud **off** the floor.

Use *into* and *out of* for small vehicles, such as cars:

> Our dog leaped **into** the convertible.
> The children climbed **out of** the car.

Use *on* and *off* for large vehicles, like planes, trains, buses, and boats:

> I was so seasick, I couldn't wait to get **off** the ship.
> I like to ride **on** the bus.

| EXERCISE **10** | **CORRECTING ERRORS IN PREPOSITIONS** |

Correct any errors in prepositions in the following sentences. Write your corrections above the lines.

1. The dinner begins on 7:30 P.M. and will be over by 9:30 P.M.

2. I studied biology during two years until I changed my major to botany.

3. Come and see me on an hour, and we can talk about old times at Thunder Bay.

4. We got into the plane two hours before it left the runway.

5. The stack of mail in the table has been sitting there since a week.

6. The restaurant is at the corner of Victoria Avenue and Edward Street, but my house is farther down at River Drive.

7. I've been studying at my room since 4:00 P.M.

8. We walked to a sunny patio with bright wicker furniture in the tile floor.

9. Take my keys off the counter and put them on your backpack.

10. How long have you lived on 5545 Hammond Lane?

CREDITS

Craig Alexander, Derek Burleton, and Francis Fong. Excerpt from "Knocking Down Barriers Faced by New Immigrants to Canada." Published by TD Bank Group, © 2012.

Samantha Bennett. "Hey, Canada's One Cool Country." *Toronto Star*. August 13, 2003. Copyright © 2003 *Pittsburgh Post-Gazette*. All rights reserved. Reprinted with permission.

Jesse Brown. "How to get a university education without paying tuition—or changing out of your PJs" in *Toronto Life*, March 28, 2013. Copyright © by Jesse Brown. Used by the permission of the author.

Amber Daugherty. Excerpt from "Cursive is dying: Kids can't sign their own names—and that's a huge problem," *The Globe and Mail*, June 25, 2013. Copyright © by *The Globe and Mail*. Used by permission of The Globe and Mail Inc.

Livio Di Matteo. "Arts Education Does Pay Off." *National Post*. May 31, 1999, C5.

Charles Gordon. "Have We Forgotten the Trojan Horse?" *Maclean's*. March 1, 1999. Copyright © 1999 by Charles Gordon. Reprinted with permission of the author.

Zora Neale Hurston. Excerpt from *Dust Tracks On A Road*. Copyright © 1942 by Zora Neale Hurston. Published by J.B. Lippincott, Inc.

Janet McFarland. "Colour-Coding a Corporate Culture." *The Globe and Mail*. March 29, 2008. B11. Copyright © 2008 by *The Globe and Mail*. Used by permission of The Globe and Mail Inc. All rights reserved.

Jim McKay. "Employers Complain about Communication Skills." *Pittsburgh Post-Gazette*. February 6, 2005. www.post-gazette.com.

Hiren Mistry. "Assimilation, Pluralism, and 'Cultural Navigation': Multiculturalism in Canadian Schools." Copyright © by Hiren Mistry. Used by permission of the author.

Megan McCafferty. "Sloppy Firsts" by Megan McCafferty, Crown Publishers 2001.

Parks Canada. *The Story of a Nation*. www.pc.gc.ca/voyage-travel/pv-vp/itm11-/page3_e.asp (accessed April 27, 2008).

Andrew Potter. "How to Get a Reference Letter." *Maclean's*. March 22, 2007. Copyright © 2007 by Andrew Potter. Used by permission of the author.

Sharda Prashad. "Mass Collaboration and Harnessing the Power of Global Ideas," *Toronto Star*, January 13, 2007. Copyright © 2007 by Torstar Syndication Services. Used by permission.

Simon Fraser University. *Fire Evacuation Procedures*. www.ehs.sfu.ca/general/details/sfu_vancouver (accessed April 28, 2008).

Daniel Stoffman. "When Immigration Goes Awry." *Toronto Star*. July 7, 2006. Reprinted with permission.

David Suzuki. "Saving the Planet One Swamp at a Time." *Toronto Star*. June 2, 2007. Copyright © by the David Suzuki Foundation. Used by permission of the David Suzuki Foundation.

Kaavya Viswanathan. "How Opal Mehta Got Kissed, Got Wild, and Got a Life" by Kaavya Viswanathan, Little, Brown and Company, 2006.

Toronto Zoo. *Request for Proposal: Architectural/Engineering Services for the Replacement of Skylight Glazing & Exhibit Refurbishment at the African Rainforest Pavilion*. January 31, 2008. www.toronto.ca/calldocuments/zoo/pdf/rfp06.pdf (accessed May 3, 2008).

Richard Wagamese. "One Caring Teacher Set Things Right." Originally published by the *Calgary Herald*, 2007. Copyright © 2007 by Richard Wagamese. Used by permission of the author.

Margaret Wente. "Who's stealing our jobs? Computers" by Margaret Wente, *The Globe and Mail*, April 13, 2013. Copyright © 2013 by *The Globe and Mail*. Used by the permission of The Globe and Mail Inc.

Elizabeth Wong. "A Present for Popo: Sometimes, it takes more than ties of kinship and culture—or even a holiday tradition—to keep a family together," by Elizabeth Wong, *Los Angeles Times*, December 30, 1992. Copyright © 1992 Elizabeth Wong. Used by permission of the author. www.elizabethwong.net.

INDEX